GCSE COMPUTER STUDIES

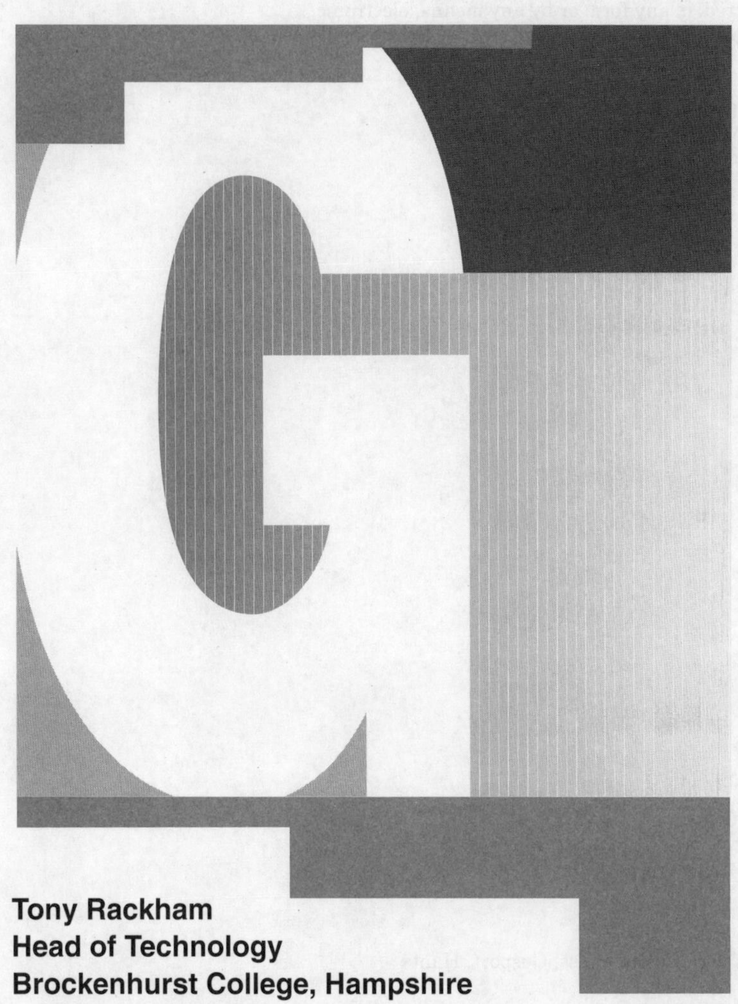

Tony Rackham
Head of Technology
Brockenhurst College, Hampshire

First published 1984
Revised 1987, 1989, 1992
Reprinted 1988, 1992, 1993, 1994, 1995

Letts Educational
Aldine House
Aldine Place
London W12 8AW

British Library Cataloguing in Publication Data
A CIP record for this book is available from the British Library.

ISBN 1 85758 303 5

Printed in Great Britain by Ashford Colour Press, Gosport, Hants

Letts Educational is the trading name of BPP (Letts Educational) Ltd

PREFACE

This book is intended as a complete revision guide for the student taking GCSE Computer Studies or one of the corresponding Scottish examinations. It is designed for use in the last six months before the examination, although I know it will probably be used by some people throughout the course.

I am indebted to Brian Kates, Paul McGee and Jack Winch who advised me throughout, and also to Geoff Attree for his research work on several units. Their differing talents and experience made an excellent combination and ensured that the work was thoroughly checked from every aspect. My thanks also to the Letts staff who, as ever, have been helpful and efficient.

I am also indebted to my wife Betty, who took most of the photographs, and to my daughter Caroline, who helped with the keyboarding and took some of the photographs.

As this book deals with applications of computers, I have needed a great deal of help from business and industry. People have been wonderful in this respect and I wish particularly to thank staff from Feeline Management Ltd, IBM, Lloyd's Bank PLC, Marchwood Engineering Laboratories, Solartron Instruments, Tecno Ltd., Thomas Cook Ltd., Research Machines Ltd., Microsoft.

My thanks also to the Examination Groups and Associations who have granted permission for the reproduction of questions from their Examination Papers: London East Anglian Group, Midland Examining Group, Northern Examining Association, Northern Ireland Schools Examinations and Assessment Council, Scottish Examination Board, Southern Examining Group and the Welsh Joint Education Committee.

Tony Rackham

CONTENTS

INTRODUCTION AND GUIDE TO USING THIS BOOK

Candidates in England, Wales and Northern Ireland can enter the GCSE examination in Computer Studies. Scotland has the Standard Grade examination in Computer Studies. The syllabuses for these stress the following:

1 The applications of computers. You study mainly what computers do rather than details of how they work and how they are programmed.
2 Practical activities. You spend more time on using computers than on theoretical work.
3 The differing abilities of pupils. You can tackle coursework and examination questions which give you an interesting challenge but are not too difficult for you.

Most of the assessment is still by written examination and so you will need a planned programme of revision. It is suggested you use this book in the way outlined below:

Using the table of analysis of syllabuses

1 There are important differences between the various syllabuses. You need to know which one you are studying. Your teacher will help you with this.

2 Find your syllabus in the table of analysis immediately after this introduction. In the appropriate column you will find:
(a) The total number of written papers set.
(b) The number of written papers you have to do. For many syllabuses there is a choice of papers depending on the type of grade you hope to get. You can tell that there is a choice if the 'number of papers candidate takes' is less than the 'number of written papers set'.

Further details of papers and questions are given in the section on the GCSE after the Table of Analysis of Examination Syllabuses.
(c) The total time for the written examinations for each candidate.
(d) Whether any of the papers includes some multiple choice questions.
(e) Whether the papers include a case study and some details if they do.
(f) Whether it is necessary to do some programming as part of coursework. All syllabuses allow programming projects but only the Scottish Standard Grade demands that they be done.
(g) The percentage of the total marks which are allocated for coursework.

3 The table also tells you which topics are on your syllabus. The symbols in your column of the table tell you which of the units of the book apply to your syllabus.

The key to the symbols in the columns is:
● unit is required for the syllabus
○ unit is only needed by those attempting higher grades (see end of table)
P unit is not needed for written papers but is useful if you are doing a programming project
a blank space means the unit is not required.

4 Further information about the various syllabuses is given in the section on the GCSE which follows the Table of Analysis.

5 The Table of Analysis is only intended as a guide. Ask your teacher if you are in any doubt about which topics to revise.

Revising

1 Select a topic. If you have enough time, tackle topics in the order in which they appear in the book. Otherwise, select one which you have been taught but are not confident about.

2 Find the appropriate unit in the main part of the book. Work through it. The units are set out so that for quick revision you can miss out the examples and the worked questions, concentrating only on the main text. However, it is better to start your revision in plenty of time and work through the complete text.

3 Do some examination questions for that unit (at the back of the book). Possible answers are provided. Exceptions to this are:

(a) Where the answer can easily be looked up in the book. In that case a reference has been given to the appropriate unit.
(b) Where the Examining Group setting the question will not allow answers to be given.

It is best not to use the answers until you have completed the set of questions for the unit.

If you cannot do many of the questions, go back and work through the appropriate unit again. Make a note of any sections you find difficult for later quick revision.

To carry out this programme properly for a summer examination you will have to start soon after Christmas. In the final week you can go through the questions again and revise the units you noted as being difficult.

General notes

You will find in the section on Projects and Coursework some useful advice about coursework.

Definitions

Throughout the book, when an important computing term is introduced it is printed in bold type and a definition is given. If you want to know what a term means look it up in the index at the back of this book. Usually one of the page numbers given there will be in bold type. This refers you to the definition and explanation you want.

Most syllabuses accept the definitions given in the booklet *A Glossary of Computing Terms for Introductory Courses* published by the CUP on behalf of the British Computer Society. Whenever possible, the definitions given here are compatible with those given in that glossary.

Table of analysis of examination syllabuses		London East Anglian Group	Midland Examining Group	Northern Examining Association	Northern Ireland Examining and Assessment Council	Scottish Examination Board Standard Grade	Southern Examining Group	Welsh Joint Education Committee
Number of written papers set		5	3	2	3	3	2	3
Number of papers candidate takes		2 or 3	1 or more	2	2	1 or 2	2	2
Time per candidate (hours)		3½ or 5	¾ or more	3¼	3½ or 4	1 to 3	2½	3½
Some multiple choice set					•			
Case Study done:		•		•		•	•	
in a written examination		•		•			•	
as a complete paper		•					•	
details known beforehand		•		•			•	
from syllabus				•			•	
OR given to candidates		•						
Coursework must include writing programs						•		
Percentage of marks for coursework		30	40	40	30	25†	30	30
1	Information processing	•	•	•	•	•	•	•
1.1	The data processing cycle	•	•	•	•	•	•	•
1.2	Encoding and decoding	•	•	•	•	•	•	•
1.3	Data collection and input	•	•	•	•	•	•	•
1.4	Processing	•	•	•	•	•	•	•
2	Representation of data	•	•	•	•	•	•	•
2.1	Binary representation of numbers	○	•	•	•	○	•	•
2.2	Binary conversion	○	•	•	•	○	•	•
2.3	Positive and negative integers	○	•	•	•		•	•
2.4	Representation of fractions in binary			•		○	•	
2.5	Accuracy		•	•		○		
2.6	Octal and hexadecimal				•		•	
2.7	Binary representation of characters	•	•	•	•	•	•	•
3	Digital logic			•	•			
3.1	Truth tables			•	•			
3.2	Simple gates – NOT, AND and OR			•	•			
4	Computer hardware	•	•	•	•	•	•	•
4.1	Digital computers	•	•	•	•	•	•	•
4.2	Microprocessors and microcomputers	•	•	•	•	•	•	•
4.3	Peripheral devices	•	•	•	•	•	•	•
5	The central processing unit	•	•	•	•	•	•	•
5.1	The fetch-execute cycle	○			•			
5.2	Registers	○			•			
5.3	Typical instruction set	○	•		•			
5.4	Typical instruction format	•	•	•	•		•	
6	Communications hardware	•	•	•	•	•	•	•
6.1	Visual display terminals	•	•	•	•	•	•	•
6.2	Other terminals	•	•	•	•	•	•	
6.3	Connecting terminals to computers	•	•	•	•	○	•	•
6.4	Interfaces	•	•	•	•	○	•	•
7	Data preparation and input	•	•	•	•	•	•	•
7.1	Use of keyboards	•	•	•	•	•	•	•
7.2	Document readers	•	•	•	•	○	•	•
7.3	Bar codes, tags and magnetic stripes	•	•	•	•	•	•	•
7.4	Input at terminals and microcomputers	•	•	•	•	•	•	•
7.5	Other input devices	•	•	•	•	•	•	•
7.6	Comparison of input methods	•	•	•	•	•	•	•
8	Output	•	•	•	•	•	•	•
8.1	Output on screens	•	•	•	•	•	•	•
8.2	Printers	•	•	•	•	•	•	•
8.3	Plotters	•	•	•	•	•	•	•
8.4	Other output methods	•	•	•	•	•	•	•
8.5	Comparison of output methods	•	•	•	•	•	•	•

Table of analysis of examination syllabuses		London East Anglian Group	Midland Examining Group	Northern Examining Association	Northern Ireland Examining and Assessment Council	Scottish Examination Board Standard Grade	Southern Examining Group	Welsh Joint Education Committee
Number of written papers set		5	3	2	3	3	2	3
Number of papers candidate takes		2 or 3	1 or more	2	2	1 or 2	2	2
Time per candidate (hours)		3½ or 5	¾ or more	3¼	3½ or 4	1 to 3	2½	3½
Some multiple choice set					•			
Case Study done:		•		•		•	•	
in a written examination		•		•			•	
as a complete paper		•					•	
details known beforehand		•		•			•	
from syllabus				•			•	
OR given to candidates		•						
Coursework must include writing programs						•		
Percentage of marks for coursework		30	40	40	30	25†	30	30
9	Storage devices and media	•	•	•	•	•	•	•
9.1	Main store	•	•	•	•	•	•	•
9.2	Backing stores	•	•	•	•	•	•	•
9.3	Comparison of storage media	•	•	•	•	•	•	•
10	Using computers to solve problems	•	•	•	•	•	•	•
10.1	Systems	•	•	•	•	•	•	•
10.2	Steps in systems analysis and design	•	•	•	•	•	•	•
10.3	Flowcharts – system flowcharts	•	•	•	•		•	•
10.4	Program design and implementation	•	•	•	•	•	•	•
10.5	Representing algorithms	•	•	•	•		•	•
10.6	Program documentation	•	•	•	•	•	•	•
11	Programming	•	•	•	•	•	•	•
11.1	Low level programming		•	•	•	○	•	•
11.2	High level languages	•	•	•	•	○	•	•
11.3	High level programming	P	•	•	•	•	•	•
11.4	Data types and structures	P	•	•	P	○	P	P
11.5	Input and output	P	•	•	•	•	P	P
11.6	Control statements	P	•	•	•	•	•	P
11.7	Subroutines, procedures and functions		•	•	•	•	•	•
11.8	Program style and layout	•	•	•	•	•	•	P
12	Errors	○	•	•	•	•		•
12.1	Program errors	○	•	•	•	•	•	•
12.2	Detection of program errors	○	•	•	•	○	•	•
12.3	Integrity of input data	•	•	•	•	○	•	•
12.4	Errors in calculation	○	○		•	•	•	
13	Files	•	•	•	•	•	•	•
13.1	Organization and access	•	•	•	•	○	•	•
13.2	Master and transaction files	•	•	•	•	○	•	
13.3	Storage and handling of files	•	•			•	•	
13.4	Updating	•	•	•	•	•	•	•
13.5	Searching, merging and sorting	•	○	•		•	•	
13.6	Security of files	•	•	•	•	•	•	•
13.7	Databases and data banks		•			•		
14	Software	•	•	•	•	•	•	•
14.1	Evaluation and use of software	•	•	•	•	•	•	•
14.2	Applications of systems programs	•	•	•	•	•	•	•
14.3	Operating systems	•	○	•	•	•	•	•
15	Processing systems	•	•	•	•	•	•	•
15.1	Real-time processing	•	•	•	•	○	•	•
15.2	Single-user systems	•	•	•	•	•	•	•
15.3	Batch processing	•	•	•	•	○	•	•
15.4	Multi-access systems	•	•	•	•	•	•	•
15.5	Networks	•	•	•	•	•	•	•

Table of analysis of examination syllabuses

		London East Anglian Group	Midland Examining Group	Northern Examining Association	Northern Ireland Examining and Assessment Council	Scottish Examination Board Standard Grade	Southern Examining Group	Welsh Joint Education Committee
Number of written papers set		5	3	2	3	3	2	3
Number of papers candidate takes		2 or 3	1 or more	2	2	1 or 2	2	2
Time per candidate (hours)		3½ or 5	¾ or more	3¼	3½ or 4	1 to 3	2½	3½
Some multiple choice set					•			
Case Study done:		•		•		•	•	
	in a written examination	•		•			•	
	as a complete paper	•					•	
	details known beforehand	•		•			•	
	from syllabus			•			•	
OR given to candidates		•						
Coursework must include writing programs						•		
Percentage of marks for coursework		30	40	40	30	25†	30	30
16	Jobs in computing	•	•	•	•	•	•	•
16.1	Data processing manager	•	•		•	o		•
16.2	Systems analyst	•	•	•	•	o	•	•
16.3	Programmer	•	•	•	•	o	•	•
16.4	Operations manager	•	•	•	•	o	•	•
16.5	Computer operating staff	•	•	•	•	o	•	•
16.6	Data preparation staff	•	•	•	•	o	•	•
16.7	File librarian	•	•		•			
16.8	Data control staff	•	•		•	•		•
16.9	Engineer	•			•	•		•
17	Applications of computers	•	•	•	•	•	•	•
17.1	Stock control		•		•	•	•	•
17.2	Payroll	•	•		•	•	•	•
17.3	Airline booking systems	•			•	•	•	•
18	Communication systems and word processing	•	•		•	•	•	•
18.1	Teletext	•	•		•	•	•	•
18.2	Viewdata networks	•	•		•	•	•	•
18.3	Comparisons	•	•		•	•	•	•
18.4	Word processing	•	•	•	•	•	•	•
19	Technical, scientific and other uses	•	•		•	•	•	•
19.1	Applications in civil engineering	•			•		•	•
19.2	Data logging	•	•		•	•	•	•
19.3	Computer-aided design	•	•		•	•	•	•
19.4	Simulations	•	•		•	•	•	•
19.5	Medical uses of computers	•	•		•	•	•	•
20	Use of computers in industrial processes	•	•	•	•	•	•	•
20.1	Process control	•	•	•	•	•	•	•
20.2	Robots	•	•		•	•	•	•
21	The social impact of computers	•	•	•	•	•	•	•
21.1	Changes in business and society	•	•	•	•	•	•	•
21.2	Personal privacy	•	•	•	•	•	•	•
21.3	The effect on unemployment	•	•	•	•	•	•	•
21.4	The effect on those in work	•	•	•	•	•	•	•

† Scottish Standard Grade: for candidates awarded grades 1 to 5, the teacher's assessment of coursework counts as 25% of the total but it will also be used as a check on the 75% of the marks which are allocated to the written papers. For candidates awarded grades 6 or 7, the coursework marks will count towards all sections of the syllabus to give altogether 62½% of the total mark.

o Section is only needed for higher grades, namely for:
LEAG – grades A,B,C; MEG – grades A,B,C,D; SEB Standard – grades 1,2,3,4.

P Section is not needed for written papers but is useful if you are doing a programming project.

Examination Boards: Addresses

To obtain syllabuses, past examination papers and further details, write to your Examining Group.

Northern Examination Association (NEA)

JMB	Joint Matriculation Board Devas Street, Manchester M15 6EU
ALSEB	Associated Lancashire Schools Examining Board 12 Harter Street, Manchester M1 6HL
NREB	Northern Regional Examinations Board Wheatfield Road, Westerhope, Newcastle upon Tyne NE5 5JZ
NWREB	North-West Regional Examinations Board Orbit House, Albert Street, Eccles, Manchester M20 0WL
YHREB	Yorkshire and Humberside Regional Examinations Board Harrogate Office – 31-33 Springfield Avenue, Harrogate HG1 2HW Sheffield Office – Scarsdale House, 136 Derbyshire Lane, Sheffield S8 8SE

Midland Examining Group (MEG)

Cambridge	University of Cambridge Local Examinations Syndicate Syndicate Buildings, 1 Hills Road, Cambridge CB1 2EU
O & C	Oxford and Cambridge Schools Examination Board Purbeck House, Purbeck Road, Cambridge CB2 1PU and Elsfield Way, Oxford OX2 7BZ
WMEB	West Midlands Examinations Board Mill Wharf, Mill Street, Birmingham B6 4BU
EMREB	East Midland Regional Examinations Board Robins Wood House, Robins Wood Road, Aspley, Nottingham NG8 3NR

London East Anglian Group (LEAG)
(now known as University of London Examinations and Assessment Council)

London office	Stewart House, 32 Russell Square, London WC1B 5DN
Colchester office	The Lindens, Lexden Road, Colchester CO3 3RL

Southern Examining Group (SEG)

AEB	The Associated Examining Board Stag Hill House, Guildford GU2 5XJ
OSEB	Oxford School Examinations Board Ewert House, Ewert Place, Summertown, Oxford OX2 7BZ
SEG	Southern Regional Examinations Board Unit 23, Monksbrook Industrial Park, Chandlers Ford, Eastleigh SO5 3RA
	South-East Regional Examinations Board Beloe House, 2-10 Mount Ephraim Road, Tunbridge Wells TN1 1EU
	South-Western Examinations Board 23-29 Marsh Street, Bristol BS1 4BP

Wales

WJEC	Welsh Joint Education Committee 245 Western Avenue, Cardiff CF5 2YX

Northern Ireland

NICCEA (formerly NISEAC)	Northern Ireland Council for the Curriculum Examinations and Assessment Beechill House, 42 Beechill Road, Belfast BT8 4RS

Scotland

SEB	Scottish Examination Board Ironmills Road, Dalkeith, Midlothian EH22 1LE

THE GENERAL CERTIFICATE OF SECONDARY EDUCATION (GCSE)

Students in England, Wales and Northern Ireland can take the General Certificate of Secondary Education examinations—the GCSE. In Scotland they can take the Standard Grade examination. This book takes into account both of these examinations and is suitable for candidates of both.

Outside Scotland, for the GCSE, the Examination Boards have been grouped together so that there are six different syllabuses. There are four Groups or Associations in England, one in Wales and one in Northern Ireland. The syllabuses are all based on a set of guidelines called 'The National Criteria'. As a result they share some common themes, although there are also some important differences between them.

For the GCSE in Computer Studies candidates are expected to be able to use computers to solve worthwhile problems, that is, ones which would be difficult to solve without a computer. Students will be encouraged to make use of available software where possible, designing and writing programs only when necessary.

Courses are intended to produce students who enjoy using computers and can do so with confidence and skill in a variety of areas. Great importance is attached to knowledge and understanding of a wide range of present-day applications. The work also emphasizes the impact of computers on our society.

Assessment Objectives

Any GCSE course in Computer Studies has to balance the main parts of the syllabus in a certain way. The candidate's abilities in these main areas will then be tested by timed written examinations and by coursework.

The abilities to be tested are set out as 'Assessment Objectives'. Each GCSE syllabus contains a list of these objectives. They are set out in the table below. The table also shows the minimum and maximum percentage of the total marks which will be given to them.

Ability	*Description*	*Minimum*	*Maximum*
A	Showing knowledge and understanding of the techniques needed to solve problems related to practical applications.	15	20
B	Using computers sensibly to produce solutions to appropriate problems and documenting the solutions.	25	30
C	Showing knowledge and understanding of the functions of the main hardware and software components of a computer system and their relationships with the representation of stored data and programs.	15	20
D	Showing knowledge and understanding of the range and scope of computer applications.	20	30
E	Showing understanding of the social and economic effects of computerized systems on individuals, organizations and society.	10	15

Each of these objectives is then further subdivided.

Examinations and Coursework

Most of the GCSE examining groups use coursework to test the ability to use computers, that is, ability B. Abilities A,C,D and E are mainly examined in written papers.

COURSEWORK

Coursework will probably be assessed by your own teacher. These assessments will be moderated by the Examination Board. (Some boards have special arrangements for external candidates, who are not attached to a school or College.)

The maximum mark a syllabus could allow for coursework would be 40% of the total marks. In practice, for most of the syllabuses, it is about 30% (see the Table of Analysis). All the syllabuses allow candidates to use existing software for projects and/or to write their own programs, although some do insist on a certain amount of programming by the candidate (see Table of Analysis of Syllabuses).

WRITTEN PAPERS

GCSE examinations cater for students of widely differing abilities. Computer Studies Syllabuses take this into consideration in their written papers.

Most boards have differentiated papers. Thus each candidate takes only some of the available papers, the ones which are at the right level for him/her. A candidate taking a particular combination of papers is only eligible for a set range of grades. A decision has to be made beforehand which papers to take. This method is used for the following syllabuses London East Anglian Group, Midland Examining Group, Northern Ireland Schools Examinations and Assessment Council, Scottish Examination Board Standard Grade and the Welsh Joint Education Committee.

Papers may have differentiated sections. The Midland Examining Group (MEG) divides each paper into sections. Each section relates to a different grade and candidates will concentrate mainly on the section they think, or have been advised, is most relevant to them.

The Northern Examining Association (NEA) and the Southern Examining Group (SEG) both use stepped questions. The early parts of these questions are relatively easy and then the later parts are harder.

The Southern Examining Group also have a stepped paper (paper 1). The questions in this paper are arranged in ascending order of difficulty, so that they get progressively harder as you work through the paper. However, the candidates must attempt all the questions.

Case Study

Many of the examining groups expect candidates to do some work on an application of computers. This is called a case study. The work may be done as part of coursework, as part of an examination paper or may take up the whole of an examination paper. If the case study is assessed in a timed examination paper, some examining groups give candidates details of the application beforehand. This may be by an explanation in the syllabus or by some details given to the candidates some days or weeks before the examination. The Table of Analysis shows what the various syllabuses say about this.

1 INFORMATION PROCESSING

Information consists of facts and items of knowledge. It can be anything that has meaning to people. Usually information is expressed in words and numbers. However, it can be expressed in other forms, such as sounds, measurements or pictures.

Examples of information

1 A list of names and addresses.
2 The contents of a letter.
3 What is said in a telephone conversation.
4 The words of a song.
5 A map.

Information processing is the organization, manipulation and distribution of information.

Examples of information processing

1 Sorting a list of names and addresses into alphabetical order.
2 Producing a letter with a word processor, saving it on floppy disc and then sending it by electronic mail.
3 Transmitting a conversation over the telephone system.

People can process information without using machines. Examples are:

1 Listening to songs and deciding which ones are best.
2 Reading a map to get from one place to another.

Data is information in a form in which it can be processed (Fig. 1.1).

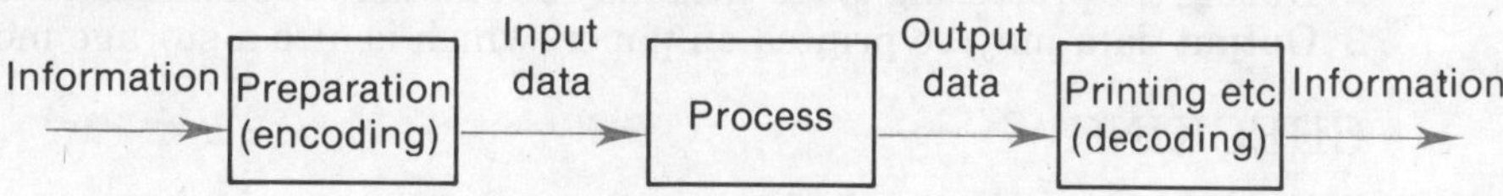

Fig. 1.1 Information and data

If information is to be processed by a computer it often has to be coded before the computer can accept it. The coded data is then input to the computer for processing. The new data resulting from the process can then be decoded and output as further information.

Examples of data

1 A set of names and addresses written out on to forms ready for typing.
2 A word-processed letter stored on a floppy disc. It is stored as a set of binary codes.
3 A telephone conversation converted to electrical signals to be sent down the wires.
4 A song written as sheet music so that it can be played.
5 A date encoded as a six-figure number – two digits each for the day, the month and the year.

Information technology (IT) is all types of equipment and programs which are used in the processing of information. The term 'information technology' is also used to refer to the uses of this technology. The main types of use involved are:

1 Communication of information. Here the technology used includes word processors and terminals (see Unit 18).
2 General information processing using computers. The uses range from printing payslips on large computers to using spreadsheets on microcomputers.
3 Using computers or electronic circuits to control machines and processes (see Unit 20). This could include a microprocessor controlling a robot or a specially designed circuit controlling a camera.

1.1 The Data Processing Cycle

When data is collected and processed, whether by a computer or by other means, a set of operations is carried out on it. This set of operations is called a **data processing sequence** or a **data processing cycle**.

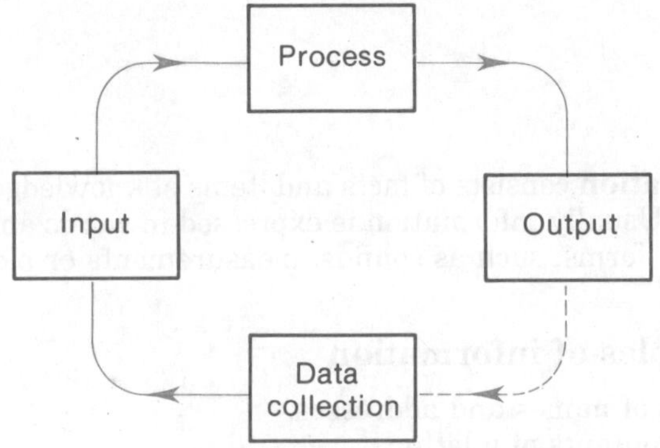

Fig. 1.2 The data processing cycle

Figure 1.2 is a very general diagram of a processing cycle. Data which is output may be used as input, perhaps at a later date, thus completing the cycle. (In the diagram OUTPUT is linked to DATA COLLECTION by a broken line to indicate that this only happens sometimes.)

Some operations may occur at different points in the cycle, between or as part of the operations shown in Fig. 1.2.

STORAGE

Data may be held for various lengths of time on a suitable material (or **medium**).

Worked question

Give three examples of data being stored, each one being at a different stage of the data processing cycle.

1 As the last stage of data collection data may be keyed on to disc, where it is stored while awaiting input to a computer.

2 During the processing stage data may be stored in the immediate access store of a computer.

3 Output data may be printed on paper, which is also a storage medium.

CHECKING

Data often has to be checked to see that it has been copied accurately and/or to see that it is reasonable (see Unit 12.3).

1.2 Encoding and Decoding

To **encode** means to convert information or data into a form ready for processing.

To **decode** means to convert data back to a form where it can be understood.

Examples of encoding where data is encoded as it is input

1 An interactive program is run on a microcomputer and data is typed in at the keyboard. Circuitry in the keyboard encodes the characters as they are typed in.

2 A microprocessor controls a chemical process. Measurements are taken by instruments connected to the processor. An interface converts the data to binary data which the microprocessor can deal with (see Unit 20.1).

Examples where data is encoded first and then input later

1 Information about foods is encoded into bar codes which are then printed on food labels. This data can then be input via a laser scanner on a point-of-sale (POS) terminal at the checkout (see Unit 7.3).

2 A school sends details of all its new pupils to a computer bureau. There they are keyed on to a floppy disc (for key-to-disc see Unit 7.1). The disc is then used on the school's computer to add the data to the main files.

Examples of decoding

1 On a school data file, the names of the teachers are stored. For this two letters of each surname are used. Thus Mr Smith is stored as SM, Miss Small as SL and Mr Sanders as SA.

The computer has a reference file of these codes. To print out a name the computer uses the reference file to decode the two letters. It can then print out the full name.
2 An electronic circuit can be made to decode binary numbers into decimal numbers (see Unit 2.1 for binary numbers).

Worked questions

1 Give three examples of encoding data in such a way that it is both briefer and standardized.
(i) Post codes – a few letters and digits are used to identify any address e.g. SO9 identifies an area of Southampton; SO9 5NH is the University.
(ii) Bank branch numbers – any bank cheque has in the top right-hand corner a number which identifies the bank branch of the person who wrote the cheque e.g. 60-18-46 is the Romsey branch of the National Westminster Bank.
(iii) Dates of birth – these are often written as three two-digit numbers e.g. 03 07 38 would be 3 July 1938.
2 Pupil records for a school include the pupils' dates of birth. A form is filled in for each pupil. Data from the forms is to be entered into a computer. The instructions say 'Enter date of birth as three two-digit numbers – DAY/MONTH/YEAR . . / . . / . .'.
For each of the following dates give a reason why they should not be accepted:
(a) 1/2/74
(b) 30/02/75
(c) 19/11/99
(a) 1/2/74 should not be accepted because the day and the month have only one digit each. The date should read 01/02/74.
(b) 30/02/75 is incorrect because this is 30th February and February has only 28 or 29 days.
(c) 19/11/99 is not acceptable as 1999 could not be a pupil's date of birth.

1.3 Data Collection and Input

DATA COLLECTION

Data collection means bringing together all the data for an application and getting it ready for processing.

Examples of data collection

1 Bank cheques are sent from branches to a central clearing house. There they are put together for sorting and updating accounts.
2 Application forms for subscriptions to a magazine are sent out to possible customers. Those who want the magazine fill in the forms and send them back. Their details are then typed into a computer via a keyboard.

DATA CAPTURE

Data capture means obtaining data for a computer. Usually the term is used in situations where a computer peripheral inputs the data automatically.

Examples of data capture

1 At a particular supermarket checkout there are POS terminals. Each product has a catalogue number that is encoded on a bar code. This can be read using a light pen (see Unit 7.4).
2 An examination candidate does a multiple choice test by marking a card with a pencil in the right places. The card is then read by a mark sensing device attached to a computer.

SOURCE DOCUMENTS AND TURNAROUND DOCUMENTS

A **source document** is the original piece of paper on which data is written when it is first recorded. A **turnaround document** is one which is produced as output at one stage of the data processing cycle, has more data added to it, and is then input for further processing.

Example of a source document and a turnaround document

A gas board uses the following system for its customer accounts. When a person becomes a customer he/she has to give details which are recorded on a source document. Using this data the computer prints forms for the meter reader which contain the customer's account number, address and probable usage of gas. These are turnaround documents because the meter reader inserts the meter reading and the forms are then input to the computer and the customer's gas bill is calculated and printed (see Fig. 1.3).

DATA PREPARATION

Data preparation is encoding data on to a medium which a computer input device can accept.

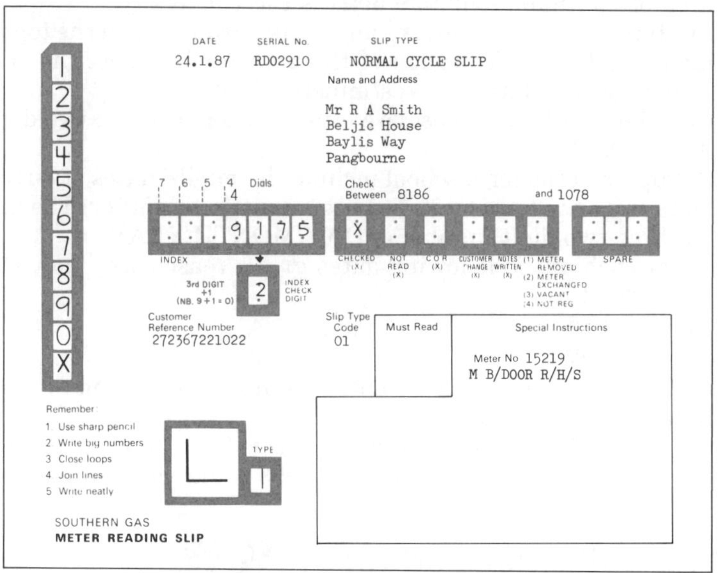

DATE 24.1.87

SERIAL No. RD02910

SLIP TYPE NORMAL CYCLE SLIP

Name and Address

Mr R A Smith
Beljic House
Baylis Way
Pangbourne

1 2 3 4 5 6 7 8 9 0 X

7 6 5 4 Dials 4

INDEX 9 1 7 5

3rd DIGIT +1 (NB. 9 + 1 = 0) 2 INDEX CHECK DIGIT

Customer Reference Number 272367221022

Check Between 8186 and 1078

X

CHECKED (X) | NOT READ (X) | C O R (X) | CUSTOMER CHANGE (X) | NOTES WRITTEN (X) | (1) METER REMOVED (2) METER EXCHANGED (3) VACANT (4) NOT REG

SPARE

Slip Type Code 01

Must Read

Special Instructions

Meter No 15219
M B/DOOR R/H/S

Remember:
1 Use sharp pencil
2 Write big numbers
3 Close loops
4 Join lines
5 Write neatly

TYPE 1

SOUTHERN GAS
METER READING SLIP

Fig. 1.3 A meter reading form

Usually the data has been written previously on to a suitable form and is typed by a skilled operator on to the medium, using a special machine with a keyboard.

Example of data preparation

Data is put on to a floppy disc by an operator using a key-to-floppy-disc station.

DATA TRANSMISSION AND COMMUNICATIONS

Data transmission means the sending of data from one place to another.

Data communications is a general term for applications which involve the transmission of data between a user and a computer or between two or more computers.

Examples of data communications

1 Electronic mail (see Unit 18.2). One user of a national computer network can send a letter to another user's 'mailbox'. This is in the store of a remote computer. The other user can then read this letter by logging in to the computer with his or her own terminal. The two users may be at opposite ends of the country.

2 A newspaper office in one country can transmit pictures to the newspaper's headquarters in another country. A special scanner is used to do this via the telephone network.

STANDARDIZED INPUT

During data collection, data may be written on to specially prepared data capture forms. The purpose of these may be:

1 To make it clear what data needs to be collected.
2 To make it easy to see what the data is.
3 To standardize the way in which data is recorded.
4 To assist in future filing of the data.

They may be used as:

1 **Index cards** – cards which can be stored in a drawer or filing cabinet for easy access.
2 **Source documents** used to prepare data for a computer system.

Examples of data capture forms

1 An index card used in a doctor's surgery to record details of patients. These are for manual filing.

2 A subscription form for a magazine. The applicant has to fill in name, address, title, etc. carefully in small squares. (see Fig. 1.4).

3 A multiple-choice answer paper.

NATIONAL BUSINESS COMPUTER MAGAZINE MEMBERSHIP ORDER FORM

The 1987 membership fee is £20.
For membership outside the United Kingdom the fee is £25.

Name

Job title

Company

Address

Post code

Principal activity of your organization (please tick)

01 ☐ Retail trade
02 ☐ Manufacturing
03 ☐ Transport
04 ☐ Printing/publishing
05 ☐ Local national government
06 ☐ Education
07 ☐ Computer services
08 ☐ Other

Size of organization (please tick)

09 ☐ 0-25
10 ☐ 26-100
11 ☐ 101-250
12 ☐ 251-500
13 ☐ 501-1000
14 ☐ 1000+

Fig. 1.4 A membership form

1.4 Processing

At the heart of the data processing cycle will be a process in which data has various operations carried out on it:

1 **Calculation** – numbers may have arithmetic performed on them.
2 **Analysis** – numbers or text may be analysed.
3 **Comparison** – data items may be compared with one another or with a set value. The process may then take a different course depending on the result of the comparison.
4 **Manipulation** – data may be rearranged into a new order (i.e. sorted), merged with other data, etc.

Examples

Without a computer

Calculation – a shop assistant uses a till to add up purchases.
Analysis – a shop manager analyses the takings to see which goods sell well.
Comparison – a car driver sees a speed limit sign, checks the speedometer and slows down if necessary.
Sort – a teacher collects examination papers and puts them into alphabetical order.

With a computer

Calculation – in running a payroll program the number of hours an employee works, his rate of pay and tax code are used to calculate his wages.
Analysis – dates of birth may be analysed to produce a graph of the population by age.
Comparison – a measuring device passes to a computer the thickness of steel plate as it emerges from the steel press. If the metal is too thick or too thin the computer adjusts the press.
Sorting – a file of accounts is put in customer number order by the computer before being stored on magnetic tape.

2 REPRESENTATION OF DATA

All storage in modern digital computers is two state. This means that the smallest unit of the store is a device which can be set to one of two states and will stay in this state for as long as required.

Examples of two-state devices used as stores

1 A circuit known as a bistable which can be put *either* into a state where it outputs 5 volts *or* into another state where it outputs 0 volts.
2 A 'magnetic bubble', a small area of material which can be magnetized *either* in the opposite direction to the surrounding material *or* in the same direction.

Usually the two states are represented by 1 and 0. A single 1 or 0 is a **binary digit** or **bit**. Each location of the immediate access store contains a number of bits. A **word** is the group of bits treated by a given computer as its working unit. Each location will contain one word.

A **byte** is a small group of bits treated as a unit. It is usually the number of bits needed to store one character. In many systems a byte consists of eight bits.

A **character** is a symbol such as a letter, a punctuation mark, a digit of a number, etc.

Alphanumeric characters are the letters of the alphabet and the digits 0 to 9. In practice an alphanumeric character set will also usually include punctuation and other symbols such as £, +, &, etc.

Graphics characters – on some systems pictures and graphs are built up by printing carefully chosen characters of various shapes. These are called graphics characters.

Control characters – some devices, particularly printing devices, can be controlled by sending them special characters called control characters. These are not printed but instead cause the device to carry out some special function.

Examples of control characters

1 A character sent to a line printer to cause it to move the paper to another page.
2 A character which causes the screen to clear on a visual display unit.

A **character set** is the complete set of all the different characters used by a given system.

Examples of character sets

1 The character set for a computer terminal is all the characters on its keyboard or which it can print.
2 The character set for a computer language consists of all the characters which can be used in writing programs in the language.

A **character string** is a group of characters which are in an ordered sequence.

A **bit string** is a group of binary digits in sequence.

What a bit string represents

If a bit string is stored in a computer there are a number of possible things it may represent including:

1 A number.
2 A character or a string of characters.
3 An instruction.
4 The address of a location in store.

Abbreviations – K and M

K is 1024 – short for kilo
M is 1 million – short for mega

Notes: 1 1024 is the nearest power of 2 to 1000: $1K = 2^{10} = 1024$.
2 In practice 1 megabyte of store in a computer would be 1 048 576 bytes. This is because $1\,048\,576 = K \times K$.

Worked questions

1 How many bits are there in 4K bytes?

Number of bytes in 4K bytes $= 4 \times 1024$
$= 4096$
∴ Number of bits in 4K bytes $= 4096 \times 8$
$= 32\,768$

2 Two computers are advertised. Computer A has 2100K bytes of memory. Computer B has 2 megabytes. Which computer has most store?

Computer A has 2100K bytes
Computer B has 2 megabytes
This is 2×1024 bytes $=$ 2084K bytes
∴ Computer A has more store

2.1 Binary Representation of Numbers

An **integer** is a whole number. It may be positive or negative. Ordinary numbers are called **real numbers**. This includes all integers and all numbers with a decimal point.

There are various ways in which integers can be represented using 1s and 0s.

The **binary notation** is a method of representing numbers using 1s and 0s (Fig. 2.1). In a binary number each 1 represents a power of 2. The powers of two are the numbers 1, 2, 4, 8, 16, etc. (see Fig. 2.2).

Decimal number	*Binary equivalent*
0	0
1	1
2	10
3	11
4	100
5	101
6	110
7	111
8	1000
9	1001

Fig. 2.1 Binary values for 0 to 9

Example

In the binary integer 110111, working from the left, the 1s represent a 32, a 16, a 4, a 2 and a 1 (the zero indicates there is no 8).

The number is equal to (in decimal) $32+16+4+2+1=55$.

If a small binary number is represented in a long storage location, the digits at the left are made zero.

Worked question

Express the decimal numbers 7 and 5 as six-bit binary numbers.

$7_{10} = 000111_2$
$5_{10} = 000101_2$

Note: A suffix is used to indicate the **base** or **radix** of the numbers – 10 for decimal, 2 for binary.

RELATIVE ADVANTAGES OF BINARY AND DECIMAL REPRESENTATION

Advantages of the binary system:

1 A binary digit has only two possible states, 0 or 1, and so is easy to represent using electrical or magnetic devices.
2 The instructions and circuitry necessary to make a machine carry out arithmetic operations in binary are very simple.

Disadvantages of the binary system:

1 Numbers represented in binary have a larger number of digits.
2 Binary numbers are difficult to write down accurately and to remember.

2.2 Binary Conversion

Some powers of 2

Power, p	2^p
0	1
1	2
2	4
3	8
4	16
5	32
6	64
7	128
8	256
9	512

Fig. 2.2 Some powers of 2

CONVERSION OF DECIMAL INTEGERS TO BINARY

Method

1 Write out powers of 2 in a line starting at the right with 1. That is write . . . 64 32 16 8 4 2 1 (as many as necessary).
2 Subtract these powers of 2 from the number. Each time subtract the largest one which will go.
3 When a power is subtracted write a 1 under that power, otherwise write a 0.

Worked question

Convert the decimal number 71 to binary.

```
64 32 16 8 4 2 1     (The line of powers)
 1  0  0 0 1 1 1     (The 1s and 0s written down while subtracting)
   71-
   64
   --
    7-
    4
   --
    3-
    2
   --
    1
```

Answer: $71_{10} = 1000111_2$

CONVERSION OF BINARY INTEGERS TO DECIMAL

Method

1 Write powers of 2 above the digits of the binary numbers. Start at the right-hand end. That is write . . . 64 32 16 8 4 2 1 (as many as necessary).
2 Write down the powers of 2 which are above a 1 in the binary number. Add them up to obtain the answer.

Worked question

Convert the binary number 1101101 to decimal.

```
64 32 16 8 4 2 1
 1  1  0 1 1 0 1
```

Number $= 64+32+8+4+1$
$= 109$

Answer: $1101101_2 = 109_{10}$

2.3 Positive and Negative Integers

The **ones complement** of a binary string is formed by replacing 0s by 1s and 1s by 0s.

The **twos complement** of a binary integer is formed by finding the 1s complement of the number and adding 1 to it.

Worked questions

1 Find the ones complement and twos complement of 000101101

To find the ones complement replace 0 by 1, 1 by 0

Ones complement of 000101101 = 111010010

Twos complement of 000101101 = Ones complement + 1

= 111010010 +

1

111010011

Answer: Ones complement is 111010010; twos complement is 111010011

2 Find the eight-bit twos complement of 110100

Make up to eight bits by adding 0s on the left: 00110100

Ones complement = 11001011

Twos complement = Ones complement + 1

= 11001011 +

1

11001100

Answer: Twos complement = 11001100

METHODS OF STORING INTEGERS

There are several methods of storing integers in a computer so that positive and negative numbers are represented. Often the bit at the left of the string indicates whether the number is positive or negative. This bit is called the sign bit:

Sign-and-magnitude method

The **sign bit** is 1 for negative, 0 for positive. The size of the number is shown in the remaining bits.

Twos complement method

The sign bit is 1 for negative, 0 for positive. For positive numbers the remaining bits show the size of the number. For negative numbers the twos complement of the number is shown.

Worked question

Express the binary integers (a) 1011 (b) −11011 in sign-and-magnitude and in twos complement form as they would appear in an eight-bit location.

(a) In sign-and-magnitude form 1011 would be 00001011
In twos complement form 1011 would be 00001011

(b) In sign-and-magnitude form −11011→10011011
In twos complement form:
Extend to eight bits 11011→00011011
Find ones complement →11100100
Add 1 →11100101

Note: Positive numbers are the same for both methods but negative numbers are different.

CONVERTING TWOS COMPLEMENT NEGATIVE INTEGERS TO DECIMAL

Method

Use the same method as that for positive integers (see end of Unit 2.2). However, treat the sign bit as a negative number.

1 Write powers of 2 above the digits of the number. Start at the right-hand end. That is write . . . 64 32 16 8 4 2 1 (as many as necessary).

2 Write down the powers of 2 which are above a 1 in the number. Add them up counting the one over the sign bit as negative.

Worked question

111011 is a negative number in twos complement form. Find its value as a decimal number.

−32	16	8	4	2	1
1	1	1	0	1	1

Number = −32 + 16 + 8 + 2 + 1

= −32 + 27

Answer: Number represented is −5

2.4 Representation of Fractions in Binary

FIXED-POINT REPRESENTATION

Fractions can be written in binary by extending the binary notation explained for integers above.

In a binary number the digits after the point represent ½, ¼, ⅛, etc.

Worked question

Give the decimal equivalents of the binary numbers

(a) 110.11 (b) 0.001

(a) $110_2 = 6_{10}$
$0.11_2 = \frac{1}{2} + \frac{1}{4} = 0.5 + 0.25$
$= 0.75$
$\therefore 110.11_2 = 6.75_{10}$

(b) $0.001_2 = \frac{1}{8}$
$= 0.125_{10}$

A **fixed-point number** is one which is represented by a set of digits with the point in its correct position.

e.g. 313.45 is a fixed-point decimal number;
1101.1101 is a fixed-point binary number.

FLOATING-POINT REPRESENTATION

The **mantissa** of a number consists of the actual digits in it. The point is put at some fixed position (often in front of the first digit).

e.g. The mantissa of 34.234 is .34234

The **exponent** of a number gives the position of the binary or decimal point.

e.g. If the position is measured from the left of the number, the exponent of 34.234 is 2.

A **floating-point number** is one which is represented by writing the mantissa and the exponent.

Examples of floating-point representation

1 The decimal number 672.4 could be written as .6724 E3.
E is for exponent. The 3 indicates three significant figures to the left of the decimal point.
2 The binary number 110.1101 could be stored with an eight-bit mantissa and a four-bit exponent as 01101101 0011.

Here 01101101 is the mantissa. The first bit is a sign bit. It has been assumed that the point is just after the sign bit. The mantissa represents 0.1101101.

The number 110.1101 has three significant figures to the left of the point. Therefore the exponent is three. Expressed as a four-bit binary number, this is 0011.

Advantages of floating-point representation

Very large numbers or very small fractions can be stored using quite a small number of bits.

Disadvantage of floating-point representation

Numbers are not stored very precisely by this method. If a number has a lot of digits some of them may be lost. The mantissa can only be allowed a certain number of bits for storage. It is therefore only correct to a certain number of significant figures.

2.5 Accuracy

Numbers are not necessarily stored in a computer with perfect precision. Each number is allowed only a certain number of bits for storage.

Usually integers are stored accurately with a limited range. Real numbers are stored with a large range but less accuracy (using floating-point representation – see Unit 2.4).

RANGE OF BINARY INTEGERS

Positive integers

As the numbers are all positive no sign bit is necessary.

The largest number which can be stored in a register with n bits is $2^n - 1$.

The smallest number which can be stored is 0.

Example

For an eight-bit word the largest number possible
$= 11111111_2$
$= 100000000_2 - 1 = 2^8 - 1$ (= 255)

Twos complement integers

If twos complement integers are represented in a register or location of n bits, then
the largest positive number possible $= 2^{n-1} - 1$
the most negative number possible $= -2^{n-1}$

Example

For an eight-bit word the largest number possible
$= 01111111$ (as the first bit is a sign bit)
$= 2^7 - 1$ (= 127)
The most negative number
$= 10000000_2$ (first bit = 1 to get a negative number; as we are complementing negative numbers, the other bits should be as small as possible i.e. 0)

This represents $-(1111111_2 + 1)$ (Taking twos complement)
$= -10000000_2$
$= -2^7$ (= −128)

i.e. The range of twos complement integers in an eight-bit register is −128 to 127

Worked question

Binary integers are represented using twos complement notation in a 16-bit register. Find their range.

Largest positive integer is $0111\ 1111\ 1111\ 1111_2 = 2^{15} - 1$
$= 32\ 767$

Most negative integer is $1000\ 0000\ 0000\ 0000_2 = -(111\ 1111\ 1111\ 1111_2 + 1)$
$= -1000\ 0000\ 0000\ 0000$
$= 2^{15}$
$= -32\ 768$

i.e. The integers represented lie in the range −32 768 to +32 767 inclusive

2.6 Octal and Hexadecimal

Octal numbers are numbers written in base 8. **Hexadecimal numbers** are numbers written in base 16.

Decimal (base 10)	*Binary (base 2)*	*Octal (base 8)*	*Hexadecimal (base 16)*
0	0000	0	0
1	0001	1	1
2	0010	2	2
3	0011	3	3
4	0100	4	4
5	0101	5	5
6	0110	6	6
7	0111	7	7
8	1000	10	8
9	1001	11	9
10	1010	12	A
11	1011	13	B
12	1100	14	C
13	1101	15	D
14	1110	16	E
15	1111	17	F
16	10000	20	10

Fig. 2.3 Conversion table for small numbers

Reasons for using octal and/or hexadecimal

Although they are stored in a computer in binary form, bit strings are often displayed by or entered into a computer in octal or hexadecimal form. This is because:

1 Binary strings are longer than their octal or hexadecimal equivalents. This means:
(a) Octal or hexadecimal strings do not take up much room when displayed.
(b) Binary strings take longer to type in.
2 Binary strings are difficult to recognize and remember.

3 As octal and hexadecimal are each based on a power of 2, they can be converted to and from binary easily.

CONVERSION BETWEEN HEXADECIMAL AND BINARY (INTEGERS)

Every hexadecimal digit corresponds to four bits of the equivalent binary number.

Binary to hexadecimal

Method

1 Starting at the right split the binary number into groups of four bits.
2 Convert each group of bits to hexadecimal.

Worked question

A location contains the value 1001101011 in binary.
How would this be displayed in hexadecimal?

	Comments
10 0110 1011	Starting at the right group into fours
2 6 B	For each group write hexadecimal equivalent

Answer $1001101011_2 = 26B_{16}$

Hexadecimal to binary

Method

1 For each hexadecimal digit write the four-digit binary equivalent.
2 Ignore any zeros at the left.

Worked question

The address of a location is 2B6A in hexadecimal. What is it in binary?

2	B	6	A	*Comment*
0010	1011	0110	1010	For each hexadecimal digit write the binary equivalent

The address is 0010 1011 0110 1010

Notes:
1 In the example addresses may occupy 16 bits so the two 0s at the left were not discarded.
2 The methods for converting between octal and binary are similar with each octal digit corresponding to three binary digits.

2.7 Binary Representation of Characters

When characters are transmitted or stored each character is represented as a binary string. The number of bits used to represent each character differs from one system to another. On punched cards there were 12 hole positions for each character, and on some paper tapes there were only 5. In most modern systems, seven, eight or nine bits are used.

In general the number of different characters which can be encoded is 2^n, where n is the number of bits used for each character.

e.g. The number of different characters you can have with an eight-bit code is $2^8 = 256$.

Worked question

Eight-bit storage locations are used to store coded characters. One bit is a parity bit. 0000 0000 and 1111 1111 both have special uses and cannot be used to code characters. How many different characters can be represented?

Seven bits are used for the actual code.
Seven bits gives $2^7 = 128$ characters.
Two codes cannot be used
$\therefore$ No. of possible characters $= 128 - 2$
$= 126$

COMMONLY USED CODES

There are many different character codes in use. Which one is used in a particular situation depends on:

1 The size of the character set being represented.
2 The number of bits available for the codes.
3 The medium being used.

Three codes commonly used in computing (Fig. 2.4) are:
1 ASCII – American Standard Code for Information Interchange
2 BCD – Binary Coded Decimal
3 EBCDIC – Extended BCD Interchange Code.

Characteristic	*Name of code*		
	ASCII	*BCD*	*EBCDIC*
Number of bits (excluding parity)	7	6	8
Maximum possible size of character set	128	64	256
Examples of where it is used	(i) Data transmission (ii) Main store of microcomputers	(i) Seven-track magnetic tape (ii) Main store of some large computers	Nine-track magnetic tape
Example codes:			
Letter A	1000001	110001	11000001
Letter B	1000010	110010	11000010
Digit 1	0110001	000001	11110001

Fig. 2.4 Character codes

EXAMPLE – CODES ON MAGNETIC TAPE

1 Audio cassettes

Standard tape cassettes are often used as a backing store for microcomputers.

Characteristics

(a) Often only one track is used, one bit lasting a given time interval, bits being stored one after another along the tape.
(b) Usually 1 and 0 are represented by sounds of two different frequencies.
(c) The code used is often ASCII, with 'start' bits and 'stop' bits in between the characters to show where each character begins and ends.

2 Standard ½-inch computer magnetic tape

Often in reels 732 metres (2400 ft) long as:
(a) a seven-track tape using BCD code and a parity bit; or
(b) a nine-track tape using EBCDIC and a parity bit.

Small areas of the tape are magnetized to produce a situation comparable with paper tape (Fig. 2.5).

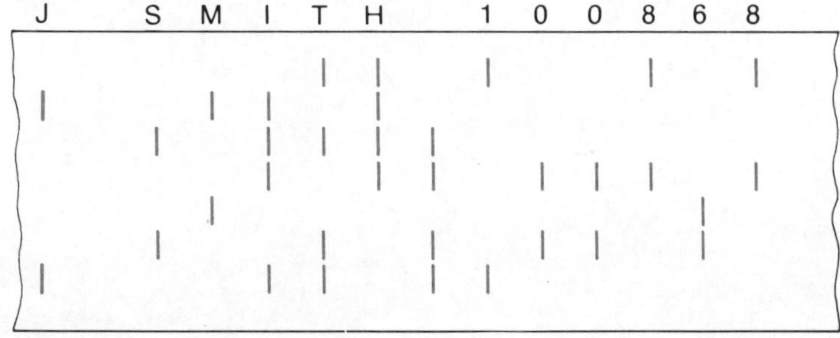

Fig. 2.5 Seven-track magnetic tape

Note: For further details of storage of data on magnetic tapes, and for details of data storage on discs see Unit 9.2.

Worked questions

1 Suggest, with reasons, two codes which could be used – one for each of the following situations.
(a) A language with a character set of 47 characters is to be used in a computer with a 24-bit word.
(b) In a microcomputer 100 different characters are used and the code must include information as to whether a character is to be printed on the screen normally or in reverse.

(a) 6 bits can hold $2^6 = 64$ different characters
5 bits can only hold $2^5 = 32$ different characters
∴6 bits are necessary to code 47 characters
BCD code could be used with 4 characters in each 24-bit word.

(b) 7 bits can code $2^7 = 128$ different characters
6 bits can code $2^6 = 64$
∴7 bits are needed to code 100 characters

Seven-bit ASCII could be used. An eighth bit could be 1 for normal printing, 0 for reverse.

2 A computer has a store of 20K 16-bit words. How many characters can be stored in it using an eight-bit character code?

Number of words = 20K
∴Numbers of characters (stored two to a word)
= 20K × 2
= 40K

3 When printed in decimal a seven-bit code gives the value 65 for letter A and 67 for letter C. Suggest values for B and D.

$65_{10} = 1000001_2$; $67_{10} = 1000011_2$
This is probably ASCII. In any case the right-hand digits seem to be the binary for the position in the alphabet (1 for A, 3 for C).
The first bit is not a parity bit. Assume it is 1 for all letters.
Probable codes are B = 1000010; D = 1000100

3 DIGITAL LOGIC

The word **logic** is used to describe systems whose members are two state. A **logic circuit** is an electrical circuit with all voltages at one of two values.

Most computer circuitry consists of logic circuits with voltages all at one of two levels called **logic 0** and **logic 1**.

One type of circuitry in widespread use in computers and similar equipment (so-called TTL circuitry) has:

logic 1 = 5 volts (or slightly less)
logic 0 = 0 volts (or slightly more)

A **logic gate** is a logic circuit with one or more inputs and one output (Fig. 3.1).

Example of a logic gate

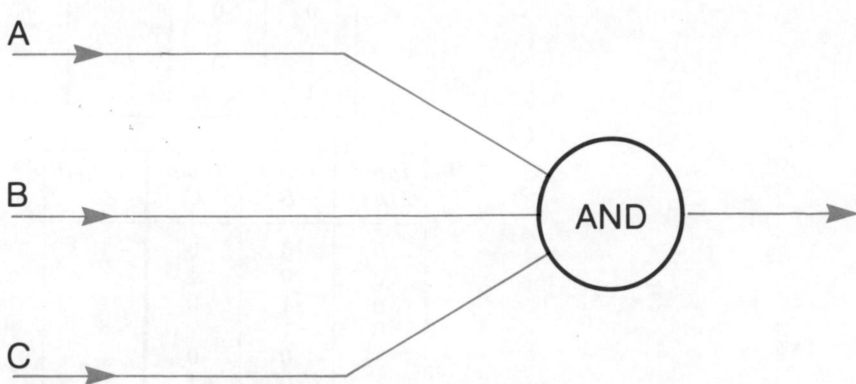

Fig. 3.1 Example of a logic gate

A **logic diagram** is a diagram showing logic elements and their interconnections (Fig. 3.2). A number of logic gates and their interconnections may be called a **logical network**.

Example of a logic diagram

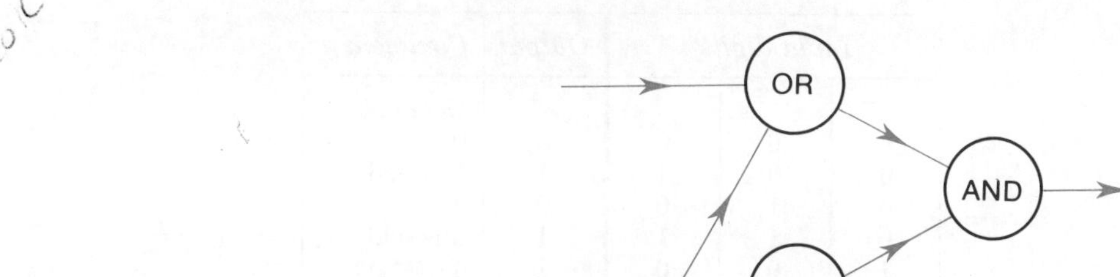

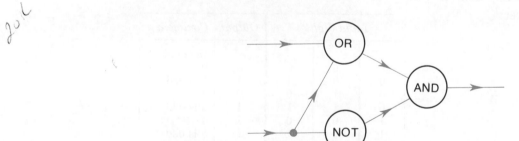

Fig. 3.2 Example of a logic diagram

3.1 Truth Tables

A **truth table** is a table which shows the result of logical operations.

Truth tables can be used:

1 To show the outputs of a logic circuit for all possible combinations of the inputs.
2 To show the result of any operations which follow logical rules.

The positions in a truth table are usually filled with 1s and 0s. Sometimes Ts and Fs are used (for true and false).

Hints for drawing truth tables

Often in questions the framework of a truth table is drawn for you. If it is not make sure you draw the table up correctly.

1 (a) Write clear headings for the columns.
(b) Sometimes it is difficult to work out the output column directly from the input columns. Don't be afraid to put in an extra column if it will make the truth table easier to work out.
(c) Draw a double line after the input columns so that it is clear which they are.
2 The number of rows down a truth table should be a power of 2 which depends on the number of inputs:
for one input there are two rows
for two inputs there are four rows
for three inputs there are eight rows
3 If the table is to be filled in with 1s and 0s write the inputs down the page in numerical order, as if you were counting in binary:
e.g. For two inputs 00, 01, 10, 11
and for three inputs 000, 001, 010, 011, 100, 101, 110, 111
(see input columns in the worked questions)

Worked questions on truth tables

1 Show all the inputs for a truth table with one output and
(a) two inputs (b) three inputs.
Answer:

(a)

Input A	*Input B*	*Output*
0	0	
0	1	
1	0	
1	1	

(b)

Input A	*Input B*	*Input C*	*Output*
0	0	0	
0	0	1	
0	1	0	
0	1	1	
1	0	0	
1	0	1	
1	1	0	
1	1	1	

2 Draw a truth table for a device which inputs three-figure binary numbers and outputs a 1 if the binary number is odd or if it is equal to 4 (decimal), outputting 0 for all other numbers.
Answer:

Input digits			*Output*	*Comment*
				Decimal
0	0	0	0	0
0	0	1	1	1 is odd
0	1	0	0	2
0	1	1	1	3 is odd
1	0	0	1	4
1	0	1	1	5 is odd
1	1	0	0	6
1	1	1	1	7 is odd

3 A simple camera will not take pictures either:
(a) When the film is fast and the day is bright (because there is too much light); or
(b) When the film is slow and the day is dull (too little light).
Otherwise it will take pictures successfully. Draw a truth table to show when the camera will take pictures. Head the columns *Fast film, Bright day* and *Picture taken*. Insert a 1 if the condition is *true* and a 0 if it is *false*.
Answer:

Fast film	*Bright day*	*Picture taken*
0	0	0
0	1	1
1	0	1
1	1	0

4 An automatic fan in a greenhouse comes on when the air is moist or when the temperature is high. Otherwise the fan is off. In the table, 1 in the *'Moist'* column means air is moist and in the *'Hot'* column 1 means temperature is high. Complete the table using 1 for *on* and 0 for *off*.

Moist	*Hot*	*Fan on*
0	0	
0	1	
1	0	
1	1	

Answer:

Moist	*Hot*	*Fan on*
0	0	0
0	1	1
1	0	1
1	1	1

3.2 Simple Gates – NOT, AND and OR

The circuits of a computer may contain millions of components, but most of this is made up by repeating a few different gates.

NOT GATE (INVERTER)

(The output is NOT the same as the input.)

Functions of NOT gate in words: a logic gate with one input. The output is logic 0 if the input is logic 1 and is logic 1 if the input is logic 0.

Truth table for NOT gate

Input	*Output*
0	1
1	0

Fig. 3.3 Truth table for a NOT gate

Note: The operation carried out by a NOT gate is referred to as **inverting**.

AND GATE

(The output is 1 only when A AND B are 1)

Functions of AND gate in words: a logic gate with two or more inputs. The output is logic 1 when both (or all) the inputs are logic 1; otherwise the output is logic 0.

Truth table for AND gate (two inputs)

Input A	*Input* B	*Output*
0	0	0
0	1	0
1	0	0
1	1	1

Fig. 3.4 Truth table for an AND gate

OR GATE

(Output is 1 when A OR B is 1 – this includes the case when both of A and B are 1.)

Function of OR gate in words: a logic gate with two or more inputs. The output is logic 1 when any one of the inputs is logic 1; the output is logic 0 when both (or all) the inputs are logic 0.

Truth table for OR gate (two inputs)

Input A	*Input* B	*Output*
0	0	0
0	1	1
1	0	1
1	1	1

Fig. 3.5 Truth table for an OR gate

Worked questions

1 Draw a truth table for the following logic diagram. Show the logic values at D, E, F and G.

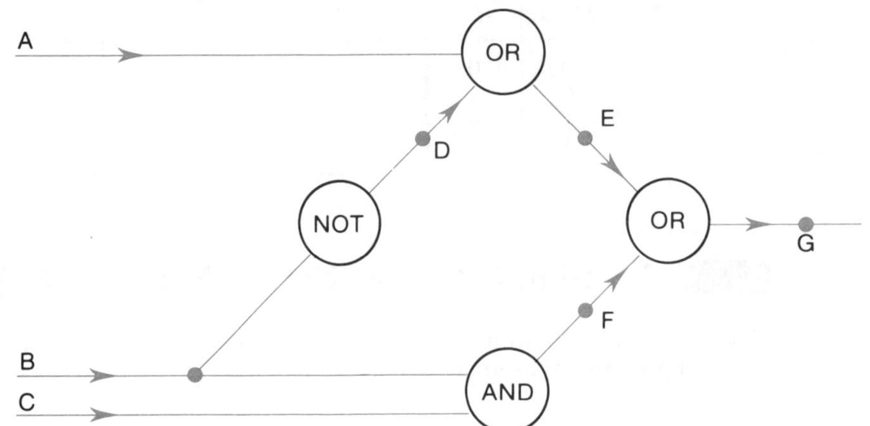

Answer: The truth table is as follows:

A	*B*	*C*	*D*	*E*	*F*	*G*
0	0	0	1	1	0	1
0	0	1	1	1	0	1
0	1	0	0	0	0	0
0	1	1	0	0	1	1
1	0	0	1	1	0	1
1	0	1	1	1	0	1
1	1	0	0	1	0	1
1	1	1	0	1	1	1

Notes: 1 A,B,C, are the inputs. The table must show all eight combinations of these.
2 D is obtained by inverting values of B.
E is obtained from the A and D columns using the truth table for OR.
F is obtained from the B and C columns using the truth table for AND.
G is obtained from the E and F columns using the truth table for OR.

2 If A = 10011, B = 10101 and C = 11001 find (A OR B) AND (NOT C), carrying out the operations on corresponding bits of A, B and C.

Answer: A OR B = 10111
NOT C = 00110
∴(A OR B) AND (NOT C) = 10111 AND 00110
= 00110

Note: Detail of A OR B: 10011
10101
10111

The bits are OR-ed one pair at a time – a bit from A with a bit from B.

3 A line to a computer is to be in use when a printer *or* a disc unit are free *and* when the computer is also free. Draw a logic diagram for a circuit which will ensure that this is so.

Assume that when a device is free it inputs 1 to the circuit, and 0 when it is not free. Assume when the circuit outputs 1 the line is in use.

Answer: The circuit is:

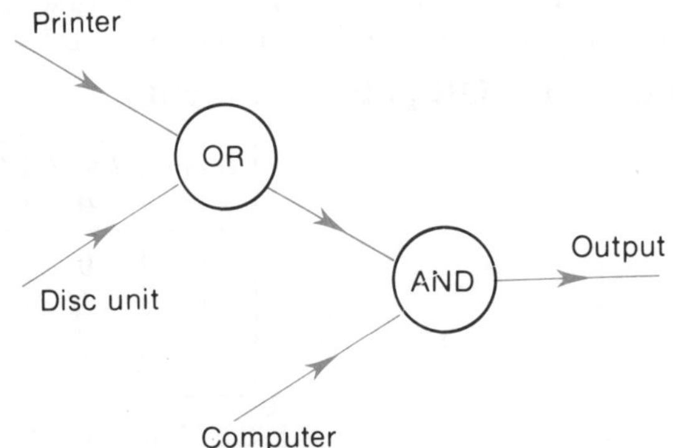

4 Draw a truth table for the following circuit:

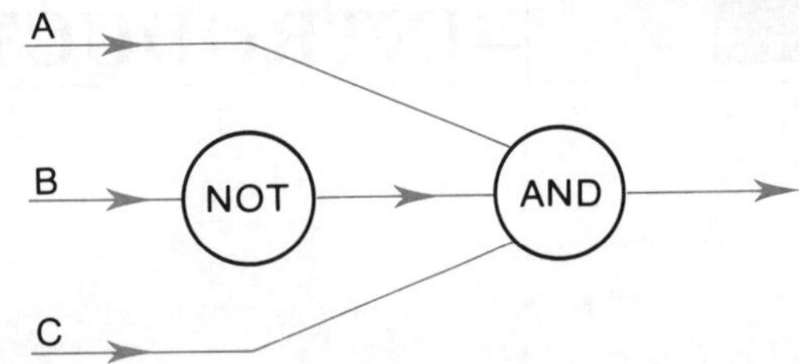

Answer: The truth table is as follows:

A	*B*	*C*	*NOT* $\bar{B}$	*Output*
0	0	0	1	0
0	0	1	1	0
0	1	0	0	0
0	1	1	0	0
1	0	0	1	0
1	0	1	1	1
1	1	0	0	0
1	1	1	0	0

4 COMPUTER HARDWARE –INTRODUCTION

Fig. 4.1 A modern computer room (*By kind permission of Central Electricity Generating Board*)

Hardware is the term used to describe all the actual pieces of equipment in a computer system.

Examples of hardware

1 Peripherals such as input, output and storage devices.
2 The central processing unit (CPU) of a computer.
3 Input and output media.

Note: Hardware may be contrasted with software, which consists just of programs (see Unit 14).

A **computer** is a machine which automatically inputs and processes data, and outputs the results. The actual process carried out is fixed beforehand, usually by a program stored in the machine (see Unit 5).

Most modern computers are **digital**.

A device is digital if some quantity in it can be set to a number of different separate values (or **discrete states**). Data and programs are then represented by combinations of these states.

In practice the quantity used has two states and is often either:

1 An electrical voltage – usually 0 volts or 5 volts, or
2 A magnetic field – in one of two directions.

Other quantities are used such as electrical capacity and light. At the moment practically all digital devices are two-state, with data and programs represented by binary codes (see Unit 2 for coding of data, Unit 5 for programs).

DIGITAL AND ANALOGUE

Some computers and computing devices are not digital but **analogue**. An analogue device is one in which data is represented by a quantity which is continuously variable. The value of a data item at a given time is represented by the size of the quantity, measured on a fixed scale.

Thus analogue data is continuously variable; digital data is discrete.

Examples of analogue and digital representation.

1 In a particular digital computer, binary digits can be represented by 0 volts or 5 volts. Numbers and characters are represented in binary codes – e.g. 4 is represented by 00000100 and 5 by 00000101.
2 In a particular analogue computer numbers from 0 to 10 are represented on a continuous voltage scale. This goes from 0 volts to 5 volts – e.g. 4 is represented by 2 volts and 5 by 2.5 volts.

Worked question

Give an example of two devices, one analogue and one digital, which are both used for the same purpose. Explain how they differ.

A digital voltmeter and an analogue voltmeter both display voltage. In a digital voltmeter the voltage is displayed as a set of digits (in ordinary decimal notation). Each digit can have any of ten separate states (the numbers 0,1,2,3,4,5,6,7,8,9).

In an analogue voltmeter voltage is shown by a needle which moves across a dial and can take any position on it. The position of the needle is continuously variable.

Examples of analogue devices

1 A mercury thermometer.
2 Kitchen scales.

4.1 Digital Computers

Practically all modern computers:

1 Are electronic.
2 Are digital.
3 Are two-state.
4 Have a stored program (see Unit 5).

A TYPICAL DIGITAL COMPUTER SYSTEM

The layout of a typical digital computer is as shown in Fig. 4.2.

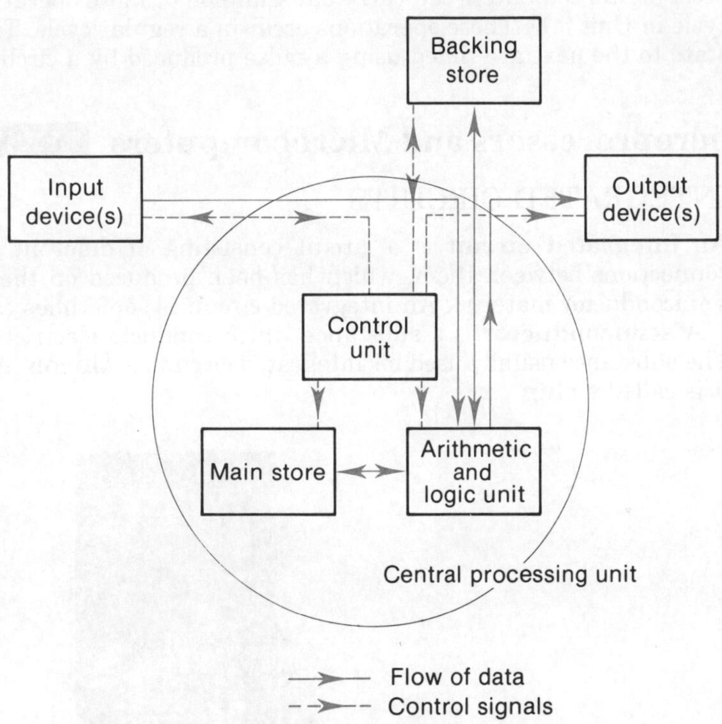

Fig. 4.2 Layout of a typical digital computer

The **central processing unit (CPU)** is the main part of the computer. It operates at a higher speed than the rest of the computer system and (in a modern computer) has no moving parts.

It is sometimes called the **central processor** and consists of the **control unit**, the **arithmetic and logic unit (ALU)** and the **main store**.

The devices outside the central processing unit but controlled by it are called **peripheral devices** or **peripherals** (e.g. input devices, output devices and backing storage devices are peripherals).

Backing store is a means of storing large amounts of data outside the central processing unit (see Unit 9.2).

The control unit

When the computer is running, the **control unit** repeatedly interprets **(decodes)** instructions rapidly, one after another. After each instruction is decoded it is carried out **(executed)**. If the instruction involves a peripheral the control unit sends signals to operate the peripheral.

Arithmetic and logic unit

If an instruction involves carrying out an arithmetic operation on data, the data is transferred to the **arithmetic and logic unit** and the operation is carried out there.

Main store

The main store of a computer is the fast access store in the central processing unit. It is also called the **main memory** or the **immediate access store** (or **IAS**).

The most important function of the main store is to hold programs and data while the programs are being executed.

The main store has the following characteristics:

1 It can be written to and read from at very high speed. This is done without any mechanical movement.

2 It is divided up into small equal sized units called **locations**. Each location can be accessed by the computer using a number called its **address**. Each location has a different address.

3 It usually consists of *two* types of store or memory:

ROM–read only memory, which can be read but not written to and

RAM–random access memory, which can be read from or written to (see Unit 9.1 for details).

Notes:

1 It is important to use the words 'location' and 'address' accurately. It is *not* correct to say that data is stored in an address–it is stored in a location.

2 Each location may contain as few as 8 bits (in some microcomputers) but often there are 16, 32 or more.

The clock

Most digital computers can carry out a million or more operations a second (see fetch–execute cycle in Unit 5.1). These operations occur in a regular cycle. The changes in the cycle from one state to the next are timed using a pulse produced by a circuit called a **clock**.

4.2 Microprocessors and Microcomputers

INTEGRATED CIRCUITS

An **integrated circuit** is a circuit consisting of different electronic components and the connections between them, which has been produced on the surface of a small flat piece of semiconductor material. An integrated circuit is sometimes called an **IC**.

A **semiconductor** is a substance which conducts electricity but not as well as metals do. The substance usually used for integrated circuits is **silicon**. A piece of silicon with a circuit on it is called a **chip**.

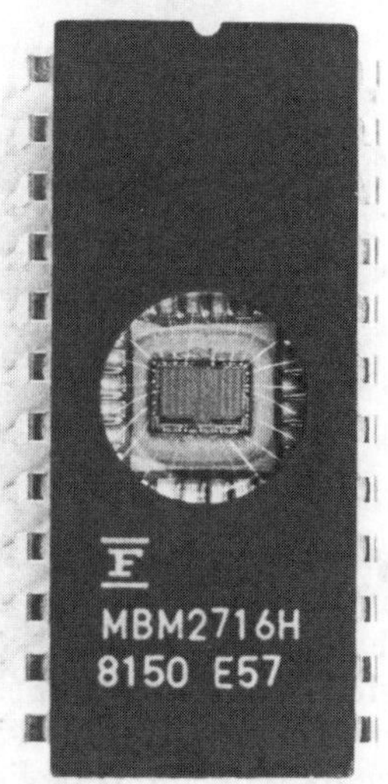

Fig. 4.3 Integrated circuit package. This particular type of package has a window, through which are visible the chip itself and the wires connecting this to the pins.

Each integrated circuit is usually encased in a rectangular plastic 'package' with two rows of pins to connect the integrated circuit to other circuits. This connection is usually done by soldering the pins into holes on a printed circuit board (see Fig. 4.3 and Fig. 4.4).

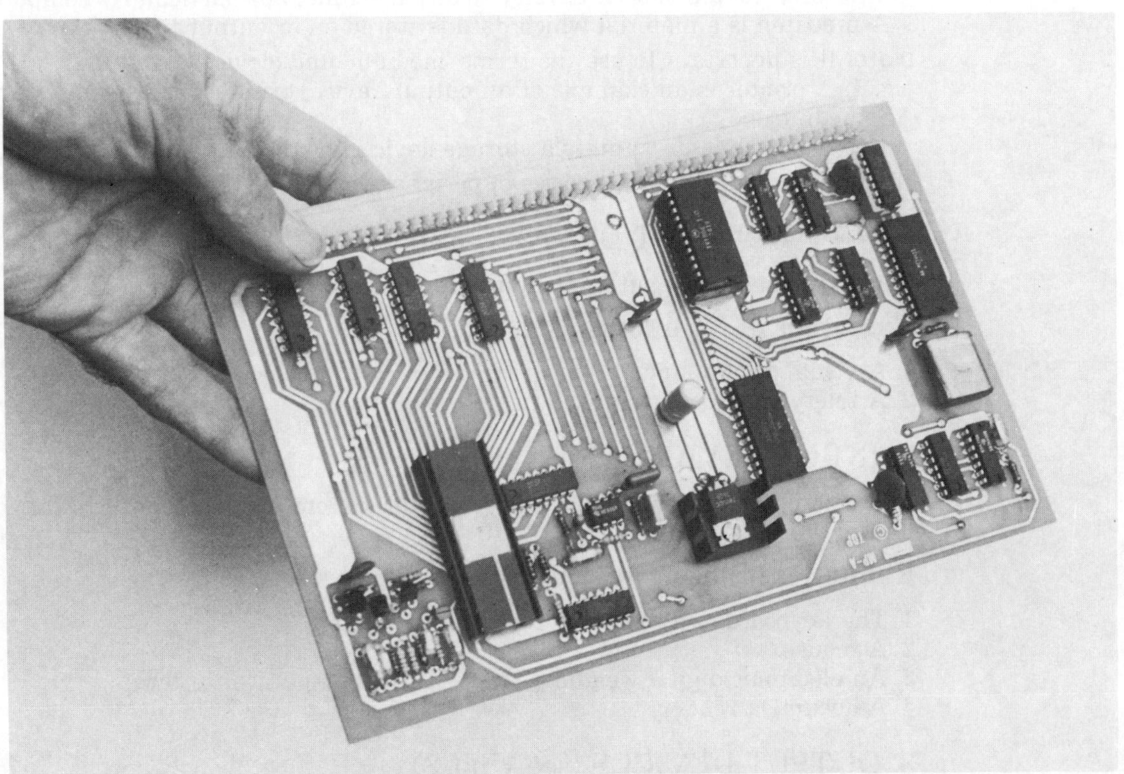

Fig. 4.4 Printed circuit board with integrated circuits soldered on to it

MICROPROCESSORS

A **microprocessor** is an integrated circuit which contains the control unit, the arithmetic and logic unit and possibly some main store for a computer.

A **microcomputer** is a computer for which the main processing is done by a microprocessor. Small computers which are not microcomputers are usually called **minicomputers**. Large powerful computers with a range of peripherals are called **mainframe** computers.

Layout of the central processing unit of a microcomputer

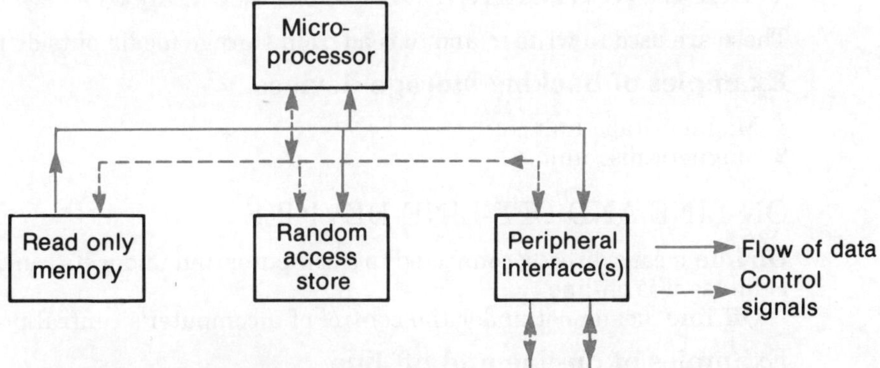

Fig. 4.5 Layout of the central processing unit of a microcomputer

Dedicated microprocessors

A **dedicated** computer is one which is just used for one particular job. Examples of dedicated microprocessors are:

1 A microprocessor can be used to operate the dashboard and some of the controls in a car. Its tasks may include:

(a) Checking that the seat belts for occupied seats are in use before the engine is started.

(b) Monitoring the fuel mixture so that the engine runs economically.

2 A camera may contain a microprocessor to control exposure calculations. This may make it possible to:

(a) Operate the camera in several different programmed modes.

(b) Select several different points in a picture and have an average exposure calculated for them.

4.3 Peripheral Devices

A **peripheral** is a device outside the central processing unit but controlled by it.

The term **device** is used to refer to any machine, but particularly computer peripherals.

A **medium** is a material which data is stored on or output to.

Note: It is important to use the terms 'medium' and 'device' carefully.

e.g. **1** A printer is an example of an output device; printer paper is an example of an output medium.

2 A magnetic disc unit is a storage device; the disc is a storage medium.

There are four main categories of peripheral:

1 INPUT/OUTPUT DEVICES (see Unit 6)

These consist of an input and an output device combined in one unit.

Examples of input/output devices

1 A visual display unit.
2 A teletypewriter terminal.

2 INPUT DEVICES (see Unit 7)

These accept data from outside the computer system and transmit it to the central processing unit.

Examples of input devices

1 The keyboard of a computer terminal.
2 A mouse.
3 An electronic digital weighing scales with a computer interface.
4 A document reader.

3 OUTPUT DEVICES (see Unit 8)

These receive data from the central processing unit and change it to a form which can be used outside the computer system.

Examples of output devices

1 A lineprinter.
2 A screen on a computer terminal.
3 A voice synthesizer.
4 A microcomputer-controlled robot which welds cars.

4 BACKING STORAGE DEVICES (see Unit 9)

These are used to write to and to read from storage media outside the central processing unit.

Examples of backing storage devices

1 Magnetic tape unit.
2 Magnetic disc unit.

ON-LINE AND OFF-LINE DEVICES

On line means directly connected to a computer and under its control. Thus when a peripheral is in use it is on-line.

Off line means not under the control of a computer's central processing unit.

Examples of on-line and off-line

1 Data is prepared and validated on a disc using a key-to-disc station. This station is on-line to a minicomputer. The disc is then transferred to another disc unit for processing. This second disc unit is on-line to a mainframe computer.
2 When a computer terminal is connected to a computer it is on-line. When it is disconnected from the computer it is off-line.
3 When a magnetic tape is stored in a rack it is off-line. When it is placed in an on-line tape drive it is on-line.

5 THE CENTRAL PROCESSING UNIT – EXECUTION OF PROGRAMS

The central processing unit consists of three main parts (see Unit 4.1):

1 The control unit. This fetches program instructions from the main store and causes them to be carried out.

2 The arithmetic and logic unit. This does calculations and comparisons.

3 The main store. This holds the program and the data being used.

In modern microcomputers the control unit and the arithmetic and logic unit are in the same chip. This chip is called a microprocessor (see Unit 4.2). Sometimes it contains some of the main store as well.

Programs

A **program** is an ordered set of instructions which a computer carries out. The program is stored in the main store while it is being executed. To carry out a task, the control unit fetches and executes the instructions in the correct sequence.

Machine code refers to the set of codes which the computer has built in to it. It can decode and execute these without any translation.

A programmer can write programs in a number of programming languages. A computer cannot execute these programs directly as they are not in machine code. They have to be either interpreted or else translated into machine code before they can be executed (see Unit 11).

5.1 The Fetch–Execute Cycle

The fetch-execute cycle (Fig. 5.1) is a timed sequence by which the control unit 'fetches' instructions from the main store. They are fetched one at a time and then decoded and executed.

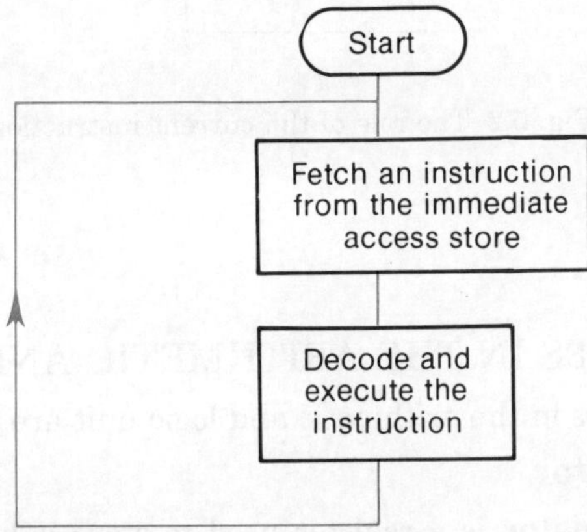

Fig. 5.1 Simplified flowchart of the fetch–execute cycle

Note: No stop has been shown in the diagram. Usually a computer does not stop fetching and executing instructions while it is switched on, although it does transfer from one program to another.

Example

When a typical microcomputer has finished executing a program which has been 'RUN', control is transferred to another program which flashes the cursor on the screen and checks the keyboard to see if a key has been pressed.

Note: In some processors (e.g. many microprocessors) an instruction may take up more than one storage location. Fetching the instruction will then take two or three operations.

5.2 Registers

A **register** is a special-purpose storage location. The computer uses registers for temporary storage of instructions, data and addresses.

REGISTERS IN THE CONTROL UNIT

1 Program counter – also known as the sequence control register (SCR)

The **program counter** holds the address of the next instruction to be fetched. As soon as the instruction (or part instruction – see note above) has been fetched the value in the program counter is increased by 1, as the control unit normally fetches instructions one after another in the order in which they are stored (see Fig. 5.2).

If the instruction executed causes a branch to an instruction in another part of the program, the value in the program counter is altered to the address of the new instruction.

2 Current instruction register

The **current instruction register** holds the instruction fetched from the store while it is being decoded and executed (see Fig. 5.2).

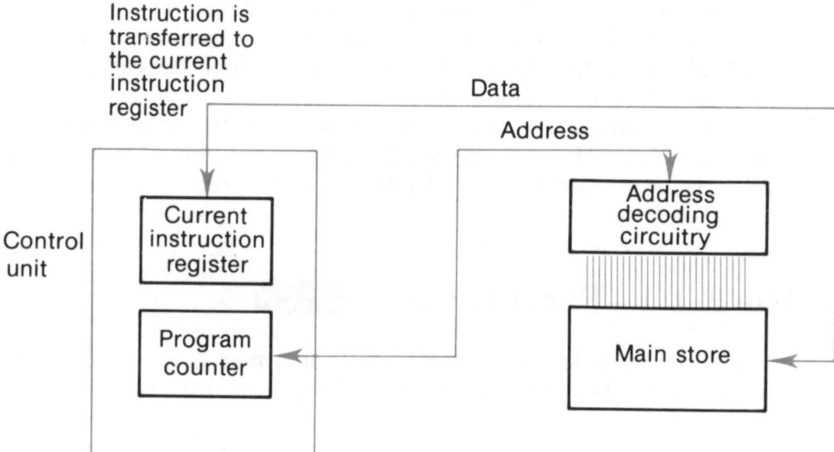

Fig. 5.2 The role of the current instruction register and the program counter

REGISTERS IN THE ARITHMETIC AND LOGIC UNIT

The registers in the arithmetic and logic unit are involved in the execution of instructions:

Accumulator

An **accumulator** is a register used to store values which are the subject of arithmetic or logical operations or of data transfers.

Examples of the use of an accumulator

1 If two numbers in locations A and B are to be added and stored in location C, instructions with the following functions will usually be fetched and executed:
(a) Load contents of location A into the accumulator.
(b) Add contents of location B to contents of the accumulator.
(c) Store contents of accumulator in location C.
2 If a character is to be printed out:
(a) A code for the character is loaded into the accumulator.
(b) The contents of the accumulator are transferred to a buffer ready for printing.
Note: A computer often has more than one accumulator.

5.3 Typical Instruction Set

The **instruction set** is the set of machine code instructions built into the computer.

Instructions are needed to:

1 Transfer data within the computer.
2 Do arithmetic.
3 Carry out logical operations.
4 Branch from one instruction to another in the program.

The following examples are written in words. The actual machine code instructions are in binary.

Transfer of data–examples

1 LOAD ACCUMULATOR–transfer a value into the accumulator.
2 COPY A B–copy the contents of register A into register B.

Arithmetic–examples

1 ADD A–add a value to register A.
2 SUB B–subtract a value from register B.

Logical operations–examples

1 SHIFT LEFT–shift all the bits in the accumulator 1 place to the left.
2 AND A,B–do the logical operation AND between the contents of A and the contents of B (see worked question 2 in Unit 3.2 for an example of this type of operation).

BRANCH INSTRUCTIONS

These are the instructions used to program the computer to make decisions. Usually the control unit fetches instructions one after another in the order they are stored. However, control can be transferred to another part of the program or to another program. This is done using a **branch** instruction (also known as a **jump** instruction).

A branch instruction is an instruction which causes a jump out of the normal sequence of a program.

There are two main types of branch instruction:

1 A **conditional branch** is an instruction which causes a jump only if some condition is met.
2 An **unconditional branch** is an instruction which always causes a jump.

Examples of branch instructions

1 JUMP IF ZERO–jump if the contents of the accumulator is zero (this is a conditional branch).
2 JUMP TO SUBROUTINE–jump to a given subroutine (this is unconditional).

5.4 Typical Instruction Format

Many computers have instructions in two main parts:

(a) function code (b) operand (or address)

The **function code** is a binary code for the actual instruction.

The **operand** is either:

1 A data item for the instruction to operate on; or
2 The address of a location containing a data item.

Example

For a particular microcomputer each function code takes up eight bits.
The code for LOAD ACCUMULATOR FROM MEMORY is 1010 1001.
The address of each location takes 16 bits.

So the instruction 1010 1001 0001 1111 1111 1111 means:
LOAD ACCUMULATOR with the contents of location 0001 1111 1111 1111

Note: The instruction would probably be displayed in hexadecimal as A9 1FFF.

Worked question

A computer has six-bit function codes for its instructions. Included in the instruction set are the following:

Function code	*Meaning*
001000	Store contents of accumulator in the given location
001101	Load the accumulator with the number given
101100	Add the number given to the accumulator

Explain the meanings of the following instructions:
1 101100 000011
2 001000 110011

1 101100 is the code for 'add the number given to the accumulator'. 000011 is the binary for 3. The instruction means 'add the number 3 to the accumulator'.
2 001000 is the code for 'store contents of the accumulator in location'. The instruction means 'store the contents of the accumulator in location 110011'.

THE NUMBER OF POSSIBLE FUNCTION CODES AND ADDRESSES

There is a limit to the number of different function codes a computer can have. This is decided by the number of bits used to store the code. The number of codes possible is the number of different values which can be stored in the available bits.

e.g. For eight-bit codes the number of different codes $= 2^8$
$= 256$

There is also a limit to the number of addresses in the same way. The number of possible addresses is the number of different values which can be stored in the number of bits available.

e.g. For 16-bit addresses, the number of locations $= 2^{16}$
$= 65\,536$

Note: In fact most 8-bit microcomputers have 16-bit addresses. This means they are limited to 65 536 (i.e. 64K) addresses for all storage. This includes the user's RAM area, the screen memory and all the ROMs.

Worked question

For a given computer, the instructions occupy 16 bits each. Of this the function code is six bits and the rest of the instruction is an address. How many different instructions could the computer have and how many locations can be addressed?

The number of different instruction codes using six bits
$= 2^6$
$= 64$

The number of different addresses which can be formed using the remaining ten bits
$= 2^{10}$
$= 1024$

6 COMMUNICATIONS HARDWARE – TERMINALS AND INTERFACES

COMMUNICATION

Generally communication is the process of transmitting data from one person or one device to another.

The term **data communication** is used particularly for transmission of data between a user and a computer or between computers (see Unit 1.3).

Telecommunications are data communications over large distances.

TERMINALS

A **terminal** is an input/output device that enables a user to communicate with a computer.

Examples of terminals

1 A visual display unit (see Unit 6.1).
2 A cash issuing terminal outside a bank (see Unit 6.2).
3 A microcomputer running a program which makes it behave as a terminal.

REMOTE AND LOCAL

Remote – a terminal which is a considerable distance from the computer is referred to as remote. A remote terminal is connected to the computer by the telephone system or by some other data link.

Local – a device or system is local if it is not using any remote links.

Examples of uses of the terms local and remote

1 A terminal is in local mode when it is not on-line to any computer but is being used off-line.
2 A terminal is said to be a local terminal if it is connected to a local area network (see below).
3 The owner of a home computer and a modem can use the computer as a remote terminal to book a holiday via Prestel (for modem see Unit 6.3; for Prestel see Unit 18.2).

An **intelligent terminal** is a terminal which has its own processor and can run some programs without linking to a central computer. It is also known as a **programmable terminal**. (Microcomputers are often used as intelligent terminals.)

Teleprocessing is processing which is carried out using a remote terminal.

NETWORKS

In data communications a **network** is a system of computers and/or terminals connected together.

A **work station** is a terminal or a computer which an operator uses to interact with the network.

There are two main types of network:

1 A **local area network (LAN)** is a network in a small area, often one building. The work stations in a local area network are connected directly by cables (see Unit 15.5).
2 A **wide area network** is a network operating over long distances. The work stations in a wide area network are connected by telephone or similar data links (see Unit 15.5 and Unit 18).

Examples of networks

Local area network – a network of computers in a school.
Wide area network – a viewdata network (see Unit 18.2).

SERIAL AND PARALLEL TRANSMISSION

Parallel transmission of data means that the bits for each character are all sent at the same time.

If the transmission is by cable then there is a separate wire for each bit. With an eight-bit code there are eight wires for the data.

Serial transmission of data means that the bits for each character are sent one after the other.

If a cable is used data could be transmitted along one wire.

SPEED OF TRANSMISSION

The speed at which data is transmitted is measured in **baud** (named after a French engineer called Baudot).

For serial transmission 1 baud is 1 bit per second.

An alternative measurement is in characters per second (c.p.s.).

Example of baud and c.p.s.

Serial terminals usually transmit ten bits for each character.

Thus 300 baud = 30 c.p.s.
9600 baud = 960 c.p.s.

6.1 Visual Display Terminals

A visual display terminal is a computer terminal which usually has a keyboard for input and a screen for output (see Unit 8.1).

A visual display terminal is also called a **visual display unit** or **VDU**. Its speed for output may vary from 10 characters per second (on a slow serial line) to 960 characters per second or faster.

Facilities on the different models can include:

1 Editing data anywhere on the screen to send it back to the computer.
2 Printing at any chosen point on the screen.
3 Storage in the terminal of data no longer on the screen.
4 Local processing.
5 Graphics (see Unit 6.2).
6 Variable-sized characters.

Advantage of a VDU over a typewriter terminal

1 Quiet
2 Usually faster – at least for a given price.
3 No paper wasted.
4 Sometimes better facilities for editing data locally (i.e. without using the computer).

Situations in which VDUs are used

1 In almost any interactive situation where a printing or other specialized terminal is not necessary.
2 Where high-speed display is needed.
3 Where noise would be annoying.

Examples of uses of VDUs

1 At an airport terminal checking on flights for passengers. Here no hard copy is needed. However, in a situation where flights can be booked at the terminal point it would be useful to also have a printing terminal available.
2 As an operator's console in a computer room. An **operator's console** is the device used by the operators to control the computer. In this situation a fast terminal is required, but no hard copy.

6.2 Other Terminals

TELETYPEWRITER

A **teletypewriter** is a computer terminal which has a slow printer for output and a keyboard for input.

Disadvantages of a teletypewriter compared with a VDU

1 The teletypewriter is noisy.
2 It is usually slower than a VDU.
3 It wastes paper. Usually a VDU has a printer available. This is used only when necessary. A teletypewriter prints all the time.
4 There are limited facilities for editing locally.

Situations in which teletypewriters are used

As an interactive terminal in situations where hard copy is needed and cannot be obtained otherwise.

Note: In recent years VDUs have improved so much that teletypewriters are now seldom used.

Fig. 6.1 Graphical display unit (*By kind permission of IBM*)

GRAPHICAL DISPLAY UNIT (GDU)

A **graphical display unit** is a visual display unit which can produce graphs and pictures on its screen as well as text (Fig. 6.1).

For input it usually has, as well as the usual alphanumeric keyboard:

1 A graphics function keyboard.
2 A light pen (or possibly a graphic tablet or a mouse – see Unit 7.4).

POINT-OF-SALE (POS) TERMINAL

A point of sale is a place, usually in a shop, where a customer pays for goods or services – e.g. the checkout in a supermarket.

A **point-of-sale terminal** is a device at a point of sale which records details of sales for computer processing.

Fig. 6.2 (a and b) A POS terminal in use in a photographic shop (*By kind permission of Tecno Ltd*)

Examples of POS terminals

1 A terminal at a supermarket checkout, with a laser scanner to read bar codes (see Unit 7.3).
2 A terminal which looks like an electronic cash till but is in fact connected to a computer. The assistant keys in code numbers for the goods sold. The computer supplies the price of the goods and the name, which is then printed on the customer's receipt (see Fig. 6.2 and Unit 17.1.).

Advantages of POS terminals over ordinary cash tills

1 The terminal records what is sold. A computer can use this data to work out how much stock is left and order more goods.
2 If the terminal is on-line the computer can hold files of the names of goods and their prices. Only a code number for the goods needs to be entered. The computer provides the name and the price to go on the customer's receipt.

CASH ISSUING TERMINALS

A **cash issuing terminal** is a terminal at a bank, building society or a post office which can be used by customers. Most of the major banks have their own names for these including 'cash point' or 'autobank'.

Customers can use a cash issuing terminal:
1 To obtain cash.
2 To obtain information about their accounts.

To use the terminal the customer:
1 Inserts a bank card.
2 Types in a password, which is usually a number.
3 Makes a choice of which service to use.

Advantages of cash issuing terminals

1 Cash or information can be obtained at any time of day or night.
2 There is no need to queue in the bank.
3 Transactions are done without any paper work.

6.3 Connecting Terminals to Computers

Methods of connection

1 By the ordinary public telephone network.
2 Direct connection by cable (not practical over long distances).
3 By private telephone circuit. The line is rented from a telephone service (such as British Telecom or Mercury).

Transmission over telephone lines

Packet-switched service (PSS). This is a special network for data communications, the data being sent in 'packets'. There is no direct link between the terminal and the computer – as there is for an ordinary telephone call. Each packet is headed by details of its destination and is switched through the network until it gets there.

System X is a new system for the telephone network which is being introduced by British Telecom. It will allow all communications, including speech, to be transmitted using digital signals instead of analogue signals. Terminals are connected to the present analogue telephone network using modems or acoustic couplers.

MODEMS AND ACOUSTIC COUPLERS

1 MODEM (MOdulator–DEModulator)

A **modem** is a device which (a) converts digital signals into analogue signals so that they can be sent along telephone lines, and (b) converts analogue signals received from a telephone line back into digital signals (Fig. 6.3). A modem can be seen beneath the telephone in Fig. 18.2.

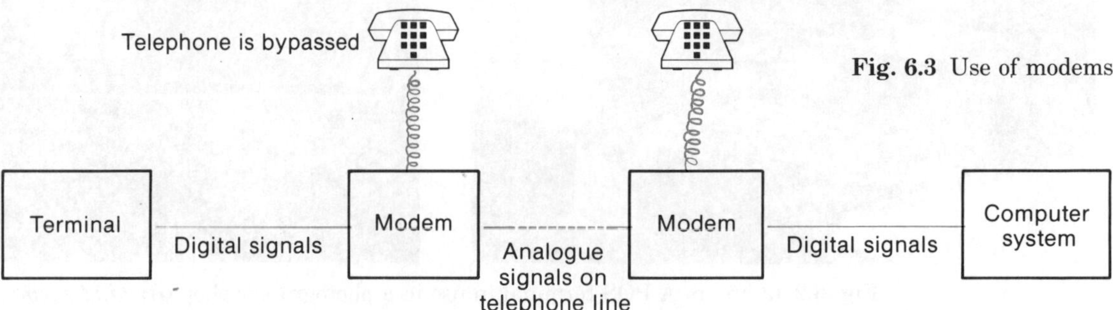

Fig. 6.3 Use of modems

2 Acoustic coupler

An **acoustic coupler** is a device which (a) converts sound from the telephone handset into digital signals, and (b) converts signals into sounds, to send data back down the line (Fig. 6.4).

The telephone handset is placed in the coupler to make the connection.

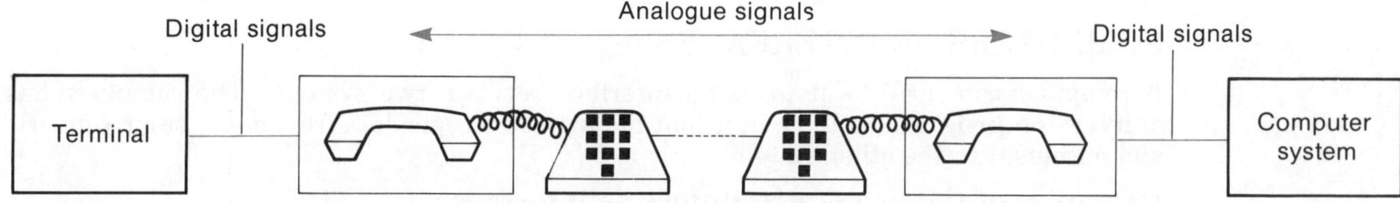

Fig. 6.4 Use of acoustic couplers

Data is transmitted usually at about 300 baud (30 characters per second).

Advantages of a modem over an acoustic coupler

1 High-speed transmission.
2 Accuracy of transmission – no interference from sounds.

Advantage of an acoustic coupler over a modem

The coupler can be used with any telephone handset. It can be moved from one telephone to another whereas a modem usually remains in one place.

MULTIPLEXORS

It is not practical to connect a large number of terminals directly to a computer because:
1 A large amount of processing time would be used up in organizing the communications.
2 It could be difficult and expensive to provide all the necessary interfaces (for interfaces see Unit 6.4).

A device called a **multiplexor** may be used. This organizes the signals to and from the computer so that only one input/output channel to the computer is used (see Fig. 6.5).

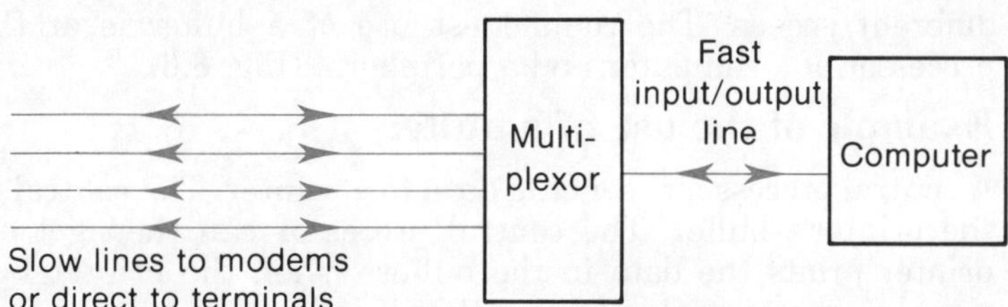

Fig. 6.5 Use of a multiplexor

6.4 Interfaces

An **interface** is some hardware, and possibly also some software, that is used to connect two devices or systems to enable them to communicate. An interface may have to:
1 Control and check the data being transmitted.
2 Convert data from one form or one code to another.
3 Allow for a difference in speed between two devices.

Examples of interfaces

1 A modem is an interface between a remote computer terminal and the telephone system.
2 When a person uses a computer the keyboard and the program are both part of the interface between the user and the computer.
3 To convert a certain computer to use floppy discs a 'disc interface' is fitted. This consists of a specially designed integrated circuit 'chip' inside the computer and a connector on the back.

Example of an interfacing problem

A particular computer is to be interfaced to a printer of another make. The problems are:
1 The printer has been set up to receive a parallel transmission, but it is to be connected to a serial port on the computer.
2 The computer is to be used for word processing. The control characters it sends out to produce underlining, bold printing, etc. are different from those used by the printer.

The interface between the two consists of:
1 A serial interface circuit board fitted to the printer so that it will receive a serial transmission.
2 A new serial lead to connect the printer to the computer.
3 A 'printer driver' program in the computer to convert the control characters to the right codes for the printer.

COMPUTERS AS INTERFACES

A computer can itself be used as an interface between two systems. The computer has a **conversion program** running in it continuously. It accepts data from one system, converts it and outputs it to the other system.

Examples of the use of computers as interfaces

1 A **front-end processor**. This is a small computer which inputs and outputs all the data for a large computer. It organizes the data so that the main computer has a simpler processing task. (Compare this with a multiplexor – Unit 6.3 – which does a similar job but a simpler one. A front-end processor deals with a variety of fast input and output devices.)
2 A microprocessor in a peripheral. Many peripherals such as printers and disc units now contain their own processors.

Advantages of having a microprocessor in a peripheral

1 Control characters sent from the computer can be used to change the way the peripheral operates – for example a printer can be sent a command to print using a different character set.
2 The main computer saves storage and processing time because the peripheral can organize the data itself.

Advantages of using a computer as an interface

1 If one of the interfaced systems is changed, the conversion program can easily be changed.
2 It is often cheaper to use a general-purpose computer than to make a different interface for each task.

BUFFERS

A **buffer** is a store in the interface between two devices which temporarily stores data which is being transmitted from one to the other. The buffer is necessary if the two devices work at different speeds. The commonest use of a buffer is at the interface between the central processor of a computer and a peripheral (Fig. 6.6).

Example of the use of a buffer

A central processor is sending data to a printer. The central processor sends enough data to fill the printer's buffer. The central processor can then get on with something else while the printer prints the data in the buffer. When the printer has printed all the data it sends a signal to the central processor that it is ready to receive more data.

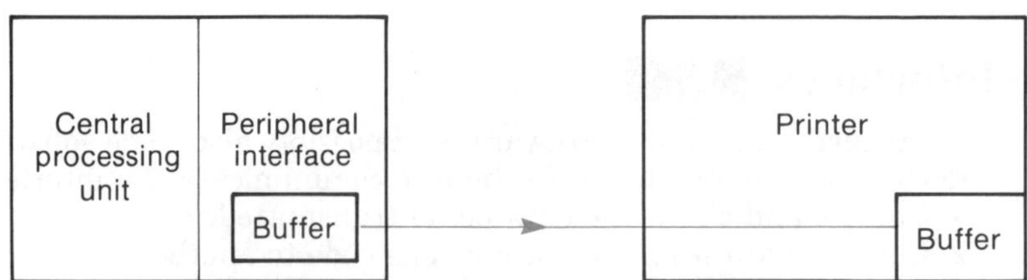

Fig. 6.6 A printer interfaced to a computer

Double buffering

Double buffering is the use of two buffers at the interface between two devices instead of just one. One device can then be emptying the first buffer at the same time as the other device is filling the second one.

ANALOGUE INPUT AND OUTPUT

Although most computers are now digital, many output and input devices are analogue (for definition of analogue see introduction to Unit 4).

Examples of analogue input and output devices

1 A joystick (see Unit 7.4) usually produces two voltages. One of these is a measure of the

movement of the stick from left to right. The other is proportional to the movement of the stick up and down.

2 The BBC Buggy (see photograph in Unit 20.3) has a light sensor which measures how much light is falling on it.

Note: This should be contrasted with a wand or light pen for reading bar codes (Unit 7.4). The wand is digital as it only registers whether light is hitting it or not.

3 A music synthesizer attached to a computer may be made to produce sounds using a steadily changing voltage from the computer.

4 The heating, watering and ventilation of a greenhouse can be controlled by a microprocessor. To control ventilation, the computer sends out a varying voltage. The vents are opened by a distance proportional to this voltage.

Conversion between digital and analogue signals

If a digital computer accepts input from an analogue device then an **analogue-to-digital (A-to-D) converter** is required.

An A-to-D converter is an interface to convert an analogue signal to a digital one (Fig. 6.7).

Usually an A-to-D converter consists of an integrated circuit which inputs a voltage. It outputs a set of two-state signals. These represent a binary number which is roughly proportional to the input voltage.

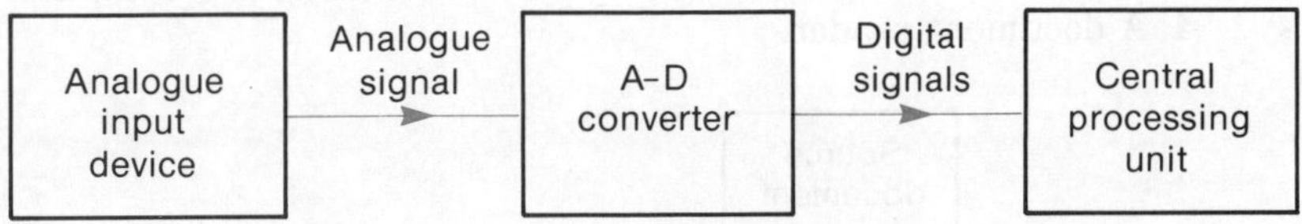

Fig. 6.7 An analogue-to-digital converter in use

If a digital computer outputs to an analogue device then a **digital-to-analogue (D-to-A) converter** is required.

A digital-to-analogue converter is an interface to convert a digital signal to an analogue one (Fig. 6.8). It converts a set of binary signals to one single varying voltage.

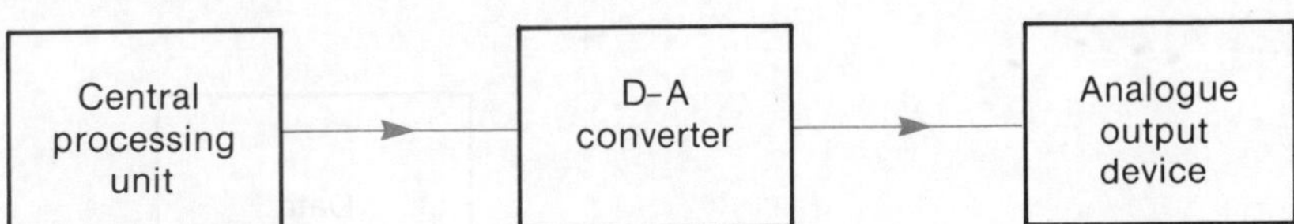

Fig. 6.8 A digital-to-analogue converter in use

7 DATA PREPARATION AND INPUT

An **input device** is a peripheral which accepts data and sends it to the central processing unit.

Data presented to an input device has to be in the right form for the device (e.g. a bar code reader will only read bar codes). The input device converts the data into a binary form which the central processor can accept.

Examples of input devices

1 The keyboard of a microcomputer.
2 A light pen.
3 An electronic digital weighing scale interfaced to a computer.
4 A document reader.

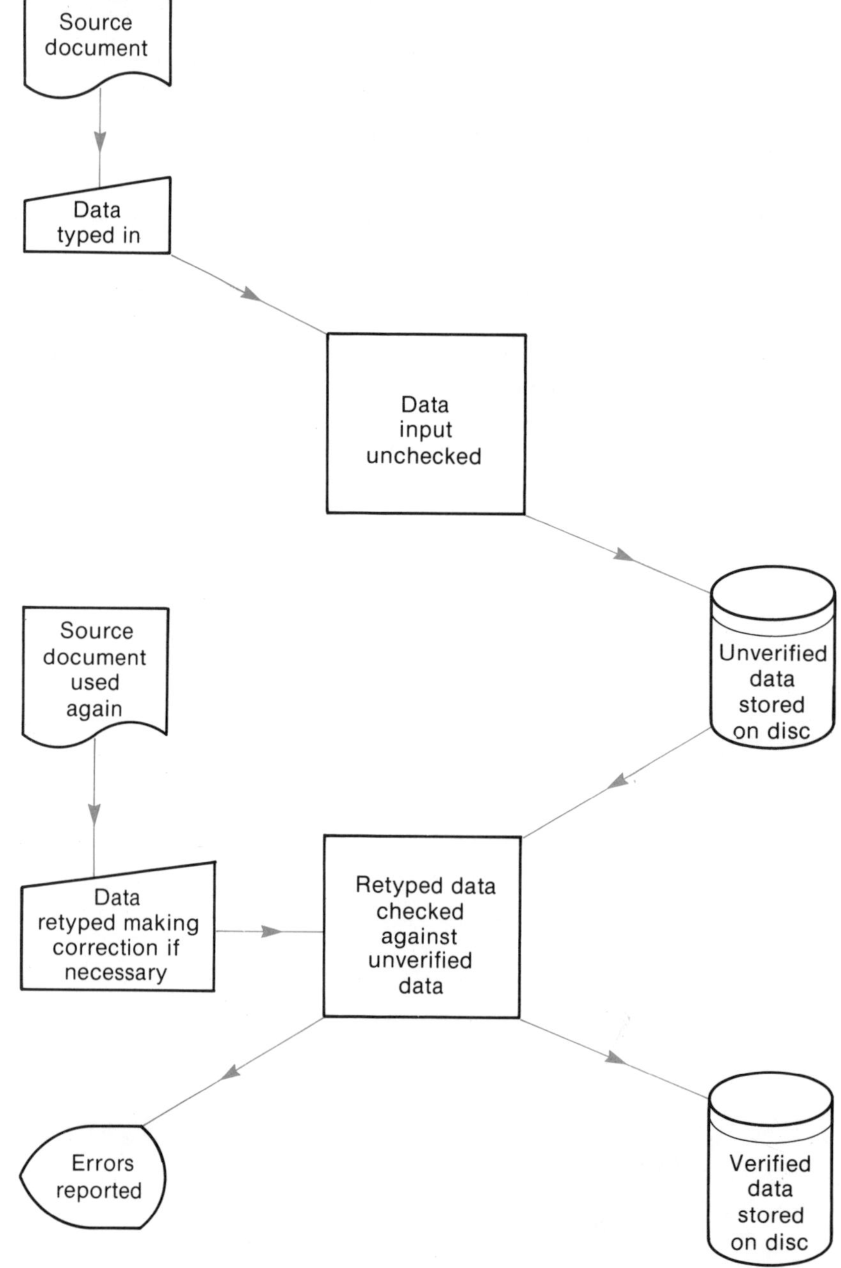

Fig. 7.1 How data is verified

PREPARATION AND VERIFICATION

For some types of input the data is handwritten on forms. It has to be typed on to disc or some other input medium by a keyboard operator. Then it has to be checked to see if the typing is accurate. Then it is ready to be read by an input device.

Data is originally written on a form called a **source document**. The process of typing the data on to an input medium is called **data preparation** (see also Unit 1.3).

Checking the data to see that it has been typed correctly is known as **verification** (see Unit 12.3).

How data is verified

When the data has been prepared the source documents from which it was typed are passed to another operator. This second operator retypes the data. However, this time the data is not encoded on to the input medium. Instead the equipment simply checks that the new data typed is the same as the data already there. The characters are retyped correctly if necessary.

Note: The data could be verified by simply reading through what has been typed to see if it looks right. However, this method is not accurate enough for commercial work.

7.1 Use of Keyboards

It will be seen in later sections of this chapter that there are now many different input devices. However, most data for computers is still typed on keyboards.

Ways in which keyboards are used

1 On-line data entry

Data is input straight to the computer which is going to process it.

2 Key-to-disc or key-to-tape

Data is prepared on tape or disc. The computer controlling the tape unit or disc unit is not the one which will process the data.

3 Off-line preparation

Data is prepared with equipment which does not use a computer.

ON-LINE DATA ENTRY

Advantages of on-line data entry

1 There is no need for special data preparation equipment.
2 There is an immediate response from the computer. Data can be checked and results obtained quickly.

Disadvantages of on-line data entry

1 Data is often not carefully prepared and verified.
2 There may be an expensive use of computer time.

Uses of on-line data entry

1 Research – where the user wants to experiment with different inputs.
2 Interactive uses of microcomputers – in education, small businesses, etc.
3 Real-time situations – booking airline tickets.
4 Using terminals to large computers – Prestel, time sharing, etc.

KEY-TO-DISC AND KEY-TO-TAPE

Keyboard operators work at **keystations**.

The media used may be floppy discs, magnetic tape, magnetic tape cartridges or magnetic tape cassettes.

Various systems are used, of which two are shown here:

1 Single station

Each keystation is independent of the others. There may be a facility for 'pooling' data from all the stations on to a magnetic tape.

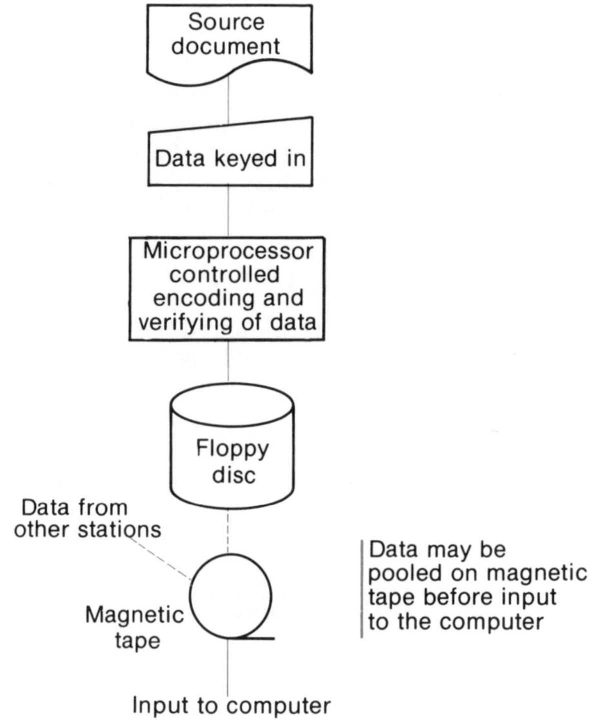

Fig. 7.2 Key-to-floppy-disc station – system diagram to show method

2 Group of keystations controlled by a minicomputer

Each keystation is in fact a terminal to a minicomputer. Usually the minicomputer can control up to 32 stations.

Often preparation, verification and editing are done with the data on disc. The data is then transferred to a tape which is input to the main computer to be processed.

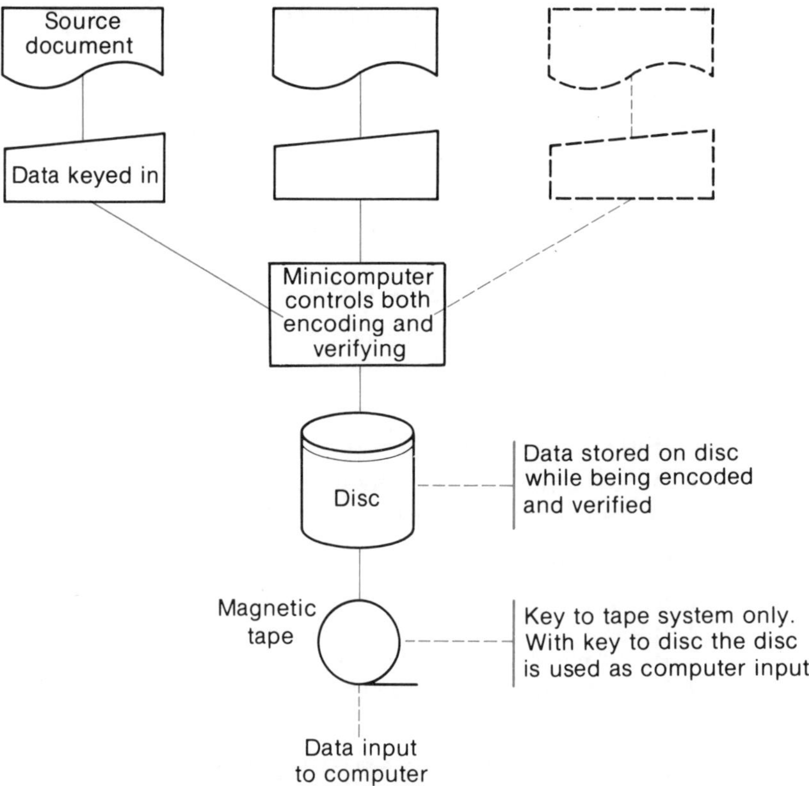

Fig. 7.3 Key-to-disc or key-to-tape system controlled by a minicomputer

Advantages

Of key-to-disc and key-to-tape systems

1 The computer controlling the stations gives good facilities for checking and editing data. Time is not wasted on the main computer which will process the data.
2 Skilled operators do the work so the data is accurate.

Of magnetic media such as discs and tapes

1 They can be used again and again.
2 They can be read quickly by tape and disc units.
3 They store a large amount of data in a small space.

Uses

1 Any situation where batch processing is used (see Unit 15.3).
2 Any situation where a large amount of data has to be input to a computer system from documents (e.g. in a school at the start of the year – records of new pupils can be sent to a bureau to be entered on floppy disc; they can then be added to the school's computer files).

OFF-LINE DATA PREPARATION

In the past most data was typed on to punched cards or paper tape using special 'punches'. These have now been largely phased out.

7.2 Document Readers

A **document reader** is a device which can read data straight from forms.

Examples of documents read by document readers

1 A card on which pencil marks are made by hand.
2 A multiple choice question paper with pencil marks to show the candidate's choices.
3 A bank cheque with numbers along the bottom in magnetic ink (see Fig. 7.5).
4 A slip filled in by a gas board meter reader (see Fig. 1.3). The customer's address and account number are printed by a line printer. The meter reading has been filled in in pencil.

Types of data read by document readers

1 Marks

Short lines made by hand – they are usually in pencil on cards or documents.

2 Handwritten characters

When documents are to be filled in by hand they are preprinted with spaces provided. The characters have to be written carefully in the right places.

3 Printed lines

The most common of these is the bar code.

4 Printed characters

Examples are:
(a) Numbers which have been output on to documents by a line printer.
(b) Magnetic ink characters on bank cheques.

MARK READING

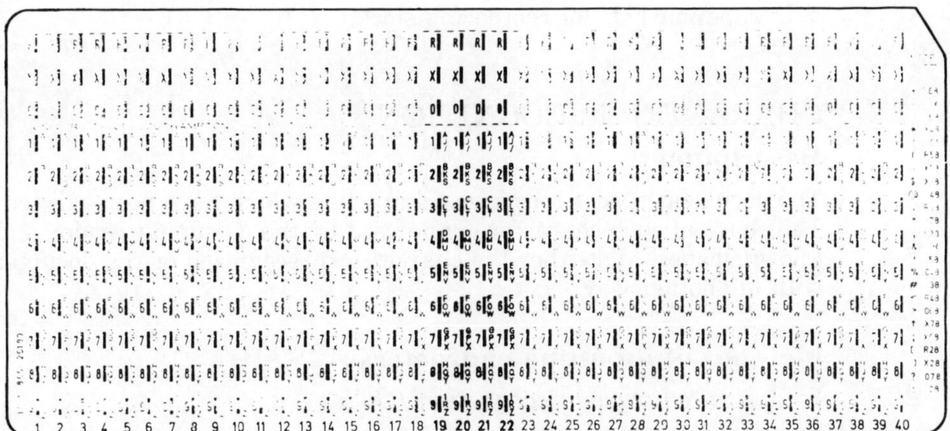

Fig. 7.4 A card designed to be read by an optical marked card reader (For clarity four columns have been intensified)

Methods of reading marks

1 Mark sensing

Small electrical 'brushes' touch the surface of the document or card. When they contact a pencil mark a circuit is completed. The marks must be in a soft pencil as this contains graphite, which conducts electricity.

2 Optical mark reading (OMR)

A beam of light is directed on to the surface of the card or document. The beam is reflected from the surface to a light sensor. When a mark passes under the beam less light is reflected back and the presence of the mark is registered.

Advantages

Of OMR compared with mark sensing

The sensitivity of optical readers can be altered to allow for different surfaces and different pencils or inks.

Of marks compared with handwritten characters

There are fewer recognition failures.

Of marks and characters compared with keyboard preparation

1 Data can be prepared at the place where it originates.
2 No machines are required for the preparation.

Disadvantages

Of marks compared with characters

Documents for mark readers are more complicated. If an item has several values then a mark space has to be allocated for each value.

Of marks compared with data prepared using a keyboard

1 Input of data to the computer is slow. For example a marked card reader is far slower than a disc unit.
2 It is difficult to verify marked data.
3 Documents for a mark reader are difficult to understand and to fill in.
4 A document reader has to be reprogrammed for each new design of document.

Uses of mark reading

In situations where:
1 The data to be input is simple.
2 The volume of data is large enough to justify designing special documents for it.

Examples of uses

1 For multiple choice examination papers.
2 For data collected 'in the field' by research workers.
3 For market research questionnaires.
4 In supermarkets for reordering stock.

CHARACTER RECOGNITION

Description

The document reader recognizes characters which have been printed by machine or by hand. The shape of each character is analysed by the document reader and compared with a set of known shapes, and either the character is recognized or the document is rejected to be dealt with in another way.

Methods of inputting characters

1 Optical character recognition (OCR)

The character shapes are recognized by sensing light reflected from the paper and from the ink (as with OMR) but the reader has to have a memory and a processing capability in order to work out what the characters are.

A **font** is a character set of a particular size and style. Practically all OCR document readers recognize at least one of two fonts known as OCRA and OCRB. Many also recognize other typed or printed fonts. Some cope with hand-printed characters (sometimes only numbers) provided that they are done carefully to copy a standard font.

2 Magnetic ink character recognition (MICR)

Characters are printed using an ink containing iron oxide. As the document passes into the reader the ink is magnetized, so that the character shapes can then be recognized electrically.

Readers usually read a font known as font E13B (at least in this country) (Figs. 7.5 and 7.6). This contains only 14 characters – the digits 0 to 9 and four special symbols.

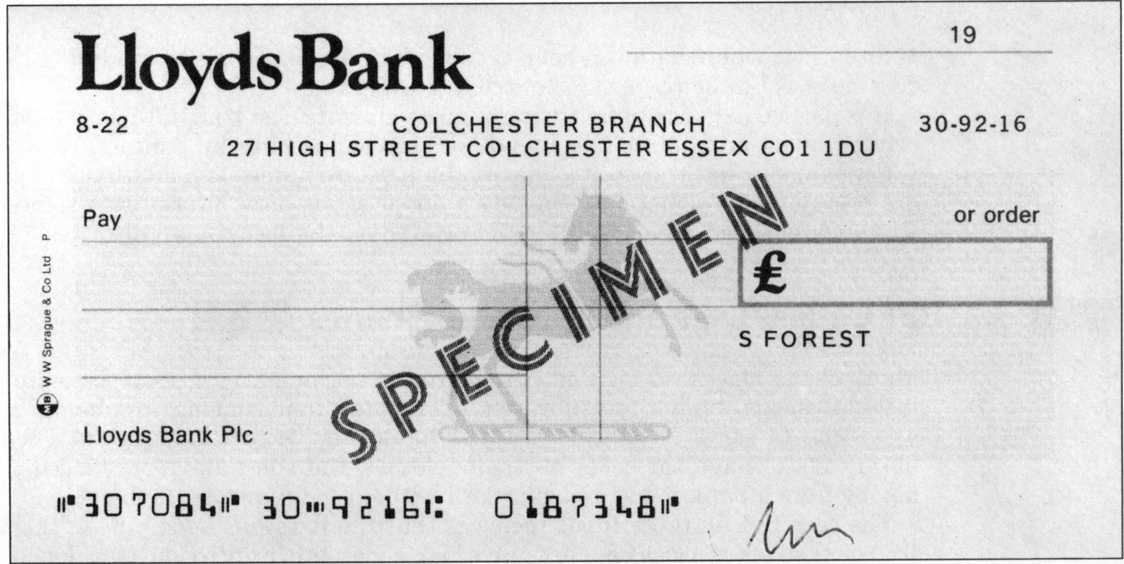

Fig. 7.5 A bank cheque showing characters in font E13B (*By kind permission of Lloyds Bank*)

1 2 3 4 5 6 7 8 9 0

Fig. 7.6 The font E13B character set

Advantages

Of MICR over OCR

1 It is difficult to forge.
2 Documents can still be read when folded, written on, etc.

Of OCR over MICR

More different fonts can be used, including sometimes handprinting and normal type.

Of characters compared with marks

Design of forms is less complicated.

Of characters over other media

Data can be read by other people.

Disadvantages

Of MICR compared with other media

1 Readers are very expensive.
2 Only certain fonts are acceptable.

Of hand-printed characters

There is a high rejection rate (perhaps 5 per cent).

Of printed characters

A high standard of printing is needed.

Uses

Of MICR

Where printed numbers in a standard format are to be read in large volume. For example the major British banks all use MICR to encode along the bottom of cheques the following information: (a) cheque number (b) branch number of the bank (c) the customer's account number (d) (after the cheque has been banked) the amount of money.

Of OCR

1 Situations where data has been typed or printed for people to read. If OCR is used the data does not need to be retyped for entry to a computer.
2 It is particularly useful for turnaround documents (see Unit 1.3), where some characters are printed by a computer printer and others are added later by hand.

For example, in the case of a charity fund, where names and addresses of prospective donors are preprinted on donation forms, each donor sends back a form with some money. The date and amount given are carefully hand printed on the form by an operator.

7.3 Bar Codes, Tags and Magnetic Stripes

Many of the places we visit as customers are becoming progressively more automated. This includes shops, banks and libraries. Computer input media are being used which allow assistants to serve us quickly without having to write things down. Food containers and library books have bar codes on them; clothes and shoes have cardboard tags; we can take money from a bank using a plastic card without going inside the bank.

The secret of all these input media is that the data has been put on them long before the transaction takes place. For example bar codes are printed on food labels before they are packed. To record the sale of the food no one has to write or type anything. All that is needed is a bar code reader (Fig. 7.7).

Fig. 7.7 A point-of-sale terminal with laser scanner for reading bar codes *(By kind permission of IBM)*

BAR CODES

Description

A **bar code** is a set of parallel printed lines of differing thicknesses (usually alternately black and white), which represent a number (Fig. 7.8). Often the number represented by the bars is also printed above or below the bar code.

When bar codes are used on shop goods, the number coded identifies the product, giving usually a number code for:

1 Country of origin.
2 Manufacturer.
3 An item number for the product.

Note: Because prices change so much they are not recorded on bar codes. The prices have to be stored in a computer, which is used when a price is needed.

Bar codes may be read by:

1 A hand-held light pen or 'wand', which is passed over the code perpendicular to the bars. The wand is attached to a computer terminal or a recording device.
2 A stationary scanner using a laser beam, which scans the bar code as the product is passed across a window (see Fig. 7.7). The scanner is part of a point-of-sale terminal (see Unit 6.2).

Fig. 7.8 A bar code

Advantages

1 Bar codes can be printed by normal printing methods.
2 The type of item or its price does not have to be repeatedly written down or typed.

Disadvantages

1 Bar codes cannot be changed, and thus are unsuitable for recording prices. Customers still have to be informed of prices (e.g. by labels or catalogues).
2 Bar codes can only be read by machine.
3 Only numbers can be coded in this way.

Uses

1 On labels on the shelves. These are then used during stocktaking.
2 Printed on the goods. These are then used at the checkout to work out the bill (see Unit 17.1).
3 Other than in shops (e.g. to identify library books).

TAGS–INCLUDING KIMBALL TAGS

A **tag** is a small ticket, usually of cardboard, which contains coded information and which is attached to goods to identify them.

Types

Data can be coded by:

1 Small punched holes (e.g. Kimball tag).
2 Magnetized spots on a small strip of magnetic material on the tag.
3 A bar code or other bar marks.
4 Characters in an OCR font.

The Kimball tag

A **Kimball tag** is in two or three parts, which can be easily separated by tearing along perforated lines. Each part has small holes punched in it which represent a code for the article. It also has some larger holes punched in it. When a garment, or other tagged article, is sold part of the tag is removed. The tags are usually stored temporarily on a spike, using the large holes.

Advantages of using tags

Stock is reordered without any writing or typing of data. Stock records can be updated using the tags as the input for the stock control program.

Disadvantage

They are small and are easily mislaid.

Uses

The tags are mainly used for the reordering of stock, a batch of them being sent to the computer centre every week or so. They can (a) be attached to an article (e.g. clothes), (b) accompany an article (e.g. shoes), (c) for cheaper items, accompany a batch of them.

MAGNETIC STRIPES

A **magnetic stripe** is a short length of magnetic tape stuck on to the surface of a tag, card or document.

On plastic tags or cards the stripe is sealed in.

Tags with stripes identify the item they are attached to.

Cards often only store enough data to enable a computer to identify the owner (e.g. bank cards).

Examples of the use of magnetic stripes

1 On cards called **visual record cards**. A special encoder is used. A keyboard operator types data which is printed on the front of the card. At the same time it is encoded on the magnetic stripes on the back of the card. People can read the printed information and a computer can read the magnetic stripe.

2 On **credit cards**. A shop or business with a terminal can have the card checked to see that the owner is creditworthy.

3 On **bank cards**. Banks issue plastic cards (Fig. 7.9) with a magnetic stripe (Fig. 7.10) for various purposes.

Examples are:

(a) For a customer to present when writing a cheque. The bank will then guarantee to accept cheques up to a certain limit.

(b) To use in a **cash issuing terminal**.

4 As tags on clothes (as in previous section).

5 As a **phone card**. Some telephones do not accept coins. Instead a card is used which has been bought previously at a post office. The value of the card is recorded on a magnetic stripe. As a user makes a call the number of units stored on the card is reduced.

Fig. 7.9 A bank card (*By kind permission of Lloyds Bank*)

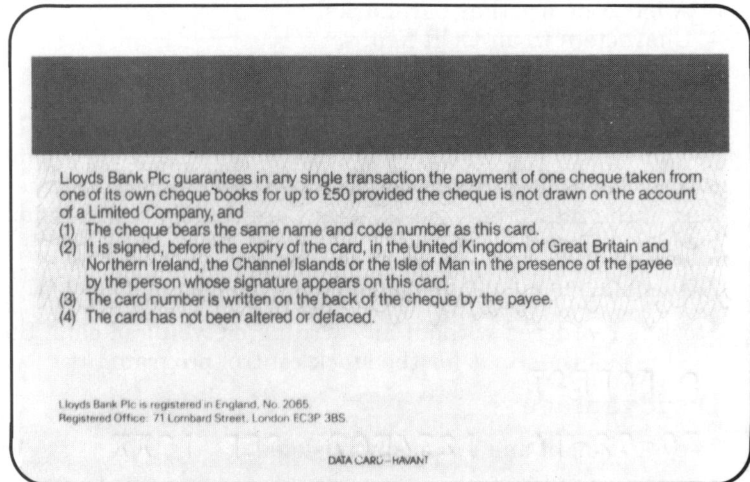

Fig. 7.10 The reverse of a bank card showing the magnetic stripe

Advantages of a magnetic stripe

1 It is simple to produce.
2 It is not easily damaged (except by magnetic fields – see disadvantage).
3 It stores a fairly large number of characters (usually about 72).

Disadvantages of a magnetic stripe

The data can be changed or erased by magnetic fields.

NEW DEVELOPMENTS

New methods of storing data on cards have become available. They include:

1 Laser cards

Data is stored on these as small holes in a polished surface. The cards are read using reflected light. Some readers contain a laser but cheaper versions do not.

One card can store over 2 million characters.

2 Smart cards

These have a very thin ROM chip sealed into them.

One card can store about 8000 characters.

7.4 Input at Terminals and Microcomputers

KEYBOARDS

Usually a VDU or a microcomputer is provided with a **keyboard** for input (Fig. 7.11). This usually has on it keys with:

1 The alphabet.
2 The numbers.

(Often numbers appear twice – once along the top as they would on a typewriter and again in a keypad at the right. The separate keypad can be used when all the data is numeric. The other row can be used for normal typing.

3 Characters for punctuation (. , ; : etc.).
4 Other text characters (mathematical symbols % & # etc.).
5 **Cursor** movements, editing functions (DELETE, COPY, etc.), control characters (ENTER or RETURN, ESCAPE, etc.).

The keyboard also has keys which change the function of other keys SHIFT, CAPS – for capital letters, CTRL – for control functions, etc.).

Often the keyboard also has a separate set of function keys. Function keys are keys whose function is set by a program.

For example a particular function key may be used to:

1 Delete a line of text for a word processing package.
2 Draw a circle for a graphics package. A graphics display terminal may have its function keys on a separate graphics function keypad (see Unit 6.2).

Fig. 7.11 A typical keyboard (*By kind permission of Research Machines Ltd*)

INPUT DEVICES OTHER THAN KEYBOARDS

As well as keyboards there is often also an extra device such as a mouse, a light pen or a joystick. This is to help the user:

1 To make selections from menus or to choose icons.
2 To position the cursor on the screen.
3 To produce graphics.
4 To move images and create windows on the screen.

Note: The terms **cursor**, **menu**, **icon** and **window** are explained in Unit 8.1.

LIGHT PEN

A **light pen** (Fig. 7.12) is a pen-shaped device, held in the hand, which can detect the presence or absence of light. It is connected by a cable to a recording device or to a computer or a computer terminal. Electrical signals are sent along the cable indicating whether or not light of sufficient intensity is being sensed.

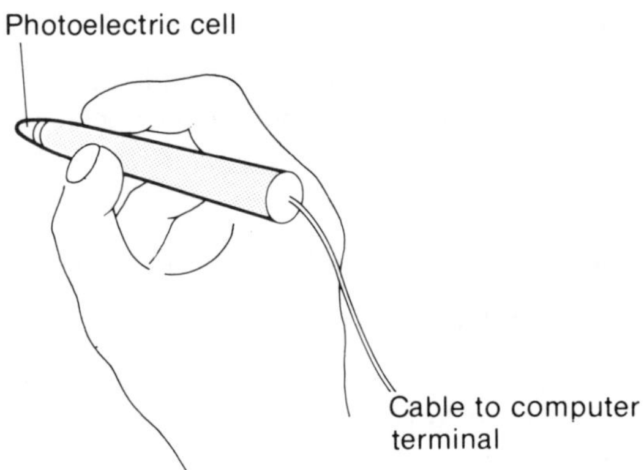

Fig. 7.12 A light pen

Types of use

1 To detect bar codes.
2 To indicate a point on a screen. The pen is pointed at the screen in the appropriate place. A television screen is 'refreshed' about every 1/50th of a second by a point of light travelling rapidly across it. When this point of light is detected by the pen a computer can work out by precise timing where the pen is on the screen.

Examples

1 The pen is used to choose one of a selection of options printed on the screen, by pointing it at the option required.
2 Drawings are produced on the screen by using a special function pad and a keyboard to indicate what the computer should draw and the pen to point out where it should draw it (see Unit 6.2).

Advantages of using a light pen

1 It removes the need to type or write.
2 It is faster than typing.

Disadvantages

1 It can record only the presence or absence of light.
2 It only works with software written for it.

Note: For screen work, light pens may eventually be replaced by **touch sensitive screens**, which enable a finger placed on the screen to indicate a position.

MOUSE

A **mouse** is a mouse-shaped object designed to fit snugly under a hand while it is moved about over a table. Moving the mouse produces movements of a cursor or a pointer on the screen. Signals indicating movements of the mouse are sent by a cable to the computer or terminal (see Fig. 7.13).

The mouse is also provided with buttons to press. These are pressed to produce action when the user has moved the cursor to the right place (see Fig. 7.14).

Different types of technology may be used to make a mouse work. Two of these are:

1 The movement of a ball-bearing is used to produce electrical signals. This type can be used on any suitable surface.

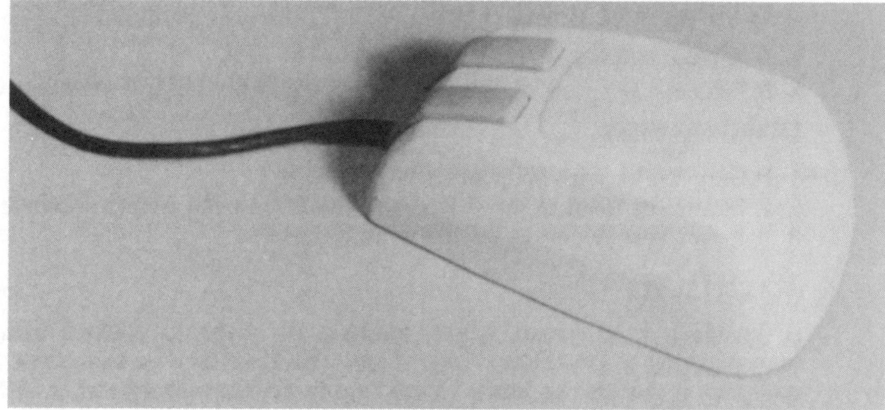

Fig. 7.13 A mouse showing two buttons and the cable joining it to the computer

Fig. 7.14 A mouse being used to select an option from a menu. The options are in boxes at the bottom of the left-hand screen (*By kind permission of IBM*)

2 Small lights under the mouse are reflected on to photoelectric cells. These detect when a line is crossed. This type of mouse only works on a grid of lines.

Uses

1 To select options from a menu or from a set of icons.
2 To position the cursor when editing text or using a design package.
3 To draw shapes.

Advantages of using a mouse

1 It is easy and convenient to use.
2 It selects a position on the screen more quickly than is possible with a keyboard.

Disadvantages

1 It only works with software written for it.
2 It cannot be used to input text – it has to be used with a keyboard.
3 It is not very accurate for drawing purposes.

JOYSTICK

A **joystick** is a device which enables the user to control movement on the screen by manoeuvring a small lever (Fig. 7.15). The lever can be moved in any direction from its zero position. It can also be made to produce faster movements by pushing it farther from the zero position. The joystick usually has buttons with which actions can be carried out once the cursor is in the right place. Some joysticks give more control on the screen by rotating the stick as well.

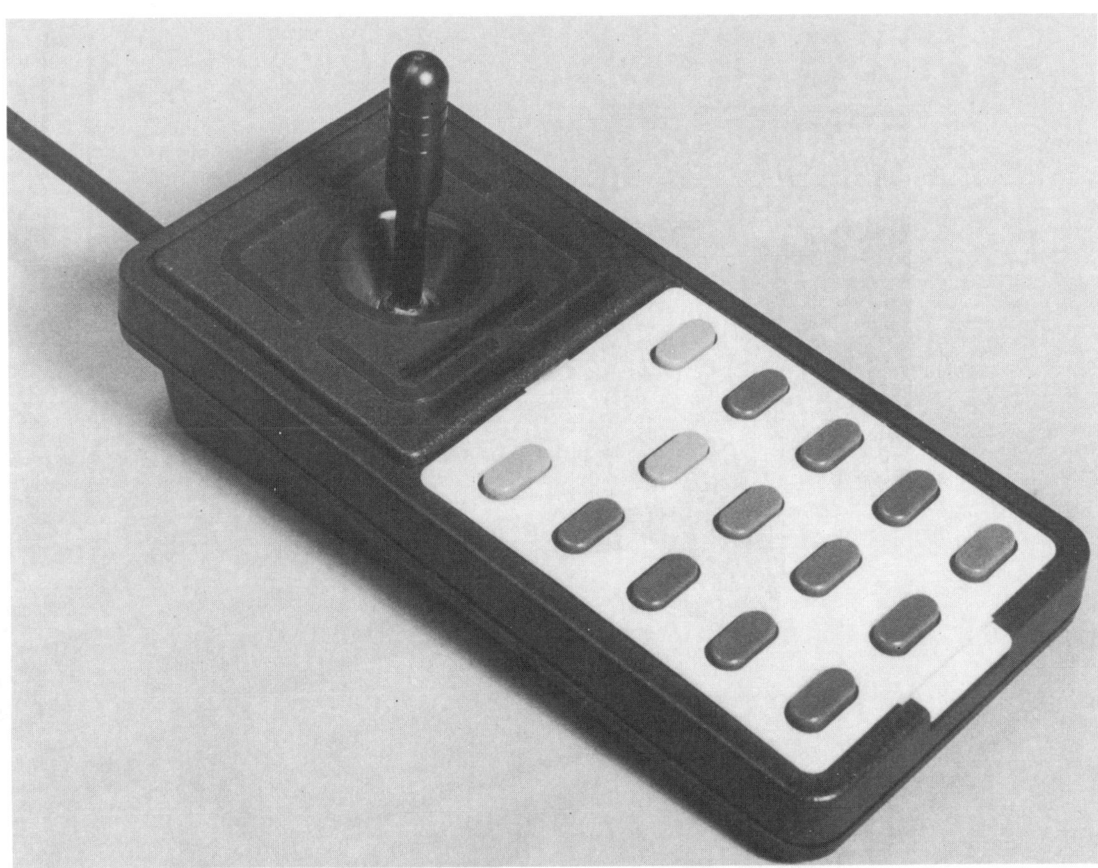

Fig. 7.15 A joystick

Uses

1 Controlling objects in computer games.
2 Producing graphics.

Comparison between a mouse and a joystick

The functions of a mouse and a joystick are similar. The joystick allows the faster interaction needed in games. The mouse is more suitable for office use. In particular, the mouse is often used with windows and icons. Programs using **W**indows, **I**cons and a **M**ouse to move a **P**ointer are often called **WIMP** packages. (The **P** can also stand for **P**ull-down menu, that is a menu which appears when you click a mouse button.)

GRAPHICS TABLET

A **graphics tablet** – also known as a **digitizing pad** or **digitizer** – is a board which can detect the position of a pen-like **stylus** on its surface (see Fig. 7.16). A design is put on to the board and its shape is traced out with the stylus. Electrical signals sent to the computer record the positions of the stylus.

To **digitize** data means to convert it from an analogue form to a digital form. The term is used particularly to describe encoding a picture into binary form.

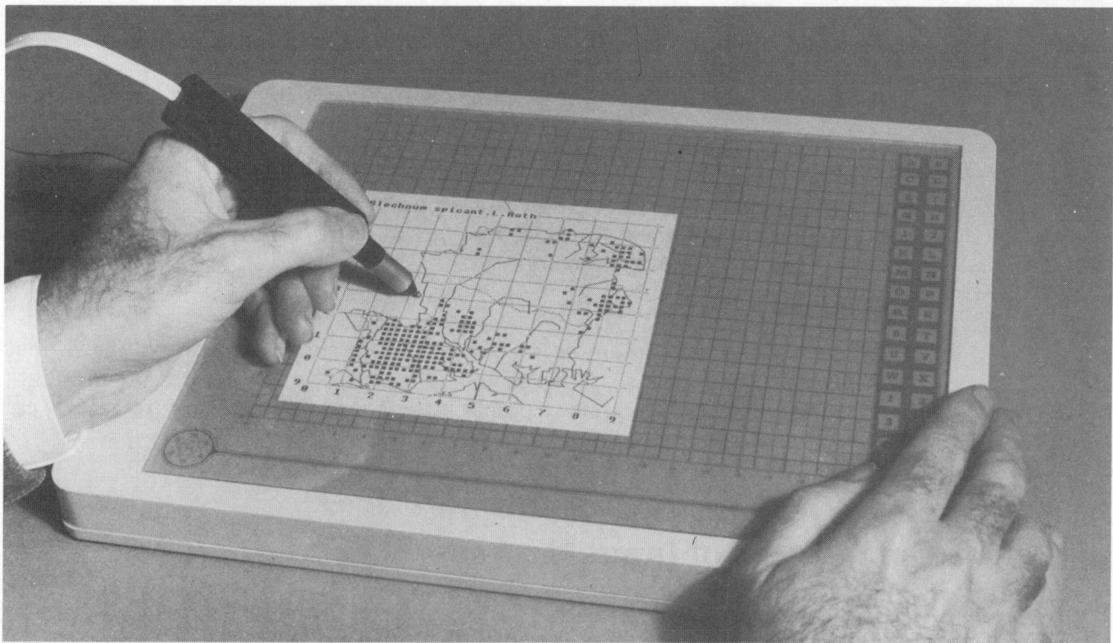

Fig. 7.16 A graphics tablet being used to digitize a map

Very accurate digitizers have a mouse-like device instead of a stylus. This is fitted with a magnifying glass and buttons for the user to press.

Advantages of a graphics tablet

It can be used to digitize drawings with great accuracy.

Uses

1 Digitizing maps – for example the Ordnance Survey is storing many of its maps on magnetic tape.
2 Reproducing drawings and designs.
3 Producing layouts for the printed circuit boards used in the circuitry of computers and other devices.

Note: Some types of graphics tablet will accept hand-written numbers and letters. This type is sometimes known as a **data pad**. It is not suitable for inputting a large amount of data. Data input in this way has to be checked on a screen as it is written to see that it has been recognized correctly.

7.5 Other Input Devices

VOICE RECOGNITION

Method

Using a microphone (or a telephone handset) human speech is coded into a sequence of electrical signals. The computer being used searches a set of stored patterns for the sound which has been input.

Advantages of voice recognition

1 No typing or data preparation is necessary.
2 It can be used remotely by telephone, or by those who are handicapped or who have their hands occupied.

Disadvantages

1 At present the method does not give good results. Relatively few words can be recognized and the error rate is high.
2 Recognition is slow.
3 It is not suitable in noisy places without a shielded mouthpiece.

Uses

1 Where only a few different commands are to be given and the hands cannot be used, for examply by a helicopter pilot to produce a display of the appropriate instruments on a screen, using simple prestored voice commands.

2 Over the telephone, for example by a bank. The computer can recognize a caller from a spoken code, tell him/her the state of a requested account (by synthesized voice – see Unit 8.4) and accept simple commands such as 'repeat'.
3 By handicapped people to control equipment.

DIRECT INPUT FROM INSTRUMENTS

Many measuring devices are now digital and electronic and can be linked to a computer. This requires special software to make use of the data coming in and, usually, a special interface between the device and the computer.

Examples of direct input

1 Thermostats or thermometers connected to a computer controlling a heating system.
2 A pressure pad on a road connected to a computer controlling traffic lights.
3 The instruments in a space vehicle interfaced with a computer which calculates the flight path and controls the rockets.
(See Unit 19 for further details and applications.)

7.6 Comparison of Input Methods

Note: Speeds are in characters per second unless otherwise stated, and refer to the rate at which the input device transfers data to the central processing unit.

Input device	*Medium*	*Preparation method*	*Verification method*	*Typical input speeds*
Disc unit	Magnetic discs	Typed at key-station	Retyping at same station	100 000 to 2 000 000
Tape drive	Magnetic tape	Key to tape or pooled from key-to-disc station	As disc or by rewinding tape	150 000
Floppy disc unit	Floppy disc	Separate key-station	Retyping at same station	20 000
Magnetic tape cartridge/cassette unit	Magnetic tape cartridge or cassette	Separate key-station	Retyping at same station	Cartridge 2000 to 1 000 000; cassette 2000 to 20 000
OCR device; document reader	Document	Handprinting or typing or computer printer or OCR encoder	Checked by eye	1 to 40 documents per second
MICR device	Document (cheque)	MICR encoder	Not applicable	15 documents per second
Mark sense reader; optical mark reader	Marked card or document	Making pencil marks in pre-printed ovals or rectangles	Difficult to verify	15 to 600 documents per minute

Fig. 7.17 Comparison of input methods

8 OUTPUT

An **output device** is a peripheral which receives data in the form of electrical pulses from the central processing unit. It then converts this data into information or into further data.

Often the information output is in a form that people can read. Examples are:

1 Payslips produced on a line printer.
2 Program listings produced on a screen.

Sometimes the information is not in the form of words or numbers. Examples are:

1 Maps or designs on a screen or on a plotter.
2 Sounds simulating a musical instrument.
3 A synthesized human voice.

Sometimes data is output which is to be read by machines. This may be used as input for computers or other equipment. Examples are:

1 Instructions to control a programmable lathe. These can be output on to a magnetic tape by a computer. The tape can then be input to the lathe, which has its own tape unit.
2 Data stored on a floppy disc by one computer to be input to another. An example of this is an insurance company where a disc of customer information is produced on a microcomputer at a branch office. This is then sent on to the company's head office to be used on their main computer.

OUTPUT ON PAPER

Printers may be adapted to accept single sheets or continuous paper. The continuous type is usually folded with perforations across it so that it can easily be torn into pages. It also has a tear-off strip at each side with holes. These are sprocket holes which enable printers to feed the paper accurately.

Preprinted stationery

Preprinted stationery consists of sets of identical forms or documents. These are fed into a computer printer instead of plain paper. Data is then printed on them in appropriate places.

The method is only suitable:

1 For computer applications which involve a large amount of similar output.
2 With a printer which can be fed different types of stationery.

Examples of the use of preprinted stationery

1 Bills for public services such as rates, gas, electricity, etc.
2 Payslips.
3 Figure 1.3 gives another example. Most of this meter reader form is preprinted. A computer printer has then added all the data which applies only to this particular form (the name, address, customer reference number, etc.). The meter reader has then handwritten the '9175', 'X' and '2' in the boxes.

8.1 Output on Screens

In recent years we have seen:

1 Better communications.
2 Faster processing.
3 Vastly increased storage.
4 Widespread use of microcomputers.

There has been a dramatic increase in:

1 The amount of data being looked at.
2 The interactive use of computers.
3 The use of graphics and animation.

Screens have been increasingly used for computer output.

DEFINITIONS

The **resolution** of a screen is a measure of how accurately data can be represented on it. Screens are usually classed as **low resolution, medium resolution** or **high resolution**.

For example, a low-resolution screen would be suitable for viewdata or teletext (see Unit 18). It would not be suitable for computer-aided design (see Unit 19.3).

A **pixel** is a very small area of the screen. It is the smallest area of the screen which the computer can change. Any display on the screen is made up by making the pixels light or dark (or by giving them the appropriate colour).

If the screen has a large number of pixels then the resolution is good.

A **monochrome** screen is one on which data is presented in one colour or tone on a background of a different colour or tone. Examples are:

1 White on black.
2 A 'greenscreen' – light green on dark green.

A **cursor** is a marker on the screen which shows the current position for printing or for entering data. Often the cursor is in the shape of an arrow or a small rectangle. With many programs the cursor flashes on and off so that it can be seen more easily.

STORAGE OF THE CONTENTS OF A SCREEN

A **screen dump** is a transfer of everything on a screen to some other medium. This is usually a printer or a plotter, but could be a disc or a magnetic tape. The dump is carried out using a special program for the purpose.

A common example is dumping a graphic design from the screen to a printer.

The data displayed on a screen has to be represented as binary codes. This is:

1 Because it is stored in random access memory while it is being displayed.
2 So that it can be transmitted – e.g. for teletext or viewdata (see Unit 18).
3 So that it can be saved by dumping it on to backing store or on to a printer.

One common way of storing the data on a screen is to store each pixel separately. Each pixel needs one bit of storage on a monochrome screen. On a colour screen each pixel needs 2 bits for 4 colours or 4 bits for 16 colours, etc. (This is in the same way that it would need 4 bits to code 16 different characters – see Unit 2.7).

Thus a large amount of storage will be required to store the contents of the screen if:

1 The screen has a high resolution.
2 Each pixel can have a lot of different colours.

Screen modes

A **screen mode** is a way a computer uses the screen for graphics and text (Figs. 8.1 and 8.2).

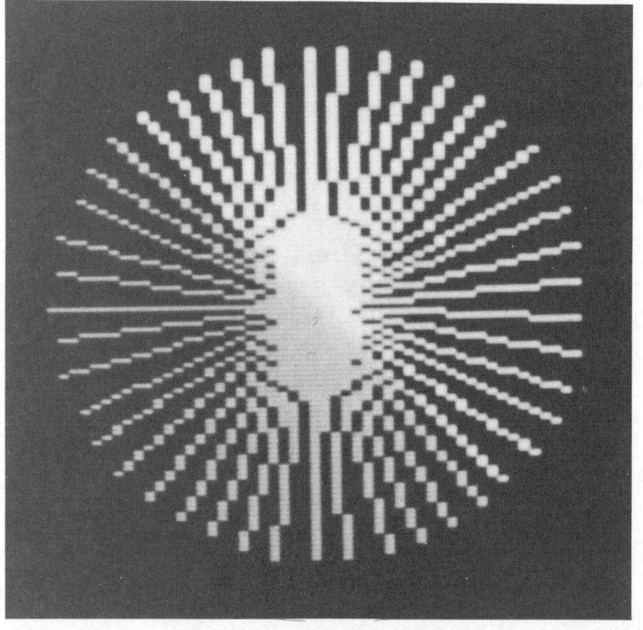

Fig. 8.1 Close-up photograph of a spoked pattern in a low-resolution mode

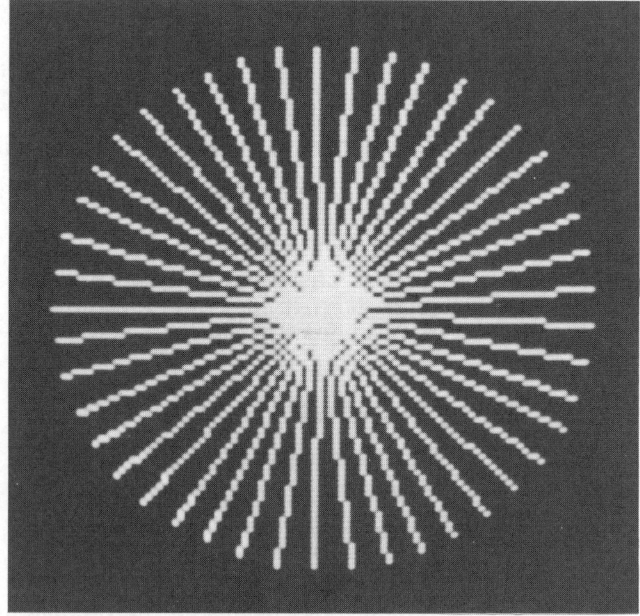

Fig. 8.2 The same pattern in a high-resolution mode

For example a particular computer can use the screen in two different modes:

1 In mode 1 there are 25 lines of text with 40 characters each; graphics are produced using 320 pixels across and 256 pixels down; 4 colours are available.

2 In mode 2 there are 25 lines of text with 80 characters each; graphics are produced using 640 pixels across and 256 pixels down; 16 colours are available.

Worked question

A particular high-resolution screen has 640 pixels across it and 512 pixels down. Each pixel can be any of 16 different colours.

How many K of bytes are needed to store the screen?

As each pixel can have 16 colours, it needs 4 bits to store it
One byte contains 8 bits
∴2 pixels can be stored in each byte
Also 1 K = 1024

$$\text{Number of K required} = \frac{1}{2} \times \frac{640 \times 512}{1024} = 160 \text{ K bytes}$$

TYPES OF SCREEN IN USE

Standard television sets

An ordinary home television can be used as a computer output. However, these sets are only designed to receive broadcast television. The pictures are not steady and have low resolution.

Uses of standard television sets in computing

1 As a cheap display device for home computers.
2 For teletext (see Unit 18).

Monitors

A **monitor** is a high-quality viewing unit. It looks like a television set but it accepts a different type of input signal. It has a far steadier, more clearly defined picture.

Uses of monitors

Almost all display screens in business and professional use are monitors.

Liquid crystal displays (LCDs)

A **liquid crystal display** consists of two thin sheets of glass with liquid crystals between them. Characters are etched on to the inner sheet but cannot be seen. The user can see them on the outer sheet only when a current is passed through them. Only a limited number of characters can be shown.

Uses of liquid crystal displays

1 As screens for small portable microcomputers.
2 As displays for electronic calculators and watches (Fig. 8.3).

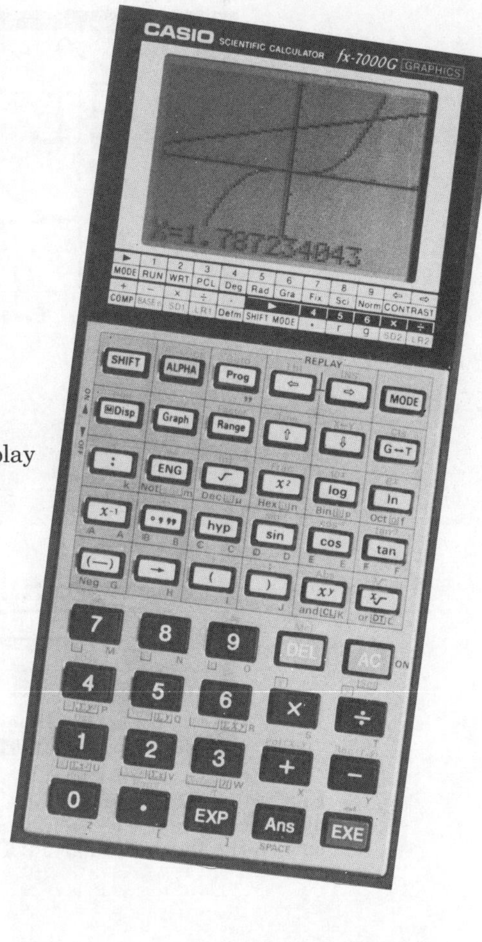

Fig. 8.3 A calculator with a liquid crystal display

Other types of screen

Various other technologies are in use. They include:

1 Displays consisting of **light-emitting diodes (LEDs)**; these use more power than liquid crystal displays but are brighter.
2 Plasma display panels; these use gas between glass plates instead of liquid and may make possible flat screens for monitors.

ORGANIZING SCREEN OUTPUT

Data on screens is often organized into **pages** (see Unit 18). Instead of the computer displaying data steadily down the screen one line after another, the screen is cleared every so often. Another page of information is then presented. In an interactive program the user can often work in selected places on the screen. To make this possible software facilities are required to:

1 Clear the screen.
2 Position the cursor at any point on the screen.
3 Split the screen up into windows (see below).
4 Use icons to make choices for action (see below).

Menus, windows and icons

A **menu** is a list of choices presented to the user by an interactive program. The user selects one of these options to say what the program should do next.

An **icon** (Fig. 8.4) is a small picture on the screen which replaces a written menu option. Instead of selecting a written choice from a menu, the user moves the cursor or pointer to an icon. A button or key is then pressed to select it. The icon may be drawn to look like the choice being made. For example for a graphics package a wide brush and a thin brush would produce lines of the appropriate widths.

A **window** is a rectangular area of the screen reserved for a particular display (Fig. 8.5).

Examples of the use of windows

1 Using a word processor an author may work on two different chapters of a book. Parts of each chapter can be displayed in two different windows on the same screen (see Fig. 8.5).
2 In a data logging application (see Unit 19.2) temperatures are being monitored in a furnace. Different windows on a screen display:

(a) A clock.
(b) A graph of the temperatures for the last hour.
(c) A table showing the values for the last minute.

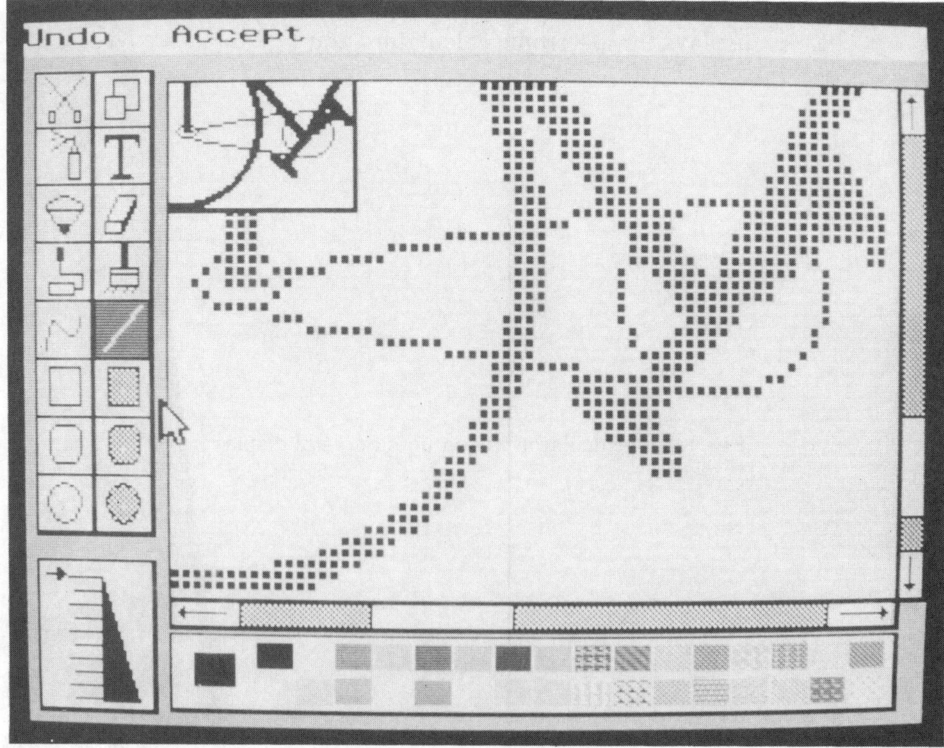

Fig. 8.4 A display screen for a graphics program. There are two windows. Both show a section of a larger diagram (of a bicycle). Changes are made in the large window. The small window shows how these will look in the finished diagram. The icons at the left and the bottom of the screen can be selected to choose colours, line thicknesses, etc.

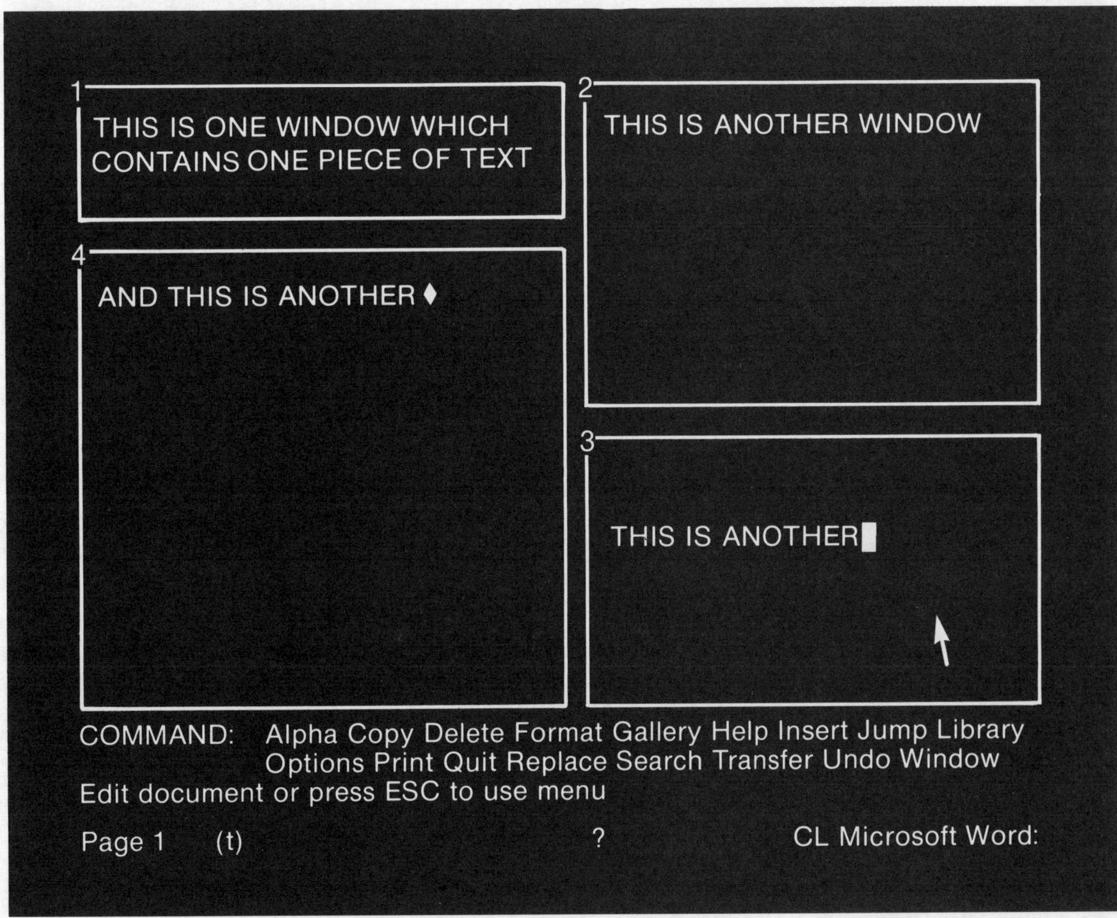

Fig. 8.5 A display screen for a word processor. There are four windows each containing a different piece of text from the same document. The bottom of the screen contains a menu. The arrow in window three can be moved using a mouse or using the arrow keys on the keyboard. (*By kind permission of Microsoft.*)

8.2 Printers

There are a large number of different types of printer used for computer output. They differ in:

1 The order in which data is printed

(a) **Character printers** – characters are printed one by one moving across and down the page.
(b) **Line printers** – Print 'a line at a time'. Strictly the line is not printed all at once but it appears to be.
(c) **Page printers** – Print a page at a time.

2 Impact or nonimpact

An **impact printer** is one in which letters are formed by forcing the paper and the printing head together to print the characters. Either (a) the printing head is pressed on to the paper or (b) a hammer hits the paper on to the character shape. An impact printer requires an inked ribbon next to the paper.

A **nonimpact printer** is one in which characters are not formed by mechanical impact (e.g. an ink-jet printer).

3 How the characters are formed – the font

The most common types are:
(a) **Matrix font** – each character is made up of dots selected from a rectangular matrix.
(b) **Solid fonts** – the characters are produced using pieces of shaped metal (or plastic) as on an ordinary mechanical typewriter.

MAIN TYPES OF PRINTER

1 Page printers

The most common of these is the **laser printer**.

In the laser printer output is produced on a light-sensitive drum. The computer controls a laser beam, which is a very narrow beam of light. The laser beam is directed very rapidly over the drum, being switched repeatedly on and off. Ink particles are then fused on to the paper wherever the laser beam hit the drum.

Large laser printers use powerful lasers and can print up to 150 pages a minute. This type are used with large mainframe printers. Recently smaller laser printers have been introduced for use in small installations and in offices. These produce up to 20 pages a minute.

Advantages of laser printers

1 They are very fast.
2 They give very high quality printing.
3 They are quiet, because they are nonimpact.

Disadvantages of laser printers

1 They are expensive to buy.
2 They are expensive to run.

2 Line printers

(*a*) *Ink-jet printers*

Very fine ink jets are directed at the paper. The ink is charged and can be directed electrically. This is similar to the way a beam of electrons is directed to make up a television picture.

(*b*) *'Band' or 'train' printers*

The character set is in a continuous loop of characters. Usually the complete character set is repeated several times round the loop.

The loop rotates in a horizontal line. There is a set of hammers across the paper. The hammer for each character position hits the paper and a carbon on to the right character as it goes past.

Advantages

Of ink-jet over band
1 They are faster.
2 They are quiet.
3 They give far better quality printing.
Of band over ink-jet
1 They are more reliable.
2 They are less expensive to buy.
3 They can print several copies at once using carbon paper between the copies.
Of line printers over character printers
They are faster.

3 Character printers

(*a*) *Dot matrix* (*impact type*)

The paper is held on a cylindrical 'platen' with a ribbon held in front of it, much as on a typewriter. Each character is produced by a printing head hitting the ribbon on to the paper. The printing head has in it a rectangular matrix of needles (Fig. 8.6). The appropriate needles are pushed forward electrically to form the shape of the letter required.

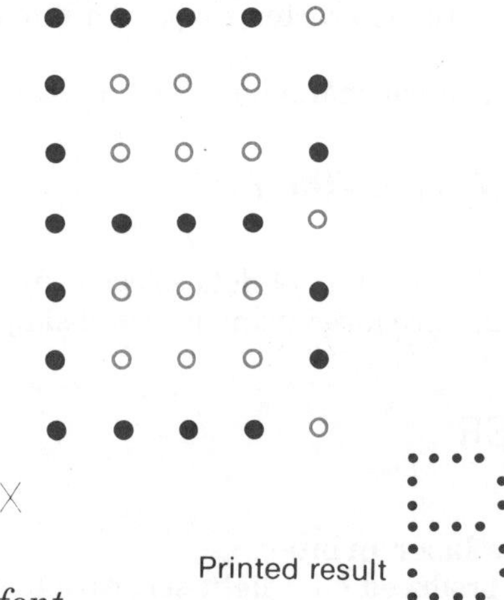

Fig. 8.6 The five by seven dot-matrix pattern for the letter B.

(*b*) *Solid font*

The paper and ribbon are held as for the dot-matrix printer, but the character set is a set of shaped characters actually on the printing head. Examples of solid font printing heads are

golfball, where the printing head is spherical, and **daisy wheel**, where the printing head is a spoked wheel, made of metal or plastic and about 80 mm in diameter, with characters at the ends of the spokes (Fig. 8.7).

Fig. 8.7 A daisy wheel

(c) *Non-impact*

Printers which rely on the paper and the print head hitting each other are noisy. Various methods have been developed of avoiding this, although at present they are not as popular as impact printers.

Advantages

Of non-impact over impact
They are very quiet.
Of impact over non-impact
They can produce multiple copies using carbon paper.
Of daisy wheel over dot matrix
1 The characters are better formed.
2 They are quieter.
Of dot matrix over solid font
They are less expensive for a given speed.
Of character printers generally
They are cheap and reliable.

Disadvantages

Of daisy-wheel printers
The daisy wheels wear quickly.
Of character printers generally
They are far slower than page or line printers.

CHOICE OF PRINTER

The following are examples of the printing requirements of two different organizations and the printers which were chosen for them:

1 A large engineering laboratory where individual research teams each have a microcomputer. These computers also act as terminals to a mainframe computer on the site. This is used for printing listings of programs and large quantities of research data. The printing facilities in the main computer room are also used to produce research documents and reports. The computer room contains three printers:

(a) An impact line printer using a band system. This produces 1200 lines a minute. It is used for listings and research data where the quality is not too important.

(b) An ink-jet printer. This produces 20 pages a minute. It is used for important documents for high-quality printing.
(c) A dot-matrix character printer. This only prints at 60 characters a second. It is used to produce a **computer room log**. This log is a record of the programs which are run and of the resources which are used during the day.

2 A college which has two networks of microcomputers. One is in the business studies department. It is used mainly for word processing. The other is in the computing department. The following printers were chosen:
(a) The computing department has one dot-matrix printer. This prints at 100 characters a second for printing program listings. However, it can produce 'near letter quality' printing if used at half speed. It can also be used to do screen dumps of graphics if necessary to record students' projects. It has a continuous feed but the paper can be divided into separate sheets.
(b) The business studies department has a daisy-wheel printer for producing high-quality typing. It takes single sheets of paper.
(c) The daisy-wheel printer is rather slow. The business studies department also has a dot-matrix printer similar to that in the computing department. It does, however, have two important improvements:
(i) It will take single sheets.
(ii) It has a wider carriage so that it can take sheets of paper sideways.

8.3 Plotters

A **plotter** (or **graph plotter**) is a device for producing graphical output on paper. By **graphical output** we mean graphs, designs and drawings output by the computer.

On most plotters characters have to be produced by tracing out their shapes, rather than by printing them. However, there are available printer/plotters designed to overcome this problem.

Plotters can be used on-line or off-line.

1 On-line

A plotting program running in the computer produces binary data which is sent directly to the plotter to control its movement.

2 Off-line

The plotting program produces the same data as before but the data is usually stored on magnetic tape (sometimes on paper tape). This tape can be used to produce a plot later, without the computer being involved, by using a reader attached to the plotter.

Advantage of off-line use of a plotter

Because of the slow movement of the pen, plotters produce output fairly slowly in comparison with other output devices. The off-line method allows plot data to be output to a high-speed medium, thus saving computer time.

TYPES OF DIGITAL PEN PLOTTER

1 Flat-bed plotter

The paper is held stationary on a flat surface. For large plotters (sometimes they are several metres in length and width) the paper may be held in place by suction from underneath.

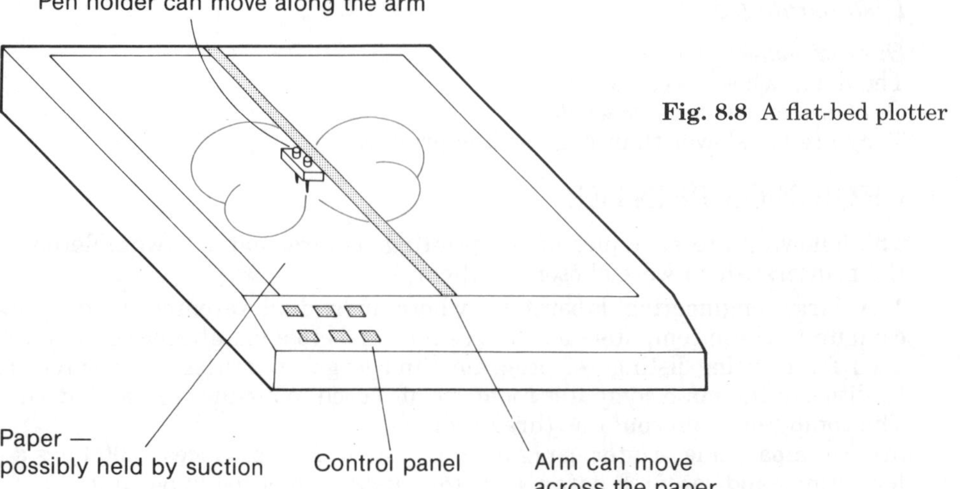

Fig. 8.8 A flat-bed plotter

The pen is held above the paper and can move:

(a) Up or down – When down it contacts the paper and draws lines.

(b) Across the width in either direction.

(c) Along the length in either direction.

By combining these movements lines can be drawn, broken or continuous, curved or straight, anywhere on the paper.

Fig. 8.9 A flat-bed plotter in use – being driven by a microcomputer

2 Drum plotter

The paper, usually a roll, is held on a drum which can be rotated backwards and forwards.

The pen is held above the paper and can move:

(a) Up (to move without drawing) or down (to draw).

(b) Left and right across the paper.

Lines can be drawn anywhere on the paper by combining drum movements with pen movements.

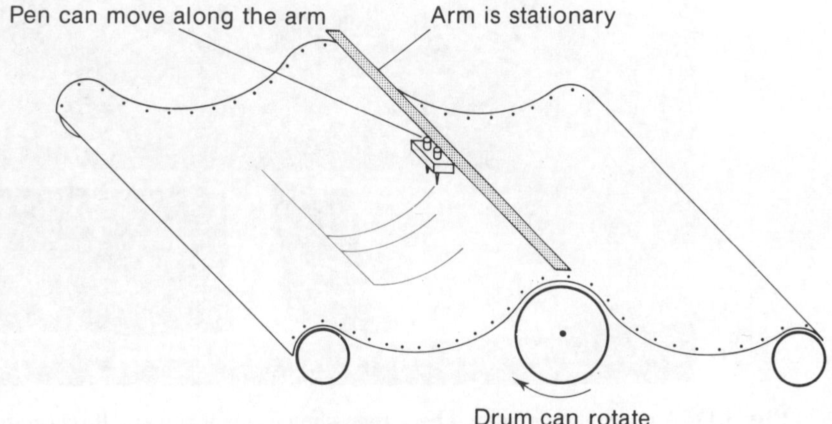

Fig. 8.10 A drum plotter

Uses of plotters

In any situation where hard copy of graphical output is required, for example to output designs which have been developed using a graphical display unit, or to produce maps.

8.4 Other Output Methods

OUTPUT ON TO MEDIA ALSO USED FOR INPUT

Media used include magnetic tapes and magnetic discs. Data is output on to them:

1 To input it to a computer again at a later date.

2 To drive a piece of equipment without the use of a computer. Magnetic tapes are often used to drive plotters, lathes, etc.

COMPUTER OUTPUT ON MICROFICHE OR MICROFILM (COM)

A miniature display screen or a laser is used to produce output, much reduced, on high-quality film. **Microfiche** is a rectangular sheet of **microfilm** large enough to contain a number of pages (or frames) of data – typically 30 to 300.

Because of the reduction in size microfilm or microfiche cannot be read without a special reader to project the image on to a screen (Fig. 8.11). With microfiche the material has to be moved into the correct position as only a small part of it is displayed on the screen. The microfiche reader is often fitted with fine adjustments to enable this to be done accurately.

Fig. 8.11 A microfiche reader. The screen shows one of the small rectangular areas of the microfiche on the plate below

Advantages of COM

Over output on to paper

1 Graphics and/or text can be produced at very high speed (see Fig. 8.12).

2 A large amount of data can be stored in a very small space.

Disadvantages

1 Cannot be read without special equipment.
2 Cannot be written on by hand.

Uses

1 To produce large quantities of output for storage in a small space.
2 To make data easy to carry around or send by post.

Examples of use of microfiche

1 A bank's computer produces statements of clients' accounts daily on microfiche, one sheet for each branch. These can then be sent cheaply by post to the branches.
2 A company may use microfiche to store old customer records.
3 To store diagrams of all the parts for a particular car. For many cars it is possible to obtain a microfiche showing all the parts together with all the part numbers. Purchasing spares is made much simpler because the assistant in the parts department has no trouble locating the correct part for that model.
4 To store library references (e.g. titles of books and extracts from them).

VOICE OUTPUT

Voice output from computers is generally easier and more successful than is voice recognition as a means of input. At first, voice output relied on the computer selecting appropriate words stored as sounds on magnetic tape. Now, however, voices can be successfully 'synthesized' by storing word patterns as bit strings. When the computer wants to 'say' something the appropriate codes are sent to a 'voice response unit' which produces the sounds.

Advantages

1 Can be accessed by telephone.
2 No reading ability is required by the user.

Disadvantages

1 It is not suitable for noisy environments.
2 There is no permanence – words not understood have to be repeated by the computer.

Uses

1 To produce a response from a computer by telephone without the need for a modem or terminal equipment at the user's end of the line. If a push-button telephone is used, coded messages can be sent by pressing combinations of the buttons and the computer replies with synthesized speech.
2 Small hand-held devices are available which produce synthesized speech and which can:
(a) Make learning more interesting.
(b) Help with the translation of foreign languages.

DIRECT OUTPUT TO OTHER DEVICES

Computers are being used more and more to control other devices. These include aircraft, robots, central heating boilers, lathes, etc. The increased use of microprocessors has increased this type of application.

Any computer-controlled system may make use of the following:

1 Digital-to-analogue converters (see Unit 6.4). This is because computers output digital signals. The devices that computers control are often analogue.
2 **Actuators** – an actuator is a device which can produce a movement when given an electrical signal.
3 Devices to switch large currents on and off. A computer only produces very low-power electrical signals. These cannot drive electrical equipment. To get a computer to do this the signal from a computer has to switch another device on and off. Devices available are:
(a) **Transistors** – a transistor can be used to switch current on and off without any mechanical movement.
(b) **Relays** – a relay is a switch which can be switched on and off by a small current. It does involve a mechanical movement, but it can be used to switch more powerful equipment than can a transistor. In particular a relay can be used to switch on and off machines which work on mains electricity.
4 **Motors** – two types of motor might be used in a computer-controlled system:
(a) A **continuous motor** – this runs continuously and evenly when it is switched on. This type of motor has the advantage that it can run at high speeds.
(b) A **stepper motor** – when a signal is sent to a stepper motor it only rotates a small amount. To make it run continuously it has to be sent repeated signals. A stepper motor has the advantage that it can be controlled more accurately.

8.5 Comparison of Output Methods

SUMMARY OF OUTPUT DEVICES

The following table (Fig. 8.12) does not show a speed for plotters, which normally produce characters by drawing them. The speeds given are all in characters per second. Where the device does not produce individual characters the speed has been approximated; for example for a line printer it has been assumed that a whole line is printed each time, whereas for many applications much of each line would be left blank.

Unit reference	*Device*	*Medium*	*Speed in c.p.s.*
8.4	Magnetic disc unit	Magnetic disc	100 000 to 2 000 000
8.4	Magnetic tape unit	Magnetic tape	150 000
8.4	COM unit	Microfilm or microfiche	120 000
8.2	Laser page printer	Paper	20 000
8.2	Line printer	Paper	200 to 6000
8.2	Impact character printer	Paper	50 to 600
8.1	Television monitor	Cathode ray tube	60 to 2000
8.3	Plotter	Paper	Not applicable

Fig. 8.12 Table of output devices

Note: There is no need for candidates to learn the speeds of devices. However, it is important to know which ones are fast and which are slow.

CHOICE OF OUTPUT METHOD

In buying or hiring output devices an installation has to consider:

1 Whether the devices purchased will cope with the needs of users for:
(a) Speed.
(b) Quality of output.
(c) Range of different types of output.
2 The cost of:
(a) The equipment.
(b) Running the devices – printers need paper but also bands or daisy wheels or ribbons, etc.
(c) Maintenance – some devices are less robust than others.
3 Adaptability – whether equipment can be adapted to fit in with future needs.

Many applications use a combination of output methods. For example:

1 A designer uses:
(a) The monitor of a graphical display unit while the design is being developed.
(b) A plotter to produce the finished designs.
2 A gas board uses the following while producing its customer accounts:
(a) Monitors on VDUs to check on individual accounts.
(b) A line printer to produce the bills.
(c) Microfiche for records of accounts which are more than 2 years old.

9 STORAGE DEVICES AND MEDIA

A **store** is a part of a computer system where data and instructions can be held, ready for later use.

Examples of stores

1 The main store of a computer.
2 A floppy disc.

To **write** data into store means to transfer it from the central processing unit to the storage medium.

To **read** data from the store means to transfer it from the store to the central processing unit.

A **volatile store** is one which loses its data when the power is switched off. The RAM in computers is usually volatile (see below), although some microcomputers have RAM which is maintained by batteries.

A **nonvolatile** or **permanent store** is one which does not lose its data when the power is switched off.

To **save** a program means to have it read from the computer's main store and written to a permanent store.

To **load** a program means to have it read from a permanent store into the computer's main store.

Note: People also refer to saving and loading data – particularly in word processing.

Examples of saving and loading

1 A programmer may load a program, correct it and then save the new version.
2 The user of a particular program has to load it from disc before running it.

To **access** data means to get ready to transfer data and then to transfer it. The term is often used to refer to reading data but can be used for writing as well.

The **access time** for a particular device is the time taken to locate data and to transfer it ready for use.

Example of access time

If data is read from a magnetic disc the access time is in three parts:
1 The **seek time** – the time to move the read/write heads across the disc to the right track.
2 The **rotational delay** – the time for the disc to rotate to the right place for reading.
3 The **transfer time** – the time taken actually to read the data.

Note: For details of how data is stored on discs see Unit 9.2.

LEVELS OF STORAGE

Store is classed into levels depending on how quickly the computer can access it. A store which can be accessed quickly is at a higher level than one which cannot.

The two main levels of storage are:

1 Main store (or main memory or immediate access store)

(a) It is divided into locations. The computer can access any of the locations directly using a number called its address. Each location has a different address.
(b) Access to it is very fast. Reading and writing are done electronically without any mechanical movement.
(c) The main store contains the **working store** of the computer. This consists of RAM (random access memory – see Unit 9.1). While a program is running, the program itself is usually stored here. So are any variables used by the program. This part of the store is usually volatile.
(d) The main store also usually contains some ROM (read only memory – see Unit 9.1). This contains certain programs which are stored permanently.

2 Backing store (or auxiliary store or secondary storage)

(a) This is storage outside the central processing unit.
(b) It usually needs mechanical read/write heads to access it.

(c) Access to it is slower than the main store.
(d) It is nonvolatile so that it can be used to store data permanently.

Usually backing storage devices are on-line to the computer. However, backing storage media such as magnetic tapes and discs may be stored off-line.

Examples of on-line and off-line storage

1 A network in a school has a hard disc unit always on-line. However, pupils may decide to buy their own floppy discs and keep their programs off-line.
2 A large computer installation keeps all regularly used files on discs which are permanently on-line. However, users may store seldom-used files in a magnetic tape library in the computer room. If a program needs one of these tapes a monitor in the computer room will show a request for it. The computer will suspend running of this program until an operator has found the tape in the library and has loaded it on to a tape unit.

REASONS FOR DIFFERENT LEVELS OF STORAGE

1 Working store is necessary:
(a) For storage of the program currently being executed.
(b) To hold data produced as the program is run.
(c) To hold data needed by the instruction being executed.

For each of these it is necessary to have a store which can be accessed very quickly. It may not matter if the store is volatile if the program and data are only in the store while the program is running.
2 Backing store is necessary:
(a) For data and programs which are to be stored for a long time. The computer may be used for other programs or may be switched off, but data on backing store will still be there.
(b) For data and programs when there is not enough room in the main store.
3 Off-line backing store is necessary:
(a) When not all the programs and data needed for a computer system can be kept on-line at once. On-line backing store is expensive and there may not be enough of it.
(b) So that programs and data can be taken away and used on other computers.
(c) When the stored data is used to operate other equipment, such as plotters.
(d) For security – important programs and data can be kept in a separate building in case of fire or theft.

9.1 Main Store

A computer's main store usually consists of integrated circuit chips. There are several types:

RAM – RANDOM ACCESS MEMORY

1 Random access memory is store which data can be written to and read from at high speed.
2 The processor accesses a location by setting the correct address for it. Decoding circuitry makes sure that the right location is accessed.
3 Usually RAM is volatile and loses data when switched off.

Uses of RAM

1 As the working store of the computer.
2 As buffers holding data being transferred to and from peripherals.
3 To store the contents of the screen in microcomputers.

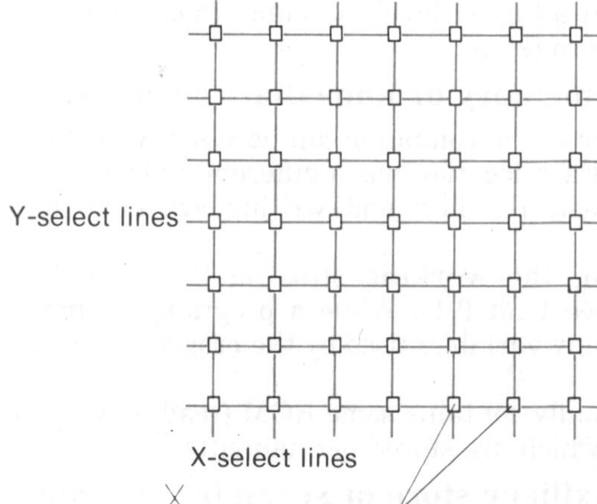

Fig. 9.1 A section of semiconductor random access memory (RAM)

How RAM works

Each bit of the store is represented in a chip as a separate storage cell. The cells are arranged in a lattice (i.e. a squared pattern) (see Fig. 9.1). Usually the bits which make up a particular storage location are each on a different lattice. Often they are on different chips. This is so that the bits for a location can all be accessed at the same time.

The lattice has X-select lines going one way and Y-select lines going the other. A cell is accessed by sending a signal along the X-select and the Y-select lines which pass through it.

ROM – READ ONLY MEMORY

1 **Read only memory** is store that can be read but nothing can be written on to it.
2 The ROM in the main store is divided into locations which are addressed in the same way as for RAM.
3 It is nonvolatile – the programs and data in it are stored there permanently.

Uses of ROM

ROM is used to store programs essential to the normal running of the computer. Usually cheap microcomputers have more programs on ROM than do large computers. This is because large computers usually have very fast backing store so that programs can be loaded easily.

Programs which might be stored on ROM include:

1 The computer's operating system or a program to load the operating system automatically (see Unit 14.3).
2 Utility programs (see Unit 14.2).
3 An interpreter or a compiler for a high-level language (see Unit 11.2).
4 A word processor program (see Unit 18.4).

PROM – PROGRAMMABLE READ ONLY MEMORY

Programmable read only memory is a form of ROM which is manufactured without anything stored on it. Programs or data can be written into and it then becomes permanent as read only memory.

EPROM – ERASABLE PROGRAMMABLE READ ONLY MEMORY

The contents of **erasable programmable read only memories** can be erased at any time using a special EPROM eraser. (One method involves shining ultraviolet light through a small window on the top of the chip – see Fig. 4.3.)

New programs or data can then be written on to the EPROM using a device called an **EPROM programmer**.

Uses of EPROMS

1 To store programs which might need to be changed.
2 To copy the contents of existing ROMs. (This should not be done without the copyright owner's permission.)

THE ROLE OF RAM AND ROM

A computer contains both ROM and RAM:

1 In powerful computers with fast backing storage devices there is not much ROM. The ROM just contains a program to load the operating system automatically when the computer is switched on. The operating system and all other programs are loaded from backing storage – usually disc. This makes the computer completely adaptable as to which software is used in it.
2 In cheap microcomputers a lot of the software is on ROM – operating system, utilities, language interpreters, word processor packages, etc. This means that the computer has all of these facilities stored in it permanently. They can be accessed without fuss and without expensive backing storage.
3 Dedicated microprocessor (see Unit 4.2). If a microprocessor is dedicated to a control task there is no need to load the program into it from backing storage. The program can be stored on ROM and the complete computer consists of the processor, some RAM, some ROM and interfaces to the devices being controlled.

9.2 Backing Stores

Backing stores are either serial access or direct access.

Direct access store is backing store for which any data item can be accessed without reading any other data first.

Magnetic discs are the most common type of direct access store.

A typical magnetic disc has two surfaces or sides. Each surface holds data in a set of circular tracks. Each track is divided into equal sections called sectors (Fig. 9.4)

Serial access store is backing store for which all data between the present read/write position and the required one has to be passed over before the data can be accessed.

Magnetic tapes are the most common type of serial access store.

DIRECT ACCESS BACKING STORES

The main types are magnetic but optical methods are being used increasingly:

1 Hard discs accessed by moving heads.
2 Hard discs access by fixed heads.
3 Floppy discs
4 Bubble memory
5 Optical storage—use of compact discs such as CD ROM.

1 Hard discs with moving heads

A For mainframe computers
Hard discs are used for on-line backing storage on large computers.

Characteristics of moving head hard discs on mainframe computers

1 There are often several discs grouped together in a disc pack. They are held parallel to one another by a spindle and all rotate together. There is one head per surface and the heads cannot move separately but move together like a comb (Fig. 9.3).

For a **disc pack**, a group of tracks vertically above one another is called a **cylinder**.

2 They are almost always exchangeable. This means the disc or pack is not permanently fixed in the drive but can be taken out and replaced by another one.

Fig. 9.2 Close-up of the inside of a modern disc unit – the IBM 9335 – showing the read/write heads (*By kind permission of IBM*)

B For microcomputers

Small hard discs are commonly installed on microcomputers. They are used to store the operating system and applications software. The user may also store his/files on the hard disc—possibly storing a backup of each file on a floppy disc (see Unit 13.6).

Characteristics of hard discs on microcomputers.

1 The discs are not exchangeable. Each is built into a sealed unit to prevent contamination by dust and moisture.

2 Access is far faster than access to floppy discs and data is transferred at a faster rate as well.

3 Hard discs store far more data than floppy discs. The capacity of one disc is often from 40 megabytes to several hundred megabytes.

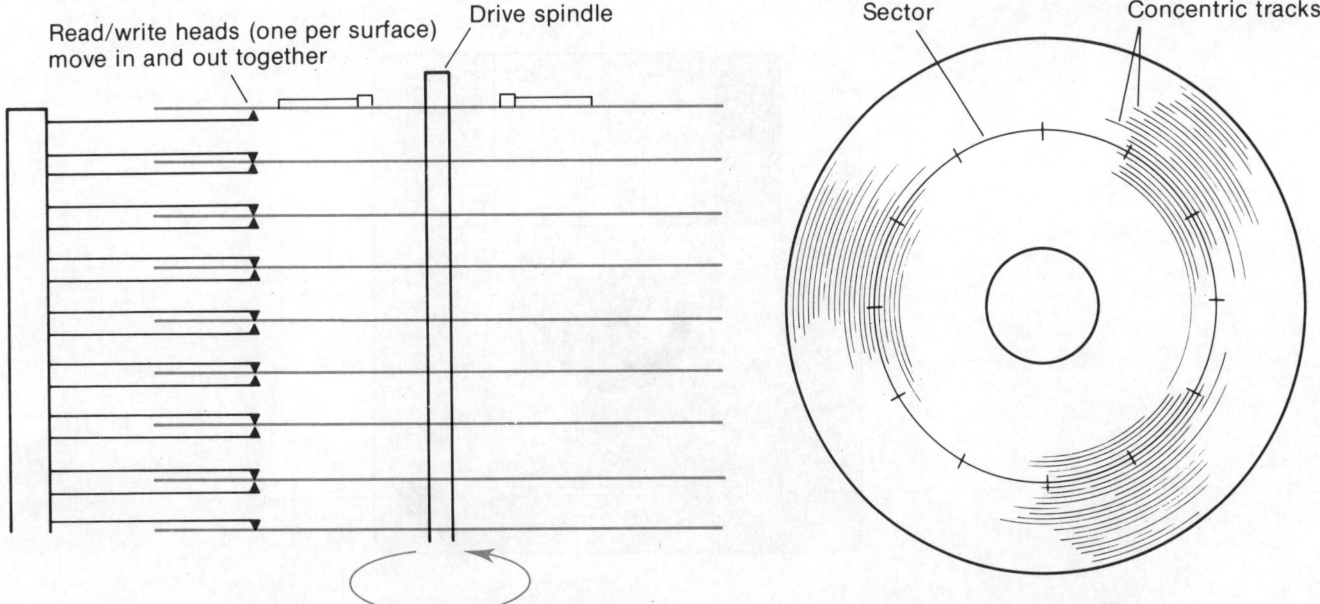

Fig. 9.3 Moving-head exchangeable disc pack in drive

Fig. 9.4 How data is stored on the surface of a magnetic disc

The access time for moving head discs is given by:

Access time = Seek time + Rotational delay + Transfer time
(See Unit 9 – introduction.)

Uses

1 General storage of users' files.
2 Storage of frequently used programs.
3 Storage of programs and data which are queueing to be dealt with by the computer.
4 Storage of data waiting to be printed.

2 Hard discs with fixed heads

These are very similar to moving-head discs except that there is a read/write head for every track of every surface.

Characteristics of fixed-head discs

1 The disc packs are usually not exchangeable, often the drive unit is a closed box and the discs are not visible.
2 The heads do not move. There is no seek time so:

Access time = Rotational delay + Transfer time
Thus access is faster than for moving-head discs.

3 They are relatively expensive.

3 Floppy discs

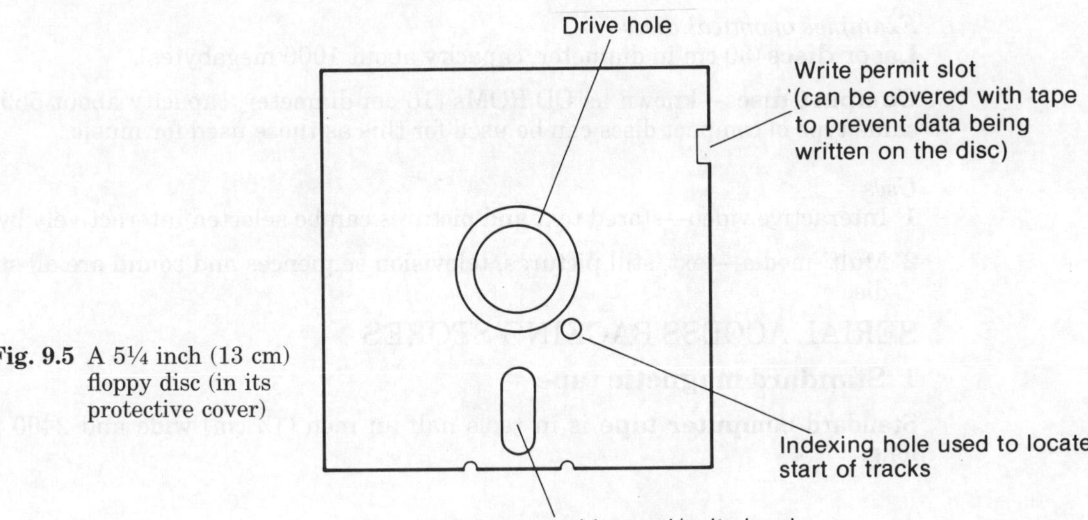

Fig. 9.5 A 5¼ inch (13 cm) floppy disc (in its protective cover)

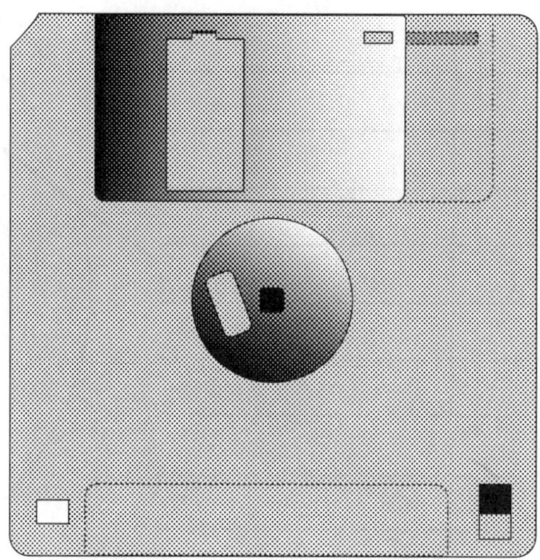

Fig 9.6 A 3 ½ inch floppy disc. The sprung metal cover protecting the disc is at the top. The disc has a small write-permit switch at the bottom right.

A **floppy disc** is a single flexible disc held in a protective jacket. Diameters vary but 8 inches, 5¼ inches and 3½ inches are common. The larger floppy discs have to be kept carefully in a small wallet. This is because part of the magnetized surface is exposed to allow contact with the read/write heads (Fig 9.5). The smaller discs are protected by a sprung metal cover (Fig 9.6).

Usually both sides of the disc are coated with magnetic material, although sometimes only one side is used. There is only one read/write head for each surface used. The discs are exchangeable. Data is stored on them in much the same way as on the larger hard discs.

Uses

1 Floppy discs were originally developed as a replacement for cards as a data preparation medium. In this role they are highly successful (see Unit 7.1).

2 They are also widely used now as backing stores for microcomputers and word processors.

4 Bubble memory

A film of magnetizable material has metal circuit patterns deposited on top of it. The bubbles consist of small areas of the material, magnetized on one of two directions to represent 1 or 0. Although the material itself does not move a bubble can effectively be 'moved' by inducing the same magnetic field in another area nearby using electric current.

5 Optical discs—CD ROM

An optical disc is a disc used to store computer data which is read using a light beam. The data is recorded on one layer of the disc by burning small pits in it, usually with a laser beam. The pitted layer is covered with another smooth layer on top to protect the data.

At the moment most optical discs are read only—data cannot be written on to them.

Examples of optical discs

Laser discs (30 cm in diameter, capacity about 1000 megabytes).

Compact discs—known as CD ROMs (10 cm diameter, capacity about 550 megabytes). The same type of compact discs can be used for this as those used for music.

Uses

1 Interactive video—stored text and pictures can be selected interactively by the user.

2 Multi-media—text, still pictures, television sequences and sound are all stored on the same disc.

SERIAL ACCESS BACKING STORES

1 Standard magnetic tape

Standard **computer tape** is in reels half an inch (1¼ cm) wide and 2400 feet (730 metres) long.

Increasingly tape is being used in the form of a **cartridge**. This is better protected from dirt and easier to use, but usually contains less tape. Cartridges are now available which are smaller than reel-to-reel tapes but store more data.

Even smaller cartridges are used in **tape streamers**. A tape streamer is a unit used to store the contents of discs as a 'back-up' – so that the data can be retrieved if there is a disc failure.

On magnetic tapes data is usually held on seven or nine parallel tracks along the tape, one frame across the tape representing one character (see Unit 2.7).

Data is stored on the tape in blocks (Fig. 9.7). A **block** is the amount of data that can be transferred as a unit between the CPU and a backing store.

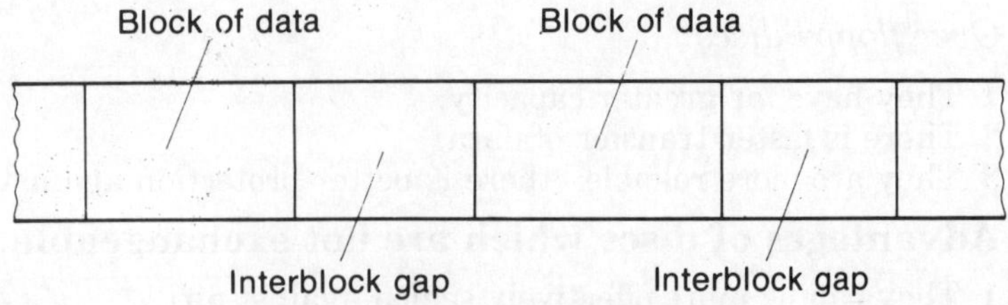

Fig. 9.7 Data stored on a magnetic tape

Reel-to-reel tape units usually have loops of tape held by a vacuum to stop the tape breaking as the unit starts and stops (Fig. 9.8). It is still necessary to have quite large lengths of blank tape in between the blocks to allow for acceleration and deceleration. These lengths are called **interblock gaps**.

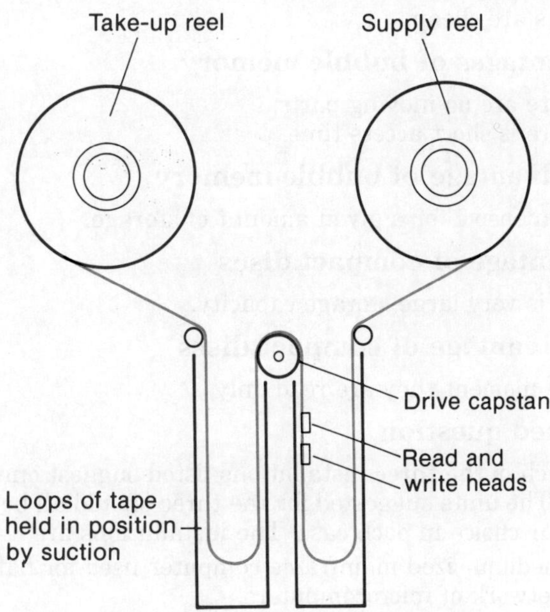

Fig. 9.8 Operation of a magnetic tape unit

Worked question

A computer file is stored on magnetic tape which has blocks of 512 characters each. The file consists of 1000 records of 25 characters each. A block cannot store parts of records – that is if there is not enough room in a block for the whole of a particular record it must go in the next block. How many blocks are needed to store the file?

512/25 is equal to 20.48
So 1 block can hold 20 records
Number of blocks needed = 1000/20
= 50

2 Tape cassettes

Standard tape cassettes are used as low-cost backing store for microcomputers.

Data is usually stored on a single track. Two different frequencies of sound are used to represent 0 or 1, the bits of each character of data following one another along the tape (see Unit 2.7). Transfer is very slow in comparison with other media – typically 30 to 120 characters per second (300 to 1200 baud).

9.3 Comparison of Storage Media

COMPARISON OF DIRECT ACCESS BACKING STORES

Advantages of exchangeable hard discs

Over fixed-head discs

1 They can be stored away from the computer.
2 Drive units are cheaper.

Over floppy discs

1 They have far greater capacity.
2 There is faster transfer of data.
3 They are more reliable – there is better protection against dirt.

Advantages of discs which are not exchangeable

1 They can be more effectively sealed against dirt.
2 More data can be stored on a given area of disc.

Advantages of fixed-head discs

Over moving-head discs

There is no seek time, so the access time is very short.

Advantages of floppy discs over other direct access media

1 Drive units are small and inexpensive.
2 Discs are cheap.

Advantages of bubble memory

1 There are no moving parts.
2 There is short access time.

Disadvantage of bubble memory

It is expensive for a given amount of storage.

Advantage of compact discs

There is very large storage capacity.

Disadvantage of compact discs

At the moment they are read only.

Worked question

For each of the three installations listed suggest one single disc unit which would be suitable for it. The units suggested for the three should all be different from one another. Give reasons for your choice in each case. The installations are:
1 A medium-sized mainframe computer used for batch work.
2 A network of microcomputers.
3 A home microcomputer.

1 The mainframe computer installation would require a hard disc unit with interchangeable disc packs. If they were only buying one unit a fixed disc unit would probably not store enough data for them.
2 The network of microcomputers would require a small fixed hard disc unit with a single disc. Exchangeable discs would not be satisfactory as different users would require different discs. In any case floppy discs would probably not hold enough data and a large exchangeable disc unit would be too expensive.
3 The most suitable storage for the home microcomputer would be a floppy disc unit. The owner might consider a small hard disc unit. However, they are expensive and also tend to be a bit noisy for home use.

COMPARISON BETWEEN MAGNETIC TAPE AND EXCHANGEABLE HARD DISCS

Advantages

Of disc over tape

1 There is direct access – data can be accessed from anywhere on a disc equally quickly. This makes it suitable for information retrieval. Tapes are not suitable for this.

2 Data is addressable – it can be accessed by giving track number and sector number (and, if necessary, cylinder number).
3 There is faster transfer of data – speeds vary widely but discs are usually faster than tapes.

Of tape over disc

1 It is light and compact. Tapes are easy to store for long periods and are easy to carry.
2 It is cheaper. Drive units vary in price but the actual tapes are far cheaper than discs.

Worked question

A computer system uses semiconductor RAM, interchangeable disc packs and magnetic tapes for storage. A program runs on this computer to plot graphs. Suggest **two** roles for each of the types of store in running this program.

The different stores are probably used as follows:

1 Semiconductor RAM as the main store which:
(a) Stores the actual program.
(b) Temporarily holds values produced by the program.
2 Interchangeable discs as the on-line backing store of the computer to:
(a) Store the program while it is waiting to be run.
(b) Store the software that the computer uses to translate and run all programs.
3 Magnetic tapes are used as off-line (external) store and:
(a) Contain the specialized software needed by graphics programs.
(b) Are used to output the actual plot data. This tape would then be used in operating the plotter off-line and producing the actual graphs.

CHARACTERISTICS OF IMPORTANT STORAGE MEDIA

In the following table no actual values have been given for access speed and transfer rate. This is because the values vary so much and are continually changing. The phrases used in the table are intended to show how devices compare with one another for speed.

Unit reference	*Medium*	*Type of access*	*Access speed*	*Transfer rate*	*Main role as storage*
9.1	RAM	Random	Very, very fast	Very, very fast	Main store in all types of computer
9.2	Fixed-head discs	Direct	Very fast	Very fast	Very fast backing store
9.2	Exchangeable hard discs	Direct	Fast	Fast	On-line backing store in large computers
9.2	Small fixed hard discs	Direct	Fast	Fast	On-line backing store for networks and expensive microcomputers
9.2	Floppy discs	Direct	Fairly fast	Fairly fast	Backing store in small computers
9.2	Magnetic tape	Serial	Slow	Fast	Off-line backing store for large computers
9.2	Tape cassette	Serial	Very slow	Slow	Cheap backing store on microcomputers

Fig. 9.9 Table of important storage media

10 USING COMPUTERS TO SOLVE PROBLEMS

As an examination candidate you have to understand how computers are used to solve problems. Assessment Objective A of the National Criteria for GCSE Computer Studies says: 'The candidate should be able to demonstrate a knowledge and understanding of the techniques needed to solve problems related to practical applications.'

(To find out about the National Criteria see the section on the GCSE on page xiii.)

INFORMATION PROCESSING APPLICATIONS

As hardware and software become cheaper, more and more problems are seen to involve information processing. The range of applications for computers and similar equipment increases all the time.

Examples could be taken from almost any human activity. Few people 30 years ago would have thought that computer technology would be used, for example, in:

1 Operating a camera – many cameras contain a microprocessor.
2 Writing a letter – word processors are now commonplace.

Units 17 to 21 of this book give details of some of the wide variety of ways in which computers are used. This unit deals with the general methods of using computers to solve problems.

STEPS IN PROBLEM SOLVING

Using a computer to solve a problem involves far more than just writing a program. In fact many computer applications are carried out without writing new programs. Exisiting software is used if possible.

Solving a problem may be seen in three main stages:

1 Defining exactly what the problem is.
2 Designing a solution to deal with it.
3 Putting that solution into practice.

In solving an information processing problem we should define:

1 The data which is to be input.
2 The data which is to be output.
3 The data which is to be stored as files.
4 The processing tasks to be carried out.

Example of a problem and a solution to it

In a particular school the pupils are divided into groups for registration and tutorials. A school list is produced by the office. This gives the names of all the pupils, arranged into tutor groups, for example:

1Sm	1Th	1Wi
Mr Smith Room 40	Mr Thomas Room 41	Miss Williams Room 4
Adams, Jeremy D.	Arden, Peter	Baines, June W.
Arnold, Helen B.	Batten, John N.	Betterton, Beryl
Biggs, Freda J.	Bostock, Jean V.	Daines, Peter C.

and so on . . .

The problem is it is difficult to use this list to find a pupil if his or her tutor group is not known. It would be much better to have two lists – the present one and another one which is alphabetical. The office staff say it would be too much work for them to produce both.

The proposed solution is to cut down the work involved by paying for a computer to be introduced. It is decided to type in data for each pupil. Most of this will be done at the start of a school year and the data will be stored on files. These can then be updated during the year for new pupils or those who leave. It would be too much work to type in for all pupils their tutor's name, their tutor group name and their room number. Instead a code will be used for the pupil's tutor.

The following will be involved:

1 Three sets of input data:
(a) The full name and tutor for each pupil. In fact the tutor's complete name will not be typed

but just a two-letter code for it e.g. Mr Smith will be Sm.
(b) The full name, tutor group name and room for each tutor.
(c) Choices of what lists are to be produced.
2 Two lists as output data:
(a) A list of all the tutor groups with the pupils in them (like the one the office produced originally).
(b) A list of all the pupils in the school in alphabetical order. Each name will be followed by the tutor's name, the tutor group name and the room they are in.
3 Two sets of data stored as files:
(a) A file storing for each pupil the full name and two-letter tutor code.
(b) A file storing for each tutor the two-letter code, full name, tutor group name and room.
4 Five main processing tasks for the computer:
(a) Inputting the pupil data and storing it in the pupil file.
(b) Inputting the tutor data and storing it in the tutor file.
(c) Updating these files when necessary.
(d) Sorting the pupils into tutor groups and printing the list of pupils in their groups.
(e) Sorting the pupils into alphabetical order and printing the alphabetical list.

To explain fully how the problem in the previous example was solved we would also have to describe:
1 Who is in charge of producing the lists and how it is organized.
2 Where the input data comes from i.e. how it is collected.
3 Who types in the data and produces the lists and how they communicate with the computer.
4 What computer equipment is used.
5 What programs are used and whether they are bought or specially written.

If we did this we would have described the **information processing system** for dealing with the problem.

10.1 Systems

A **system** is a set of components which works as a unit. An **information processing system** consists of everything required to carry out a particular processing task.

Examples of information processing systems

1 The stock control system for a shop (see Unit 17.1). The system comprises:
(a) The methods of checking on stock levels, of ordering new goods, of recording their delivery, and so on.
(b) The means of communicating with suppliers.
(c) The computer hardware and software if the system is computerized.
2 The working system in an office. This would include:
(a) The methods of communication – whether by letter, by telephone, by electronic mail.
(b) The methods of storage of information – whether on computer discs or in filing cabinets.
(c) The methods of producing letters – perhaps they are dictated to a secretary who later produces them on a word processor.
(d) The equipment – word processors, copiers, etc.

COMPUTERIZED INFORMATION PROCESSING SYSTEMS

In general a computerized information processing system includes:
1 Computers and other hardware.
2 Computer **software** – software is a general term for programs which are written to help computer users (see Unit 14).
3 Methods of (a) collecting, (b) checking and (c) inputting data.
4 Methods of communication (a) for data transmission, (b) between people in the organization.
5 Data files – the data held and the methods of (a) updating files and (b) of keeping them secure.
6 Processing operations carried out on data.
7 Methods of outputting data.

OTHER USES OF THE TERM 'SYSTEM'

The word 'system' can be used to mean just a set of equipment or, in computing, just hardware and/or software.

Examples

1 A camera system – the camera together with all its lenses, filters, flashguns, etc.
2 A central heating system – the boiler, pipes, radiators, thermostats, pumps and control box.
3 A computer system – the central processor, the peripherals and the software.
4 The operating system of a computer – the software which keeps it running (see Unit 14.3).

10.2 Steps in Systems Analysis and Design

In business and industry new systems are produced by a person called a **systems analyst** or a **systems consultant** (see Unit 16.2).

The analyst's task consists of three main parts:

1 Analysis – finding out what the present situation is.
2 Design – working out a new system.
3 Implementation – creating the new system and getting it into working order.

ANALYSIS

Defining the problem

It is necessary to set out very clearly the problem to be solved. What is wrong with the present system? What will the new system be expected to do?

Analysing the present system

The people involved are used to the present system so it is important for the analyst to understand it. In some cases there will be a good manual system which can be improved by the use of computers. It will be necessary to:

1 Observe the present system in use.
2 Interview the people who work with it.
3 Read any existing documents which explain how the system should work.
4 Work out the requirements of the system in terms of input, output, files, etc.

DESIGN

Feasibility study

Following the analysis of the present system the analyst will produce a **feasibility report**. This is an investigation into whether a new system is realistic. It will enable the people requiring the new system to decide whether to go ahead with it.

It will:

1 Propose the outline for a new system (possibly with alternatives).
2 Summarize the costs and the benefits of this proposal. This summary will consider money, manpower, equipment and software.

Detailed design

This is the stage at which all parts of the new system must be thought out. (These parts are listed as items (1) to (7) under computerized information processing systems in 10.1).

Particular attention is given to:

1 Structure, organization and security of data files (see Unit 13).
2 Human considerations.
The new system should make good use of the skills of existing employees. The new system should be 'user friendly':
(a) Manuals should be simple and clear. They should be easy to use for reference.
(b) Computer programs should be easy to use. They should not irritate users by printing out too few instructions and headings, or too many.
(c) If a user enters the wrong data it should be easy to recover the situation and correct the data.
3 Whether it is necessary to purchase new hardware. The possibilities are:
(a) Buy a new computer system for the new application.
(b) Improve the existing computer system to cope, or possibly manage with existing hardware.
(c) Use the services of a **computer bureau**. A computer bureau is a firm which sells or hires out computer services. It has its own computing equipment and staff. Facilities offered may include:
(i) Software – the bureau may write software or make available program packages bought from elsewhere. The cost of this type of service is often shared by a group of firms all with the same requirements.
(ii) Computer time – the bureau may provide a batch processing service and may prepare the data for users. It may run a multi-access service for users with terminals (see Unit 15 for batch processing and multi-access systems).
(iii) Expertise – a bureau usually provides an advisory service.
4 Whether computer programs should be specially written or whether existing software should be bought.
(a) It is very expensive to have programs written specially.
(b) An existing software package may not exactly fit the user's situation. (See Applications Packages – Unit 14.2.)

IMPLEMENTATION

1 Purchase of new equipment if necessary.
2 Development or purchase of suitable programs.
3 Testing of the new system.
4 Documentation of the new system.
5 Staff retraining.
6 Gradual introduction of the new system. This may be carried out by running the old system and the new system together in parallel for some time. The advantage of this is that if the new system gets into difficulties, the old system is still running. The disadvantage is that the users have to work harder to keep both systems going at once.
7 Maintenance – the new system has to be monitored and problems solved as they arise.

RELEVANCE TO COMPUTER STUDIES COURSEWORK

The above account deals mainly with the solving of commercial problems. However, many of the same principles apply to Computer Studies coursework.

Assessment Objective B of the National Criteria for GCSE Computer Studies says:

'The candidates should be able to use computers sensibly to produce solutions to appropriate problems and be able to document their solutions. This includes the design of a simple system.'

1 In using a computer to solve a problem it is a mistake to spend most of the time on program writing. A large amount of time needs to be devoted to:
(a) Getting the problem clear. The system you design is to solve a problem for a user. What does that user want from it?
(b) Designing a complete system – not just a program.
(c) Designing the system to be robust and user friendly.
(d) Testing.
(e) Documentation.
2 Consider carefully whether a new program is needed at all.
Perhaps the problem can be solved by using a program that your school already has or can acquire, for example:
(a) File processing problems can often be solved using a database package (see Unit 14.1).
(b) Producing tables of figures on the screen can be done with a spreadsheet program (see Unit 14.1).

Most examining boards are quite happy for candidates to produce as a project a solution to a problem which uses existing software (see the Table of Analysis of Examination Syllabuses on page ix).

10.3 Flowcharts – System Flowcharts

FLOWCHARTS

A **flowchart** is a diagram representing the operations involved in a process. It consists of a combination of:
1 **Symbols** (or **boxes**) to represent the operations. There are standard shapes for the different types of operations which should be remembered and used.
2 Messages in the symbols. These state briefly what the operations are.
3 **Annotation** This is the explanation given in the margin (usually at the right of the flowchart). It allows the messages in the symbols to be kept brief.
4 Lines connecting the symbols. These lines may have arrows.

There are two completely different types of flowchart:
1 System flowcharts. These represent the operations on data in a system.
2 Flowcharts of algorithms. These represent the sequence of operations and include program flowcharts (see Unit 10.5 for algorithms and program flowcharts).

SYSTEM FLOWCHARTS

A **system flowchart** (or **data flowchart**) is a diagram representing the operations on data in an information processing system.

On a system flowchart the symbols represent data or operations on data. Usually the symbol used for each data operation looks like the medium involved (Fig. 10.1).

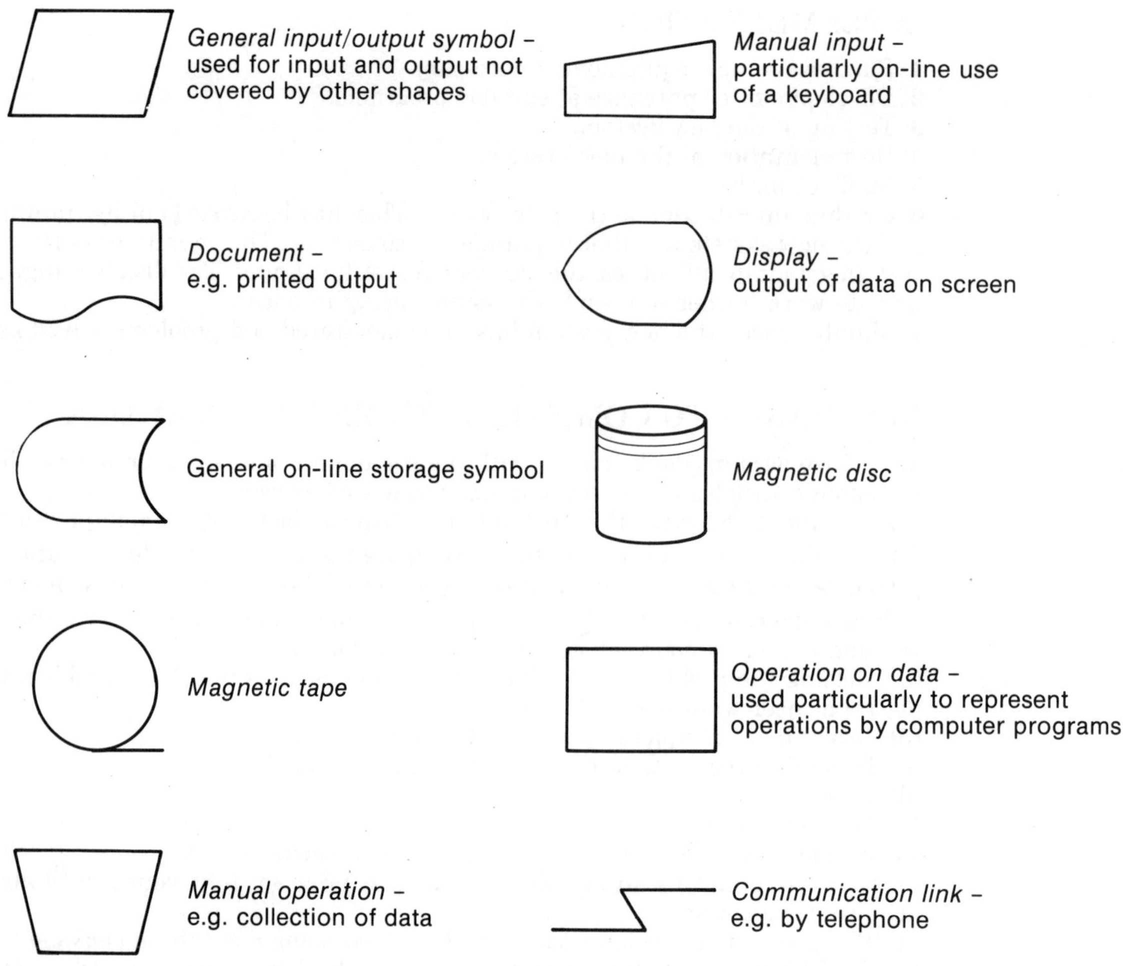

Fig. 10.1 Standard shapes of symbols used in system flowcharts

The general symbols for input/output and for on-line storage can be used for methods which do not have their own shapes. They can be used for all input/output or storage but syllabuses seem to prefer the style shown in Figures 10.3 and 10.4.

If the general symbols are used, they usually have the device used written in the strip along the bottom, as in Fig. 10.2.

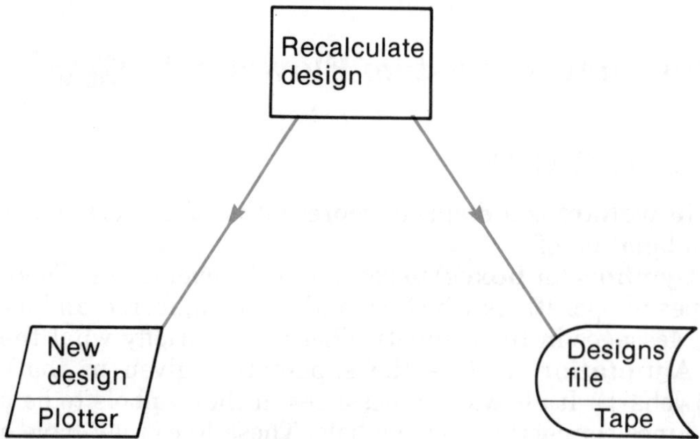

Fig. 10.2 Example of the use of the general symbols for input/output and for on-line storage

Drawing system flowcharts

1 System flowcharts are quite different from other flowcharts:

(a) In a system flowchart the arrows and lines show the flow of data within the system. They do **not necessarily** show the order in which operations are carried out.

(b) A system flowchart does not have a START symbol or a STOP symbol.

(c) System flowcharts should not show details of how computer programs work. They should not contain decision boxes. Usually each process box shows the operation of a complete program.

2 There are no definite rules about the layout of a system flowchart but it is a good idea to:

(a) Represent programs in process boxes (rectangles) in order down the middle of the page.
(b) Show data collection and input at the top left.
(c) Show files and output towards the left or right of the page.
(d) Put annotation (comments) at the far right of the page.

Examples of system flowcharts

1 A payroll system for a firm. A firm pays some of its employees weekly on the basis of the number of hours worked The employees punch a clock card on arriving at work and on leaving. Data from these is prepared on magnetic tape encoders. Some of the employees are paid through the bank and some in cash (see Unit 17.2). The system flowchart in Fig. 10.3 is a simplified version of the computerized system used.

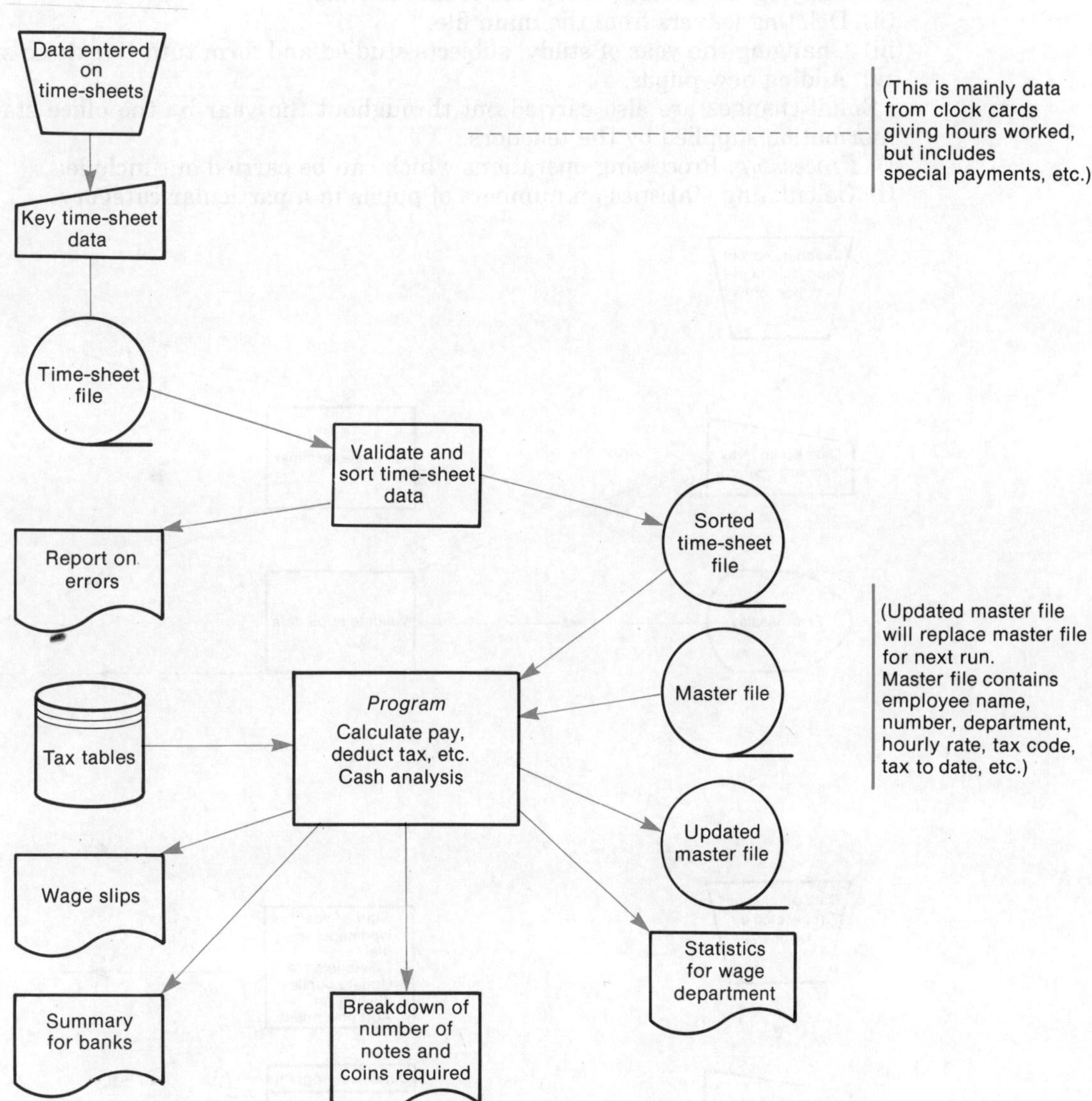

Fig. 10.3 System flowchart for a payroll application (see Unit 17.2)

2 A pupil records system for a school. The system is described first in words and then in the flowchart (Fig. 10.4), so that you can make a comparison.
(a) *Hardware*. The school office has a microcomputer with both a hard and a floppy disc unit and a printer. There is also a modem connected to an outside telephone line.
(b) *Software*. (For Software see Unit 14.) The records are maintained using a database program.
There are also separate programs for tasks such as:
(i) Validating data as it is typed in,
(ii) Updating all the records at the beginning of each year so that first year pupils become second year pupils, etc.
(iii) Connecting the microcomputer to the local authority's main computer.
(c) (i) *Collection of data*. Part of the data on the pupils comes from the local authority's main computer. The rest comes from forms completed by the pupils and their teachers.

(ii) *Checking of data.* The forms are checked for accuracy by the teachers. Data is also validated by the computer as it is input.
(iii) *Input of data.* Input of the large amount of data from the forms at the start of the year is achieved by using a local computer bureau.
Data from the local authority's computer is input direct using the modem. Minor changes to the data during the year are made by the office staff.
(d) *Communication. Data communication* with the main computer is achieved using modems. The school's microcomputer acts as an intelligent terminal to the main computer.
(e) *Files.* (For Files see Unit 13.) The main data file includes – for each pupil at the school – name, year of entry, date of birth, address, phone numbers, medical problems, test results from the previous school, year of study, subjects studied, form tutor.

Files are *updated* at the start of the year by:
(i) Copying the records of leavers to another file.
(ii) Deleting leavers from the main file.
(iii) Changing the year of study, subjects studied and form tutor for those staying on.
(iv) Adding new pupils.

Small changes are also carried out throughout the year by the office staff on the basis of information supplied by the teachers.
(f) *Processing.* Processing operations which can be carried out include:
(i) Calculating statistics on numbers of pupils in a particular category.

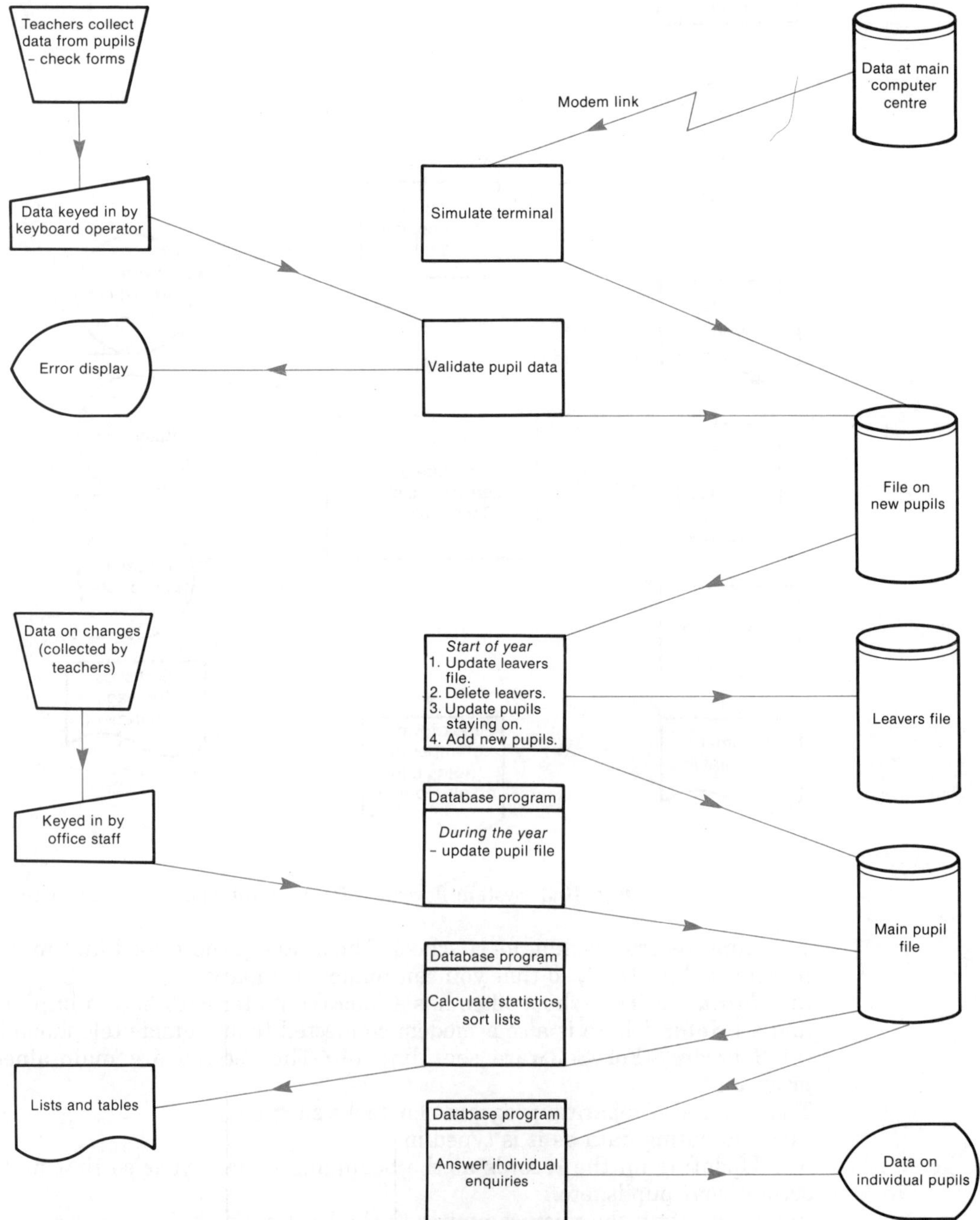

Fig. 10.4 System flowchart for a school pupil records system

(ii) Working out lists in a chosen order, for example, lists of pupils as in the example in the introduction to this unit.
(g) *Output.* Output can be produced on the printer and/or a screen.
Most lists and tables of statistics are produced on the printer. However, the screen may be used for enquiries about individual pupils.

10.4 Program Design and Implementation

TOP-DOWN DESIGN

Usually a **top-down** method is used for designing and writing a program. In top-down design the main function of a program is expressed as simply as possible. This function is then split up into more detailed separate procedures. These are then further split and so on. The process finishes when the program has been split down to the level of the separate statements of the computer language being used.

The process of dividing parts of a program into gradually more detailed parts is called **stepwise refinement**.

Simple example of stepwise refinement

Program function: input three numbers and print out their average.
First level of refinement:
(a) Input three numbers
(b) Calculate total and average
(c) Print numbers and their average
Second level of refinement:
In this simple example the next level would be separate program statements.

A program for the above example is written below in the language Pascal. Note that in Pascal:
1 Statements end with a semi-colon.
2 All variables used in a program have to be declared first in a VAR statement.
3 The first level of refinement is shown at the end of the program, after the final BEGIN statement.
If you are not familiar with Pascal you may find COMAL easier to understand. The same program has been written in COMAL at the end of Unit 11.7.

```
PROGRAM Average_Three_Numbers;
                    (* Input three numbers and print out their average *)
VAR
  Num1, Num2, Num3, Total, Average: REAL;

PROCEDURE Input_Three_Numbers;
BEGIN
  WRITELN ('The Average of Three Numbers');
  WRITELN;
  WRITE ('Please type your first number    '); READ (Num1);
  WRITE ('Please type your second number    '); READ (Num2);
  WRITE ('Please type your third number    '); READ (Num3);
END;

PROCEDURE (Calculate_Total_and_Average;
BEGIN
  Total := Num1+Num2+Num3;
  Average: = Total / 3;
END;

PROCEDURE Print_Numbers_and_Average;
BEGIN
  WRITELN ('The Numbers are:-' ,Num1,Num2,Num3);
  WRITELN ('Their average is  :-' ,Average);
END;

BEGIN
  Input_Three_Numbers;
  Calculate_Total_and_Average;
  Print_Numbers_and_Average;
END.
```

STEPS IN PRODUCING A PROGRAM

If it is decided that the solution of a problem requires a new program then the main steps followed are:

1 Program design.
2 Program writing.
3 Testing and debugging.
4 Documentation, implementation and maintenance.

Program design

1 *Function definition*

The general system design is used to decide precisely what the program is to do. This design may be in the form of system flowcharts. In any case it is necessary to define:
(a) The data requirements of the program – inputs, outputs and files.
(b) The processing function – what the program is to do with the data.

2 *First level of refinement*

(a) The data to be used is defined in detail. This includes arrays (see Unit 11.4) and files (see Unit 13).
(b) The main operations of the program are defined – possibly using a structure diagram or an outline program flowchart (see Unit 10.5).

Program writing

1 Each operation is worked out in detail. If necessary this may be done using detailed program flowcharts or structure diagrams.
2 The program is then coded. To **code a program** means to write it out in a suitable language.
3 The program is entered into a computer. (This may be done as the program is coded.)

Testing and debugging

1 If a compiler is used, errors are first eliminated which prevent the program from being compiled (see Unit 11.2 for compilers, Unit 12.2 for compilation errors).
2 Any further errors are eliminated which prevent the program from running.
3 The program is run with test data.

Test data is data which has been carefully chosen to try out every feature of a program (or flowchart) to make sure that it carries out its intended function. It is important to make sure that:
(a) The test data provides a check on every possible situation.
(b) The correct results of running the program with the test data have been worked out manually beforehand.
4 The programmer uses various debugging aids to correct the program until the expected output is produced when the test data is used (see Unit 12.2).

Note: For a complex program it is very difficult to test every possible situation. Professional programmers concentrate on designing and writing programs methodically so that they do not have errors.
1 The time saved in debugging is well worth the extra work in the early stages.
2 Programs with a lot of errors which need patching up are not as easy to read and to maintain as those which are well written to start with. Examination candidates writing project programs would do well to note this.

Documentation, implementation and maintenance

1 Before a program can be made available for use it is necessary to produce documentation for users and programmers (see Unit 10.6).
2 The new system of which the program forms part then has to be implemented and maintained (see Unit 10.2).

10.5 Representing Algorithms – Flowcharts and Structure Diagrams

ALGORITHMS

An **algorithm** is a series of instructions or steps for the solution of a problem.

Examples of algorithms

1 A computer program.
2 A set of instructions in a kit telling you how to put the kit together.
3 A knitting pattern.
4 A cooking recipe.

5 A key of the type used in science to identify a specimen.

An algorithm is made up of three main types of component:

1 **Sequence** – a group of steps is carried out once each and in order.

2 **Selection** – a selection has two or more parts, but a choice has to be made and only one of the parts is carried out.

3 **Repetition** (or **iteration**) – part of the algorithm is repeated, usually a fixed number of times or until some condition is met.

Example of a sequence

In the following recipe for Sweet and Sour Prawns steps 1 to 14 are to be carried out in order and once each.

1 Place the prawns in a bowl with the sherry and seasonings.
2 Marinate for one hour.
3 Slice the onion.
4 Cut the pepper into wedges.
5 Put the oil in a saucepan.
6 Add the vegetables.
7 Fry gently until softened.
8 Add the pineapple.
9 Mix together the cornflour, soy sauce, vinegar and sugar and add.
10 Bring to the boil, stirring constantly.
11 Simmer for 3 minutes.
12 Add the prawns and sherry.
13 Bring to the boil.
14 Serve.

Example of selection

The following is a key for classifying vertebrate animals. Each of the numbered steps is a selection with two parts. For a given animal only one of the parts will apply.

1 Does the animal have a backbone?
If YES it is a vertebrate – go to 2.
If NO it is an INVERTEBRATE.
2 Does it have internal gills AND fins?
If YES it is a FISH.
If NO go to 3.
3 Is part of its life history spent in water and part on land?
If YES it is an AMPHIBIAN.
If NO go to 4.
4 Does it have feathers?
If YES it is a BIRD?
If NO go to 5.
5 Does it have scales?
IF YES it is a REPTILE.
If NO go to 6.
6 It is a MAMMAL.

Example of repetition

The following is an extract from a knitting pattern. In the first row the sequence **Purl 2, Knit 2** has to be repeated until the last 3 stitches in the row. There is another repetition, of **Knit 2, Purl 2**, in the second row. Then these two rows have to be repeated until the knitted piece is 7 cm long.

1st row (RS facing) K1, * P2, K2, rep from * to last 3 sts, P2, K1.
2nd row P1, * K2, P2, rep from * to last 3 sts, K2, P1.
Rep last 2 rows until rib measures 7 cm ending with a first row.

REPRESENTING ALGORITHMS USING DIAGRAMS

Structure diagrams

A **structure diagram** is a diagram which shows how an algorithm is broken down into more and more detailed steps.

A structure diagram is ideal when an algorithm has been designed top down. It can then show the refinement into more and more detailed steps.

Notation for structure diagrams

(**Note:** There are several methods of drawing structure diagrams. The one used in Fig. 10.5 is based on the Jackson Method.)

1 All steps are shown in rectangles, each containing a brief statement of the step.
(a) The detailed steps making up a step are shown below it and joined to it by lines.
(b) A sequence is shown in order from left to right across the page.
2 Selection is shown by:
(a) Drawing a small circle in the top right of each of the choices and
(b) Writing the condition for selecting that box just above it.
3 Repetition is shown by:
(a) Drawing an asterisk in the top right of the step being repeated and
(b) Writing the condition for repeating just above it. (See Fig. 10.6)

Example of a simple structure diagram

In the knitting pattern on page 81 the K2, P2 sequence is called a double rib. Double rib consists of Knit 2, Purl 2. Knit 2 consists of Knit, Knit.

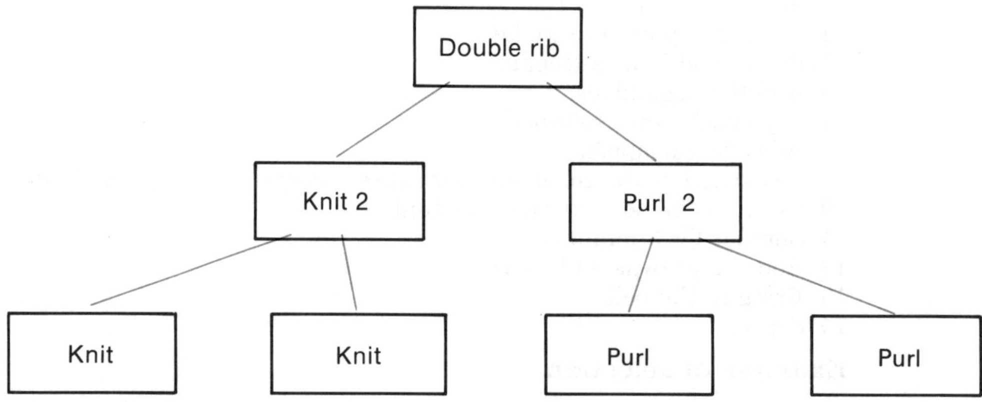

Fig. 10.5 Structure diagram for double rib

Example of a structure diagram showing repetition

In the knitting pattern on page 81 the 2nd row consists of Purl 1, a repeat of the double rib, followed by Knit 2, Purl 1.

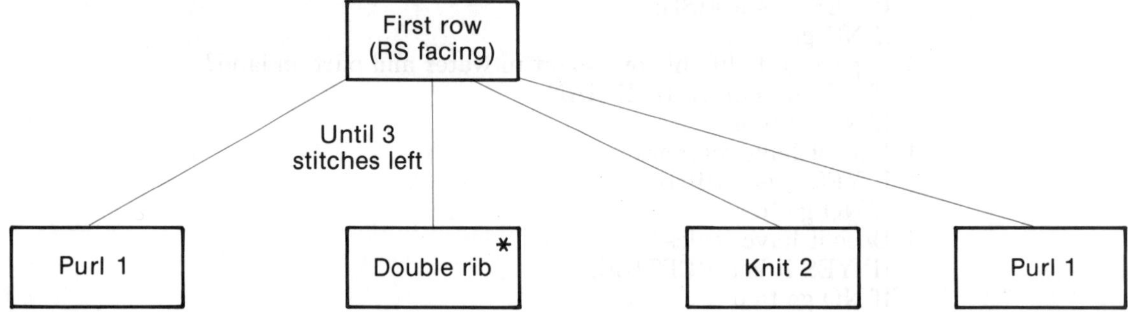

Fig. 10.6 Structure diagram for first row of knitting pattern

Example of structure diagram showing selection

In the animal key on page 81 the selection between vertebrate and invertebrate would be represented as in Fig. 10.7.

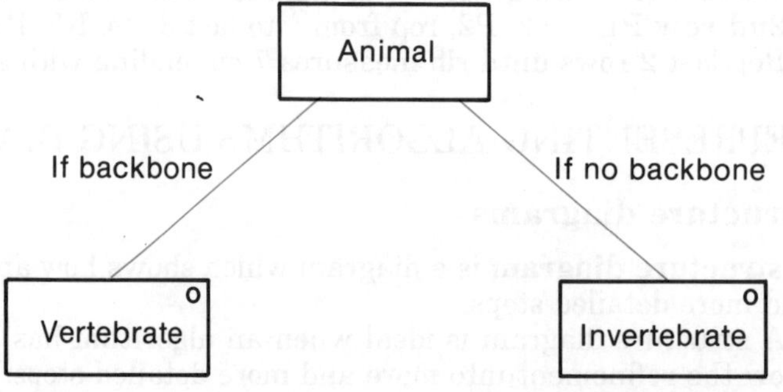

Fig. 10.7 Structure diagram for start of animal key

Note: If a condition or a message is rather long, it can be replaced by a number and explained in the margin.

Flowcharts

In a flowchart of an algorithm:
1 The lines and arrows show the order in which steps are to be carried out.
2 The messages in the symbols are the steps of the algorithm. (See Fig. 10.8.)

Example of a flowchart of an algorithm

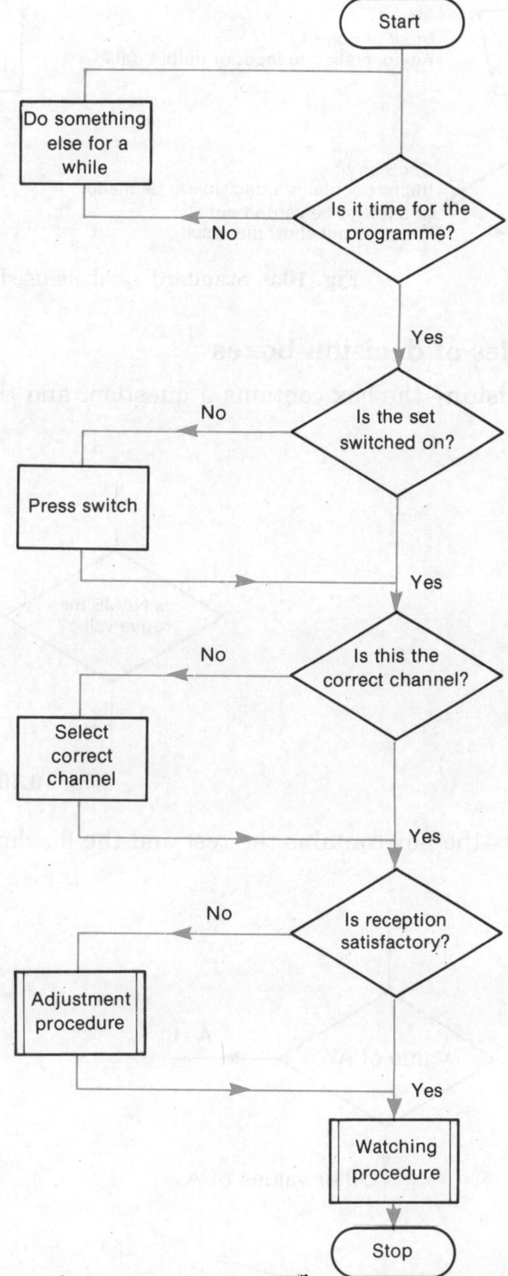

Fig. 10.8 Flowchart giving instructions for switching on the television

A **program flowchart** is a flowchart showing the sequence of operations performed by a computer program.

An **outline program flowchart** is a flowchart showing only the general operations carried out by a program. It should show:
1 all input and output operations,
2 the main modules of the program,
3 where execution of the program starts and stops.

A **detailed program flowchart** shows all operations carried out by a computer program. It should:
1 Show enough detail for someone to be able to write a program directly from it.
2 Avoid using messages aimed at a particular programming language. (See Fig. 10.9 for the standard symbols used in program flowcharts.)

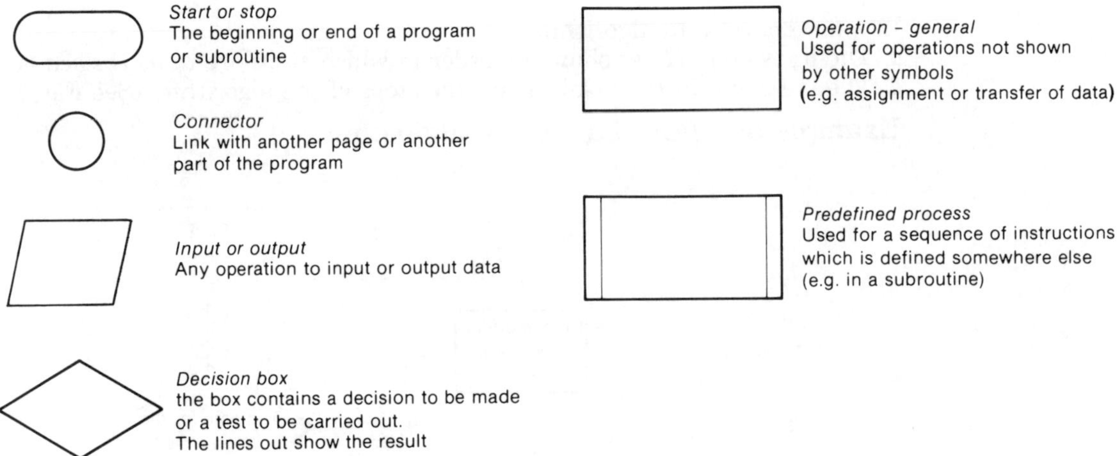

Fig. 10.9 Standard symbols used in program flowcharts

Examples of decision boxes

1 A **decision** – the box contains a question, and the flowlines out say 'yes' or 'no'. (See Fig. 10.10.)

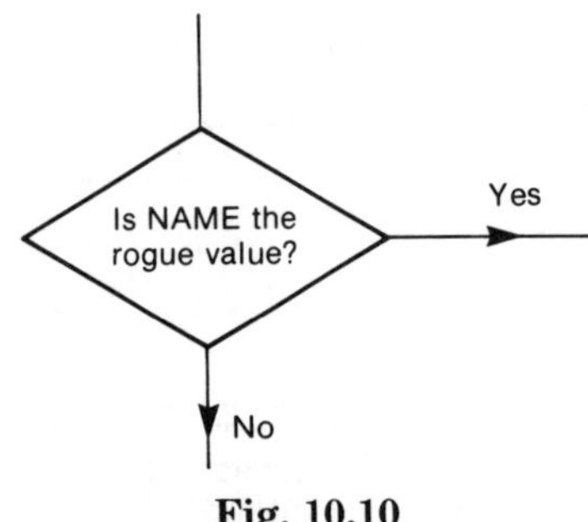

Fig. 10.10

2 A **test** – the box contains the test and the flowlines out show the possible results. (See Fig. 10.11.)

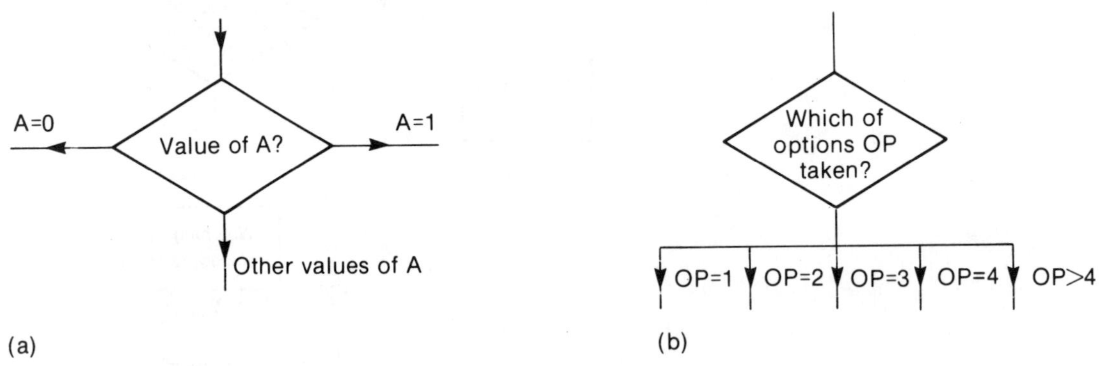

Fig. 10.11

Notes on drawing program flowcharts

1 Use a template if possible – this has box shapes on it which you can draw round.
2 Draw all flowlines in either a vertical or a horizontal direction.
3 Use arrows where the direction is not clear. (If there are no arrows it is usually assumed that vertical lines are downwards and horizontal ones are left to right.)
4 Do not draw more than one line going in to a box.
5 Use ordinary English where possible.
6 Add notes in the right-hand margin if necessary.
7 Show only one entry point (e.g. a START symbol) and one exit point (e.g. a STOP symbol).

Example comparing a structure diagram and a program flowchart

The program represented in Figs. 10.12 and 10.13 is used in the systems flowchart Fig. 10.3 (labelled 'Calculate pay, deduct tax, etc'). It calculates the pay of a group of employees.

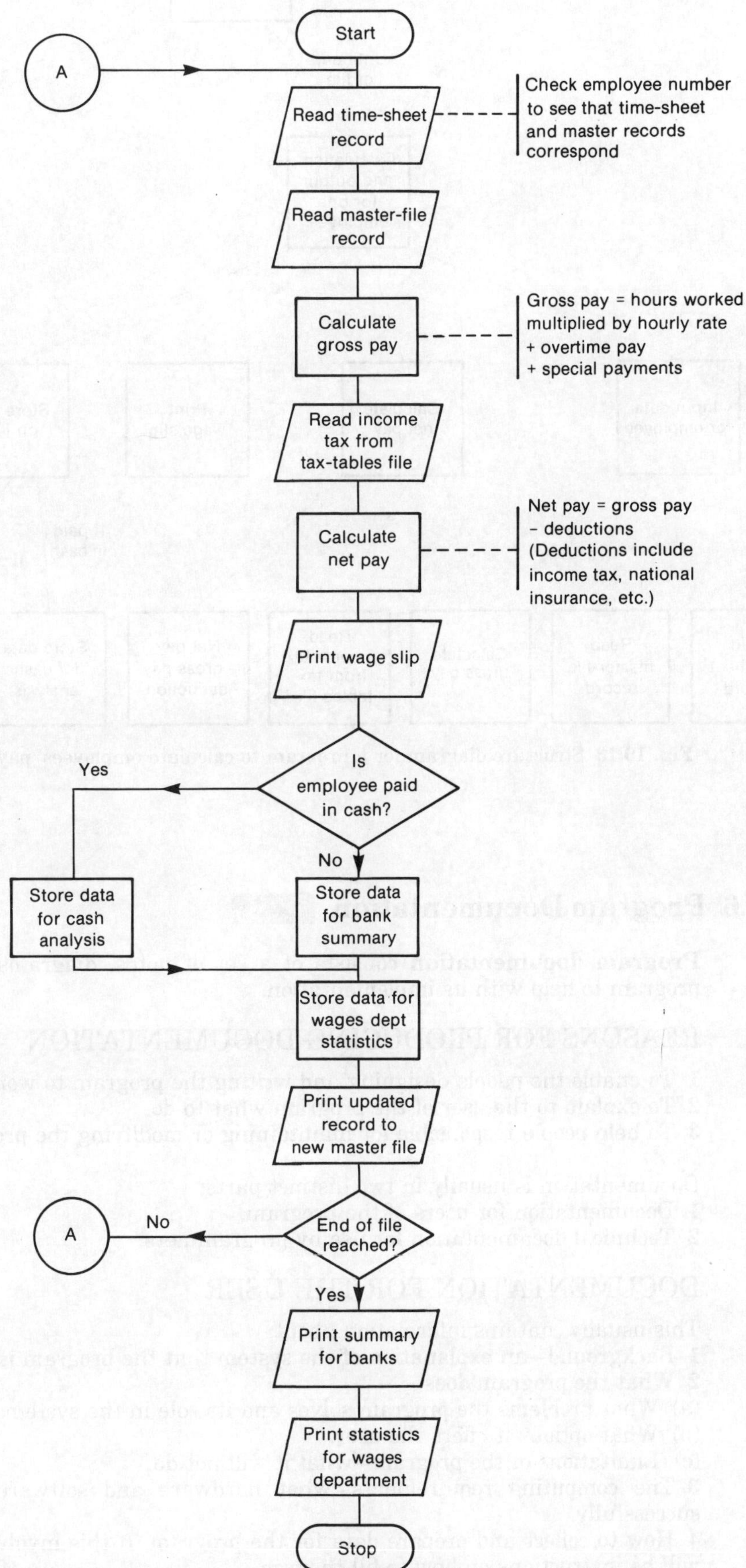

Fig. 10.12 Outline program flowchart for a program to calculate employees' pay (see Fig. 10.3 and Unit 17.2 for payroll application)

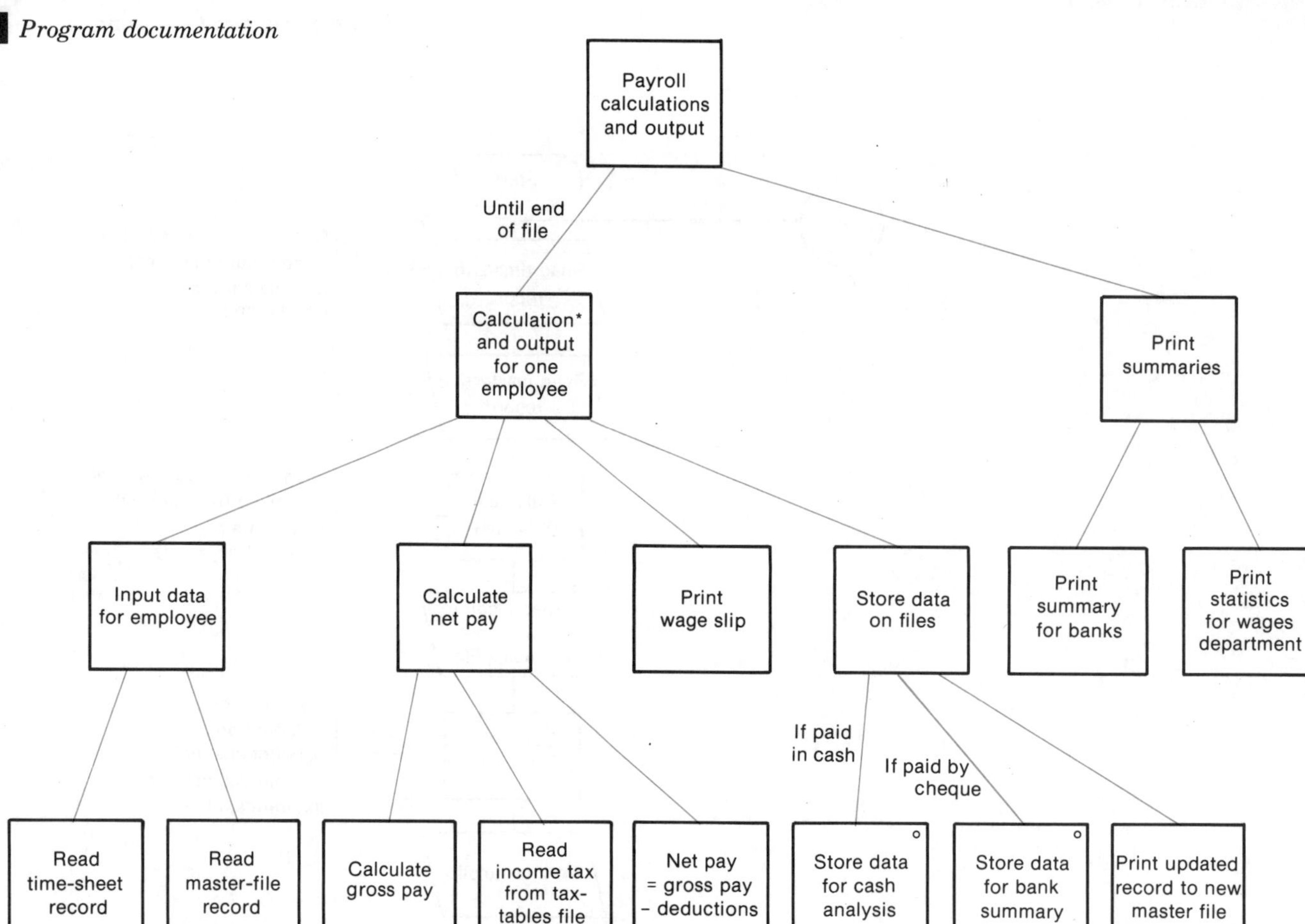

Fig. 10.13 Structure diagram for a program to calculate employees' pay (see Fig. 10.3 and Unit 17.2)

10.6 Program Documentation

Program documentation consists of a set of notes, diagrams, etc., which accompany a program to help with its implementation.

REASONS FOR PRODUCING DOCUMENTATION

1 To enable the people designing and writing the program to work together.
2 To explain to the user of the program what to do.
3 To help people responsible for maintaining or modifying the program.

Documentation is usually in two distinct parts:
1 Documentation for users of the program.
2 Technical documentation for use by programmers.

DOCUMENTATION FOR THE USER

This usually contains information about:
1 Background – an explanation of the system that the program is designed to work within.
2 What the program does:
(a) What problems the program solves and its role in the system.
(b) What options it offers the user.
(c) Limitations of the program – what it will not do.
3 The computing requirements – what hardware and software are necessary to run it successfully.
4 How to collect and prepare data for the program. If this involves special documents there will be instructions on how to fill them in.
5 How to operate the program. For a batch program the system control cards necessary to get it to run. For an interactive program there will also be details of the conversation when it is run.
6 How to interpret the output.

Note: the user documentation for a software package is called a **User Manual**.

DOCUMENTATION FOR A PROGRAMMER

This documentation may be used by:

1 The programmer who wrote the program, or
2 People working with the programmer, such as the systems analyst and the programmer's supervisor, or
3 A programmer responsible for maintaining or modifying the program.

The documentation would usually include:

1 A system flowchart with annotation (see Unit 10.3).
2 Program flowcharts with annotation (see Unit 10.5).
3 Technical details of any limitations, special features, different versions, etc.
4 A program listing accompanied by a list of the variables used in the program and an explanation of their purpose.
5 Details of data structures used – e.g. files and arrays.
6 A set of test data and expected output with which to check that the program operates successfully.

11 PROGRAMMING: LANGUAGES AND STYLE

PROGRAMMING AND COURSEWORK

GCSE candidates are expected to be able to use computers to solve problems. In many cases this does not mean you have to be able to program.

If you are not doing any programming in your coursework then ask your teacher for advice about this unit. It may only be necessary for you to study part of it.

PROGRAMS

A computer works by carrying out a program of instructions stored in its main store. To do this it fetches and then executes machine code instructions quickly one after another. (Machine code instructions are dealt with in Units 5.3, 5.4.)

It is not practical for programmers to write their programs in machine code. Instead instructions are usually written in a language which is easy to understand. This language then has to be translated because the computer can only execute machine code instructions. This is done using another program – which may be an assembler, a compiler or an interpreter. (See Unit 11.1 for assembler and Unit 11.2 for compiler and interpreter.)

A **source program** is a program in the form originally written by the programmer.

An **object program** is the machine code program which results when a source program is translated.

PROGRAMMING LANGUAGES

A **low level** programming language is a computer language which is based on the machine code of the computer being used.

For a low level language:

1 Each instruction usually translates into one machine code instruction.

2 The fixed words of the language stand for machine code functions (see 'mnemonics' in Unit 11.1).

Examples of low level languages include: 6502 Assember and 80186 Assembler.

A **high level** programming language is a computer language which is based on the problems being solved. It does not depend so much on the computer being used. (Unfortunately some high level languages have so many different versions that they do depend on the computer used, e.g. BASIC.)

For a high level language:

1 Each instruction usually translates into a number of machine code instructions.

2 The fixed words of the language are words that the person programming uses normally – such as technical terms in their job or just plain English.

Examples of high level languages include: BASIC, COMAL and Pascal.

Comparison of high and low level languages

Advantages of high level over low level

1 High level programs are easier to write.

2 They are also easier to understand and to modify.

3 High level programs are portable. A **portable** program is one which can be run on a number of different types of computer with only minor changes.

Advantages of low level over high level

1 A low level program is efficient. If a high level program and a low level program are written to do the same thing:

(a) The low level program will run faster.

(b) When the two programs are translated into machine code the high level program will use more store than the low level one.

2 Low level programs make full use of the computer's capabilities. A high level language program written to run on any computer will not allow for the special features of a particular one.

Choice of level

Applications programs (see Unit 14.2) are normally written in a high level language unless there is an important reason for writing them at low level.

Programs are normally written at low level when efficient use of store and high speed are essential, for example:

1 Systems programs such as a computer's operating system (see Unit 14.3).
2 Programs which are to be stored on ROM (e.g. a word processing program).
3 Interactive graphics programs such as computer games.

Worked question

Give an example of a program for a microcomputer:
1 Written in a high level language.
2 Written in a low level language.
In each case explain the reason for the choice of level.

1 One example for which a high level language would be used is an interactive program to help pupils to understand the formulae for connecting resistors together in physics. Using it the computer draws a circuit diagram and the pupil has to calculate the value of one resistor. If the pupil cannot do it, the computer gives some help.

This program would be written in a high level language because it does not have to be particularly fast in execution. Also it would be far simpler to write at high level and the teacher might well want to modify it to fit the teaching situation.

2 A low level example is a commercial word processing program. This must make it possible to produce, edit, store and output text.

It would be written at a low level because it has to be fast and efficient at carrying out operations such as inserting passages, or transferring them from one place in the text to another. Once sold it would not be modified and the sales would be great enough to justify the programming effort to produce it in a low level language.

11.1 Low Level Programming

Programmers writing low level programs do not usually write in machine code. Instead they write in a language which is then translated into machine code.

Each instruction in machine code contains a function code and one or more addresses or operands (see Unit 5.4).

An **assembly** language is a low level language which allows the programmer to use:
1 Mnemonics instead of the function codes; and
2 Symbolic addresses.

A **mnemonic** is a word or set of letters which can be used to represent a function code and which is easy to remember. The programmer writes the mnemonic instead of having to look up or remember the actual binary function code.

A **symbolic address** is a name invented by the programmer to identify a location. Without this idea the programmer would have to use absolute addresses, which are in binary (see Units 2.1 and 5.4).

Symbolic addresses are used so that:
1 There is no need to remember, or even to know, where each location is in the store.
2 If a program is changed parts of it will be moved in the store; the absolute addresses of the instructions may change but their symbolic addresses will stay the same.

Examples of mnemonics and symbolic addresses

The mnemonics used here are like those in some real low level languages. However, there are many languages which use different ones.

1 LDA can often be used as a mnemonic for LOAD ACCUMULATOR.
2 JMP PRNT. Here JMP is a mnemonic for 'jump to the instruction'. PRNT is the symbolic address the programmer has chosen to represent the first instruction of a print routine.
3
```
LOOP   ADD   VALUE   * Add VALUE to accumulator
       JMP   PRNT    * Print contents of accumulator
       INX           * Add 1 to X register
       BNE   LOOP    * Branch to LOOP if (X) is not 0
```
Here LOOP, VALUE and PRNT are symbolic addresses. ADD, JMP, INX and BNE are mnemonics.
The explanations at the right are programmer's comments.

Example of a low level language program with mnemonics

Note: For simplicity it can be assumed that the addresses and data in this example are decimal numbers. It has been assumed that each instruction takes up one location of the store.

Address of instruction	*Mnemonic*	*Address or operand*	*Explanation*
100	LDA#	100	Load the number 100 into accumulator
101	DEC		Decrement accumulator
102	BNE	101	If accumulator is not zero, branch to location 101
103	RTS		Return from subroutine

This small section of program seems to do little. The accumulator starts at 100 and is reduced to 0 as the program keeps executing the instructions in 101 and 102. Then it 'returns from subroutine'. In fact the purpose of it is merely to delay the computer for the small fraction of a second that it takes to do this.

ASSEMBLERS

An **assembler** is a program which translates a program written in an assembly language into one in machine code. Assemblers were given this name because of the way they put together the machine code program in the store.

The main functions of an assembler are to:

1 Translate an assembly language source program into a machine code object program.
2 Work out where to store the object program and its data.
3 Detect errors in the source program and say what they are.
4 Link the program to any other programs or routines it uses.
5 Print a listing of the source and object programs.

Example of an assembly language program

The following program compares two numbers, A and B, and subtracts the smaller from the larger. It then stores the difference in RESULT. The language used is made up, but it is very similar to a number of actual assembly languages.

```
/ORIGIN = 1025
* PROGRAM TO FIND THE POSITIVE DIFFERENCE BETWEEN TWO NUMBERS
      LDA  A       * LOAD A INTO THE ACCUMULATOR
      SUB  B       * SUBTRACT B FROM THE ACCUMULATOR
      BPS  STORE   * IF ACCUMULATOR IS POSITIVE BRANCH TO STORE
      LDA  B       * OTHERWISE LOAD B INTO THE ACCUMULATOR
      SUB  A       * SUBTRACT A FROM THE ACCUMULATOR
STORE STA  RESULT  * STORE THE ANSWER IN RESULT
      HLT          * HALT THE PROGRAM
/END
```

Notes:

1 '/' indicates an instruction which is a directive. A **directive** is an instruction which tells the assembler how to deal with the rest of the program. Directives are carried out while assembling and are not translated into machine code.
/ORIGIN = 1025 means 'store the object program starting at location 1025'.
/END means 'there are no more instructions to translate'.

2 '*' indicates the start of a comment (or a remark). A **comment** is a statement written by the programmer to explain the program to anyone reading it. Comments are not translated into machine code.

USE OF A TABLE TO SHOW THE EFFECT OF A PROGRAM

One way to demonstrate or to check the running of a program with certain data is to draw a table. The table should show the instructions carried out and the values in important locations and registers. (See also Unit 12.2 – Trace Tables.)

Example of the use of a table to show the effect of a program

Assume that the program in the previous example is run twice:
1 For the first run A is 21 and B is 32.
2 For the second run A is 45 and B is 15.
The following table shows what happens:

First run: A = 21, B = 32

Current Instruction	Accumulator	Result	Comments
LDA A	21	?	
SUB B	−11	?	Subtract B from A
BPS STORE	−11	?	Accumulator negative. No jump
LDA B	32	?	
SUB A	11	?	Subtract A from B
STORE STA RESULT	11	11	
HLT	11	11	

Second run: A = 45, B = 15

Current Instruction	Accumulator	Result	Comments
LDA A	45	?	
SUB B	30	?	Subtract B from A
BPS STORE	30	?	Accumulator positive. Jump to STORE
STORE STA RESULT	30	30	
HLT	30	30	

11.2 High Level Languages

A program written in a high level language can be dealt with by a computer in two main ways.
1 It can be translated into machine code by a compiler and then run.
A **compiler** is a program which translates a high level program into a machine code program. There are two separate operations:
(a) Compiling the high level (source) program into machine code.
(b) Executing the machine code (object) program.

In fact once a program has been compiled and runs successfully, there is no need to keep compiling it. It can be run just by executing the object program. The source program will only be needed again if the program has to be changed.

2 The program can be run directly using an interpreter. An **interpreter** is a program which interprets a high level program, one line at a time, as it is being run.

Using the interpreter the computer recognizes each instruction. It then runs a machine code routine corresponding to that instruction.

FUNCTIONS OF COMPILERS AND INTERPRETERS

1 To translate or interpret source code written in a high level language.
2 To detect errors in the program and print error messages.
3 To organize the storage of variables used by the program.
4 To link the program with any other software it uses.

COMPARISON BETWEEN COMPILERS AND INTERPRETERS

This is shown in Figs. 11.1 and 11.2.

Advantages of a compiler over an interpreter

1 Once a program is compiled, it can be used again and again without any further translation being necessary. With an interpreter the program is translated every time it is run.
2 Each line of a program has to be translated only once during a compilation, but an interpreter interprets a line each time it is executed. If a line is part of a loop it will be interpreted each time round the loop. Thus running a compiled program is normally faster than interpreting the source program.

Advantages of an interpreter over a compiler

When an interpreter is used, the source program is always in the store (sometimes in an abbreviated form). This means:
1 That the program can be changed easily if a run is unsatisfactory.
2 The version of the program which is in the store is relatively short – a high level program is generally shorter than its machine code equivalent.

USES OF COMPILERS AND INTERPRETERS

An interpreter is used for interactive computing. High level programming on microcomputers

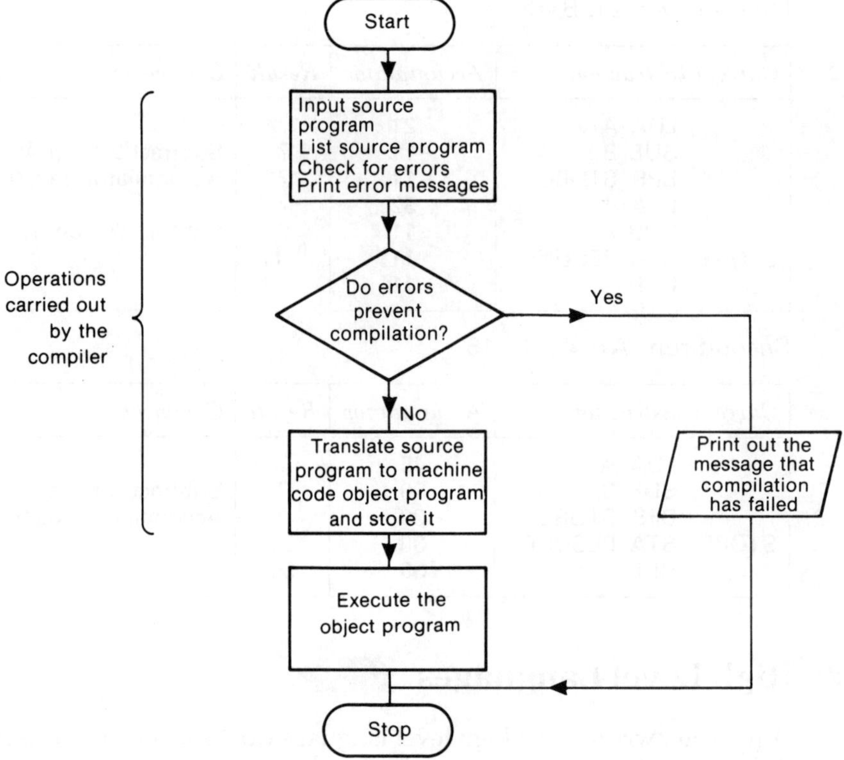

Fig. 11.1 Operation of a compiler
(**Note:** The flowchart shows a program being compiled and then executed immediately afterwards. Compilation and execution can be quite separate operations. In particular it is not necessary to compile the program again every time it is run.)

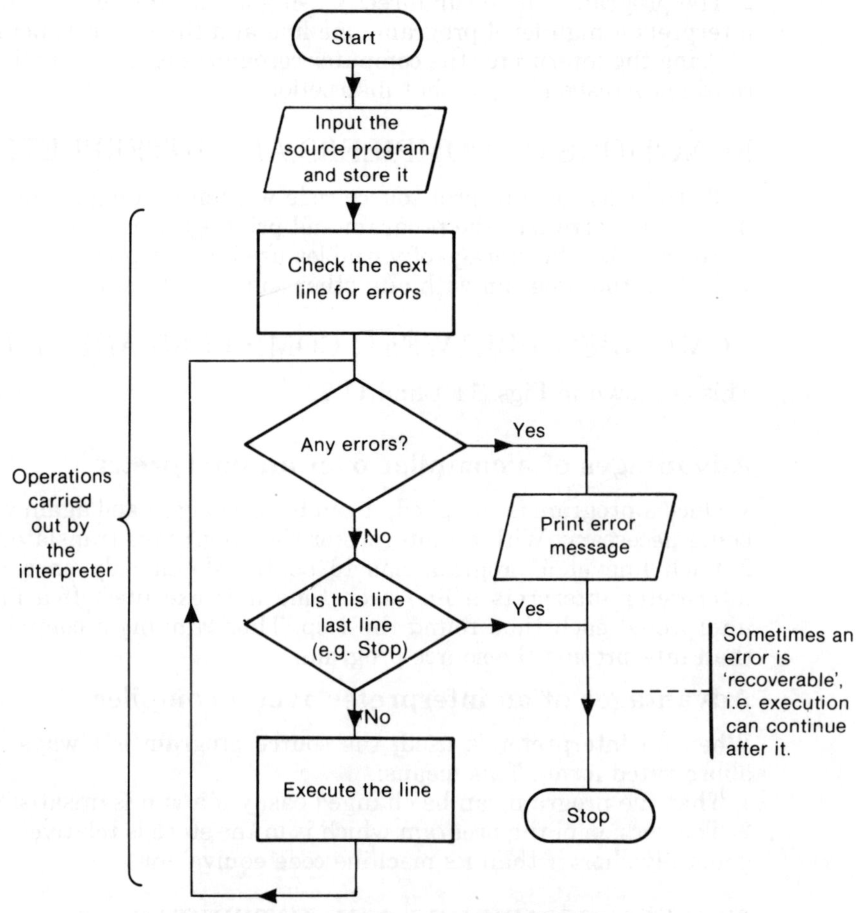

Fig. 11.2 Operation of an interpreter

is often done with an interpreter, particularly if BASIC is used. High level programs on school or home computers are often interpreted.

A compiler is usually used when:

1 Programs are being batch processed (see Unit 15.3).
2 It is important that a program executes quickly. High level programs on large computers in business and industry are usually compiled.

Worked question

A compiler, an interpreter and an assembler are all programs. State what each of them has as input data. Your answer should make clear how these inputs differ.

For a compiler the input data is a complete high level source program. For an interpreter the input data consists of the lines of a high level program, taken one at a time in the order they are executed. The input data for an assembler is a low level source program.

REASONS FOR THE VARIETY OF LANGUAGES

There are very many different languages for various reasons.

1 Some languages are more suitable in particular programming situations. BASIC can be used for beginners using computers interactively. COBOL is good for commercial applications.
2 Some applications programs become so complicated that a new language is needed in order to use them – for example file enquiry packages (such as QUEST).
3 As new and improved languages are introduced, the old ones are still used. Often they are changed to fit the new ideas (for example, FORTRAN was improved in 1977).

Examples of general purpose high level languages

BASIC – Beginners **A**ll-purpose **S**ymbolic **I**nstruction **C**ode
Purpose: Originally a teaching language for interactive work. Since extended.
Features: 1 Every line has to be numbered.
2 Easy for beginners to learn.
3 Difficult to write programs which are easily understood.
4 Many different versions.

COBOL – COmmon **B**usiness **O**rientated **L**anguage
Purpose: An easily understood language for commercial data processing applications.
Features: 1 Statements look like English sentences.
2 Good facilities for file handling.

COMAL – COMmon **A**lgorithmic **L**anguage
Purpose: Originally an extension of BASIC to allow a clear structure. It has since dropped some BASIC statements.
Features: 1 Every line is numbered as in BASIC. Numbers are just used for editing. They are not used for reference by program statements.
2 Extra words to allow structuring similar to those in Pascal.

FORTRAN – FORmula **TRAN**slator (Produced in 1956 – but still widely used.)
Purpose: For scientific use. Usually batch work.
Features: 1 Designed to be used with cards as input and a line printer as output.
2 Lack of statements which make program structure clear.
3 Some statements which are difficult for beginners to learn – e.g. FORMAT, which is used to define layout of input and output.

LOGO
Purpose: An educational language to encourage logical thinking.
Features: 1 Enables the programmer to make a 'turtle' perform planned tasks. Originally a turtle was a device to run around on the floor, but it may be just a pointer on a screen.
2 New instructions can be defined and added in.
3 Facilities to process lists.

PASCAL
Purpose: To allow clear structuring of data and program.
Features: 1 All data (variables, etc.) have to be declared before they can be used.
2 Encourages clear structure and stepwise refinement.
3 New procedures, functions and data types can be defined and added in.

SPECIAL PURPOSE LANGUAGES

In some cases a high level language is only used for one particular type of application. It is made up of words which are used in that type of application and is not suitable for other purposes.

Such languages may be used in various situations:

1 Making database enquiries or file enquiries. (See Unit 13.)
2 Producing computer simulations. (See Unit 19.4.)
3 Robot control. (See Unit 20.2.)

There are many such languages.

11.3 High Level Programming

NOTES

1 Programming examples in this unit are in three different languages.
(a) BASIC – chosen because most candidates know it. The examples should be accepted by most school microcomputers. However, BASIC does not have many of the programming facilities which some syllabuses require.
(b) COMAL – recommended by some examining boards. It allows good program structure. Most of the BASIC examples given here will run in COMAL with very little alteration.
(c) Pascal – used mainly where COMAL and BASIC are inadequate.
2 The examples should be clear enough even where you are not familiar with the language. If you are not familiar with it, try to write the equivalent piece of program in the language you do know.

DEFINITIONS

Statement A program statement is a single instruction.
Line In some languages, such as BASIC and COMAL, a program is divided up into numbered lines. Each line has a line number and contains one or more statements.
Variable A variable is a quantity named in a program and whose value can change.
Constant A constant is a value that does not change. In a program it may or may not be given a name.
Identifier An identifier is a name invented by the programmer for some data. An identifier can be a name for a variable, a constant, a file, an array, etc.
Reserved words A reserved word is a name which has some special significance to the compiler or interpreter. The programmer can only use it for its special purpose and cannot use it as an identifier.
Expression An expression is a set of variables, constants and operators (such as +,−, etc.) which is to be evaluated by the computer. An example is set out below.

The following is a line of a BASIC program:

```
100 INPUT NUM: PRINT 3.1*NUM*NUM + 5
```

In this line:
100 is a line number.
INPUT NUM is a statement because it is a single instruction.
PRINT 3.1*NUM*NUM + 5 is also a statement.
PRINT and **INPUT** are reserved words and cannot be used as identifiers.
NUM is a variable because it can have any value which is a number.
NUM is also an identifier as it was chosen by the programmer.
3.1 and **5** are constants.
3.1*NUM*NUM + 5 is an expression which the computer has to work out before the result can be printed.

Assignment An assignment statement is one which gives a variable a value. Usually an expression on the right hand side of the statement is worked out and the result is assigned to a variable on the left of the statement. For example:

1 In BASIC: 100 LET **Area = Width * Length**
or just: 100 **Area = Width * Length**
In COMAL: 100 **Area: = Width * Length**
In Pascal: **Area: = Width * Length;**

Notes:
(a) In BASIC the **LET** is usually optional – you don't have to use it.
(b) Pascal and COMAL use := in assignments, using = on its own only in other situations.
(c) statements in Pascal end with a semi-colon (except the last END statement, which ends with a full stop).

2 In BASIC:

```
100 Name$ = Forenames$ + Surname$
110 HeightCms = 2.54*(Feet*12 + Inches)
```

11.4 Data Types and Structures

The variables and constants used by a program can be of various different types. Data types may differ:
1 In the way they are stored, for example, decimal fractions are usually stored as floating point numbers but integers are not (see Unit 2.4).
2 In the operations which can be done on them, for example numbers can be multiplied but strings cannot.

REALS, INTEGERS AND STRINGS

The common data types are:
1 REAL numbers – all ordinary numbers including decimals.
2 INTEGERS – all whole numbers including 0 and the negative numbers.
3 STRINGS – groups of charactes including letters, digits and others.

Uses and advantages

1 (a) Integers are used whenever the variable involved is always a whole number. This is because:
(i) Integers can be stored exactly, whereas real numbers are stored approximately (see Units 2.4, 2.5).
(ii) Operations on integers can be done more quickly.
(b) In particular integers are useful when counting and as the variable in FOR loops.
2 Real numbers are used:
(a) Where there is a large range of numbers – numbers are either very big or very small.
(b) Where decimals are involved – for instance, where division is done.
3 Strings are used:
(a) For data which is not numeric or is not going to be used in calculations.
(b) For inputting numeric data so that it can be checked that it is in fact a number.

Examples

1 The following is a line of a BASIC program:

```
200 IF Name$="***" THEN Average=TotalMark / N
```

Here

Name$ is a string variable. We can tell this because it ends in $;
"***" is a string constant;
Average is probably REAL and **TotalMark** and **N** are probably INTEGERS.

In BASIC many versions do not allow you to declare which variables are REAL and which are INTEGER.

2 The following is a statement from a Pascal program:

```
IF Name=Rogue_Value THEN Average:=Total_Mark/N;
```

In Pascal all variables and constants have to be 'declared' before they are used. This seems a lot of trouble but at least anyone reading the program can understand it clearly. Thus in the program in this example the following statements appear near the beginning:

```
CONST
  Rogue_Value='***';
VAR
  Name       : STRING[10];
  Average    : REAL;
  Total_Mark : INTEGER;
  N          : INTEGER;
```

DATA STRUCTURES INCLUDING ARRAYS

A **data structure** is a set of data items organized together. The data items making up the structure are its **elements**. The structure is defined by a set of properties linking the elements.

Examples of data structures

1 A file. In a file the items are grouped into records. The records are then organized into a file (see Unit 13).
2 A string. This can be thought of as a data structure composed of separate characters.

An **array** is a data structure in which the elements all have the same name. Each element is distinguished from the others by means of one or more numbers.

These numbers are called **subscripts**. The subscripts provide the programmer with a means of referring to individual elements.

The number of **dimensions** an array has is the number of subscripts attached to each element, for example, if each element has two subscripts, then the array has two dimensions.

Declaring an array

Usually the programmer has to declare the size of an array before using it. This is done by giving the range of values which can be taken by each subscript. In some languages this is done in a DIMENSION statement. In BASIC and COMAL a DIM statement is used.

Example of an array in BASIC

```
100 REM *** Fill the array num with the odd numbers from 1 to 19 ***
110 DIM num(10)
120 FOR subs = 1 TO 10
130 num(subs) = 2*subs - 1
140 NEXT subs
```

Line 110 declares a one-dimensional array, **num**, with 10 elements. In line 130 **subs** is a subscript. The FOR . . . NEXT loop gives **subs** the values 1,2,3 . . . up to 10 (see Unit 11.6 for FOR . . . NEXT). The expression **2*subs − 1** gives 1 when **subs** is 1, 3 when **subs** is 2, 5 when **subs** is 3, etc. Thus the program sets **num(1)** = 1, **num(2)** = 3, **num(3)** = 5, etc.

Advantages of using arrays

1 The same operation can be done on each of a group of variables using only one instruction. The instruction is repeated in a loop using the same name but varying the subscript. (See line 130 in the example above.)
2 In some languages the whole array can be treated as a unit, as if it were one variable.
3 Arrays can be used to store tables, lists, etc.

11.5 Input and Output

In a program to input or output data it may be necessary to supply information about:
1 The input or output device to be used. (In BASIC on a microcomputer the input is usually assumed to be from the keyboard and output to the screen. However, the programmer can specify other devices if required.)
2 The **format** of the data on the input or output medium – i.e. the way the data is to be set out. (In BASIC output format is mainly controlled within PRINT statements.
e.g. `100 PRINT TAB(10); "HELLO THERE";Name1$,"AND";Name2$` might print:

```
          HELLO THERE Fred          AND Jim
```

The **Tab(10)** would cause HELLO THERE to start after column 10. The semicolon causes the next item to be printed without the cursor moving. The comma causes the next item to be printed in the next 'zone' of the screen. The screen is divided up into a number of equal zones of about 10 to 20 columns each depending on the computer.)
3 The variables being used to store the data being input or output. In BASIC input these appear in a list separated by commas, for example,

```
100 INPUT SNAME$,MONTH,YEAR
```

ROGUE VALUES

A **rogue value** or **data terminator** is a special value put at the end of a list of data items so that the end of the list can be detected. The computer has to check every item read to see if it is the rogue value.

The rogue value:
1 Has to have a value that cannot be mistaken for real data.
2 Is in the same format as the rest of the data, so that it will be read without producing an error.

Example of a rogue value

The following is part of a BASIC program. Here the rogue value is ***.

```
130 REM /// Convert heights to centimetres ///
140 PRINT "For each one type in name,feet,inches. Type '***,0,0' to finish"
150 INPUT name$,feet,ins
160 IF name$ = "***" THEN GOTO 500 : REM /// CONTINUE REST OF PROGRAM ///
170 PRINT name$;" has height ";(feet*12 + ins)*2.54;" cms "
180 GOTO 150
```

11.6 Control Statements

Programmers need to be able to use the 3 main types of component of algorithms:
1 Sequence.
2 Repetition.
3 Selection. (See Unit 10.5.)

SEQUENCE

Each of the statements in a group is carried out once and in the order given.

In most high level languages statements are normally executed in sequence unless the programmer does something to change that. (See Fig. 11.3.)

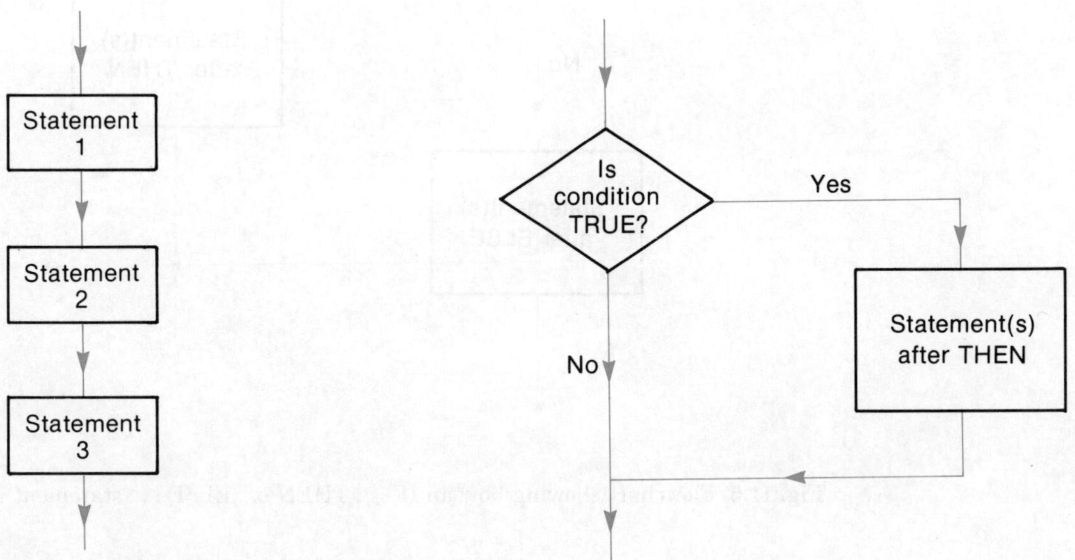

Fig. 11.3 Flowchart showing statements executed in sequence

Fig. 11.4 Flowchart showing how an IF . . . THEN . . . statement is executed

In a language such as BASIC the programmer can transfer control out of the sequence to another part of the program.

Examples of BASIC statements which transfer control

```
1 300 GOTO 500
2 250 GOSUB 1000
3 110 IF A > 3 THEN GOTO 200
```

Statements containing GOTO are easy to use. However, programs which contain them are often difficult to understand. It is good programming practice to avoid using GOTO if possible.

SELECTION

A choice is made between two or more different options. Only one of the options is carried out.

1 *IF . . . THEN . . .*

Test the condition after the IF. If the condition is TRUE then carry out the statement(s). If it is FALSE ignore the statement(s) and carry on. (See Fig. 11.4.)

2 *IF . . . THEN . . . ELSE . . . – carry out one of two possible actions.*

Test the condition after the IF. If the condition is TRUE carry out the statement(s) after the THEN. If the condition is FALSE carry out the statement(s) after the ELSE. (See Fig. 11.5.)

Examples of IF . . . THEN . . . statements in BASIC

```
1  150 IF A1=A2 THEN Comparison$="EQUAL"
2 1000 IF age > 100 OR name$="LAST" THEN PRINT TOTAL
```

Example of IF . . . THEN . . . ELSE . . . in COMAL

In COMAL an IF statement taking up more than one line ends with an ENDIF:

```
100 IF age >=17
110     THEN PRINT "You may apply for a provisional licence"
120 ELSE
130     PRINT "Sorry, you are still too young to drive"
140 ENDIF
```

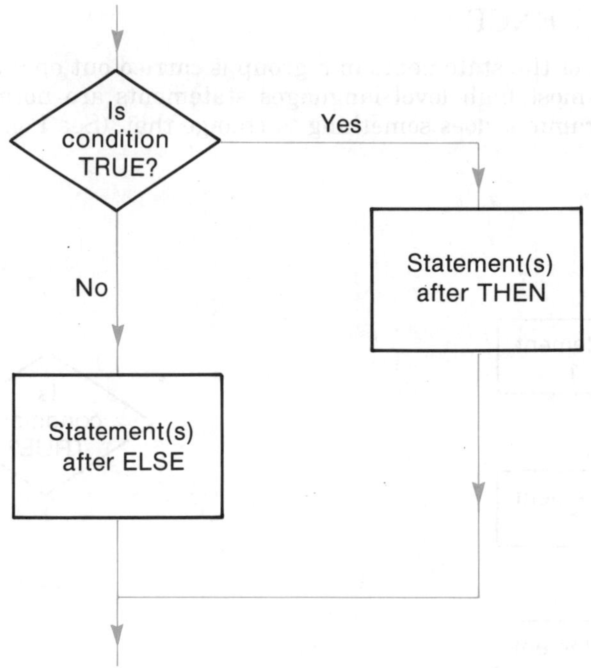

Fig. 11.5 Flowchart showing how an IF . . . THEN . . . ELSE . . . statement is executed

CASE

This is a statement to carry out one of a number of possible actions.

The facilities for selecting one of a number of alternatives differs from one language to another. In COMAL the statements are:

```
CASE (Expression) OF
WHEN (List1 of expressions) (Action1)
WHEN (List2 of expressions) (Action2)
etc. ..............................................
OTHERWISE (Action)
ENDCASE
```

The expressions in the lists after WHEN all give possible values of the expression after CASE. If the value chosen is in List1 then the computer will take Action1, etc.

Usually the expression after CASE is just a variable and the expressions after the WHENs are just values of it.

The OTHERWISE is not necessary. It is used if there are some cases not covered in the other lists.

Example of CASE statement in COMAL

The example is part of a program to find how many letters, words and sentences there are in a piece of text. Each character is checked in turn.

```
500 CASE character$ OF
510 WHEN " "
520 words := words + 1
530 WHEN "."
540    sentences := sentences + 1
550 WHEN   "A","B","C","D","E","F","G","H","I","J","K","L","M","N","O","P",
         "Q","R","S","T","U","V","W","X","Y","Z"
560    letters := letters + 1
570 OTHERWISE
580    oddments := oddments + 1
590 ENDCASE
```

REPETITION

In repetition a statement or a sequence of statements is repeated.

A **loop** is a sequence of statements which is repeated until some condition is met.

In a language such as BASIC the programmer can write loops using GOTO and IF statements.

Example of a loop in BASIC

```
100 REM **** Program to print out 10 numbers and their squares ****
110 LET I=0
120 LET I=I+1
130 PRINT "The square of ";I;" is ";I*I
140 IF I <=10 THEN GOTO 120
```

BUILT-IN LOOPING STRUCTURES

Most languages have special looping structures built in. In many languages there are three main types of looping structure:

1 *The FOR loop*–Repetition a given number of times. (See Fig. 11.6.)

2 *The REPEAT . . . UNTIL loop*–Repetition until a condition is met.
The loop is always carried out at least once. This is because the test to see whether it should finish is at the end of the loop. (See Fig. 11.7.)

3 *The WHILE loop*–Repetition while a condition is true.
Here the condition is tested at the beginning. So if it is not true to start with then the loop will not be executed at all. (See Fig. 11.8.)

Examples of a FOR loop

1 The following BASIC program performs the same task as the first loop example (above).

```
100 FOR I=1 TO 10
110     PRINT "The square of ";I;" is ";I*I
120 NEXT I
```

2 The previous program (example 1) would also work in COMAL (using := in the FOR statement). COMAL also allows a FOR loop which only repeats one statement to be done without a NEXT. A DO is placed between the FOR statement and the repeated statement. The previous example becomes:

```
100 FOR I := 1 TO 10 DO PRINT "The square of ";I;" is ";I*I
```

3 Loops are often used with arrays (see Unit 11.4). The following BASIC example is a module of a program. The array MARK has been dimensioned and had values read into it earlier in the program. This module finds the highest mark in the array and prints it out.

```
                                           Comments
500 LET highest=0                          highest is highest mark so far
510 FOR I=1 TO numval                      numval is number of marks
520 If mark(I) < highest THEN GOTO 540
530 highest=mark(I)
540 NEXT I
560 PRINT "the highest mark is "; highest
```

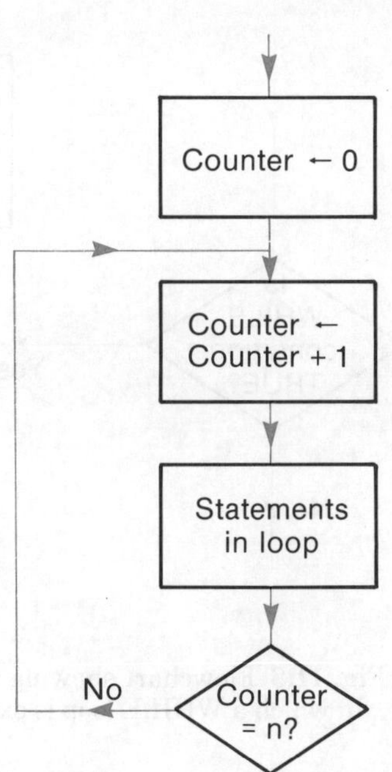

Fig. 11.6 Flowchart showing the order in which a FOR loop is executed

Example of a REPEAT . . . UNTIL loop in COMAL

```
100 REM *** Selecting from a menu–correct options are 1 to 7 ***
110 PRINT "Type ";
120 REPEAT
130    PRINT "a whole number from 1 to 7, please";
140    INPUT Option
150 UNTIL Option>0 and Option<8 AND INT(Option)=Option
```

Notes:
1 INT is a function (see Unit 11.7). INT(X) produces the whole number below X. The condition in the UNTIL statement will only be fulfilled if OPTION is a whole number between 1 and 7 inclusive. The loop will be repeated until this happens.
2 This example would also be correct in some versions of BASIC.

Example of a WHILE loop in COMAL

```
100 // To find the total of a set of marks //
110 Total :=0
200 PRINT "Type in the marks, pressing RETURN after each one"
210 PRINT "After the last mark enter –1"
220 INPUT "First mark ": Mark
240 WHILE Mark >= 0 DO
250 Total := Total + Mark
260 INPUT "Next mark ": Mark
270 ENDWHILE
280 PRINT "Total mark is "; Total
```

Notes:
1 In COMAL a WHILE loop is ended with an ENDWHILE.
2 –1 is a rogue value for the input data (see Unit 11.5).

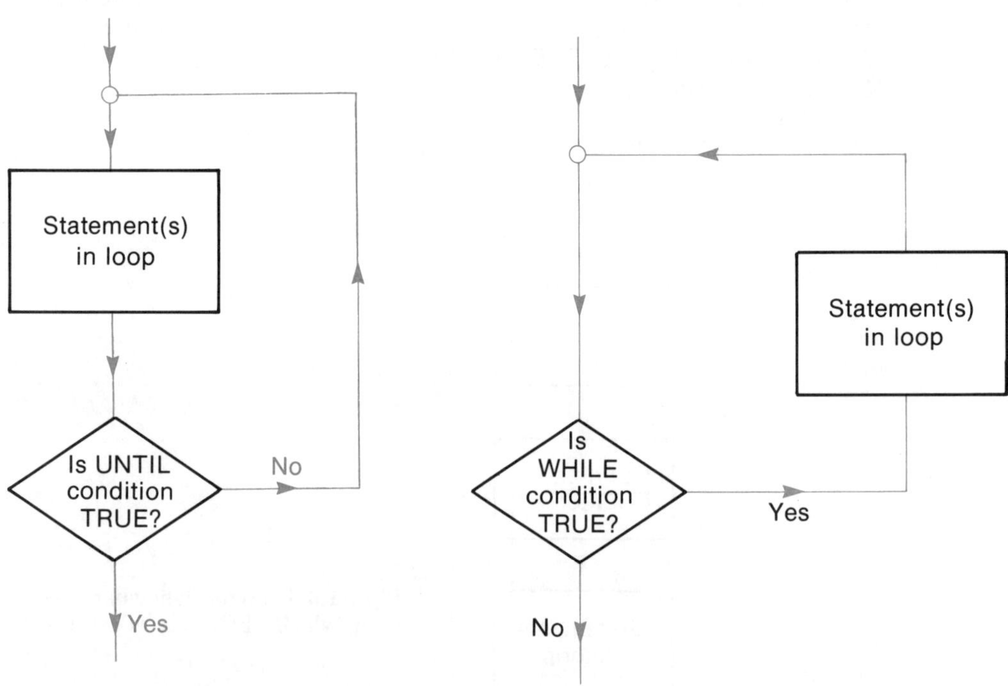

Fig. 11.7 Flowchart showing the order in which a REPEAT . . . UNTIL loop is executed

Fig. 11.8 Flowchart showing the order in which a WHILE loop is executed.

11.7 Subroutines, Procedures and Functions

ROUTINES AND SUBROUTINES

A **routine** is a sequence of instructions to carry out a particular task. A routine is a general term for a relatively small self-contained set of instructions. It may refer to:
1 A complete short program; or
2 A part of a program; or
3 A set of instructions used by other programs.

A **subroutine** is a routine which is used by one or more programs. A subroutine is not itself a complete program. It has to be **called** by other programs.

A program calls the subroutine and the subroutine's task is carried out. Control then **returns** to the correct place in the calling program, which continues from where it left off.

Often a computer system has a library of subroutines available for programmers to use.

A **library subroutine** is a subroutine which is available to all users of a computer system as part of the software.

PARAMETERS AND LOCAL VARIABLES

A **parameter** or **argument** is a value passed between a program and a subroutine. Most languages (though not some versions of BASIC) allow a programmer to do either of the following:
1 Use one name for a parameter in a subroutine and another name for the same parameter when it appears in the calling program.
2 To have a variable in a subroutine and another one in the calling program, both with the same name. This is made possible by having **local** variables.

A **local** variable is one whose name is restricted to one subroutine.

A **global** variable is one which has the same name throughout a program and all its routines.

Advantages of these arrangements are:
1 A subroutine can be used in more than one program without worrying
(a) Whether names in the subroutine and the program clash; or
(b) Whether the right names have been used for the parameters.
2 Subroutines from subroutine libraries can be used without a problem over names.
3 The same subroutine can be used to operate on two different variables in the same program.

PROCEDURES

Languages such as COMAL and Pascal (and some versions of BASIC) allow a type of subroutine called a **procedure**. Procedures are generally used in stepwise refinement of a program (see Unit 10.4).

In COMAL

1 Procedures are executed using an EXEC statement.
2 A procedure is defined between a PROC and an END PROC.
3 Parameters are put in brackets after the name of the procedure.
4 All variables in a procedure are made local using CLOSED.

Example of variables and parameters in COMAL

The following COMAL routine produces an introductory pattern for a game of noughts and crosses. It simply prints a pattern made of alternate blocks of o's and x's. In fact it repeats the following 3 times down the page:

```
oooooooooooooooooooo
oooooooooooooooooooo
oooooooooooooooooooo
oooooooooooooooooooo
xxxxxxxxxxxxxxxxxxxx
xxxxxxxxxxxxxxxxxxxx
xxxxxxxxxxxxxxxxxxxx
xxxxxxxxxxxxxxxxxxxx
xxxxxxxxxxxxxxxxxxxx
```

```
100 // ROUTINE TO PRINT ALTERNATELY BLOCKS OF o'S AND x'S //
200 FOR I := 1 TO 3
210 EXEC BLOCK("o")
220 EXEC BLOCK("x")
230 NEXT I
299 //
300 PROC BLOCK(CHAR$) CLOSED
310 FOR I := 1 TO 4
320 EXEC ROW(CHAR$)
330 NEXT I
340 END PROC BLOCK
399 //
400 PROC ROW (CH$) CLOSED
410 FOR I := 1 TO 20
420 PRINT CH$;
430 NEXT I
440 PRINT
450 END PROC
```

Notes:

1 Because the procedures BLOCK and ROW are both CLOSED the variables in them are local. In particular the changes of I in ROW and BLOCK do not affect the I in the main program.

2 The variable CHAR$ in BLOCK is a parameter which takes first the value "o" and then the value "x".

FUNCTIONS

In high level programming a **function** is a sequence of instructions used by a program to supply a value in an expression.

There are two main types of function:

1 Built-in functions (or **standard** functions). These are functions which are always available to users of a particular language.

2 Programmer-defined (or **user-defined**) functions. These are functions written by the programmer.

Examples in BASIC

1 Built-in functions.

(a) LEN

```
100 LET N1=LEN(A$)
```

LEN is a function giving the number of characters in a string. For example, if A$ is the string "HELLO", N1 will be assigned the value 5.

(b) INT

```
110 IF Num=INT(Num) THEN PRINT "Whole number"
```

INT gives the whole number below the value of the expression in the brackets. For instance INT(2.6) is 2 and INT(−3.4) = −4

Num will only be equal to INT(Num) if Num is a whole number.

2 Programmer-defined functions.

The following function C would correct a value to the nearest whole number. It uses the built-in function INT mentioned above.

Definition of the function C:

```
100 DEF FNC(N)=INT(N+.5)
```

Use of the function C to correct the values of H and W:

```
500 PRINT "Approximate height and weight are "; FNC(H), FNC(W)
```

Using functions and procedures in top-down programming

In structured languages it is usual to write first the main structure of a program. The details are then filled in by defining functions and procedures. In other words these structures make stepwise refinement easier while doing top-down programming (see Unit 10.4).

Example of the use of procedures in COMAL

The following program is a COMAL version of the program discussed in Unit 10.4. It has been written top-down in three levels as suggested there:

1 The function of the program is expressed in line 100.

2 This function is refined into procedures in lines 110 to 130.

3 The procedures are written in detail in lines 200 to 430.

```
100 //PROGRAM : Input three numbers and print out their average.//
110 EXEC Input_Three_Numbers
120 EXEC Calculate_Total_And_Average
130 EXEC Print_Numbers_And_Their_Average
140 END
199 //
200 PROC Input_Three_Numbers
210 PRINT "The Average of Three Numbers"
220 PRINT
230 INPUT "Please type your first number ": Num1
240 INPUT "Please type your second number ": Num2
250 INPUT "Please type your third number ": Num3
260 END PROC Input_Three_Numbers
299 //
300 PROC Calculate_Total_And_Average
310 Total := Num1 + Num2 + Num3
320 Average := Total / 3
330 END PROC Calculate_Total_And_Average
399 //
400 PROC Print_Numbers_And_Average
410 PRINT "The Numbers are :- ";Num1,Num2,Num3
420 PRINT "Their average is :- "; Average
430 END PROC Print_Numbers_And_Average
```

11.8 Program Style and Layout

Programs should be written in such a way that they are:
1 Easy to understand.
2 Well structured.
3 Easy to modify.

Programs written with these points in mind:
1 Are easier to debug.
2 Are far less likely to contain errors in the first place.
3 Can be worked on by teams.
4 Can be modified to fit new situations.

A program must be carefully designed and planned (see Unit 10). Even then a large program cannot be written successfully by starting at the beginning and working through it instruction by instruction. It should be written top down (see Unit 10.4). The main operations of the program should be worked out first.
1 In a structured language such as COMAL or Pascal these operations can then be refined using procedures (see program examples in Unit 11.7).
2 In an unstructured language, as in many versions of BASIC, the program can still be divided up into distinct parts or modules.

To make a program easier to read the programmer can also:
1 Include helpful **comments** in the program.
2 Choose names of variables, procedures and functions which make their purpose clear without further comments.

USE OF COMMENTS

Comments are also known as **remarks** or **narrative**.

In BASIC any part of a line after the word REM is assumed to be comment.

In COMAL, REM can be used or just //.

Comments can be used:
1 To highlight the modules of the program.
2 To explain the function of modules.
3 To explain the variables used.

Examples of the use of comments in BASIC

1
```
100 REM ******************************************************
110 REM *****            IDENTIFICATION MODULE           *****
120 REM ******************************************************
130 REM               HOUSE PURCHASE PROGRAM
140 REM                   VERSION 5     15/1/87
```

2
```
500 LET high  =0        : REM high is highest mark so far
510 LET pnum=K-1        : REM there are K-1 names
```

USE OF HELPFUL IDENTIFIERS

The name given to a variable (or a file, etc.) can be chosen in such a way that anyone reading the program can see what the variable represents from its name. Some languages, including some versions of BASIC, make this difficult because they only allow short names.

Example in BASIC

Part of a program to calculate the area of a triangle:

```
100 INPUT BASE,HEIGHT
110 LET AREATR=0.5*BASE*HEIGHT
```

Even if only one letter is allowed for names, the following would still be of some help.

```
100 INPUT B,H
110 LET A=0.5*B*H
```

PROGRAM LAYOUT

Where the language allows procedures, programs should be set out to show top down structure (as in the two short COMAL programs shown in Unit 11.7).

Even in BASIC you could still use the GOSUB statement to produce a similar effect. In any case try to keep to the following rules:

1 Break the program up into modules. Usually the modules would match the boxes in the outline program flowchart.

2 Keep branching between modules to a minimum. In BASIC this is difficult, but GOTO should be used sparingly and subroutines should each have only one exit point.

3 Set the statements out in a clear manner, for example, spaces can be used to separate words and to show up loops.

Example

The following is a section of a program which reads a table of values and column headings and prints the table out.

```
100 REM ******************************************************
110 REM *****     INITIALISE VARIABLES,DIMENSION ARRAYS    *****
120 REM ******************************************************
130 LET NCOL=5   : REM NUMBER OF COLUMNS
140 LET NROW=10 : REM NUMBER OF ROWS
150 DIM HEAD$(NCOL)
160 DIM TABLE$(NROW,NCOL)
200 REM ******************************************************
210 REM *****          READ HEADINGS AND TABLE              *****
220 REM ******************************************************
230 FOR I=1 TO NCOL
240    READ HEAD$(I)
250    FOR J=1 TO NROW
260        READ TABLE(J,I)
270    NEXT J
280 NEXT I
300 REM ******************************************************
310 REM *****               PRINT HEADINGS                  *****
320 REM ******************************************************
```

etc.

Notes:

1 Lines 240 to 270 have been indented (i.e. moved in from the side of the page) to highlight the fact that this is a loop within a loop.

2 The same result could have been achieved with a program section written as follows (in many versions of BASIC):

```
10 DIMA$(5),B(10,5)
20 FORI=1TO5:READA$(I):FORJ=1TO10:READB(J,I):NEXTJ:NEXTI
```

It is true that the longer version would:

(a) Take a greater time to type on a keyboard.

(b) Take up more store in its source form.

(c) Take more time to load into the computer or to print.

But the longer version is:

(a) Easier to understand.

(b) Easier to adapt.

12 ERRORS

An **error** is a condition which causes a computer to fail to produce the expected results.

Errors occur at all stages of developing and implementing a program and a large proportion of computing effort is aimed at detecting or avoiding them.

The main causes of errors are:

1 Faulty system design.
2 Hardware failure.
3 Errors in the program.
4 Errors in the data.
5 Inaccurate calculation.

12.1 Program Errors

An error in a program is called a **bug**. Bugs may be one or more of the following.

SYNTAX ERRORS

A syntax error occurs when a language is not used correctly. A compiler or interpreter will not be able to translate statements with syntax errors because they do not make sense.

Syntax errors usually occur because:

1 The programmer has misunderstood the rules of the language; or
2 A transcription error has been made. A **transcription error** is a mistake made in writing or keying.

Examples of syntax errors in BASIC

1 300 LET A=2(X+3)
This should read '300 LET A=2*(X+3)'. The programmer probably did not realize that an asterisk was needed.
2 100 IF A$="***" TEN 200
This should read '100 IF A$="***" THEN 200'. This was probably a transcription error.

LOGICAL ERRORS

A **logical error** occurs when the program designer or the programmer makes a mistake in working out the sequence of instructions required to produce a particular result.

Examples of logical errors

1 The following BASIC program module is intended to print 'INCORRECT MONTH' whenever the value of MONTH is not between 1 and 12, inclusive.

```
100 REM *******   MONTH CHECK *******
110 IF MONTH>12 THEN 200
120 IF MONTH<1  THEN 200
200 PRINT "INCORRECT MONTH"
```

In fact there is a logical error because it will still execute line 200 and print 'INCORRECT MONTH' if MONTH does lie between 1 and 12. A GOTO statement is required at line 130, so that line 200 is not executed if the month is acceptable.

2 The following module is intended to input a set of names into the array SNAME$:

```
200 REM ***** INPUT SURNAMES *******
210 PRINT "TYPE EACH SURNAME, THEN PRESS 'RETURN'"
220 PRINT "AFTER THE LAST NAME, ENTER'***'"
230 LET COUNT=0
240 LET COUNT=COUNT+1
250 INPUT SNAME$(COUNT)
260 IF SNAME$(COUNT)="***" THEN 500
270 GOTO 230
```

When this module has been run SNAME$(1) will have the value "***". All the other elements of SNAME$ will be blank and no names will have been stored. This is because line 270 says 'GOTO 230', which sets COUNT=0 every time round the loop. Line 270 should read 'GOTO 240', so that COUNT is incremented.

12.2 Detection of Program Errors

To **debug** a program means to find and to correct errors in it. There are a number of methods of detecting errors.

COMPILATION ERROR MESSAGES

When a source program is compiled, syntax errors can be detected by routines, called **diagnostic** routines, and messages are printed out giving the type of error and where it occurs in the program.

Examples of compiler error messages

1 ERROR 25 AT LINE 200 – MISMATCHED PARENTHESES

Parentheses are brackets. Line 200 probably contains different numbers of opening and closing brackets.
2 LINE 160 – NEXT WITHOUT FOR ERROR

EXECUTION ERROR MESSAGES

An **execution error** or **run-time error** is an error which occurs when a computer is running a program and is unable to carry out an instruction. The computer has been asked to do something which is not possible in that situation.

Examples of execution error messages

1 File not open error

This would occur if the program tried to write data to, or read data from, a file without opening it first.

2 Division by zero at line 200

It is possible to divide by a very small number to get a very large answer, but it is not possible to divide by 0, for example, the message would arise if N has the value 1 and line 200 is

```
200 NEWVAL=6/(N-1)
```

3 Device not present error

This would occur if the program tried to use a device such as a printer and the device was not connected up or not switched on.

Common causes of execution errors

1 Incorrect data. A well-written program should validate the data and prevent execution errors.
2 A logical error in the program can lead to the computer trying to carry out some operation which was not intended.
3 The hardware system not being set up correctly, for example, the wrong devices or too little memory, etc.
4 The user giving the wrong instructions to the operating system.

TRACES

A **trace** is a printout of the steps taken by all or part of a program. Usually the trace is produced while the program is running. Common types of trace are:

1 Arithmetic trace – prints the results of each calculation as it is performed.

2 Transfer trace – shows which statements in the program are executed.

A trace is produced by a **trace routine** or a **trace program**. This adds extra instructions to the program which is being traced.

DRY RUNS

A **dry run** (or **desk check**) is a check for errors in a program by working through a flowchart or program by hand, i.e. without a computer.

A dry run is useful:
1 So that the results of running a program with test data are known beforehand.
2 To help check the logic of a program.

A dry run is often carried out by drawing a **trace table**. A trace table is a table which shows the instructions which are being executed and the results they produce. (For a low-level example see Unit 11.1.)

Worked question

The following is a module of a BASIC program. It should input a set of lengths and print out their total and average. In fact it gives the right total and wrong average.

1 Draw a trace table for the input data 10, 14, 0.
2 State the correct output with these values.
3 Suggest a change to one line of the program to correct it.

```
610 PRINT "Enter lengths, one after another, in cms. Type 0 after last one"
620 I=0
630 Total=0
640 I=I+1
650 PRINT "Next length ";: INPUT Length
660 IF Length=0 THEN GOTO 700
670 Total=Total+Length
680 GOTO 640
700 PRINT "Total length    ="; Total
710 PRINT "Average length="; Total/I
```

1 The trace table is as follows:

Line	*I*	*Total*	*Length*	*Comments, results of instructions*
610				PRINT "Input lengths . . . ." message
620	0			
630	0	0		
640	1	0		
650	1	0	10	PRINT "Next length ". INPUT 10
660	1	0	10	Length is not 0.
670	1	10	10	
680	1	10	10	GOTO 640
640	2	10	10	
650	2	10	14	PRINT "Next length ". INPUT 14
660	2	10	14	Length is not 0.
670	2	24	14	
680	2	24	14	GOTO 640
640	3	24	14	
650	3	24	0	PRINT "Next length ". INPUT 0
660	3	24	0	Length = 0. GOTO 700
700	3	24	0	PRINT "Total length = 24"
710	3	24	0	PRINT "Average length = 8"

2 The output should be: Total length = 24
Average length = 12

3 The average is incorrect because the division is done by I in line 710. In fact the number of values is I−1. Change line 710 to

```
710 PRINT "Average length="; Total/(I-1)
```

12.3 Integrity of Input Data

The **integrity** of data means its accuracy and completeness. Data has integrity if it has not been lost or corrupted in any way. (See also Unit 13.6–Security of files.)

In business and industry a great deal of time and effort is devoted to making sure that data is accurate and that it is not corrupted.

CAUSES OF INACCURACIES IN INPUT DATA

The following are common causes of errors in input data.

Mistakes or inaccuracies in collecting the data

Example

A computer is used to control the temperature at which a chemical process takes place. A digital thermometer connected to the computer is faulty and as a result the computer sets the temperature to the wrong value.

Failure to organize the data in the way required by the program

Example

If a program expects names to be entered as "Christian name, Surname" and "JOHN SMITH", "BARRY JONES" is entered then the computer will take JOHN SMITH to be the Christian name and BARRY JONES the surname of the same person.

Hardware errors

Common examples are:
1 *Transmission errors*–data sent from one device to another is changed due to a hardware failure.
2 *Read errors*–failure by an input device to read the input medium correctly.

Examples

1 A letter C is transmitted in ASCII code by a telephone line. One bit is changed and the character is read as a letter A. (IN ASCII letter C = 1000011, letter A = 1000001 – see Fig. 2.4).
2 Exactly the same type of error could occur if the letter C is encoded in ASCII on magnetic tape and there is dirt on the reading head of the magnetic tape unit.

Errors in preparing data

Common types are:
1 Simple typing errors.
2 Misreading characters on coding sheets.

Examples

1 *Transposition*–typing digits or letters in the wrong order (for example, 3256 instead of 3526).
2 *Misreading a 2 as a Z.* Often the Z is crossed to distinguish it from 2–i.e. Ƶ. Similarly 0 (zero) is often crossed to distinguish it from O (the letter)–i.e. Ø. The letter I is given a bar at the top and the bottom to distinguish it from 1–i.e. I.

METHODS OF AVOIDING OR DETECTING INPUT ERRORS

Organized methods of data collection

If a large amount of data is to be collected for a system then data integrity can be improved by organizing the data collection, for example
1 Pre-printed forms–forms are printed with spaces provided for the data to be filled in (see Unit 1.3–Fig. 1.4).
2 In some situations the data itself can be pre-printed, for example, in bar codes (see Unit 7.3).

Adding a value to data just as a check

A calculation is done on data which produces a value to add on to it. Then if the data is transmitted or typed, etc., the value can be checked by doing the same calculation again. If the value is different then the data itself must have been corrupted in some way.

Some commonly used examples are:
1 A **parity bit.** This is a method of ensuring the integrity of bit strings.
The **parity** of a bit string depends on the number of 1's in it.
A bit string has **even parity** if the number of 1's in it is an even number. It has **odd parity** if the number of 1's in it is an odd number.
A **parity bit** is a bit added to a bit string to adjust the parity. In most systems which have a parity bit the parity is even.
If a bit string has even parity and one bit gets changed (i.e. a 1 becomes a 0 or a 0 becomes a 1) then the parity becomes odd. A computer can check all the bit strings. If one string has odd parity then there must be an error in it.
2 A **check digit.** A check digit is an extra digit added to a number to ensure that, if the number is changed by mistake, the error will be detected. Check digits are most commonly added to numbers which it is very important to get right, for example, customer account numbers, international book numbers.
3 **Control total.** A control total is the sum worked out for a group of records by adding up particular items. The addition is done before and after an operation to check that all of the records are in fact processed. A **hash total** is a control total for which the sum used does not have any actual meaning–a 'nonsense total'.

Worked question (parity bit)

Add a parity bit at the left of the following bit strings to give them even parity:
1 1011011.
2 1011010.

1 Parity of 1011011 is 5 and is odd.
Parity bit is 1 to make the parity even.
String with parity bit added = 11011011.
2 Parity of 1011010 is 4 and is already even.
Parity bit is 0.
String with parity bit added = 01011010.

Worked question (check digit)

Five-figure account numbers have a digit added to them according to the following rules:
1 Starting from the right, multiply the first digit by 1, the second by 2, the third by 3, etc.
2 Add the result together.
3 Use the last digit of the result as a check digit to add to the end of the number.
Find the new value, with the check digit added, of (a) 56037 (b) 50637
Comment on the result.

(a) For 56037 rules (1) and (2) give:
$5\times5+6\times4+0\times3+3\times2+7\times1=62$
From rule (3) check digit = 2
New version of the number = 560372

(b) For 50637 rules (1) and (2) give:
$5\times5+0\times4+6\times3+3\times2+7\times1=56$
From rule (3) check digit = 6
New version of the number = 506376

Comment: The only difference between the two numbers 56037 and 50637 is that the digits 6 and 0 have been transposed. However this method gives them different check digits. Thus it would be a useful method for detecting transposition errors.

Example of a control total

For a file of customer accounts the actual account numbers can be added up and used as a check. The sum of the account numbers does not mean anything but, after any operation, the account numbers can be added up again. If the total is the same it can be assumed that all the right records were used.
Note: This is also an example of a hash total.

Verification

Verification is the checking of data which has been copied from one medium to another to see that it still represents the original data.

Examples of verification of data

1 When data is encoded onto disc, a keyboard operator reads the data from a source document and types it at a keystation, the data being recorded on disc. This data is then verified by a second operator, who retypes it all. The computer controlling the keystation checks the data stored against the data now being typed and reports differences, so that any errors can be corrected (see Unit 7.1).
2 A magnetic tape cassette can be used to store the contents of part of a computer's main store. If the tape is rewound, the computer can then read what is recorded and verify that the contents have been 'saved' correctly.

Validation

Validation is checking of data before the main processing to see that it is acceptable for the process.

Validation may include checks that the data is:
1 In the right format.
2 Of the right type.
3 Complete.
4 Within the range of possible values.

Examples of validation checks

1 A **type check.** A set of numbers which are to be totalled can be checked to make sure that:
(a) All the characters are either decimal digits or decimal points.
(b) There is at most one decimal point per number.
2 A **range check.** The month of a date of birth can be checked to see that it is a whole number between 1 and 12 inclusive.

12.4 Errors in Calculation

Common causes of calculation errors are as follows.

When the program attempts an operation which is impossible

Examples

1 Division by zero.
2 Attempts to find the square root of a negative number.
Note: Usually, in a high level language, attempting either of these operations would result in an execution error message.

Overflow

This occurs when the result of a calculation is too large for the store reserved for it. In a digital computer only a certain number of bits are used to store any given number.

Loss of accuracy

This again is because of the limited amount of store available for each number. Each number may be inaccurate because some of its digits cannot be stored. If arithmetic operations are then performed on these inaccurate numbers the result may be even more inaccurate.

If not all of the digits of a number can be stored the number can be truncated or rounded. If a number is **truncated** the digits which cannot be stored are simply lost. If a number is **rounded** the last digits which can be stored are adjusted to make the number as accurate as possible.

Worked question

In a certain machine only 4 digits of any decimal number can be stored. For the numbers **1** 53.647 and **2** 65.2145 give the result (a) if the numbers are truncated and (b) if they are rounded.

1 (a) 53.647 truncated to 4 figures = 53.64.
(b) 53.647 rounded to 4 figures = 53.65.
2 (a) 65.2145 truncated = 65.21.
(b) 65.2145 rounded = 65.21.

13 FILES

A **file** is an organized collection of related records.

In computing a file is usually on backing store but the term can be used for data being input or output.

A **record** is a group of related items of data which together can be treated as a unit. The records are usually similar to one another in the type of data they contain and the way they are set out.

A **field** is an area of a record reserved for one particular type of data. Each field contains one, or possibly more, data items.

An **item** of data here means the smallest piece of data that would be dealt with separately – a single name or a single number, etc.

Examples of files, records, fields and items

1 Each record of a file of student records has the following fields:

Surname Forenames Date of Birth Address

One of the records is:

WALTERS DAVID ANDREW 21/02/75 3, BURNSIDE GARDENS, BISHOPSWICK

The Date of Birth field contains the item 21/02/75.

2 A payroll file of a firm's employees. One record would be all the data on one employee. The separate items in a record could include the employee's (a) works numbers, (b) name (c) tax code, etc.

3 A file stored on the Police National Computer giving data on stolen cars. One record would be all the data on one car.

The items in a record could include the car's (a) registration number, (b) legal owner, (c) make, (d) colour, etc.

4 Any organized collection of data held on backing store. The following can be regarded as files:

(a) A computer program.

(b) A piece of text stored by a word processor.

5 Any organized set of data even if it is not on a computer medium, for example, a set of index cards in a doctor's surgery. Each record is the data on one patient. The items consist of the patient's name, history of symptoms and treatment.

REASONS FOR USING FILES

Files can be used:

1 In any situation requiring a permanent source of data which is readily accessible.

2 In a computer when the main store is too small for the amount of data being processed.

FIXED AND VARIABLE LENGTH FIELDS

Fields may be of **fixed length** or **variable length**.

If the fields are of **fixed length** then a given field in a record has a set number of character positions reserved for it.

If the fields are of **variable length**, the number of characters in each is not determined beforehand.

Advantages of variable over fixed length

There is no waste of storage space (there is wastage for fixed length fields because a given field has to be as long as the longest item to go in it, and space is wasted for short items).

Advantages of fixed over variable length

1 Computer operations such as searching can be carried out quickly.

2 Allocation of storage space is more straightforward.

3 Updating of files is simpler – if one record is changed it still takes up the same amount of space, so that other records do not have to be moved to make room for it.

Keys

Usually one particular field of each record of a file contains an item which is used to identify the record uniquely. This field is called the **key field**, and the item in it is called the **key** to that record. In a file the keys must all be different from one another, so that there is no confusion over which record is which.

Examples illustrating field lengths and keys

1 A stock file for the sales department of a garden centre. The fields are fixed length and are as follows:

Field	*Number of characters*
catalogue number	6
name of plant	20
minimum height (feet)	2
maximum height (feet)	2
price (pence)	5
number in stock	3

The key field is catalogue number and the records are in the order of these keys.

Four of the records are as follows:

```
002103ABIES GEORGEI       2 3  250 23
002104ABIES GEORGEI       3 4  350 14
002113ABIES GRANDIS       2 3  250  3
002114ABIES LASIOCARPA    3 4  420  6
```

2 A BASIC program stored on a floppy disc is an example of a file e.g.

```
20 FOR I=1 TO 20
30 PRINT N$
100 NEXT I
```

Here each record is a line of the program. It has two variable length fields – the line number and the BASIC statement.

The key item is the line number and is used by the computer to search for a line when editing or running the program.

13.1 Organization and Access

The method of **organization** of a file refers to:

1 The way in which the records are arranged within the file.

2 The method of working out where each record is stored in the file.

There are various different ways of organizing computer files.

The method of **access** to files refers to the way in which a program reads data from a file or writes data to it.

The different methods of access to files include the following.

SEQUENTIAL ACCESS

Access to a file is **sequential** when records can only be written to or read from it in order, one after another.

Sequential files can be stored on *either* a serial access medium (such as magnetic tape) *or* a direct access medium (such as magnetic disc).

DIRECT ACCESS (ALSO CALLED RANDOM ACCESS)

Access to a file is **direct** when any record can be accessed without having to access other records first.

Direct access files can *only* be stored on a direct access medium (such as magnetic disc).

Advantages of direct access over sequential

1 Selected records can be accessed far more quickly from direct access files.

2 Records can be accessed in any chosen order.

3 Records do not have to be put into any particular order before the file is created.

Advantages of sequential access over direct

1 For the user: sequential files can be stored on most media including magnetic tape, paper tape and punched cards as well as magnetic discs.

2 For the programmer: it is usually easier to write programs to handle sequential files.

FACTORS AFFECTING CHOICE OF METHOD OF ACCESS

1 How many records are to be accessed. If records are to be accessed singly or only a few at a time, then sequential files would be inefficient. Direct access should be used.

2 How large the file is. If a file is small, the time delay in searching it is not important therefore a sequential file is acceptable.
3 Whether the application is interactive. Sequential access is often suitable for batch applications. On-line applications such as information retrieval usually need direct access.
4 The type of storage medium being used. If magnetic tape is to be used, then files will have to be sequential.

Examples of uses

1 Sequential access

A payroll application where the main file of employee details is to be stored on tape. Each employee has an employee number which can be used as a key.

The main operations to be done are (see Fig. 10.3):
(a) Weekly pay run – the computer goes through the employees in sequence working out their pay.
(b) Update run – a file of changes is produced in employee number order and the computer goes through this file and the main file in sequence, making changes to the main file (as described in Unit 13.4).
Note: It does not matter for either of these operations that individual records cannot be accessed quickly. In case (a) the whole file is processed anyway.

2 Direct access

Maintenance records for a lift repair firm. Engineers from the firm service the lifts in buildings and keep records of what they do. The data is stored in a computer file in the order of the dates on which the services take place. An index is held in the computer's main store which shows where each record is stored. If the computer is given a date it searches the index to find whereabouts the records are for that day and retrieves them directly.

A typical record includes the date, building, name of customer, address, type of contract (3 or 6 months): 11/04/87 SABRE HOTEL MORLEY FOODS BRYANT SQUARE, MOSSTOWN 6

A direct access use of this system is to find out which lifts to service on a particular day. The lifts are on either six-month or three-month contracts. The computer checks only the two dates, 6 months and 3 months before that day. It then prints out all the six-month contracts on the first date and the three-month contracts on the second date.

Note: The file has sequential organization but direct access. In fact it can also be accessed sequentially. This facility is used to find all the repair and service calls made to the lifts in a particular building. To do this the computer reads the whole file, a record at a time. It checks the second field in each record for the building in question. Each time the right name appears that record is printed out.

13.2 Master and Transaction Files

MASTER FILE

A **master file** is a file used as a reference for a particular computer application. It may be updated when necessary.

TRANSACTION FILE

A **transaction file** is a file of temporary data which has been prepared in order to carry out a processing operation with the data on a master file. Usually the transaction file is being used to update the master file.

Example of a master and a transaction file

A file holds details of the goods stored by a chain of food shops. Each record consists of: product code, name of goods, price, minimum number to be held in stock. This file is the master file. Another file is prepared containing product code and new price for some of the goods on the master file. This is the transaction file and it is used to update the prices on the master file.

13.3 Storage and Handling of Files

To **create a file** means to organize data into a file.

STORAGE OF FILES

Files on tape are usually stored with extra information both
1 Before the first record in a **header label**, for example, file name, date written, etc., and
2 After the last record in a **trailer label**, for example, number of records in the file, etc.

Sequential files have an **end of file marker**, so that programs can recognize the last record.

Discs usually have a **directory** which is used by the operating system to locate files.

A **directory** is a file containing a list of names of files and the information needed to access those files on the disc.

The operating system locates files using an addressing system for the tracks and sectors (and cylinders on a disc pack). This addressing may be built-in at the manufacturing stage or may be added later by formatting the disc.

To **format** a disc means to prepare it for subsequent file storage by adding control information to it. In microcomputers this is usually done by running a program which writes track and sector numbers on the disc. Only blank or unwanted discs should be formatted as the operation will effectively erase any data already on them.

FACILITIES FOR FILE USERS

A computer's operating system usually allows users to:
1 Create and access sub-directories. A **sub-directory** is a part of the main directory which can be accessed separately.
2 Obtain a catalogue of a given directory. A **catalogue** is a list of the files in a directory.
3 (a) **save**, (b) **load**, (c) delete, (d) rename and (e) copy files.
(a) To **save** a file means to copy all the records from the main store onto a permanent store.
(b) To **load** a file means to read all the records from a permanent store into the main store.
(c) When a user deletes a file it can no longer be used. Usually the file is not actually erased from the disc. The reference to it is erased from the directory and the space on the disc is made available for other data.
(d) When a user renames a file, the name of it is changed in the directory. The file itself is not altered.
(e) When a file is copied, it is read into the main store, in sections if necessary, and a copy of it is written onto a new disc or another part of the same disc. After the operation there are two identical files, although the user may choose to give the new file a different name.

13.4 Updating

To **update a file** means to alter it with new information. Updating can involve:
1 Adding new records.
2 Deleting existing records.
3 Changing the items within existing records.

Direct access files are sometimes updated one record at a time by a keyboard operator using a file updating program interactively on line. Otherwise files are usually updated by using a transaction file. The method for updating sequential files on magnetic tape is given here.

UPDATING A SEQUENTIAL TAPE FILE

1 A transaction file is prepared containing all the updating information. It contains details of all records which are to be added, deleted or changed.

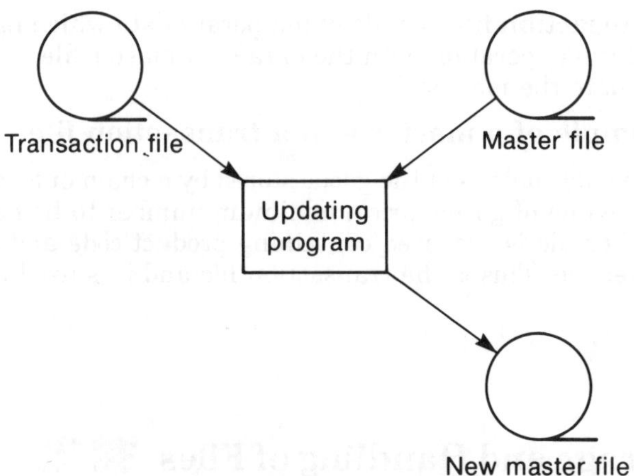

Fig. 13.1 Updating a sequential file on magnetic tape

The records on this file are in the same order as the records on the master file (the one being updated). This is done by having both files arranged with their keys in ascending order.

Note: The files are arranged with their keys in the same order because otherwise the updating would take an impractically long time and involve much winding and rewinding of tapes.

2 An updating program is run which reads the master file and the transaction file one record at a time. At the same time a new, updated master file is written; the old master file is not changed. (See Fig. 13.1.)

Note: The old master file is not changed because:

(a) It is not practical to try to insert, change or delete records on an existing sequential file, particularly on tape.

(b) The old master file can still be useful for security purposes (see Unit 13.6).

13.5 Searching, Merging and Sorting

SEARCHING

To **search** a file means to scan it methodically looking for a given item. The simplest method of searching is a **linear search**. A linear search is one in which each record is read in turn and checked for the item. If the end of the file is reached without finding the required item then the search has failed.

Word processor and editor programs allow the user to search for a word in a passage of text, and to replace it with another word if necessary (see Unit 18.4).

File enquiry packages are available which allow the user to search a file for items or combinations or selected items (see Unit 14.1).

Example

The following is part of a file detailing the name and colouring of cat breeds.

Name	*Colour 1*	*Colour 2*	*Colour 3*	*Eyes*
Birman	Blue	Chocolate		Blue
Blue-cream long-hair	Blue	Cream		Orange
Blue Persian	Blue			Orange
British Blue	Blue			Orange
Brown Burmese	Brown			Yellow
Calico	Black	Red	Cream	Orange
Chinchilla	White			Green
Havana Brown	Brown			Green

An enquiry program is used to find the names of cats with certain colour combinations.

1 The search pattern : Colour 1 = Brown
produces the names : Brown Burmese, Havana Brown

2 The search pattern : (Colour 2 = Cream OR Colour 3 = Cream) and (Eyes = Orange)
produces the names : Blue-cream long-hair and Calico

MERGING

Two files are **merged** by interleaving their records to form one file which still has its records in order.

A common example of merging is when two sequential files have their records in order and they have to be combined into a single file (see worked question below).

Example of a situation where files would be merged

A firm selling car parts has a master file of all the stock. Details of each part are stored in one record with the part number as key item. The file is stored sequentially in the order of the part numbers. When a new car model is introduced a file detailing all its parts is supplied to the firm. This file is then merged with the existing master file to produce a new file which includes parts for the new car.

SORTING

To **sort** data means to arrange it into order. Usually alphabetical data is sorted into alphabetical order and numbers into ascending order.

Files are sorted because:

1 File operations on two or more files are simpler if the files are in the same order (see updating and merging).

2 An operation on a serial file may be easier if the keys are in order (e.g. searching for a record if the key is known).
3 People reading files printed out on paper find them easier to use if they are in order.

Worked question

For the two files A and B, the first item of each record is to be taken as the key by which they are sequenced. The files are:

File A

256023	A.F.SMITH	234.56
403214	J.P.JONES	156.25
207888	L.C.JACKSON	2478.00
365142	P.JONES	89.50

File B

864512	P.R.TAYLOR	105.23
956421	A.FREEMAN	325.20
125642	S.ARBER	1025.60
320147	P.R.WEBER	68.25
403215	M.PALMER	512.00

Show the result of:
1 sorting the two files into correct sequence,
2 merging the sorted files.

1 File A when sorted is:

207888	L.C.JACKSON	2478.00
256023	A.F.SMITH	234.56
365142	P.JONES	89.50
403214	J.P.JONES	156.25

File B when sorted is:

125642	S.ARBER	1025.60
320147	P.R.WEBER	68.25
403215	M.PALMER	512.00
864512	P.R.TAYLOR	105.23
956421	A.FREEMAN	325.20

2 The two files when merged give:

125642	S.ARBER	1025.60
207888	L.C.JACKSON	2478.00
256023	A.F.SMITH	234.56
320147	P.R.WEBER	68.25
365142	P.JONES	89.50
403214	J.P.JONES	156.25
403215	M.PALMER	512.00
864512	P.R.TAYLOR	105.23
956421	A.FREEMAN	325.20

SORTING SEQUENTIAL FILES

In a computer, data can only be sorted when it is in the main store. Usually a file is too large to store all at once in the main store.

Such a file can be sorted as follows:
1 The file is read into the main store, a group of records at a time.
2 Each group is sorted and written back onto the backing store.
3 When all the groups have been sorted, they are merged again to produce a completely sorted file.

METHODS OF SORTING DATA IN THE MAIN STORE

A set of data items can be sorted into order by many methods. The methods below have been described for numbers, but can also be used to sort names and other strings.

Insertion

Build up a new set of numbers by taking each number in turn and inserting it into its correct place in the new set.

Selection

Search through the set, select the smallest and place it first. Then search again to find the next smallest, place it second and so on until they have all been selected.

Exchange

1 Compare two of the numbers to see if they are in the correct order.
2 If they are, leave them alone; if not, exchange them.
3 Carry on until all the numbers are in the correct order.

BUBBLE SORT

A **bubble sort** is an exchange sort in which a number is always compared for possible exchange with the one next to it in the set.

13.6 Security of Files

Security of files refers to the protection of files.

POSSIBLE DANGERS

Files may be in danger of accidentally or intentionally:
1 Being destroyed, for example,
  (a) By fire.
  (b) By hardware failure such as scratches on a disc caused by dirt.
2 Being modified, for example,
  (a) By being unintentionally written over,
  (b) For malicious reasons such as fraud,
  (c) By being updated with incorrect data.
3 Being accessed by unauthorized people.

METHODS OF PROTECTING DATA

Keeping copies

Data can be protected from destruction or modification by keeping copies, although care has to be taken that this does not make unauthorized access easier. Methods include:
1 Dumping files periodically onto backing store or onto an output device.
2 **Back up** files. When a file is saved on disc a second copy is made, preferably on another disc.
3 Keeping generations of a file

When a file is updated, the new file is called a **son**. The previous master file, from which it was produced is called a **father** and the one before that a **grandfather**. When the son becomes a father, the father becomes a grandfather (as you might expect) (See Fig 13.2).

Usually three generations are always kept (son, father and grandfather) so that if data is lost or incorrectly updated it can be recovered.

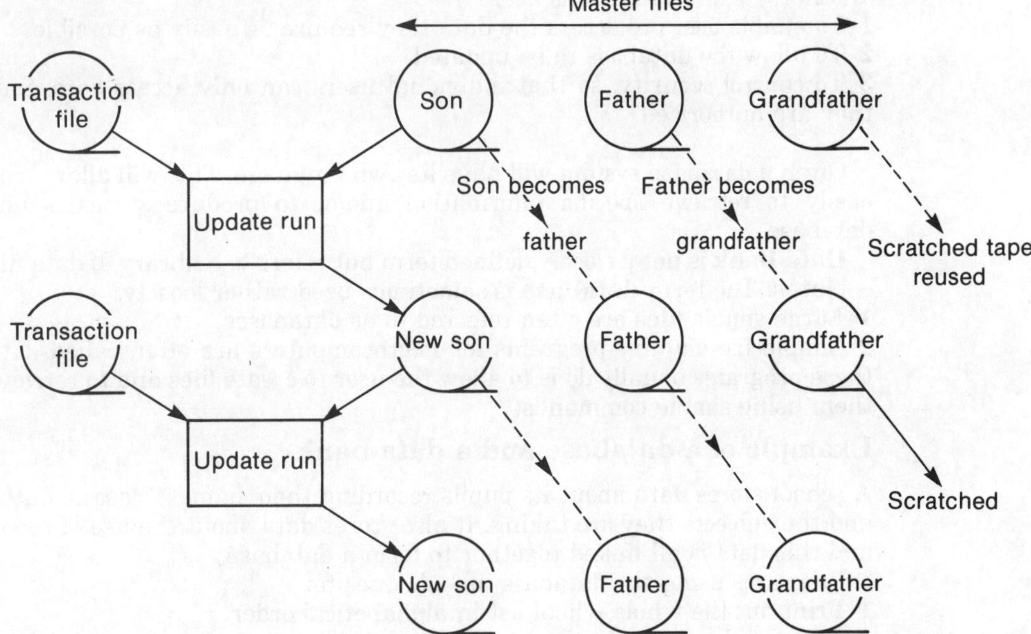

Fig. 13.2 Generations of files

Physical safeguards

1 To safeguard against fire or theft, important files and software are often kept in another building in a fireproof safe.

2 Magnetic tapes often have to be fitted with write permit rings before data can be written on them. Similar measures can be taken for other media.
3 Only authorized personnel are allowed in certain areas of many computer installations.

Software safeguards

The computer's operating system may be used to restrict access to the system:
1 Anyone using the computer may have to use a password (see Unit 14.3).
2 Some files may only be accessible to certain passwords.
3 On networks users may be able to give files an **access code**. This is a code which they add to the filename to indicate which users are allowed access to the file.

13.7 Databases and Data Banks

A **database** is a large collection of data structured in such a way that it can be used in different ways for different applications.

A **database management system (DBMS)** is a set of programs which organizes the use of a database. (See Fig. 13.3.)

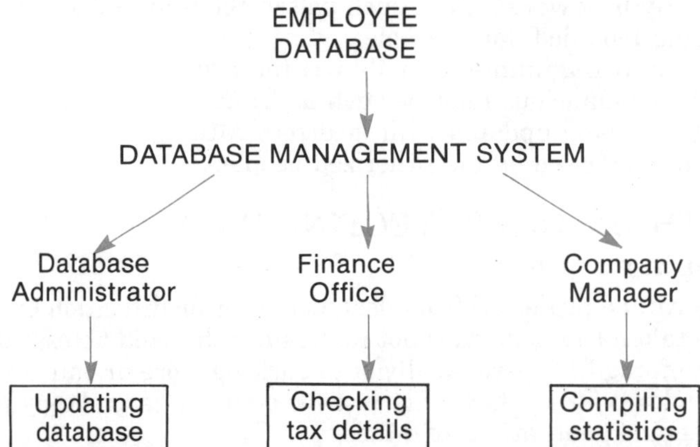

Fig. 13.3 Example of a database management system – the database contains details of employees of a company. The diagram shows only 3 of many applications which use the database

The database management system allows the different users to work independently of one another. Its main functions are:
1 To enable users to access the data they require as easily as possible.
2 To allow the database to be updated.
3 To control security, so that individual users can only access data and facilities for which they are authorized.

Often a database system will have its own language. This will allow users to write enquiries easily to retrieve specific information and/or to produce statistics and graphs from the database.

Data bank is not a closely defined term but refers to a library of data files and or databases.

Notes: The term **database** is sometimes used rather loosely:
1 Large simple files are often referred to as databases.
2 Simple file enquiry programs for microcomputers are often called database packages. All these programs usually do is to allow the user to create files and to retrieve selected data from them using simple commands.

Example of a database and a data bank

A school stores data about its pupils recording their names, classes, dates of birth, addresses and the subjects they are taking. It also stores data about the use of rooms and the timetable and this data is all linked together to form a database.

Programs using the database include ones to:
1 Print out the whole school list in alphabetical order.
2 Prepare class lists for the teachers.
3 Find out how many pupils are in various age ranges.
4 Work out the number of chairs and tables required in each room.
5 Produce statistics about the numbers of pupils in the 4th year opting for different subjects.

The school also has separate files stored on the same computer containing its tuck shop accounts and details of its stock of library books. All of this data taken together forms a data bank.

14 SOFTWARE

Software is a general term for programs which are written to help computer users.

A **software package** is a program or set of programs together with a full set of documentation. (Compare this with **hardware** – see the introduction to Unit 4.)

PROGRAM LIBRARIES

A computer installation usually has a centrally held set of software. This is available to authorized users and is referred to as a **library** of programs.

A **program library** is a collection of useful working programs and routines which are available to authorized users of the computer system.

A **library program** is a program which is readily available to users of a computer system as part of its software.

This software may come from:

1 The computer manufacturer – this includes software which is 'bundled', i.e. sold as part of the price of the computer system.
2 **Software houses** – a software house is a commercial organization specializing in the design and preparation of software packages.
3 Within the computer installation.

Programs would not normally be included in the library unless they are:

1 Full tested.
2 Properly documented.

The programs and their documentation would be kept up to date by the computing department. They would receive updates from the people who produce the software.

14.1 Evaluation and Use of Software

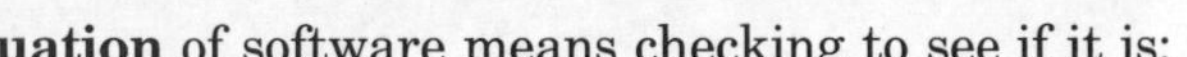

Evaluation of software means checking to see if it is:

1 Of a good standard.
2 Suitable for a particular application.

Candidates need to evaluate and to use software as part of their coursework. Projects and coursework are also dealt with more generally at the end of the book.

GCSE COURSEWORK

As a GCSE candidate part of your coursework will consist of using a computer to solve a problem. One way you can do this is by writing one or more programs. Alternatively you can, if you prefer, use existing software.

The idea of giving you the choice of using an existing package or writing one yourself is that it is realistic. You are faced with the same kind of situation as people solving problems in business and industry:

1 You have a problem to solve.
2 You design a solution (see Unit 10.2).
3 You investigate what software is available for this kind of application.
4 Having found a possible package you evaluate it – you see whether it is suitable.
5 If the package is satisfactory, then you use it to solve your problem. If no known package is satisfactory, then a program has to be written.

EVALUATION OF SOFTWARE

To see whether a package is suitable for a given problem you should:

1 Read the documentation to see whether:
   (a) The program can be used to solve the sort of problem you have in mind.
   (b) It is easy to use. Does it tell you clearly what to do? Is it easy to look up things you want to know? Are there good examples?
2 Run the program. Think of some suitable test data first. The data should be chosen to investigate all aspects of the program.
   (a) Is the program user friendly?
      (i) Are the messages clear? When data has to be entered, is it easy to understand what is required?

(ii) Does it sometimes make you wait an unreasonably long time or without explanation?
(iii) Does it make you do more typing than is necessary?
(iv) Can you get the program to do what you want?
(b) Are the methods of input and output the best for your problem? If the program is interactive, is the way you interact with it suitable? A program can be 'driven' in several different ways:
(i) By menu. Whenever the user needs to make a decision a set of choices appears on the screen and the user takes one of them.
(ii) By command. The user types a command whenever he/she wants a change in action. This may involve typing words or just pressing function keys on the keyboard. This method requires the user to know what the commands are. You should see whether it is easy to find out what they are if you forget. Possible methods of finding the commands might be:
A 'HELP' command you can type to obtain a list of commands. A reference card with the commands on it, supplied with the manual.
A system for labelling keys on the keyboard so that their function is clear.
In any case you should check that the method used is reasonable.
(iii) By icons. Often accompanied by use of a mouse.
In this case you should check that the meaning of all the icons is clear.
(See Unit 7.4 for mouse, Unit 8.1 for icons.)
(d) Is the program robust? A program is **robust** if it can cope with errors in data while it is running.

Try to make the program go wrong. Enter incorrect data for each response.

A good program will validate all data before processing it. If the data is not sensible, it should find this out and ask you to re-type it.
(e) Is the program versatile and adaptable? Can it cope with a variety of different situations?
(f) Is the program reliable? A program is **reliable** if it does what the manual says it does.

If your project is to design and write a software package yourself be sure to apply the above tests to your own program. For example, a programming project should be provided with good documentation and the program should be robust and user friendly.

In writing a program it is important to remember that compilers and interpreters are software packages. These also have to be evaluated. At school you may have little choice in this but in business or industry it is an important decision:
1 Which operating system to use. **2** At what level to program – high or low. **3** Which language to use. **4** Whether to use a compiler or an interpreter. **5** Which compiler or interpreter to use. There are often several different compilers of the same language available for a given machine.

USE OF PACKAGES

Because this topic is particularly important to candidates' project work the examples have been looked at from the point of view of two GCSE candidates.

Examples of use of software packages decided in projects

Spreadsheet

For a GCSE project, Caroline decided to produce price lists for her mother, who is a photographer. Her mother charges for weddings as follows. There is a set fee (at present £80). Customers then pay for each batch of 10 prints. VAT then has to be added at 17.5 per cent.

Caroline's idea was to make the computer print out a table showing the cost to the customer for different numbers of prints.

She investigated the idea of writing a BASIC program to do this. However, this seemed quite difficult and would take a long time to do. She finally decided to use a **spreadsheet** package.

A **spreadsheet** is a program which provides the user with a large grid. The rows and columns are numbered or lettered so that the user can refer to the slots in the grid (see Fig. 14.1). For example if the columns are lettered A,B,C, . . . and the rows are numbered 1,2,3,4 . . . then the 3rd slot across in the 4th row down is referred to as slot C4.

Each slot in the spreadsheet can be filled by one of:
1 A label, i.e. a word or words, usually used to describe the purpose of a row or a column.
2 A value, i.e. a number,
3 A formula. This enables the user to define how slots are linked together. Thus if slot D1 is always found as the sum of slot B1 and slot C1 then slot D1 can have the formula B1+C1 put into it.

With the spreadsheet program Caroline used, it is possible to **replicate** slots. This means that slots can be copied into other slots. Formulae can also be replicated **relative**. This means the formula is not copied exactly but changes as you go across a row or down a column.

Thus if slot D1 contains B1+C1
slot D2 becomes B2+C2
slot D3 becomes B3+C3, etc.

The spreadsheet Caroline produced was as shown in Fig. 14.1.

	A	B	C	D	E
1	*No. of*	*Set*	*Prints*	*VAT*	*TOTAL*
2	*prints*	*fee £*	*cost £*	*£*	*COST £*
3	10	80.00	12.00	16.10	108.10
4	20	80.00	24.00	18.20	122.20
5	30	80.00	36.00	20.30	136.20
6	40	80.00	48.00	22.40	150.40
7	50	80.00	60.00	24.50	164.50
8	60	80.00	72.00	26.60	178.60
9	70	80.00	84.00	28.70	192.70
10	80	80.00	96.00	30.80	206.80
11	90	80.00	108.00	32.90	220.90
12	100	80.00	120.00	35.00	235.00

Fig.14.1 Caroline's spreadsheet

The rows and columns took a long time to work out because it is planned so that it can be changed easily. This is so that if any of the prices change not many changes have to be made to the spreadsheet. She actually wrote the spreadsheet as in Fig. 14.2.

	A	B	C	D	E
1	*No. of*	*Set*	*Prints*	*VAT*	*TOTAL*
2	*prints*	*fee £*	*cost £*	*£*	*COST £*
3	10	80.00	A3*1.2 (B3+C3)	*.175	B3+C3+D3
4	A3+10	B3			
5					
6					
7					
8					
9					
10					
11					
12					

Fig. 14.2 The formulae used for Caroline's spreadsheet

In the package Caroline used, the formulae did not actually appear in the slots, but they have been shown here to show how it was done. The formulae were worked out as follows:

1 The prints cost £1.20 each so the formula for C3 is A3*1.2.

2 VAT is 17.5 per cent of the sum of the Set Fee and the Prints Cost. Seventeen and a half per cent is the same as 0.175 so the formula for D3 is (B3+C3)*0.175.

3 The Total Cost=Set Fee+Prints Cost+VAT. The formula for E3 is B3+C3+D3.

4 The number of prints in column A increases by 10 for each row down. The formula for A4 is A3+ 10.

5 The 'Set fee' in column B does not change. The formula for B4 is just B3.

Caroline then obtained formulae for all the other slots by replicating the ones done already. Fig. 14.3 shows the formulae after this had been done.

	A	B	C	D	E
1	*No. of*	*Set*	*Prints*	*VAT*	*TOTAL*
2	*prints*	*fee £*	*cost £*	*£*	*COST £*
3	10	80.00	A3*1.2	(B3+C3)*.175	B3+C3+D3
4	A3+10	B3	A4*1.2	(B4+C4)*.175	B4+C4+D4
5	A4+10	B4	A5*1.2	(B5+C5)*.175	B5+C5+D5
6	A5+10	B5	A6*1.2	(B6+C6)*.175	B6+C6+D6
7	A6+10	B6	A7*1.2	(B7+C7)*.175	B7+C7+D7
8	A7+10	B7	A8*1.2	(B8+C8)*.175	B8+C8+D8
9	A8+10	B8	A9*1.2	(B9+C9)*.175	B9+C9+D9
10	A9+10	B9	A10*1.2	(B10+C10)*.175	B10+C10+D10
11	A10+10	B10	A11*1.2	(B11+C11)*.175	B11+C11+D11
12	A11+10	B11	A12*1.2	(B12+C12)*.175	B12+C12+D12

Fig. 14.3 Caroline's spreadsheet after all the formulae have been replicated

The computer was then given the instruction to calculate the spreadsheet. This produced the full table with numbers shown in Fig. 14.1.

Finally the spreadsheet was printed out but without the letters A,B,C . . . above the columns or the row numbers.

File handling

There are many program packages which allow the user to:
1 Design and create data files.
2 Retrieve selected information from these files.

These may be described as **file management** or **file enquiry** or even **database** packages. The title 'database package' is really too grand for many of these, particularly those for microcomputers. (See Unit 13.7 for database management packages.)

Chris wanted to create a file containing details of his music collection. This consists of records, cassettes and a few compact discs, as his parents have a CD player. His idea was to store data describing each album and where it is kept in his music cupboard. He would then be able to retrieve information such as:
1 Where an album is kept or
2 How many albums there are by a particular artist, etc.

Chris tried to design a program which would store the data in a sequential file. He would write three separate programs:
1 To create the file in the first place.
2 To update the file. **3** To retrieve data from it.

The second of these programs was going to be difficult because a sequential file cannot be updated directly. A new file has to be written each time (see Unit 13.4). Chris did not know how to program direct access files. Also the third program was going to be long if it was going to allow the user a large number of choices.

Chris's teacher then showed him a file enquiry package which seemed to do all the things that Chris wanted. He decided to use it.

He then had to carry out the following steps, using the manual and the instructions from the program:

1 To run the program taking the 'FILE CREATE' option. Then type in as requested:

Filename	:	CHRISMUSIC
Maximum number of records	:	50
Number of fields	:	6

2 To define the different fields in one record of the file. The program asked for:
(a) The name of the field – this would be used later when retrieving information.
(b) Its length – the largest number of characters in the field.
(c) A description – this is an explanation that the user can read if it is not clear what a field represents.

Chris typed these in as follows –

Fieldname	*Fieldlength*	*Description*
TITLE	20	Title of the album
ARTIST	20	Singer or group
LABEL	12	Producing company
MEDIUM	1	T(Tape cassette), R(Record) or C(Compact Disc)
YEAR	4	Year of production
SLOT	2	Number of slot in music cupboard

3 To type in the actual data. The computer goes through the file requesting data. The first few records which Chris typed in are given below:

```
RECORD NO.    1
  TITLE       ?   ACHTUNG BABY!
  ARTIST      ?   U2
  LABEL       ?   ISLAND
  MEDIUM      ?   R
  YEAR        ?   1991
  SLOT        ?   11

RECORD NO.    2
  TITLE       ?   DIAMONDS AND PEARLS
  ARTIST      ?   PRINCE
  LABEL       ?   PAISLEY PARK
  MEDIUM      ?   C
  YEAR        ?   1991
  SLOT        ?   15

RECORD NO.    3
  TITLE       ?   STARS
  ARTIST      ?   SIMPLY RED
  LABEL       ?   EAST WEST
  MEDIUM      ?   T
  YEAR        ?   1991
  SLOT        ?   3
```

RECORD NO.	4	
TITLE	?	GREATEST HITS
ARTIST	?	DIANA ROSS
LABEL	?	MOTOWN
MEDIUM	?	R
YEAR	?	1990
SLOT	?	11

Once the data was entered Chris could easily update any records using the 'EDIT' facility on the program.

He was also able to make enquiries about the file as follows:

1 The program has a 'FIND' option which will find all the records which fit a given set of conditions.

2 It also has a 'PRINT' option so that only some of the field are printed. For example, with the instructions:

PRINT : TITLE, ARTIST, YEAR, SLOT
FIND : ((YEAR=1991) OR (YEAR=1990)) AND MEDIUM=T

Chris was able to find all his cassettes which were produced in 1991 or 1990. The records found with this enquiry included:

TITLE	ARTIST	YEAR	SLOT
STARS	SIMPLY RED	1991	3
SEAL	SEAL	1990	4
WE CAN'T DANCE	GENESIS	1991	4

Both Caroline and Chris had to produce a fully documented project including a report on what they did, their test data and evidence of their output. Details of what to do to produce this type of project are given later under the heading *Projects and Coursework* at the end of the book.

14.2 Applications Programs and Systems Programs

Software programs are usually one of two types: applications programs or systems programs.

APPLICATIONS PROGRAMS

An **applications program** is a specialized program which allows a computer to be used for a specific application. An **applications package** is an applications program or set of programs together with all the documentation for its use (see Unit 10.6 for documentation).

Examples of applications programs

1 A payroll program. As this is a common requirement for a firm, there are many payroll programs to choose from.

2 A **desktop publishing (DTP)** package. This is a program which makes it possible to produce text and pictures and to organise them into pages to produce newspapers, posters, books, etc. Usually a DTP package makes use of a mouse and a laser printer.

3 A program to produce graphs of experimental results for a research biologist. This is a more specialized type of program and may have to be specially written.

SYSTEMS PROGRAMS

A **systems program** is one of the programs which controls the performance of a computer system or provides commonly used facilities. Systems software is frequently supplied by the computer manufacturer.

Examples of systems programs

1 A compiler (see Unit 11.2).
2 A trace program (see Unit 12.2).
3 The operating system of a computer (see Unit 14.3).

A **utility program** is a systems program which performs one, usually simple, task.

Examples of utility programs

1 A program to transfer data files from a magnetic tape to a disc.
2 A program to transfer the contents of a VDU screen to a printer (often called a **screendump**).
3 A program to sort a file so that the keys are in numerical order (see Unit 13.5).
4 A program to merge two files into one large file (see Unit 13.5).

14.3 Operating Systems

An **operating system** is software which controls the general operation of a computer. It consists of a set of programs and routines and for large computers is very complex.

Usually part of the operating system is stored in the main store all the time the computer is running. Those parts which are not often used are stored on disc and only loaded when required.

On a microcomputer the operating system is the part of the software which deals with, for example:

1 Instructions to save, load, delete, rename and copy files.
2 Instructions to run and list programs.
3 Error messages telling you a device is not present.

In some microcomputers the operating system is stored on ROM.

PURPOSE OF AN OPERATING SYSTEM

1 To provide a background in which users programs are run.
2 To keep the computer running without the operator having to intervene too much.
3 To make the best use of resources such as the store and the peripherals.

FUNCTIONS OF THE OPERATING SYSTEM

For computers generally

1 To control the use of peripherals such as disc units and printers.
2 To avoid the use of devices which need attention.
3 To control the loading and running of programs.
4 To deal with execution errors, keeping the computer running when they happen.

For larger computers and networks

1 To communicate with users and operators:
(a) Carrying out users' requests.
(b) Carrying out instructions from operators.
(c) Telling operators of necessary actions, such as putting paper in a printer or loading a magnetic tape which is needed by a program.
(d) Producing a log, i.e. a record of the programs as they are run.
2 To maintain security (see item below).
(a) Seeing that users give the right identification and password to use the system.
(b) Checking that users trying to access files have authority to use them.
3 To organize the use of storage. Mainframe computers often have several programs running at the same time. The storage has to be shared between them.
4 To work out what resources have been used by each program. If the user is paying for the service, then the computer works out the cost of running the program and charges the appropriate account.

SECURITY

A large computer system may have many users and many access points such as terminals. Use has to be restricted.

Only certain people are allowed to use the system. Each one of these needs:

1 A **user identification (or ID)**. This is a name or number by which the system knows that user. Each user is given an area of backing store in which to store files. Usually the user can decide which other users can access these files.
2 A **password**. A **password** is a set of characters which a computer associates with a particular user ID. The password is known only to the user and usually he or she selects it. A password is usually kept secret and the computer does not display it on the screen as it is typed in.

Users of a multi-access system (see Unit 15.4) have to **log in** and **log out** every time they use it.

To **log in** means to gain access to a system by giving the correct instructions and responses. This usually includes typing in a user ID and password.

To **log out** means to exit from a system by giving the correct instructions. This usually includes typing some instructions such as 'BYE' or 'EXIT'.

15 PROCESSING SYSTEMS

There are many different ways of organizing a computer system. Anyone designing a system has to decide on:
1 The hardware – computers, storage, input and output devices.
2 Communications – between computers and between terminals and computers.
3 The operating system – this very important software organizes the running of the computer system (see Unit 14.3).
4 Other software – this includes utilities, languages and applications programs.

15.1 Real-time Processing

A **real-time** system is one which processes data without significant delay.

CHARACTERISTICS OF REAL-TIME SYSTEMS

1 The computer is waiting for input. As soon as the data is received it is processed, and results can be output straight away.
2 Because the output can be produced quickly it may be used to influence the input. For example, if a computer oversteers a spaceship (example 5 below) it can be adjusted back before any harm is done.
3 The computer is usually running the same program all the time. In fact the computer is often **dedicated** to the real-time application.
A **dedicated processor** is one which is working on a particular application and on nothing else. It just runs the same program all the time.

Examples of real-time systems

1 An analogue computer (see Unit 4).
2 A machine controlled by a computer, e.g. a 'robot' used in car manufacture.
3 A network controlled by a computer, e.g. the pipelines and pumping stations owned by a Gas Board. The controlling computer communicates with the stations by microwave transmissions at regular intervals, and pressures are adjusted when necessary. (See Fig. 20.1)
4 An interactive game where the user has to react to what is happening on a computer screen by pressing keys quickly.
5 A computer controlling a space flight.
6 An airline flight-booking system.

Advantages and disadvantages of real-time processing

Advantage

Fast response. Output from the computer may be used to adjust and improve the input.

Disadvantage

A computer being used for a real-time application often cannot be used for anything else.

15.2 Single-User Systems – Microcomputers

A **single-user system** is one where only one person can use the computer at a time, interacting directly with its operating system to run programs. Microcomputers are usually used in this way. A typical system would have a keyboard, a screen, a floppy disc unit and a character printer.

Examples of the use of a microcomputer as a single-user system

1 As a 'home' computer.
2 In a newsagent's shop to store details of the newspapers required by customers, to organize the newspaper rounds and to work out customers' accounts.
3 In an office as a word processor (see Unit 18.4).

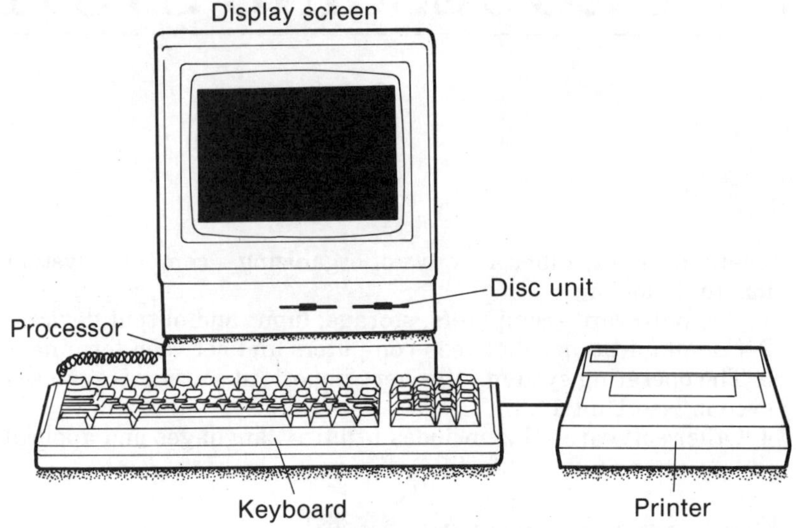

Fig. 15.1 A typical single-user system based on a microcomputer

Advantages and disadvantages of single-user systems

Advantages

1 Inexpensive – cheap enough to be used:
 (a) As a home computer.
 (b) By a small business.
 (c) In schools for teaching and administration purposes.
 (d) Dedicated to one application, such as process control or word-processing.
2 The user has better control over:
 (a) The uses to which the computer is put.
 (b) What changes are made to the system.
 (c) Security.
 (d) Maintenance.
3 Mobile and small – a microcomputer can be:
 (a) Moved from place to place.
 (b) Attached to equipment in order to control it.
4 Robust and reliable – microcomputers can function in more variable conditions than larger computers.

Disadvantages

In comparison with a mainframe computer a single-user system often has:
1 Slower processing.
2 Less storage.
3 Fewer and slower peripherals.
4 Less sophisticated software.

These disadvantages can be partly overcome if the single-user system is able to communicate with larger systems. For example, it may be used as a workstation in a network (see Unit 15.5).

15.3 Batch Processing

A **batch processing** system is one where programs and data are collected together in a batch before processing starts. Each piece of work for the computer to do is called a **job**. Often a job just consists of a program to be run and the data for it. A **job queue** is a number of jobs waiting to be processed.

CHARACTERISTICS OF BATCH PROCESSING SYSTEMS

1 Jobs are stored in job queues until the computer is ready to deal with them.
2 There is no interaction between the user and the computer while the program is being run. Computers which do batch processing often operate all night so the user might be at home asleep.
3 Batch processing is often used where a large amount of data has to be processed on a regular

basis. The program is not changed and it is so routine that there is no need for anyone to be present while the program is running.
4 Batch processing is normally done on large mainframe computers.

The following is a typical way of preparing and running batch jobs (see also Fig. 15.2):
1 The user writes out what has to be done on pre-printed sheets.
2 A keyboard operator prepares and verifies the work by key-to-disc or key-to-tape.
3 The job is put together with other jobs and input to the computer.
4 The job waits in a queue and is then processed.
5 The output is stored on disc (or 'spooled') and then printed later.
6 The printout is returned to the user.

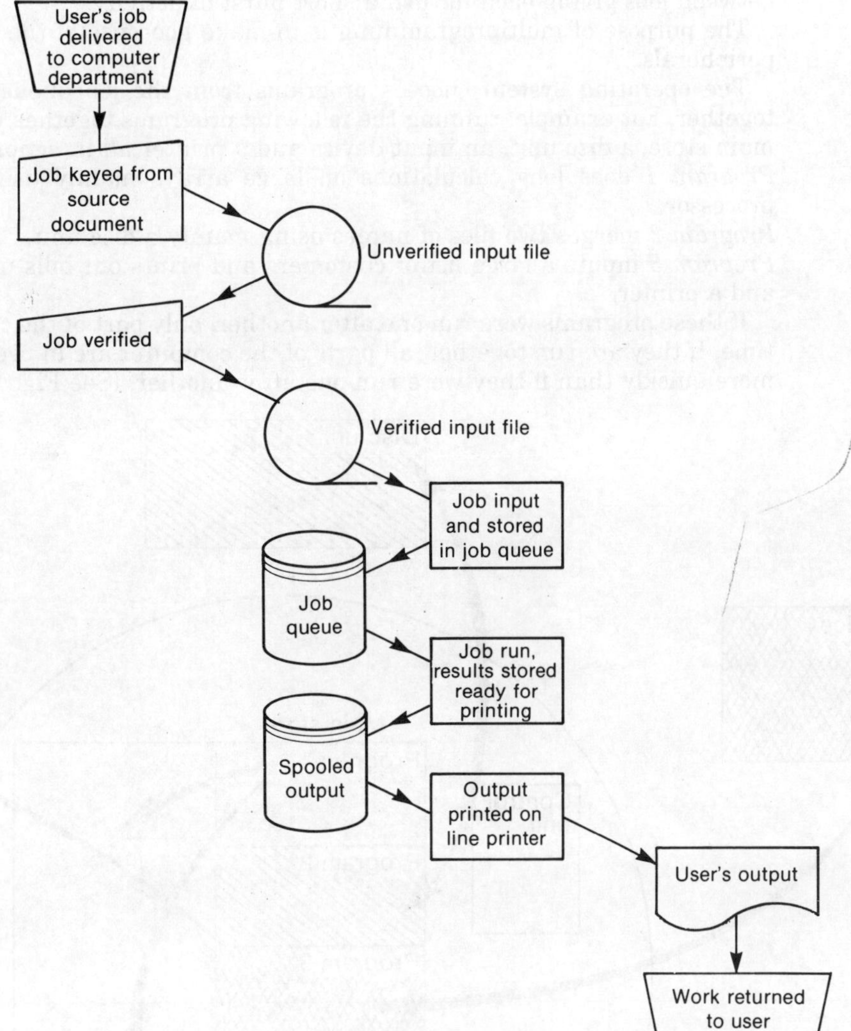

Fig. 15.2 Example of a batch processing system (system flowchart). In this example jobs are keyed onto magnetic tape and discs are used for spooling work before and after processing

Examples where batch processing would be used

1 A weekly payroll run (see Fig. 10.3 for system flowchart).
2 A run at a Gas Board to produce bills for customers. The input data is a batch of meter reading slips completed in pencil by the meter reader and accompanied by a batch header.
3 An updating run in which a transaction file is used to update a master file (see Fig. 13.1).
4 A programmer developing a batch program edits it on-line at a terminal and then uses the terminal to submit the program into a batch job queue.

Advantages and disadvantages of batch processing

Advantages

1 There is no need for the user to be present when the job is run.
2 Preparing the work and operating the computer are done by trained people and not by the user.
3 Less expensive than time-sharing on large systems.

Disadvantages

1 There is always a delay before work is processed and returned.
2 The user cannot take action if anything is wrong – he has to re-input the job.
3 Batch processing usually involves an expensive computer and a large staff.

MULTIPROGRAMMING

Large computers used for batch processing often employ a technique known as **multi-programming**.

Multiprogramming is a process which enables two or more jobs to run, apparently at the same time. In fact, the computer can only execute one program at a time. It actually switches between jobs giving each in turn a short burst of activity.

The purpose of multiprogramming is to make good use of the processor, the store and the peripherals.

The operating system chooses programs from the job queue which are suitable to run together. For example, running the following programs together would keep the processor, its main store, a disc unit, an input device and a printer all in action:

Program 1 does long calculations on large arrays mainly using the main store and the processor.

Program 2 merges two files of names using mainly a disc unit.

Program 3 inputs a large list of customers and prints out bills using mainly an input device and a printer.

If these programs were run one after another, only part of the computer would be busy each time. If they are run together, all parts of the computer are in use. The three jobs are finished more quickly than if they were run one after another. (See Fig. 15.3.)

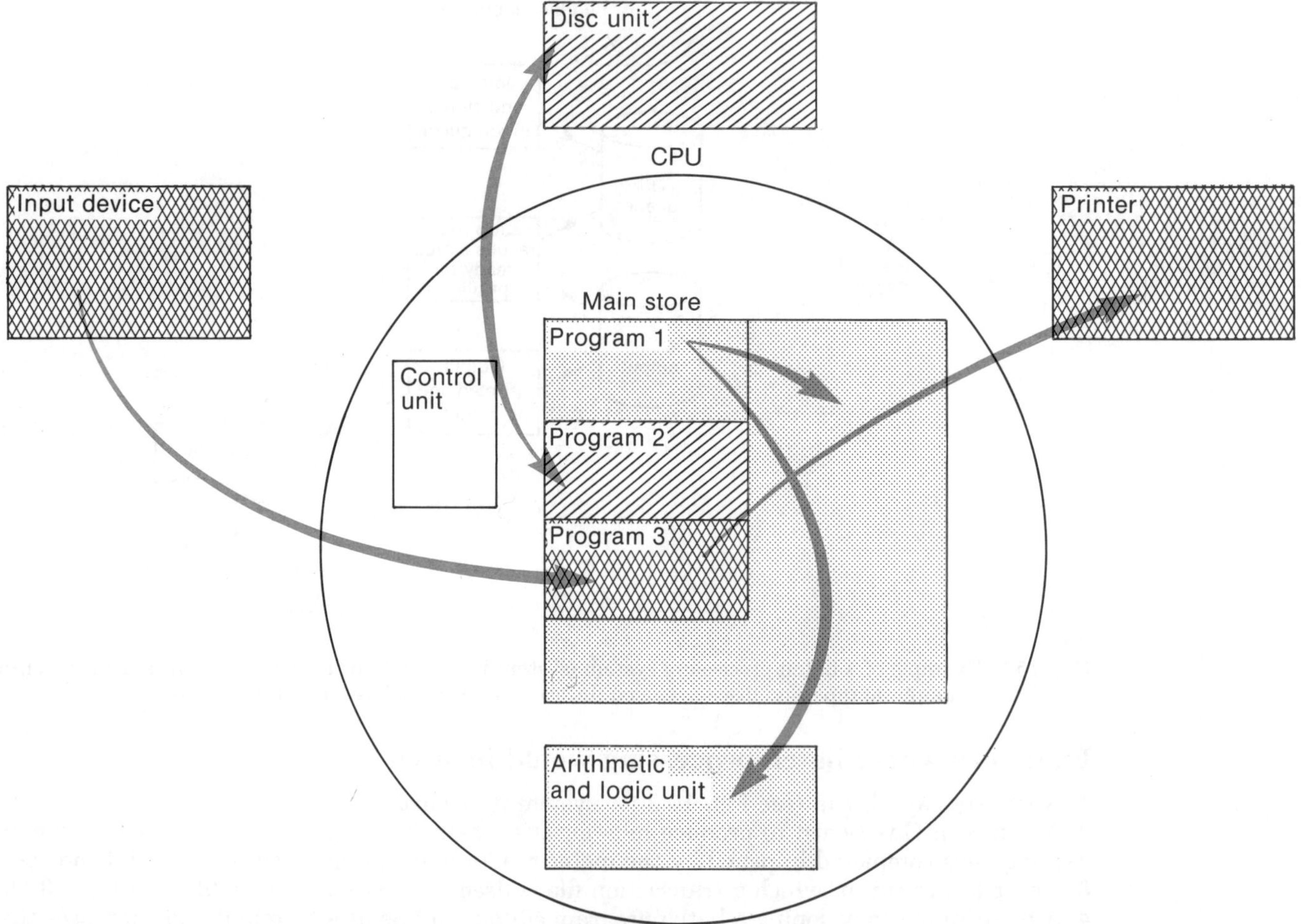

Fig. 15.3 Multiprogramming – use of resources by programs 1,2,3

15.4 Multi-access Systems

A **multi-access** system is one which allows a number of users with on-line terminals to interact with the same computer at the same time. (See Fig 15.4.) Use of a terminal to a multi-access system is called **on-line interactive computing**.

In fact, the computer can only run one program at a time. However, it is so fast compared with the terminals that it can do work for each terminal very quickly one after the other. Usually each user is able to interact with the computer as if he or she were the only user.

RESPONSE TIME

The **response time** of a multi-access system is the time the computer takes to start an operation which is requested. Usually it is the time between pressing the 'RETURN' key and getting a reply.

If a computer has too little processing power for the number of terminals on-line, it can happen that the response becomes very slow.

TIME-SHARING

One way of organizing a computer for multi-access is by **time-sharing**. Time-sharing is a system where the computer allows each terminal in turn a small amount of processing time before it goes on to the others.

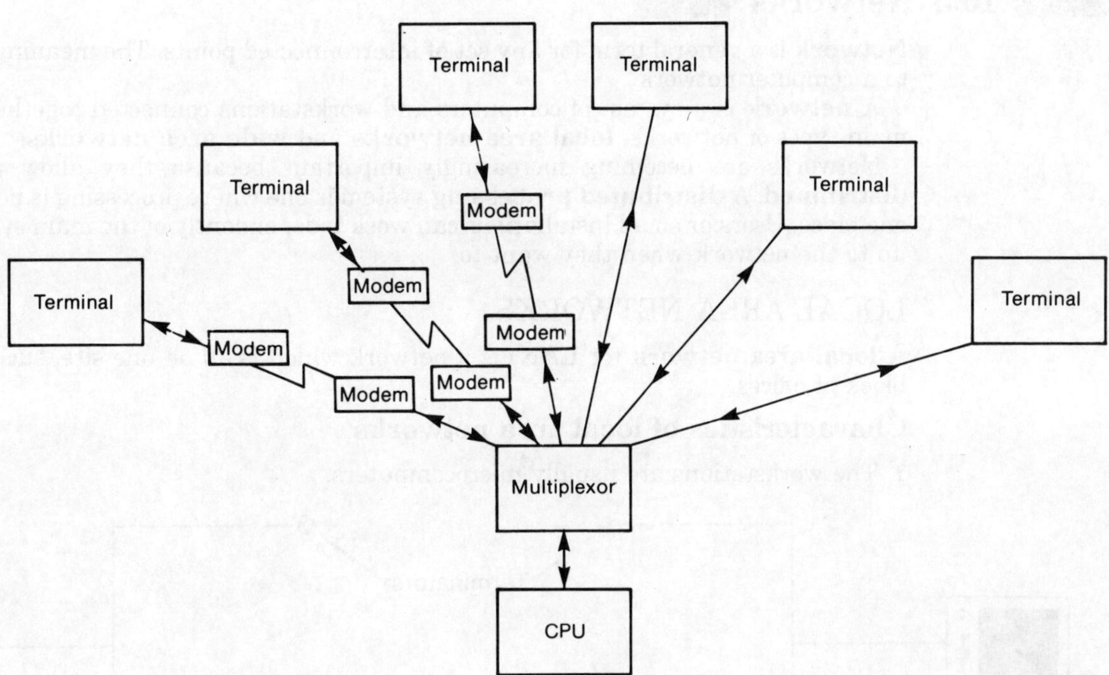

Fig. 15.4 Example of a multi-access system (hardware). In different systems the terminals may vary in type and number (see Unit 6.). They may be connected to the computer by any of a number of different methods (see Unit 6.3). The diagram shows a system with six terminals, of which three are connected directly to a multiplexor, and three are connected using modems and telephone lines

Examples of multi-access systems

1 An on-line airline flight-booking system. (See Unit 17.3.) This is an example of a multi-access system which is also a real-time system. If a ticket is booked from a terminal, this will be put into effect immediately. If someone else then tries to book the same seat from another terminal, they will be told it is taken.
2 A university or polytechnic main computer with a large number of terminals. Many of the users would be students learning to program. Most of their terminals would be linked to the computer directly by cable.
3 A national network such as CAMPUS 2000. Most of the users of this system are schools using the telephone system via a modem. They usually use microcomputers programmed to act as terminals.
4 Bank cash points. These are in fact cash issuing terminals connected to the bank's main computer (see Unit 6.2).

Advantages and disadvantages of multiple access

Advantages

1 Allows interactive use of a powerful computer.
2 Can be used at large distances from the computer (e.g. using modems and a telephone line).
3 Needs little action by computer operators.

Disadvantages

1 Time consuming for the user, who has to be available to run the program.
2 Response time may be too slow for many real-time operations.
3 It is often not practical to run jobs with large amounts of input or output data.

INTERACTIVE COMPUTING

Interactive computing is a method of computer use where the user and the computer communicate with one another in the form of a conversation.

Examples of interactive computing

1 On-line conversational use of a terminal which is linked to a time-sharing system.
2 Using a microcomputer via a keyboard and screen.

15.5 Networks

Network is a general term for any set of interconnected points. The meaning used here refers to a computer network.

A **network** is a system of computers and workstations connected together. There are two main types of networks, **local area networks** and **wide area networks**.

Networks are becoming increasingly important because they allow processing to be **distributed**. A **distributed processing** system is one where processing is not concentrated at one place. Users or small installations can work independently of the main system but can link up to the network when they want to.

LOCAL AREA NETWORKS

A **local area network** (or **LAN**) is a network which is all on one site, such as a school or a block of offices.

Characteristics of local area networks

1 The workstations are usually microcomputers.

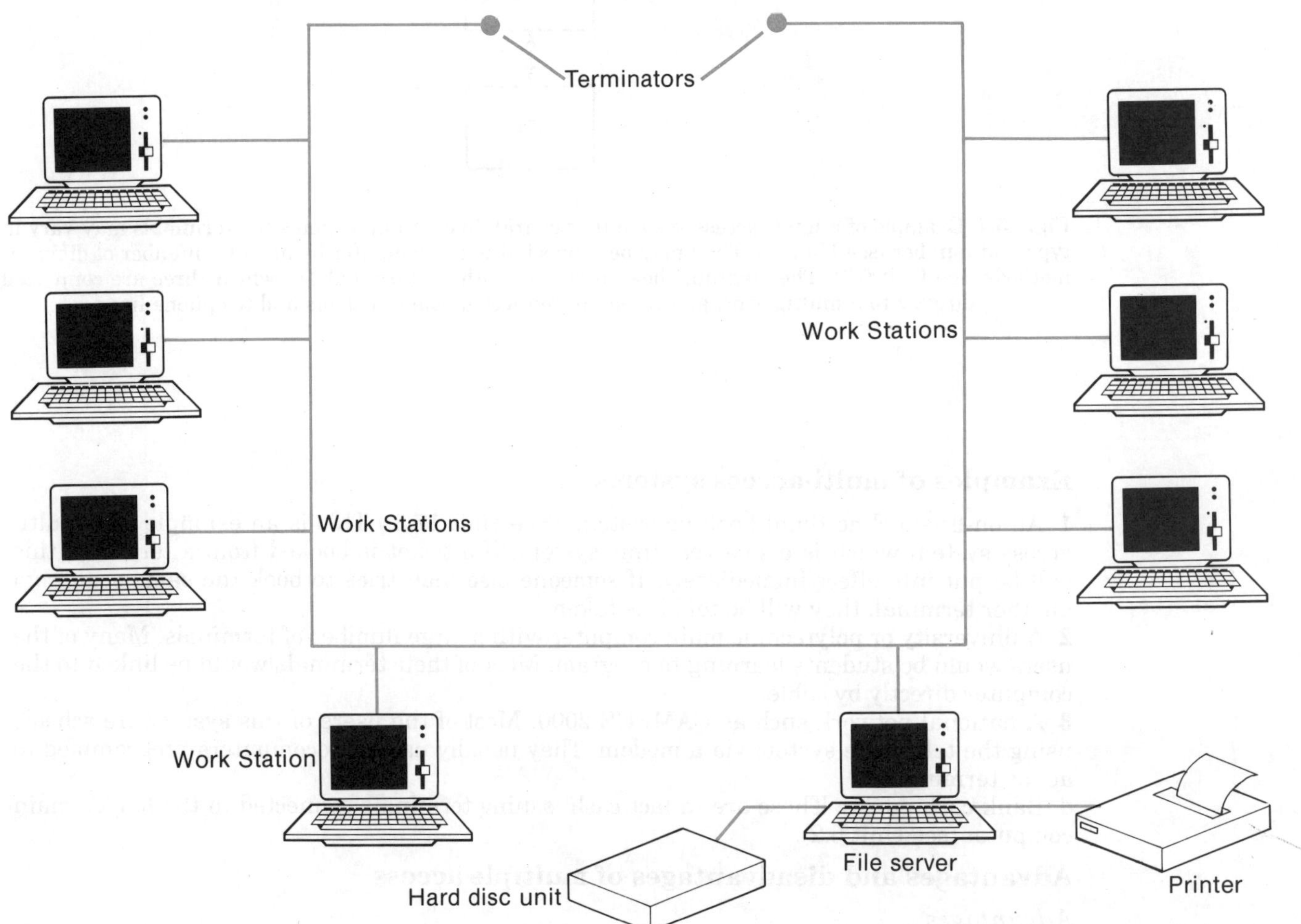

Fig. 15.5 Diagram of a typical local area network. In this example there is only one file server, which also serves the only printer. More printers, disc units, file servers and work stations can be added

2 The communication between workstations is usually along cables.
3 The network usually contains peripherals such as hard-disc units and printers to which all users have access via the network.
4 There is no central powerful computer (see multi-access systems in Unit 15.4). The workstations can operate on their own, without the network. However, there may be one or more stations dedicated to controlling the work of the main disc unit(s) and printer(s).

A **file server** is a computer on a network dedicated to handling users' files.

A local network may be arranged in various ways. Fig. 15.5 shows the type of network common in schools. The stations are all connected to one cable. Each end of the cable has a terminator. The example shown has one computer controlling both the printer and the hard-disc unit. Other networks may not have this arrangement.

Examples of local area networks

1 In a school (see Fig. 15.5). The stations are microcomputers and the network has a dot-matrix printer and a hard-disc unit. Most of the computers are in one room but the file server is in a separate office. There is also one workstation at the front of a classroom with a large screen so that the teacher can show it to a whole class. The network is used by Computer Studies pupils to do coursework and also by classes in other subjects.
2 In the Business Studies department of a college. The workstations are microcomputers used mainly for word-processing. The network has a laser printer which can produce high-quality printing of letters. A hard-disc unit is used mainly for storing files of text.
3 In a small company which sells, services and repairs cars. Each office has a workstation and so do the stores, the salesroom and the service area. The system is used mainly to deal with:
(a) Communication between management and secretaries dealing with correspondence.
(b) Stock control for parts in the stores.
(c) Sales of cars.

For example, the stations in the stores and service areas are usually running a stock control program. However, they can, if necessary, interrupt this and send messages to sales or office staff.

Advantages and disadvantages of local area networks

Advantages

1 The workstations are usually separate computers. If the network breaks down, they can each still be used on their own.
2 The stations can share peripherals. Disc units and printers can be of better quality because they do not have to be bought for each station.
3 Users do not need to have separate discs. They can sit down at any of the work stations and access their own files from the file server.
4 A number of stations can all access and run the same program.
5 The stations can communicate with one another.

Disadvantages

1 If the file server for a network breaks down, the users will have no files to work with. However, they may still be able to use the stations as separate computers.
2 If only a small number of stations is required, then a network is expensive. The file server is usually more expensive than an ordinary station. It is also usually dedicated to the network and cannot be used for anything else while the network is running.

WIDE AREA NETWORKS

A **wide area network** (or **WAN**) is a network which connects large numbers of computers and terminals over long distances. (See Fig. 15.6.)

Characteristics of wide area networks

1 The workstations are terminals or microcomputers.
2 The network is usually nationwide or even worldwide.
3 Computing power for the network may be provided by a number of mainframe computers. These may be remote from one another, connected by high-speed data links.
4 Users will usually be able to connect to a point on the network near to them. For example a user connected by telephone will often be able to make a local call.

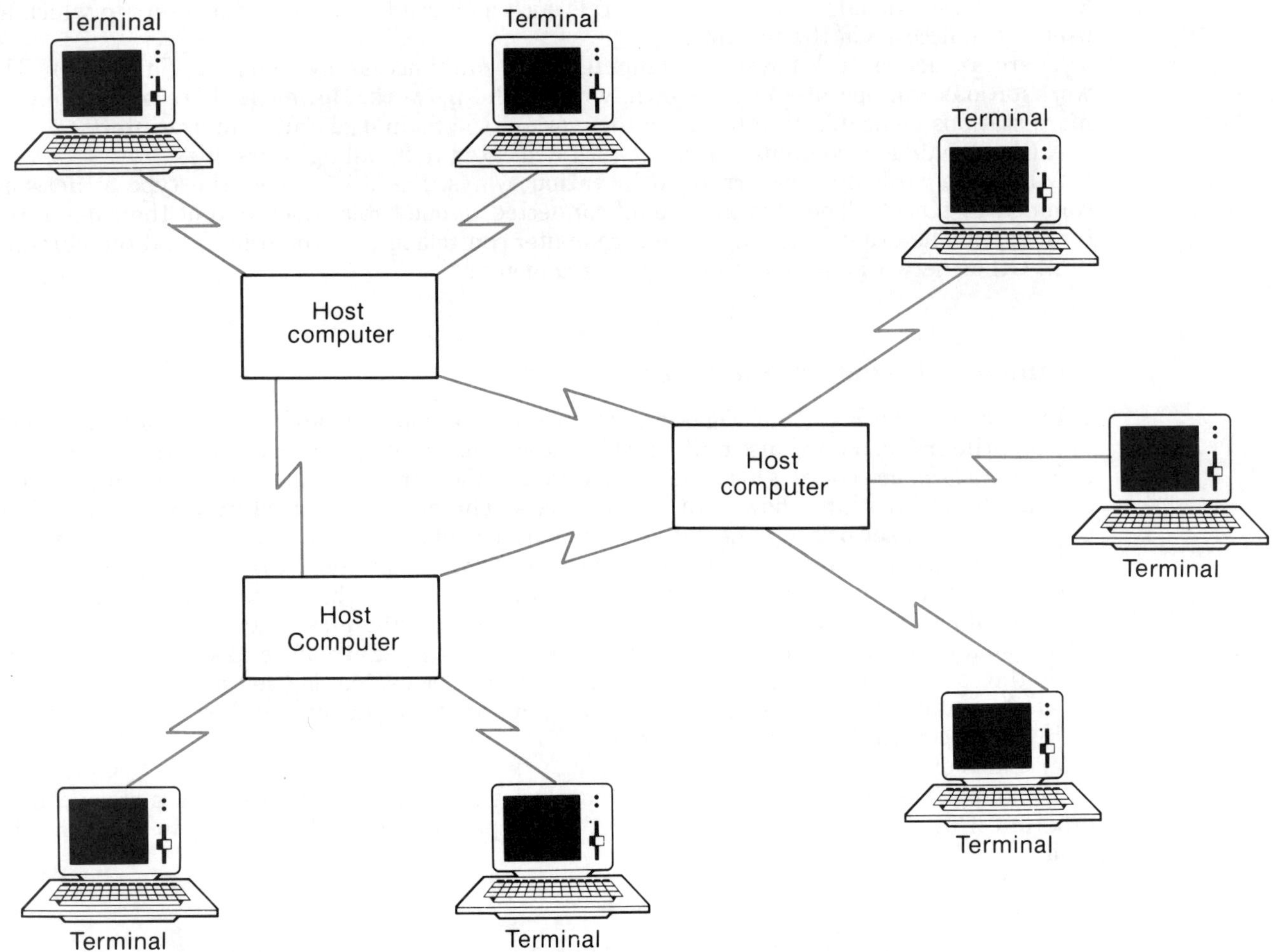

Fig. 15.6 Diagram of a typical wide area network. The network shown has three host computers. A user connects to the nearest host and can then be connected to any other host or leave messages for any other user

Examples of wide area networks

1 A large international company has mainframe computers in a number of countries. These are networked together so that employees in all the countries can:

(a) Communicate with one another by electronic mail (see Unit 18.2).

(b) Keep a personal diary on the network so that other people can easily arrange meetings with them.

(c) Use a noticeboard facility to find out about research, courses, and so on in the other countries.

(d) Use software and databases available anywhere in the company.

2 A public Viewdata network. In Britain (and other countries) there are a number of networks available to the public. They are usually accessed using the telephone system. The user needs a terminal and a modem and has to pay a subscription. Examples are PRESTEL and CAMPUS 2000 – see Unit 18.2 for details.

Advantages and disadvantages of wide area networks

Advantages and disadvantages of viewdata networks are dealt with in Unit 18.3.

Advantages

1 The user has a fast means of communication with other users wherever they are.
2 Access is provided to large databases and other mainframe facilities.

Disadvantage

You can only communicate with someone over the network if they are a member and if they use it regularly.

16 JOBS IN COMPUTING

A very large number of people use computers as part of their work. This unit is about those people whose jobs are entirely concerned with computers and computing. Even here there is a wide variety of jobs. This variety has increased recently with the widespread use of microcomputers and networks. The situation is changing all the time.

For simplicity this unit describes the jobs of people working in a large installation. (See Fig. 16.1.) It is assumed that the department:

1 Designs and maintains much of the software itself.
2 Runs both a batch and a multi-access system.

In a smaller installation there would be fewer employees and some of the jobs would be combined together.

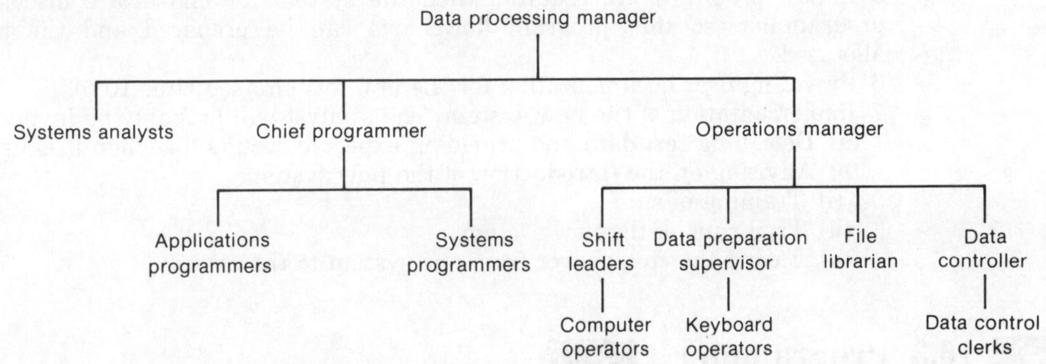

Fig. 16.1 Organization of a fairly large data processing department

16.1 Data Processing Manager

The **data processing manager** (or **DP manager**) is the person responsible for the overall running of a data processing department. In a department too small to have a separate operations manager he/she is often known as the computer manager.

The DP Manager has responsibility for all aspects of the department's work:

1 Design, production, and maintenance of programs.
2 Data preparation.
3 Reception and control of data.
4 Operations.
5 Hardware maintenance.

DUTIES OF A DATA PROCESSING MANAGER

1 Liaison with other departments about computing work to be done for them.
2 Allocation of duties and tasks to staff in the department.
3 Partial responsibility in employing new staff.
4 Meetings with staff to maintain the smooth running of the department.
5 Helping to decide general data processing policy and requesting equipment and other changes if necessary.
6 Keeping up to date with new developments in software and hardware.
7 Working out the cost of running the department.

16.2 Systems Analyst

A **systems analyst** is a person who analyses an information system and considers the practicality of using computers to improve it. Usually if the analyst's report is approved, he/she also designs and helps to implement the new system.

DUTIES OF A SYSTEMS ANALYST (see also Unit 10.2)

1 Defining the client's problem.
2 Analysis of the present system:
(a) Studying documentation of how the system should work.
(b) Observing how it actually works.
(c) Interviewing management and employees.
(d) Preparing a report:
(i) Defining inputs and outputs to the system.
(ii) Detailing the existing resources – hardware, software and people.
(iii) Describing the system with system flowcharts, etc.
3 Carrying out a feasibility study and producing a report:
(a) On making best use of existing resources.
(b) On software and hardware requirements of a new system.
Note: This work is carried out with full discussions, so that positive recommendations can be made with a good chance of acceptance.

If the report is accepted and the systems analyst is to be involved with design and implementation, then the work also includes:
4 Design of the new system including:
(a) Defining methods of data collection and preparation.
(b) Defining all clerical procedures and documents.
(c) The production of system flowcharts and program specifications.
5 If new programs are required then the system flowcharts are discussed with the chief programmer, so that program flowcharts can be prepared and the programming work allocated.
6 Providing user documentation for the new system (see Unit 10.6).
7 Implementation of the new system. The analyst will probably be involved in:
(a) Designing test data and providing expected results for when it is used.
(b) Advising on the introduction of the new system:
(i) Training of staff.
(ii) Trial runs of the new system.
(iii) Easing the changeover from one system to the other.

16.3 Programmer

A **programmer** is a person who produces or amends computer programs.

There are two main types of programmer:
1 Applications programmer – a programmer who writes programs to carry out specific applications for computer users. The applications programmer:
(a) Has to have an understanding of the application itself.
(b) Usually works in a high-level language.
2 Systems programmer – a programmer who writes systems software (see Unit 14.2). The systems programmer:
(a) Has to be very familiar with a particular computer and operating system.
(b) Often works in a low-level language.

DUTIES OF A PROGRAMMER

1 Discussing the program specifications with the designer.
2 Producing detailed program flowcharts.
3 Coding, ie. writing the source program.
4 Testing and debugging.
5 Producing program documentation (see Unit 10.6).
6 Program maintenance:
(a) Eliminating errors not discovered during testing.
(b) Making improvements.
(c) Making modifications to allow for changing business methods or new equipment.

DUTIES OF MORE SENIOR PROGRAMMING STAFF

Many large installations have programmers with special responsibilities. These people may include **senior programmers**, **chief programmers**, perhaps a **programming manager**. Their special duties would include:
1 Liaison with the data processing manager and the operations manager about general programming needs, for example:
(a) Training for junior programmers.
(b) Languages and equipment needed.
(c) Need for more staff.

2 Liaison with systems analysts about programs.
3 Allocation of work to programmers.
4 Supervision of programmers.

Notes:

1 Programmers write programs. They are not usually involved with designing them. Those programmers who are involved with design work are called **analyst/programmers**.
2 Programmers are not usually involved with operating computers.
3 Programmers usually work on a project as a team. This is why it is so important to write good documentation and to produce programs that are easy to understand.

16.4 Operations Manager

The **operations manager** (or **computer manager**) is the person responsible for the day-to-day efficiency of data processing operations.

DUTIES OF AN OPERATIONS MANAGER

1 Supervising and coordinating:
(a) Data reception and control.
(b) Data preparation.
(c) Operations in the computer room
2 Planning:
(a) Organizing the solution of any problems the staff cannot deal with.
(b) Working out procedures to deal with emergencies.
(c) Working out staff timetables.
3 Liaison with the data processing manager or other management staff about, for example:
(a) Staff problems.
(b) Staff training.
(c) Possible improvements in methods of working or in equipment.

16.5 Computer Operating Staff

A **computer operator** is a person who controls and operates the hardware in the computer room.

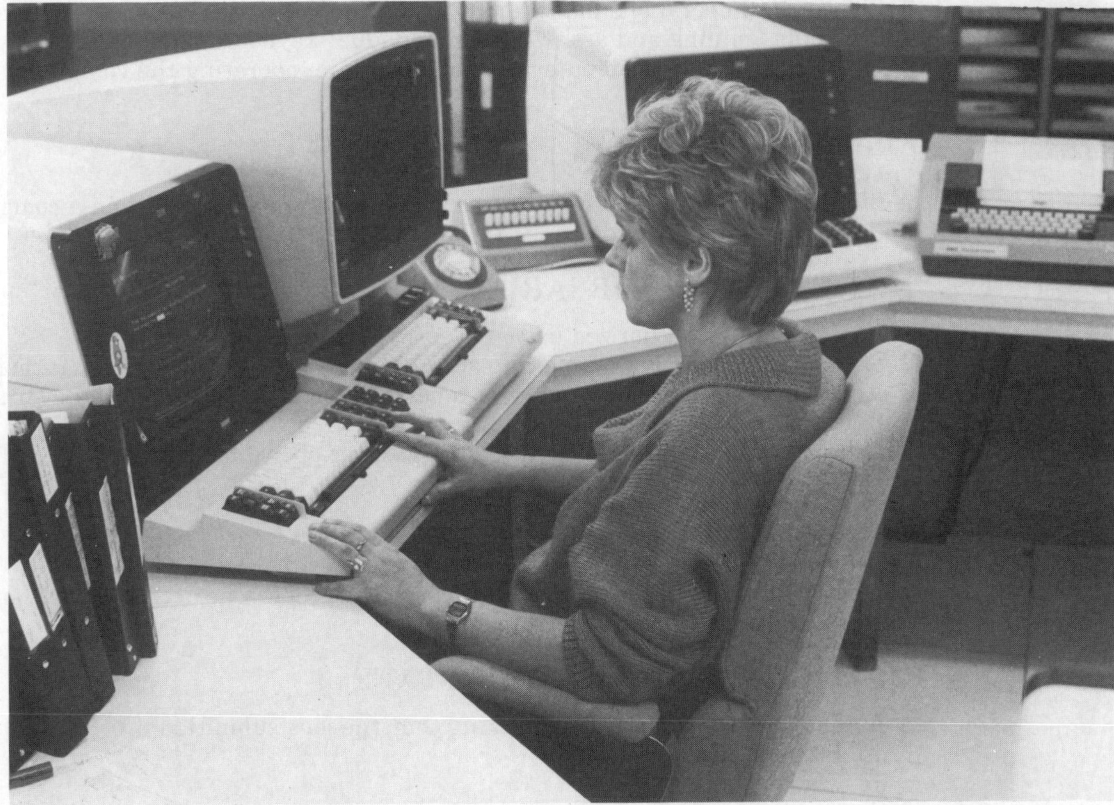

Fig. 16.2 A computer operator at work. The operator is working at a control terminal. Behind her to the right is a printing terminal which is producing a log of the jobs done by the computer. The telephone is for user enquiries. (By kind permission of Marchwood Engineering Laboratories)

DUTIES OF A COMPUTER OPERATOR

1 Starting up the computer.
2 Running programs.
3 Putting materials into appropriate peripherals e.g.
(a) Paper into printers.
(b) Magnetic tapes into tape drives.
Note: This will usually be in response to messages on a terminal. These come from the operating system, but originate from users or from the peripherals themselves.
4 Monitoring the progress of individual jobs and of the computer system in general.
5 Dealing with malfunctions where possible – otherwise reporting them.
6 Carrying out cleaning and simple maintenance.
7 Maintaining a log of what happens to supplement the log produced by the computer.

16.6 Data Preparation Staff

KEYBOARD OPERATOR

A **keyboard operator** is a person who operates a key station to prepare data. The keyboard operator may also be known as a **punch operator** or a **data preparation operator** and may be specialized in the use of one type of data preparation device, for example, a key-to-disc station.

DUTIES OF KEYBOARD OPERATOR

1 Keying in contents of forms or documents.
2 Responding to messages, etc., from the equipment.
3 Keeping a record of data dealt with.
4 Reporting to the supervisor any problems with the data or the equipment.
5 Verification of previously keyed data.

DATA PREPARATION SUPERVISOR

A **data preparation supervisor** is the person responsible for immediate supervision of the data preparation area.

DUTIES OF A DATA PREPARATION SUPERVISOR

1 Allocating work to the keyboard operators.
2 Monitoring the quality of work produced.
3 Liaison with operations manager.
4 Providing training and assistance to individual keyboard operators.
5 In the case of a minicomputer controlled system, operating the computer.

16.7 File Librarian

A **file librarian** is the person who keeps all the tape and disc files in a computer installation up to date and in good order.

DUTIES OF FILE LIBRARIAN

1 Issuing files for authorized use.
2 Storing files securely and making sure they are not available for unauthorized use.
3 Arranging regular maintenance of tapes and discs, i.e. cleaning and overhaul, etc.
4 Keeping records of the files and of their use.
5 Liaison usually with data control supervisor or operations staff.

16.8 Data Control Staff

The **data control staff** in an installation are the people who accept work from users, ensuring that it is processed and returned to them.

DUTIES OF DATA CONTROL STAFF

1 Accepting work from users, checking that the jobs submitted are:
(a) Properly authorized.
(b) Complete.
2 Seeing that work gets to the right place at the right time. Usually this will be either:
(a) The computing area for the job to be run, or
(b) The preparation area for data to be keyed in.
3 Seeing that output is returned to users.

16.9 Engineer

Data processing departments that do not have their own team of engineers will contract out the work to either the hardware manufacturers, the retailers or a specialist maintenance company.

DUTIES OF ENGINEERS

1 Attending to breakdowns. The response to breakdowns must be prompt and in a large computing department there will always need to be one engineer on call.
2 Carrying out preventative maintenance. All the hardware in the department will need regular maintenance in order to cut down the chances of a breakdown. Such maintenance will probably take place monthly.

17 APPLICATIONS OF COMPUTERS – COMMERCIAL APPLICATIONS

A **computer application** is any particular use made of a computer.

A large part of the Scottish Standard and the GCSE Computer Studies syllabuses and examinations are devoted to applications. All of the GCSE syllabuses contain Assessment Objective D of the National Criteria for GCSE Computer Studies. This says that a candidate for GCSE should be able to: 'demonstrate a knowledge and understanding of the range and scope of computer applications'.

It is hoped that you will have already gained this knowledge and understanding by activities during your course. You may have:

1 Been able to go into business or industry and see computers being applied.
2 Watched some of the videos which are available and which give a clear picture of various computer applications.
3 Used some of the software which is available for most school computers to allow you to simulate actual applications.

There follows a list of computing activities to simulate actual applications. Look through the list and try any which you have not already done. Your teacher will help you find out what programs and equipment you can use.

If you have not already done all of your coursework, one of these activities might be turned into a project you can submit.

SUGGESTED ACTIVITIES TO HELP UNDERSTANDING OF APPLICATIONS

1 Run programs to simulate commercial applications such as:

(a) An airline booking system, or
(b) A stock control program.

2 Run programs to simulate any other situation – you may have a program to simulate running the country or perhaps driving a car.
3 Try a file enquiry package – retrieve information from a file. There is probably a sample file supplied with the package. If you have time create a file yourself (see the example project in Unit 14.1).
4 Run a spreadsheet program – (see the example project in Unit 14.1).
5 See and, if possible, use CEEFAX or ORACLE on a television set which has been adapted for teletext.
6 See a microcomputer being used with a modem as a terminal for a viewdata system such as Prestel or The Times Network for Schools. You should look particularly at electronic mail and access to databases.
7 Use a wordprocessor – there should be computers in your school which can be used for wordprocessing.
8 Run a computer-aided design (CAD) package. There is a temptation to doodle with this type of package. Find or sketch a definite design or drawing and then try to produce it on the screen.
9 See if you can get a computer to input data from an external measuring device. Some schools have interfaces which can be connected to a computer – often in one of the science departments. These can be connected up to a digital thermometer for instance but you need the right software as well as hardware. Other schools have little robots with light sensitive devices. In any case you will need a teacher's help with this.
10 Control an external device with a computer – the robot mentioned above would do. Failing this you might be able to obtain software which simulates controlling a device such as a crane, for instance.

The applications corresponding to these activities are explained in Unit 14.1 (spreadsheet and file enquiry) and in Units 17 to 20 inclusive. The applications described in Units 17 to 20 follow fairly closely the lists given in most of the GCSE syllabuses.

It is important to understand the general principles of a given application and not concentrate on the particular equipment used. The work in Units 1 to 16 should help you to understand these better.

COMMERCIAL AND ADMINISTRATIVE DATA PROCESSING

Computers were first used commercially in the 1950s. The computers were expensive and were used by large companies to carry out routine tasks such as:
1 Stock control – checking and reordering goods.
2 Payroll – calculating the employees' pay each week or each month.
3 Customer accounts – checking on the money paid by customers and sending out statements, bills and reminders.

Now that computers and software are much cheaper, more firms are able to use computers for this kind of application. It still accounts for a large proportion of the use of computers today. Stock control (Unit 17.1) and payroll (Unit 17.2) are dealt with in this chapter.

In the 1960s computers were put to a wider range of commercial uses. One of the first was the airline booking system, introduced in America in 1962. This is dealt with in Unit 17.3.

Characteristics of commercial applications

Commercial applications generally:
1 Deal with very large amounts of data.
2 Use the same program in the same way on similar data on a regular basis.
3 Involve very simple operations – mostly input, output and file operations; any arithmetic involved is very uncomplicated.

When studying a commercial application you should be clear about:
1 The general background.
(a) The situation in which the computer is used (e.g. to understand how an airline booking system works you have to understand something about the airline itself).
(b) The problem which the computer helps to solve.
2 The overall system. The general way in which the system operates, including the work carried out by the people involved. What does the computer do?
3 The collection and input of data. Also the checking of data – verification and validation.
4 The files used. Most commercial applications involve the use of large data files.
5 The role of the computer. The kind of operating system used and the operations carried out by the computer.
6 Computer output.

17.1 Stock Control

The general background

The **stock** of a shop or firm means all the goods it has for sale. **Stock control** means managing sensibly the amount of goods in stock. The aims are to:
1 Keep enough of each item in stock so that they do not run out.
2 Avoid having too much of any item.
It is bad for trade to run out of goods a customer wants. It is also bad for profits to have large quantities of items that won't sell. They take up storage space and represent money spent for no return. All the items which are in stock have had to be bought.

The main jobs of a stock control system are:
1 To keep a check on exactly what goods are in stock.
2 To work out what goods are selling and to fix maximum and minimum stock levels for each item.
3 To reorder goods to replace the items which are sold so that stocks are kept between the maximum and minimum levels.

Example of a stock control system

The following example is about a chain of photographic shops. The shops deal mainly in cameras and photographic materials such as films. They also sell specialized items used for photography such as tripods and camera bags. The company has a computer at its head office, which has a warehouse adjoining it. There is a point of sale terminal in each shop and a terminal in the warehouse (see Figure 6.2 in Unit 6.2).

The overall system

The computer controls the stock in the shops and in the warehouse (Fig. 17.1). The shops are supplied by a delivery twice weekly from the warehouse. The company orders goods to stock the warehouse from a number of different suppliers.

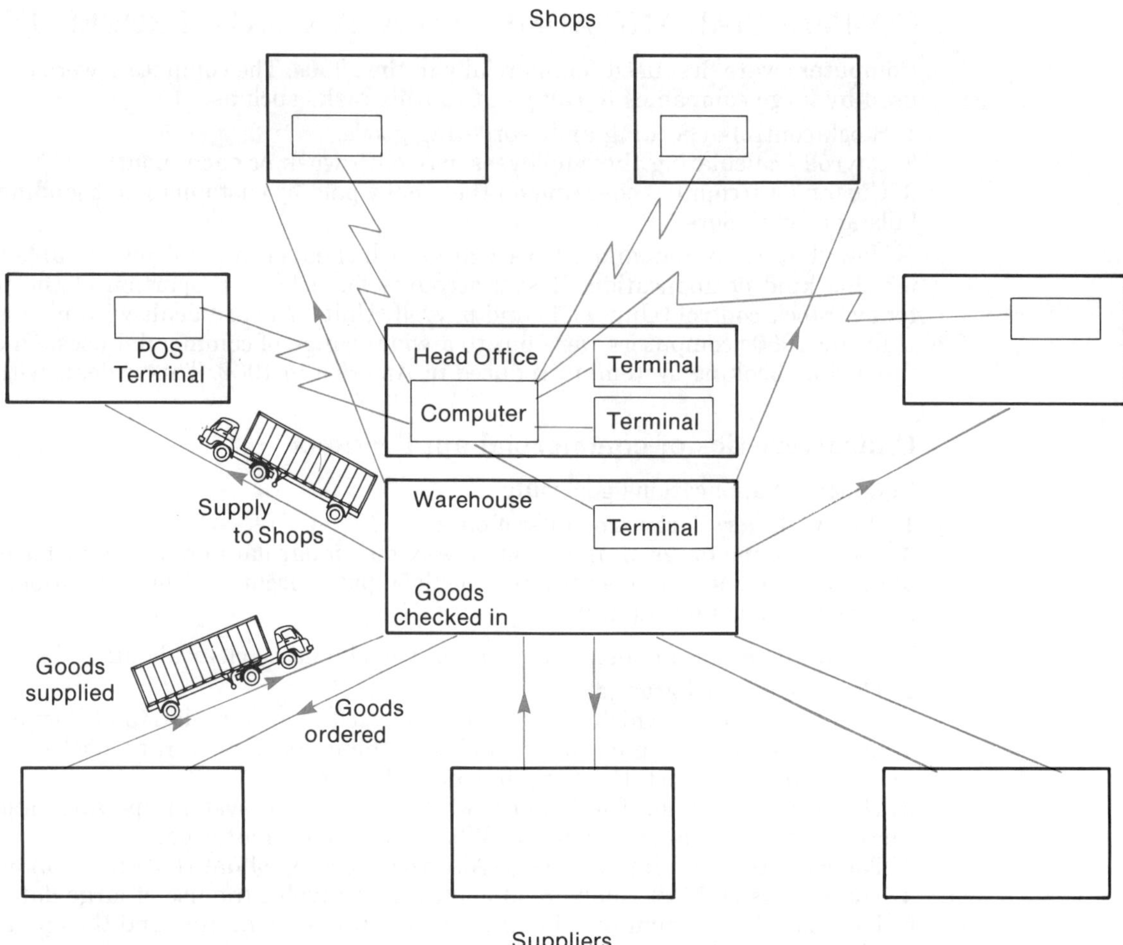

Fig. 17.1 The supply of goods for a chain of photographic shops

The collection and input of data

Data is collected and input:

In the shops

As each item is sold the sales assistant types in a code for it at the terminal. The terminal contains a microprocessor and some storage. This is used:

1 To store details of all the day's transactions. These are stored during the day and sent to the main computer in the evening. The terminal is left connected to a telephone line overnight. The main computer phones each terminal in turn automatically for its information. The computer uses the information to keep its file of the stock levels in each shop up to date. In this way the computer has a record of what items should still be on the shelves in the shop.

2 To store a list of the names and the prices of most goods in the shop. The terminal uses this when printing the receipt for the customer (Fig. 17.2).

```
          TECNO SOUTHAMPTON
          89 COMMERCIAL ROAD
             SOUTHAMPTON
210287 1233 ASSNT-S T04502 R0000

1 31PAT23  ACULUX 250ML      1.70

      TOTAL TO PAY           1.70
      CASH TENDERED          1.57
      DISCOUNT               0.13

           NOTHING TO PAY

ALL PRICES ARE INCLUSIVE OF VAT
         PHONE 0703 229227
          VAT 232 6329 79
```

Fig. 17.2 A receipt produced by a POS terminal. Note that the assistant typed in '1 31 PAT 23'. The terminal had stored the name of the item, ACULUX 250 ml, and the price, £1.70
(*By kind permission of TECNO*)

The sales assistants do sometimes have to fill in forms to be sent to the main computer centre:
1 If a mistake is made in entering data and not discovered until later.
2 If the terminal breaks down.
3 When they do a stock check in the shop – which they do occasionally in case any errors have been made.

At the warehouse

Entries have to be made of goods leaving or arriving:
1 When items are delivered from the suppliers to the warehouse.
2 When items are sent from the warehouse to the shops.

For standard items such as films and cameras a delivery form arrives with the goods from the supplier. The data from this form is then sent to the head office to be input by a keyboard operator working at a VDU.

For special one-off orders the storekeeper keys the details in at the terminal.

In the office

The management make decisions about new products or items which are to be discontinued. This information is typed into a terminal to update the files.

The files used

1 The **stock master file**. This contains data on the stock in the warehouse. It has details of all items which are stocked on a regular basis. Each of these is given an item number. The file is a sequential file and is in order of the item numbers. Each record refers to one item and contains:

Item number	– this is a key field for the record.
Description of the item	– the name and details such as size, etc.
Present stock level	– the number of the item in the warehouse.
Reorder level	– item is reordered when stock falls below this.
Maximum stock level	– used to decide how many to order.
Minimum reorder number	– this is the smallest number which can be ordered from the supplier.
Date of previous order	
Supplier	– this is a code indicating which supplier the item can be reordered from.
Reorder situation	– this is a code indicating whether the goods are discontinued or to be reordered, etc.

2 The **suppliers master file**. This contains data on all the suppliers which the company uses. Each record consists of:
Supplier code as stored on the master stock file.
Name and address of the supplier.
Status of orders from that supplier.
3 There is also a stock file kept for each shop. These stocks files are similar to the master file for the warehouse.

The role of the computer

The computer carries out many tasks including:
1 Checking stock levels in each shop and working out what goods are to be sent to the shop.
2 Checking stock levels in the warehouse and working out what goods are to be ordered from the suppliers.
3 Storing orders so that goods from each supplier are together. Producing orders using the suppliers master file.
4 Adjusting stock levels in the files for the warehouse and the shops when a delivery is made from the warehouse to the shop. The computer produces a list of the items to be sent. The storekeeper indicates on the terminal when the items have been sent.
5 Adjusting stock levels in the files for the warehouse when a delivery is made to the warehouse from the suppliers.

Computer output

The computer output includes:
1 Lists of goods to be ordered from each supplier.
2 Lists of goods to be sent to each shop.
3 Records of sales and forecasts for management so that decisions can be made about discounting products and introducing new ones.

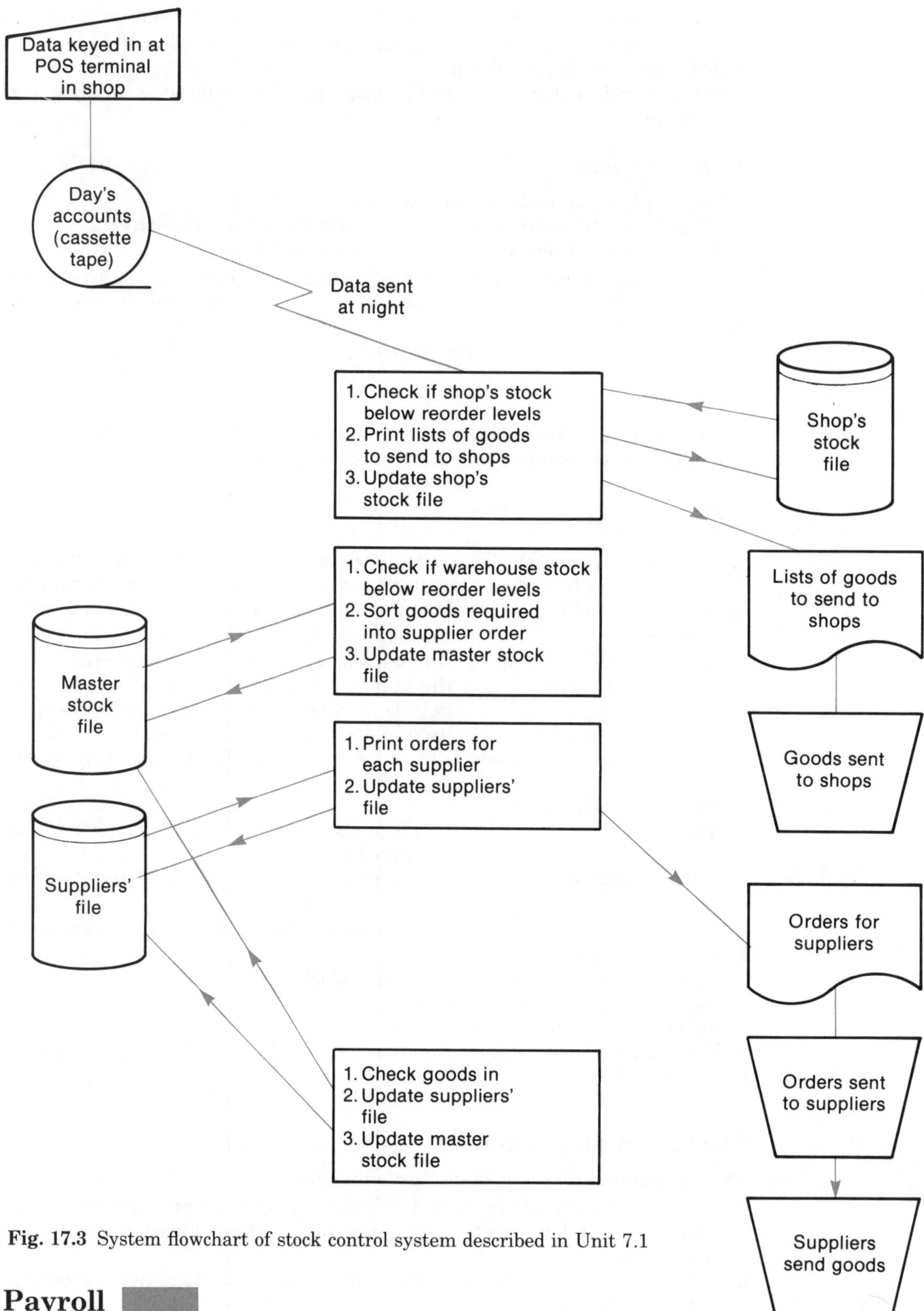

Fig. 17.3 System flowchart of stock control system described in Unit 7.1

17.2 Payroll

General background

1 Employees are usually paid either weekly or monthly.
2 Two common methods of working out a person's pay are:
(a) As a salary – a fixed amount per year is divided up and the employee is paid the same amount, usually each month (although there may be extra payments for overtime, etc.).
(b) Based on an hourly rate. The pay for the week (or month) is worked out by multiplying the number of hours worked by the hourly rate. The rates of payment are higher for overtime, weekends, etc.
3 People usually receive their pay:
(a) In cash, or
(b) As a cheque, or
(c) By a payment to their bank.

4 Various deductions have to be made from pay including:
(a) Income Tax, which is complicated to work out, and depends on the amount already paid in the year,
(b) National Insurance contributions.

Example of payroll

The overall system

The following example, which agrees with the system flowchart of Fig. 10.3 and the program flowchart of Fig. 10.12 assumes that the employees have an hourly rate, are paid each week, and receive their money as cash or as a direct payment to the bank.

The work is done by batch processing on a large computer whose peripheral devices include magnetic tape drives, magnetic disc drives and line printers.

Collection and input of data

1 The employees punch a clock card on arriving at work and on leaving.
2 Using this card a clerk fills out a time sheet for the employee, adding details about overtime, special payments, sickness, etc.
3 This data is encoded on to magnetic tape and verified.

Files

1 A master file on magnetic tape of data about the employees, including their employee number, name, department, hourly rate, tax code, tax paid to date, total pay to date, etc.
2 The magnetic tape file which has been prepared from the time sheets, giving details of the current week's work.
3 A sorted version of the file of current week's details, also on magnetic tape, with the record keys in the same order as the master file.
4 A file of tax tables from which income tax can be calculated using a person's tax code and pay to date. For speed this file has to be stored on disc for direct access.

Updating

1 The master file has to be updated before the payroll run takes place, if there have been any changes to employee details. An update file is prepared with its records in the same order as those in the master file and a program is run which uses one file to update the other (see Unit 13.4). Employees' tax-to-date is updated during the main payroll run (see programs below).
2 The tax tables file is updated only when the Government changes the tax rules.

The role of the computer

The main computer programs are:
1 A program which validates the data from the time sheets and produces a new magnetic tape file sorted into order.
2 The main program which:
(a) Calculates the employees' gross pay (i.e. pay before deductions).
(b) Calculates tax and other deductions, and hence calculates the actual pay.
(c) Updates the tax-to-date and the total pay-to-date on the master file.
(d) Prints wage slips and details for the wages department and for the banks (of money to be directly credited to employees' accounts).
3 A 'coin analysis' program which works out how many of the different coins and notes are required from the bank. Employees paid in cash will then receive the correct money.
4 An update program which updates the master file to allow for new employees, or for people leaving or for changes in rates of pay.

Printed output

This is all produced on a line-printer:
1 Wage slips – using preprinted stationery.
2 Coin analysis.
3 Summary for the banks of money to be transferred to employees' accounts.
4 Statistics for the wages department.

17.3 Airline Booking Systems

The general background

A large airline may operate planes throughout the world. In most cases these planes fly on routes and at times which are worked out a long time ahead. Passengers can book seats on these flights in advance and from almost anywhere in the world. Immediately a flight is fully booked any further requests for it have to be refused.

Such a system requires:

1 A network of points from which requests can be made.
2 A centre where data is stored and from which the network is coordinated.
3 Very fast communication between the points and the centre.

This is an obvious situation in which to use a computer and was one of the first major commercial uses of computers.

The main tasks of an airline booking system are:

1 To keep up-to-date information on all flights and bookings.
2 To provide information on availability of flights and seats.
3 To accept bookings for flights until all seats are taken.
4 To deal with cancellations.
5 To store and provide details of fares.
6 To prepare and issue tickets.

The same computer system which deals with bookings will also handle other tasks.

1 The information about passengers is used to:
(a) Prepare in-flight meals.
(b) Prepare passenger lists.
(c) Organize the checking in of passengers at the airport.
2 The information on planes and flights is used to:
(a) Plan the timetables.
(b) Plan individual flights – working out the flight path and detailed times of departure and arrival.
(c) Calculate fuel requirements.
(d) Make available details of flights. This includes providing the information on display boards in the airports. These show passengers when flights are expected to depart and when to board their plane.

The overall system for bookings

A customer can use one of several methods to book flights.

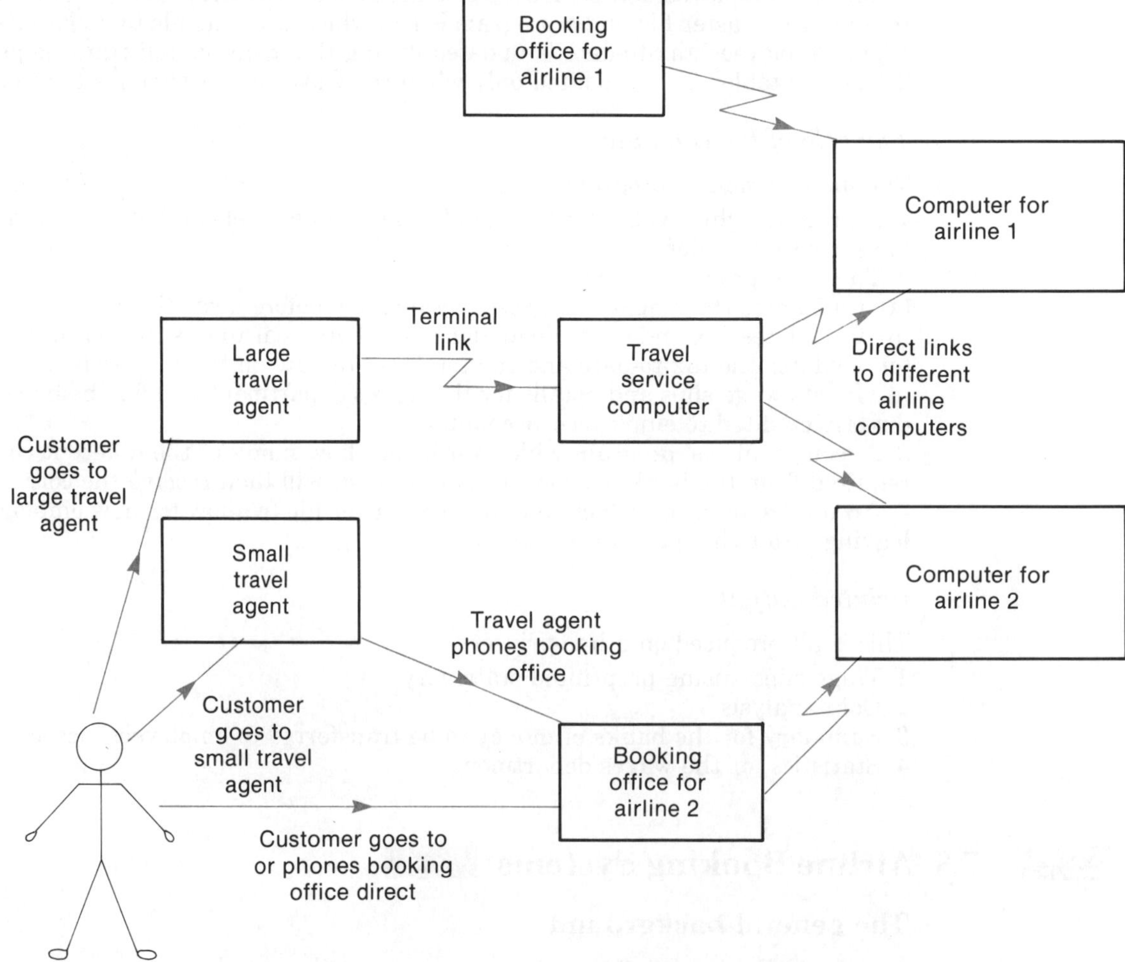

Fig. 17.4 The different ways of connecting to the airline computers

1 Each airline has visual display terminals at its booking offices. Customers can go to these offices or phone them.
2 Customers can use a travel agent:
(a) A small travel agent will then simply telephone the airline booking office.
(b) Each local office of a larger travel agent usually has its own terminal. This terminal is linked to a computer which can then connect to the computer of any individual airline.

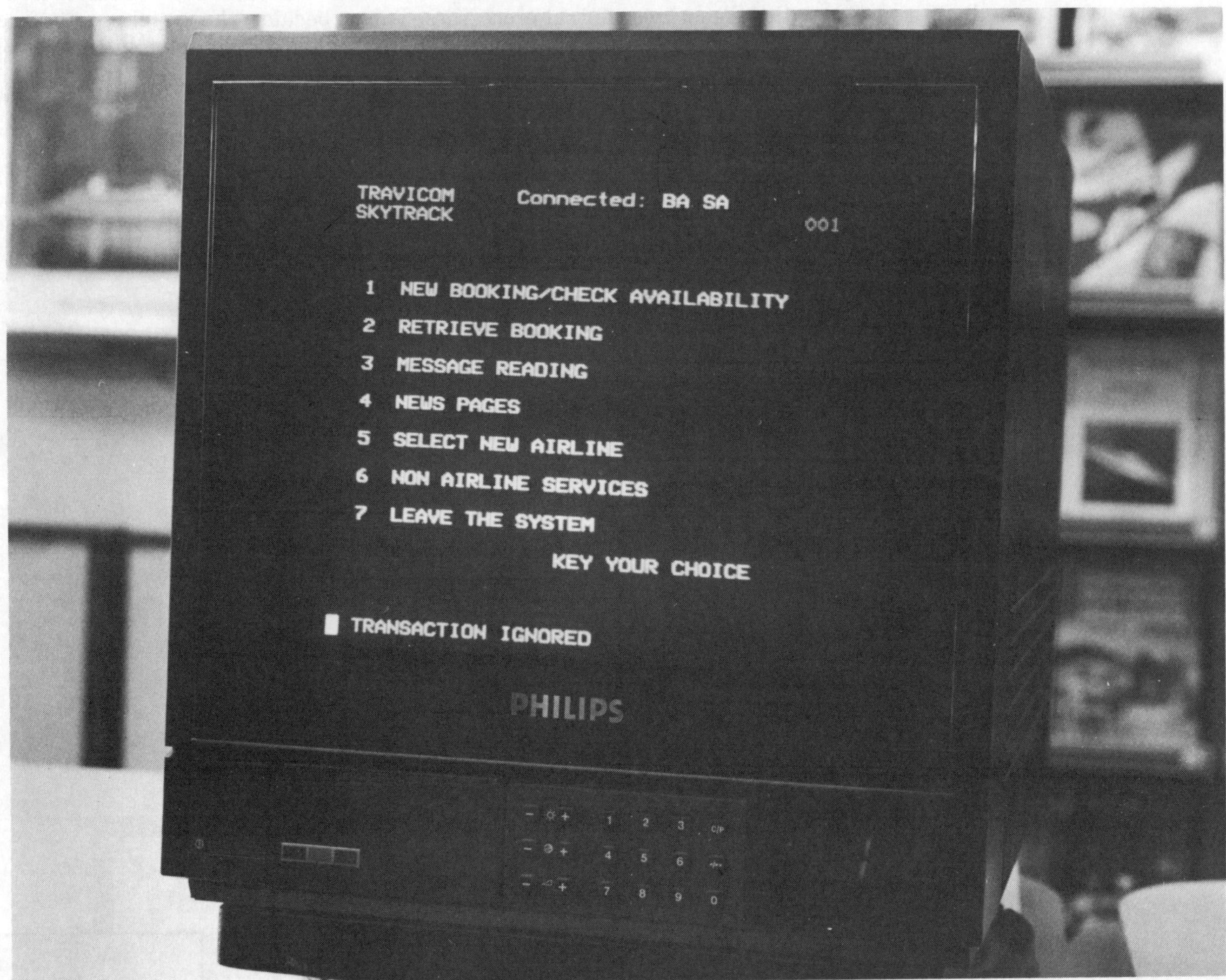

Fig. 17.5 A terminal in a travel agent's office
(*By kind permission of Thomas Cook Limited*)

Input and output at the terminals

When a customer wishes to book a flight:
1 The booking clerk logs on to the airline computer, giving the appropriate codes.
2 The clerk types in the intended date for the flight and the destination. The computer gives details of possible flights. This includes arrival and departure times, type of aircraft and cabin services available.
3 The customer selects a suitable flight. The flight number is typed in at the terminal. The computer gives the number and class of seats available.
4 The booking clerk requests a reservation, typing in the class of seats and the number of seats required.
The computer repeats the request for the clerk to check it.
5 If this is accepted the computer makes the booking by altering its files. It then shows on the screen that the booking has been made.
The computer also deals later with payment and the issue of a ticket.

The files used

Any such system will have a large number of disc files. These will include:
1 A timetable file containing details of flights and times for some months ahead.
2 A bookings file containing data for each flight of seats in each class that are already booked.
3 A passenger file showing for each passenger necessary details such as:
(a) Name, address and phone number.

(b) Flight number, class of seat, cabin service required.
(c) Whether ticket has been paid for, issued, etc.
4 A file of travel agents and booking offices. This contains details of the transactions made by each travel agent or booking office.

The role of the computer

The type of computer used for an airline booking system is a large mainframe computer. It usually is a system with at least two central processors. This is because the system is running continuously and the airline cannot afford to have the computer stopped completely because of breakdown or for servicing.

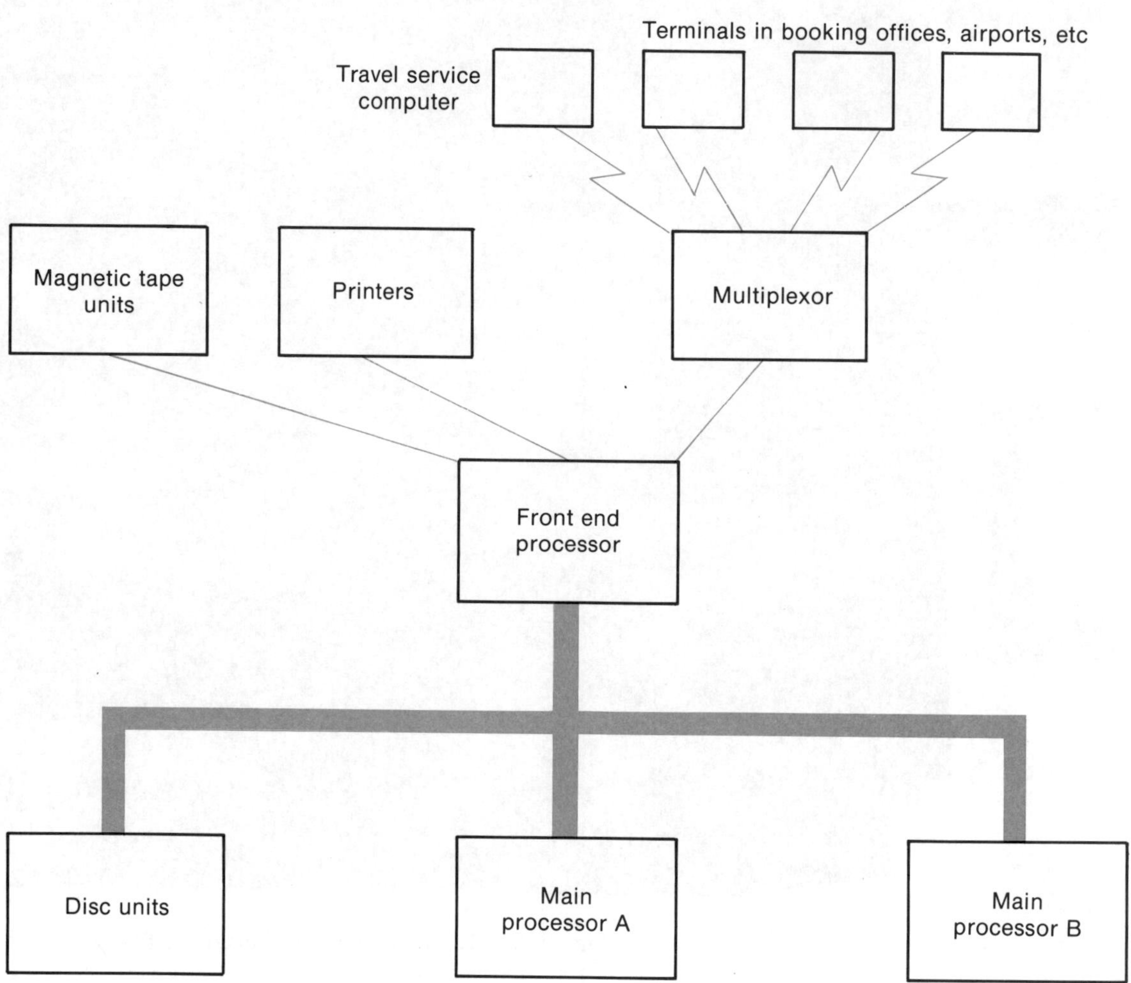

Fig. 17.6 An airline computer system with two processors

The computer performs many tasks including:
1 Running the interactive booking system to the travel agents and booking offices. This is a real-time system (see Unit 15.1) because bookings have to be dealt with immediately. As soon as a booking is made the bookings file, the passenger file and the travel agents file have to be updated straight away. Then if another booking office tries to make a reservation just afterwards the computer can take the first booking into account.
2 Providing information on flights to the airports either:
(a) In response to requests from terminals, or
(b) For display on passenger display boards.
3 Providing passenger lists to the airports for use in checking in passengers.
4 Providing information to the booking offices and travel agents on the bookings they have made.

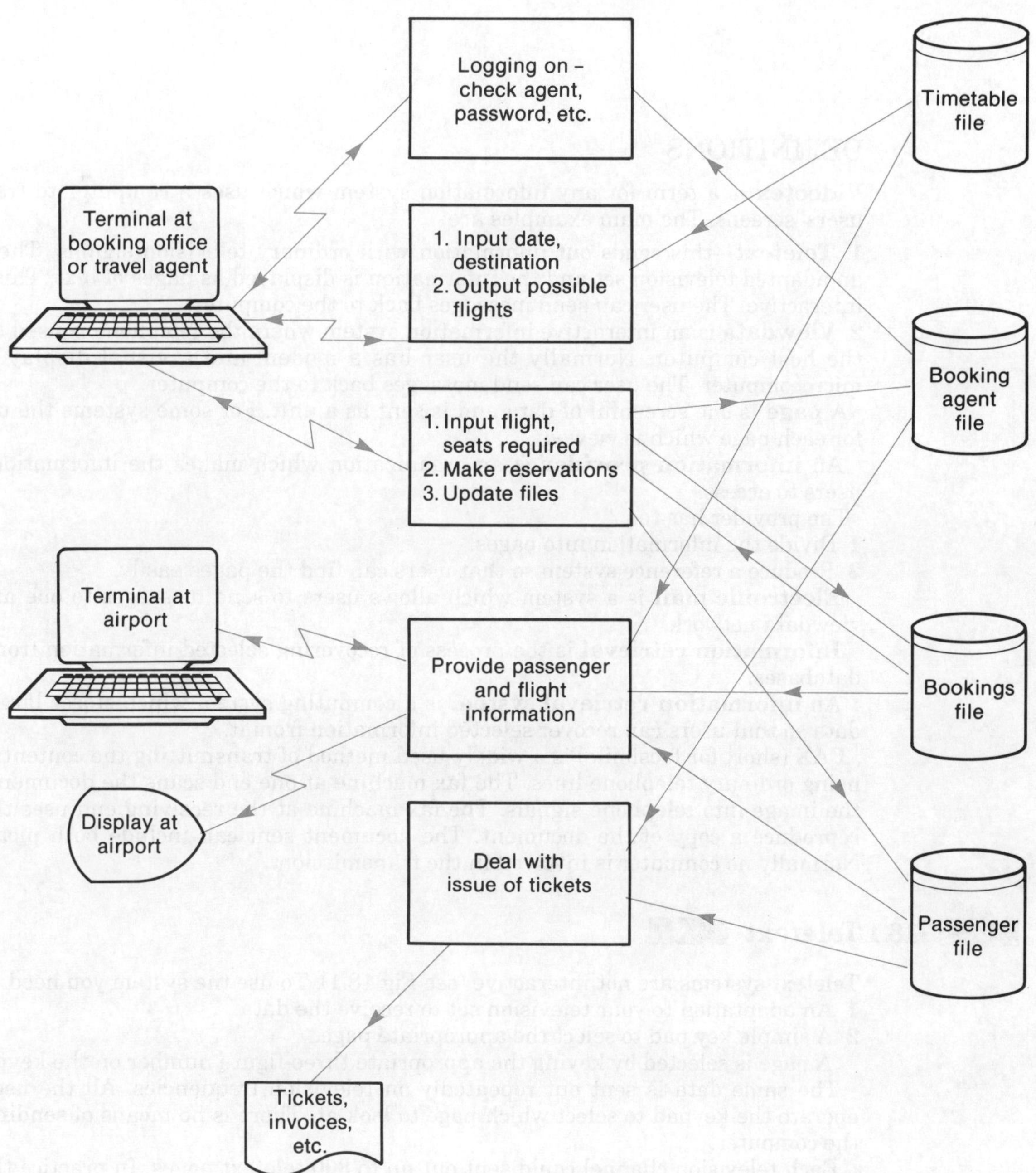

Fig. 17.7 System flowchart showing the main operations in an airline booking system

18 COMMUNICATION SYSTEMS AND WORD PROCESSING

DEFINITIONS

Videotex is a term for any information system which uses a computer to transmit data to users' screens. The main examples are:

1 Teletext—this sends out information with ordinary television signals. The customer has an adapted television set and the information is displayed as pages of text. This system is not interactive. The user can send messages back to the computer.

2 Viewdata is an interactive information system where the telephone is used to link users to the host computer. Normally the user has a modem and a visual display terminal or a microcomputer. The user can send messages back to the computer.

A **page** is one screenful of data and is sent as a unit. For some systems the user has to pay for each page which is viewed.

An **information provider** is an organization which makes the information available for users to access.

The provider has to:

1 Divide the information into pages.

2 Produce a reference system so that users can find the pages easily.

Electronic mail is a system which allows users to send messages to one another using a viewdata network.

Information retrieval is the process of recovering selected information from large files or databases.

An **information retrieval system** is a computing system which stores large quantities of data so that users can recover selected information from it.

FAX (short for facsimile) is a widely-used method of transmitting the contents of documents using ordinary telephone lines. The fax machine at one end scans the document and converts the image into telephone signals. The fax machine at the receiving end uses these signals to reproduce a copy of the document. The document sent can include both pictures and text. Normally no computer is involved in the transmission.

18.1 Teletext

Teletext systems are not interactive (see Fig 18.1). To use the system you need:

1 An adaptation to your television set to receive the data.

2 A simple key pad to select the appropriate page.

A page is selected by keying the appropriate three-figure number on the keypad.

The same data is sent out repeatedly on television frequencies. All the user can do is to operate the keypad to select which page to look at. There is no means of sending data back to the computer.

Each television channel could sent out up to 800 teletext pages. In practice they send fewer than that.

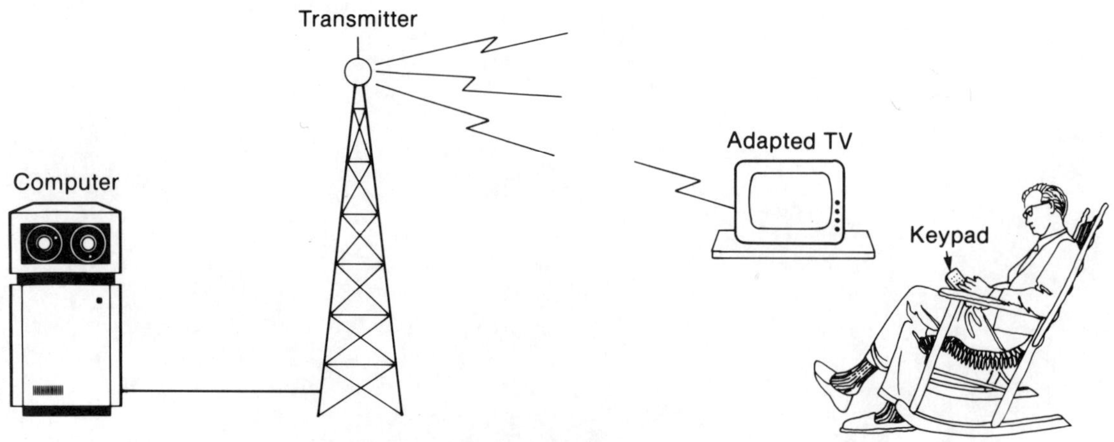

Fig. 18.1 A teletext system

Examples of teletext systems

1 The BBC system – called CEEFAX.
2 The IBA system – ORACLE.

Examples of information available from CEEFAX or ORACLE

1 Up-to-date news.
2 Latest sports results.
3 Weather information.
4 Details of radio and TV programmes.
5 Stock exchange prices.
6 Money exchange rates.

18.2 Viewdata Networks – Information Retrieval and Electronic Mail

EQUIPMENT AND SETTING UP FOR VIEWDATA

Viewdata systems use telephone lines and a packet switching service (see Unit 6.3). The host computer is running a multi-access system (see Unit 15.4).

The user needs:
1 A visual display terminal (see Unit 6.1). Very often a microcomputer is used for this. A program is run in the microcomputer so that it behaves as a terminal.
2 A telephone line which can be used for fairly long periods.
3 A modem.

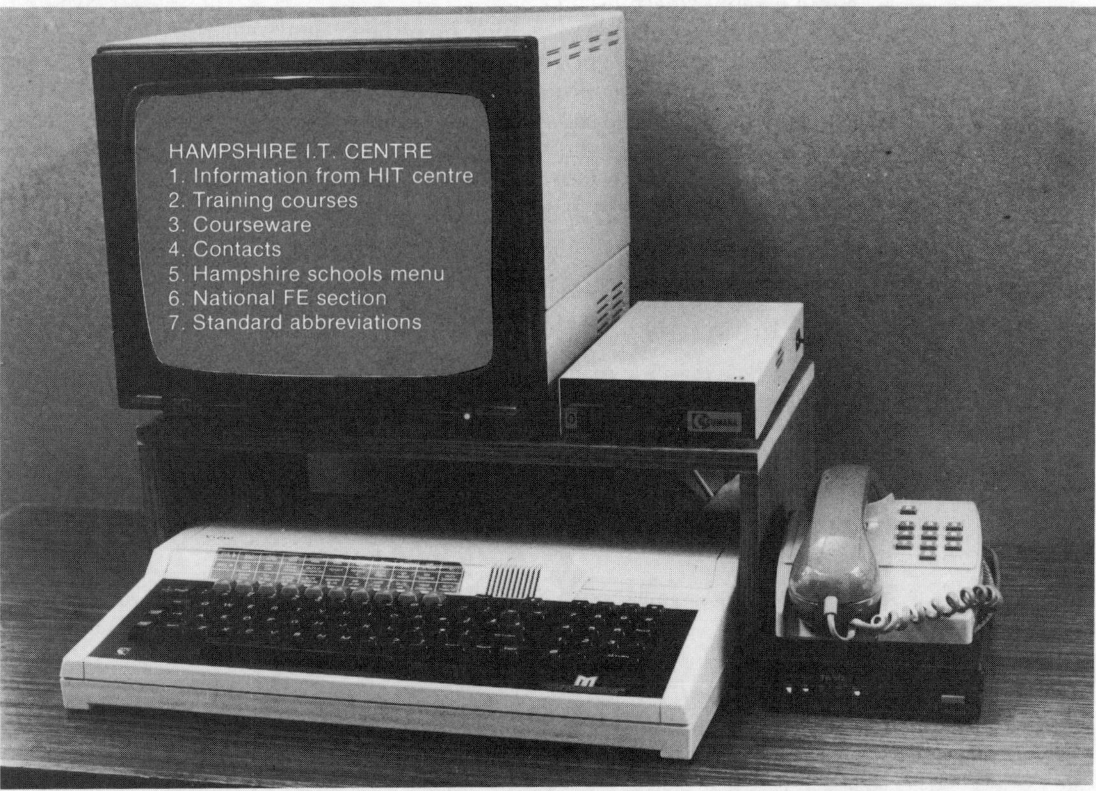

Fig. 18.2 A microcomputer being used as a viewdata terminal

Users have to decide which viewdata service or services they wish to use and pay subscriptions to them. For each service they will usually be given:
1 A manual of instructions and lists of services available.
2 A telephone number for the service.
3 An account number and password (this password can be changed by the user later).

Users with microcomputers can also obtain the software needed to make their computer behave as a terminal. This software, known as **communications software**, will usually enable the microcomputer to:
1 Make the phone call automatically.
2 Carry out most of the logging-in conversation – the user still has to type in the password (see Unit 14.3).
3 Send and receive data in the same way as an ordinary terminal does.
4 Carry out the logging-out sequence.

CHARGES FOR VIEWDATA

1 Users of a viewdata service usually pay a regular subscription to use it.
2 They also have to pay telephone charges.
3 They may also have to pay for separate pages of information or for access to particular databases.
4 Firms or organizations can pay to become information providers.

TYPES OF SERVICE AVAILABLE ON VIEWDATA

1 Access to databases

A user can search files of data for information. The files may be provided:
(a) Locally by members of a group of users.
(b) Nationally by information providers of the viewdata company. Or
(c) Nationally by arrangement with another viewdata company.
For example subscribers to Prestel can use databases on other systems.

2 Electronic mail

Each user has a 'mailbox'. This is an area of the main computer's memory where messages can be stored. With each message is recorded the name of the sender and the date when it was sent.

A user can:
(a) Send a message to another user.
(b) Scan the mailbox, printing out a list of the messages in it.
(c) Read any message which seems important.
(d) Print messages out on paper.
(e) Send a reply to a message.
(f) Delete or retain messages which have been dealt with.

A long letter can be typed beforehand, using a wordprocessor, and stored on disc. This is done with the terminal off-line. The user then logs on to the computer and the letter is transmitted quickly. This saves money because the telephone call is shorter.

Note: Unlike telephone and telex systems, two people using electronic mail do not have a direct conversation. One person sends a message and the other receives it later. It is rather like sending letters but is faster.

3 Telesoftware

Telesoftware means computer programs which are transmitted via viewdata or teletext.

4 Bulletin boards

A bulletin board is an area where one user of a viewdata system can leave messages and information which is then available to all other users.

5 Ordering goods and services

A user can order airline or theatre tickets using viewdata.

Examples of viewdata services available in Britain

Telecom Gold

This is a public service run by British Telecom mainly for electronic mail.

Prestel

This is a British Telecom service which is mainly an information retrieval system with over a quarter of a million available pages. Subscribers can also use the system to buy goods and services.

Prestel is designed so that any page can be accessed using only the numbers 0,1,2,3,4,5,6,7,8,9 and the characters * and #. This is so that if necessary the system can be used without having an actual terminal. It is possible to use just an adapted television set, selecting pages by pressing the buttons on a push-button phone.

Prestel has over a thousand information providers. These include travel agents, transport companies such as British Rail, airlines and car ferry companies, universities, unions, insurance companies, building societies, etc.

Campus 2000

This is a service for education.

The data users are schools and colleges throughout the United Kingdom. They can use the service for electronic mail, access to databases and for telesoftware.

The data providers are local authorities, schools themselves but also organizations such as the Stock Exchange and the Army. During the summer the polytechnics use CAMPUS to publish details of places available for prospective students.

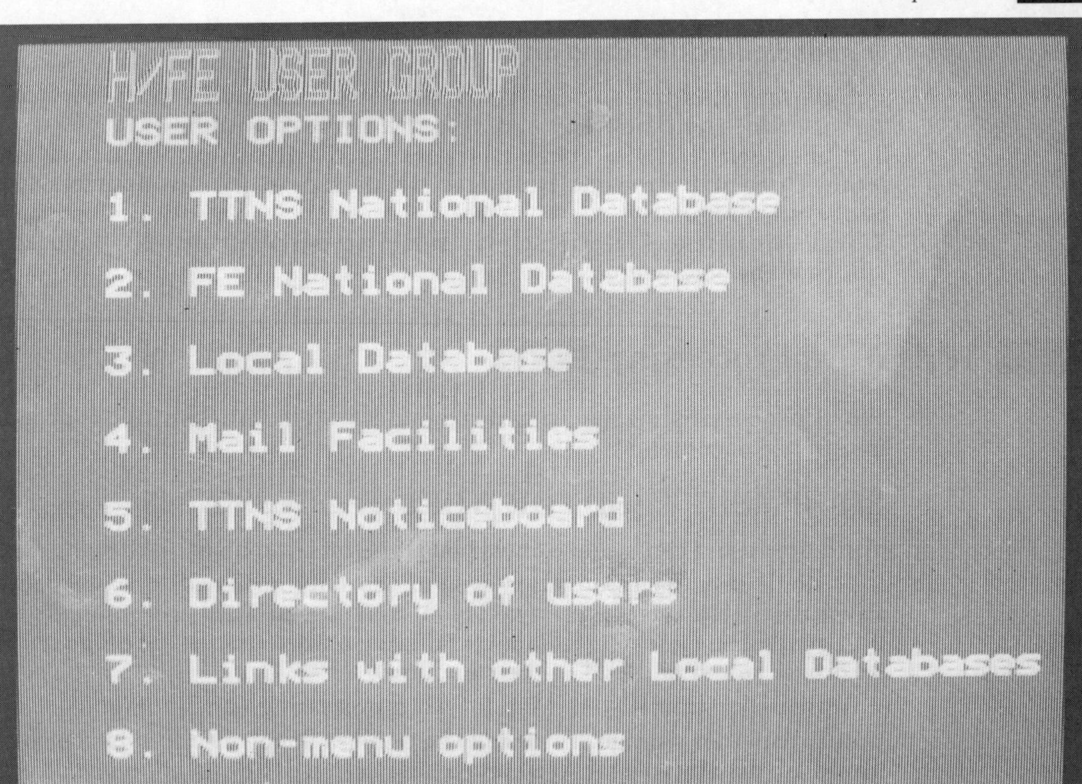

Fig. 18.3 A menu on CAMPUS

18.3 Comparisons

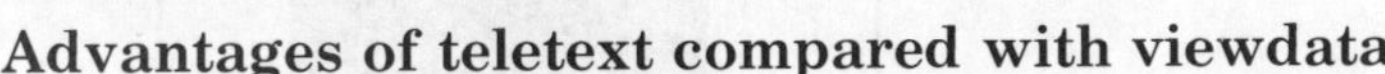

Advantages of teletext compared with viewdata

1 It is relatively easy to select the information you want.
2 The equipment required is fairly inexpensive.
3 No money is needed to use the system once you have the equipment.
4 Teletext data can be added to ordinary television pictures. For instance deaf people can have subtitles added to television programmes by this method.
5 Pages can be changed easily so that information is up to date.

Disadvantages of teletext

1 Only a limited number of pages can be looked at.
2 There is no interaction with the computer.

Advantages of viewdata

1 A wide variety of interactive services. They range from electronic mail to travel information and facilities for ordering goods.
2 The amount of information available is very large.

Disadvantages of viewdata

1 On some systems response is slow and the method of searching is cumbersome.
2 Cost of telephone calls and of charges for using the system.

Viewdata in Britain has not increased as much as was expected originally. There are still only about 60 000 Prestel subscribers. This compares with over 3 million users of the corresponding French system, which has started much more recently. This is partly because the French system is heavily subsidized.

Advantages of electronic mail over post

1 Less use of paper. It is possible to read and reply to correspondence without it being printed out. A letter can be written using a word processor and transmitted direct.
2 Speed. A message transmitted to a user's mailbox can be read almost immediately.
3 Simplicity. If an employee of one company sends a letter by post to an employee of another, a chain of people is involved. Electronic mail only involves the computer system and the two people concerned.

Disadvantages of electronic mail

1 Electronic mail can only be sent to people who subscribe to the service.
2 A user does not know any mail is in the mailbox until he or she logs on to the system.
3 It is expensive to use a public network (see Charges for viewdata in Unit 18.2).
Note: These first three disadvantages are not significant for subscribers who use an electronic mail system regularly.
4 Widespread use of electronic mail would be worrying for postal and office workers as their jobs could be endangered.

18.4 Word Processing

Word processing means using a computer system to help with the production and editing of letters and documents.

EQUIPMENT USED FOR WORD PROCESSING

Word processing can be done on various types of equipment. Two methods commonly used are:
1 A single user microcomputer system specially designed as a word processor. This has a keyboard with a typewriter-style layout and special word-processing keys.
2 A general purpose microcomputer running a word-processing program. The program may be on disc or stored on ROM in the computer.

A microcomputer system used for word processing usually has:
1 A disc unit for storage. There may be either a floppy disc or a hard disc unit or possibly both. Tapes are not suitable for word processing because they do not allow direct access to text files.
2 A good quality printer. This could be a daisy wheel printer or a laser printer.

A dot matrix printer may be suitable for some word processing applications if:
(a) It allows 'letter quality' printing. Or
(b) It is only used to produce internal documents.

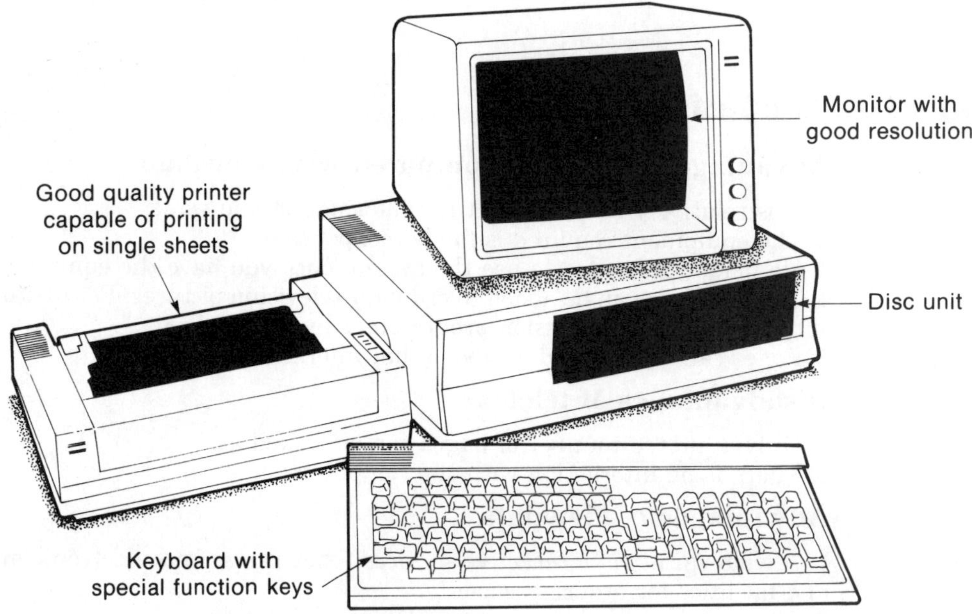

Fig. 18.4 A microcomputer system suitable for word processing

WHAT A WORD PROCESSOR DOES

A word processor allows the user to:
1 Type in text without having to worry about:
(a) The ends of lines – the computer automatically moves on to a new line when the next word will not fit on to the present line.
(b) Making mistakes – it is very easy to correct errors before the document is printed out.
2 Edit text on the screen. There are usually facilities to:
(a) Delete or insert letters and words.
(b) Move or copy paragraphs.
(c) Find all the occurrences of a word and replace them with another one.
3 Store text on disc:
(a) Files can be stored to be printed or sent by electronic mail later.

(b) Files can be combined.
(c) Frequently used text can be inserted in a letter – for example the firm's address.
(d) Letters can be 'personalized' – names and addresses from a list can be added to a standard letter. This makes it look as though each letter has been specially typed for the person addressed.
4 Control the **format** of text for printing. The **format** of output means the way it is set out. The user can decide on:
(a) Numbering and headings at the top and bottom of each page.
(b) The width of the margins at the sides of the page and at the top and bottom.
(c) Spacing between the lines.
(d) Whether to **right justify** the text.

To **right justify** text means to space the words out so that the right hand ends of the lines are all in a straight line down the page.

Methods of operation

The user of a word processor types not only text, but also instructions – to carry out the operations described above.

This can be done:
1 Using menus, from which the user chooses; a menu may be on the screen all the time or may be 'pulled down' using a mouse.
2 Using special function keys; these may be labelled to say what each of them does.
3 By typing commands or combinations of keys which the user has to remember.

A word processor often allows the user to have more than one piece of text in the main store at the same time. In some cases the user can display two passages on the screen at the same time using windows.

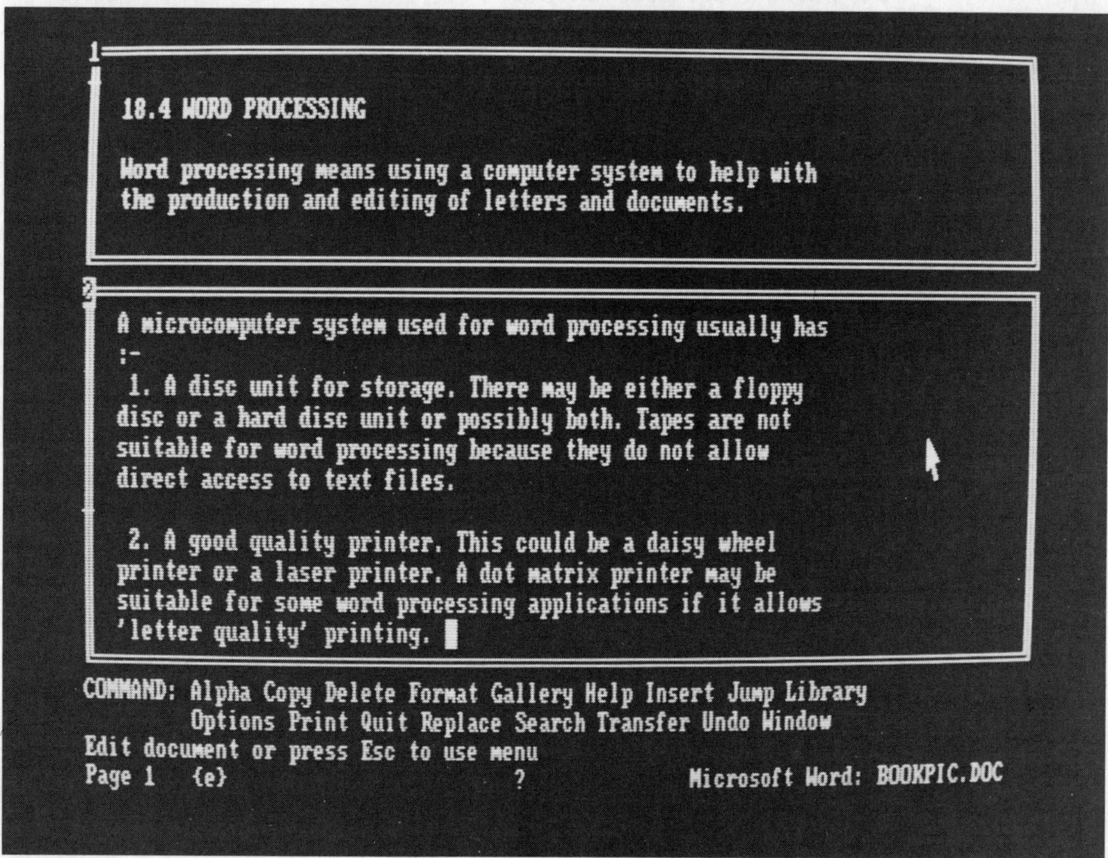

Fig. 18.5 A word processor screen showing a menu and windows
(By kind permission of Microsoft)

Examples

In the following examples word processing operations have been carried out on a piece of text. You could try typing out the first version on a word processor. Then use the word processor to carry out the steps which were carried out in the examples.

The original passage was as follows:
'A Muprocessor is a processor contained on a single integrated circuit chip. Many modern Mucomputers are based on 16-bit and even 32-bit Muprocessors.

By 1971 we had Large Scale Integration (LSI). It was possible to put 10 000 elements on the same chip. The first Muprocessor was produced – the INTEL 4004.

A succession of 8-bit Muprocessors followed. These included the ZILOG Z80, the MOSTEK 6502, the INTEL 8008 and the Motorola M6800. Many current Mucomputers are still based on these Muprocessors.'

1 In the first example the passage was edited as follows:

(a) The short-hand 'Mu' was changed to 'micro' throughout the passage. This was done using a 'find and replace' option. The computer found each occurrence of the word 'Mu' and asked if it was to be replaced or not. The word was changed whenever the reply was 'Y' for 'Yes'.

(b) The word 'current' in the last sentence was changed to 'present-day'. It was not worth using the 'find and replace' option for this. The cursor was just moved to the right place and the word retyped.

(c) The second sentence was moved to the end of the passage. To do this block markers were set at the beginning and end of the sentence. The cursor was then moved to the end of the passage and a 'block move' instruction carried out.

The text then looked like this:

'A microprocessor is a processor contained on a single integrated circuit chip.

By 1971 we had Large Scale Integration (LSI). It was possible to put 10 000 elements on the same chip. The first microprocessor was produced – the INTEL 4004.

A succession of 8-bit microprocessors followed. These included the ZILOG Z80, the MOSTEK 6502, the INTEL 8008 and the Motorola M6800. Many present-day microcomputers are still based on these microprocessors. Many modern microcomputers are based on 16-bit and even 32-bit microprocessors.'

2 The passage was then formatted for printing. The left margin was set at column 10 and the right margin at column 50. The passage was also right justified. This looks rather odd but the passage is to be printed in a book with narrow columns.

The final passage looks like this:

> A microprocessor is a processor contained on a single integrated circuit chip.
> By 1971 we had Large Scale Integration (LSI). It was possible to put 10 000 elements on the same chip. The first microprocessor was produced – the INTEL 4004.
> A succession of 8-bit microprocessors followed. These included the ZILOG Z80, the MOSTEK 6502, the INTEL 8008 and the Motorola M6800. Many present-day microcomputers are still based on these microcomputers. Many modern microcomputers are based on 16-bit and even 32-bit microprocessors.

Spelling

Some word processors can check spellings. The word processor has a file of words which is a dictionary. When the user runs the spelling check the computer stops at any word which is not in the dictionary. It stops at abbreviations and names as well as at spelling mistakes. The user can then choose whether to change the word or not. Words can also be added to the dictionary if necessary.

THE ELECTRONIC OFFICE

The new information technology has made possible the **electronic office**. This is an office where most information such as documents, diagrams, finance and correspondence is handled electronically. It is stored digitally in computers, rather than on paper in filing cabinets.

An electronic office may contain:

1 Word processors for the input and storage of all letters and other documents.
2 Viewdata networks to send letters by electronic mail and for other communications.
3 Local networks for communication within the company.
4 Local and national databases for the storage and retrieval of facts.
5 Graphics, spreadsheet and other packages for the display and manipulation of data.
6 A fax machine to send and receive copies of documents.

19 TECHNICAL, SCIENTIFIC AND OTHER USES

This unit covers the topics in the GCSE National Criteria for Computer Studies under Assessment Objective D section (ii). This is on 'technical, mathematical and scientific uses (e.g. civil engineering calculations, data logging, computer-aided design, simulations).

Unit 19.1 gives a summary of some important applications in the field of civil engineering.

Units 19.2, 19.3 and 19.4 deal with some techniques used in many applications. These are data logging, computer-aided design and simulation. The examples given have not been restricted to the technical, mathematical and scientific fields as these techniques are widely used in other areas as well.

Unit 19.5 explains some of the medical uses of computers. This topic is not included in the GCSE National Criteria but it is included in a number of syllabuses. (See the table of analysis of syllabuses at the start of this book for details.)

CHARACTERISTICS OF TECHNICAL AND SCIENTIFIC APPLICATIONS

The type of application dealt with in this unit generally requires one or both of the following:

1 Ability to respond to signals from external devices,
2 Complex calculations to be done quickly and accurately.

(Contrast this with the characteristics of commercial applications – see introduction to Unit 17).

Note: Speed and accuracy produce a conflict. For calculations to be done accurately each number needs a large number of bits to store it. This makes the calculations slower (see also Unit 2.5).

19.1 Applications in Civil Engineering

Civil engineering is the construction and maintenance of works such as bridges, roads and buildings.

Computers are used in civil engineering in an increasing number of ways.

MATERIALS EVALUATION

Materials evaluation involves:

1 Testing materials to find out how strong they are.
2 Testing materials to find out how long they last – their endurance.
3 Deciding which is the best material for a particular job.

Example of materials evaluation

A multistorey car park is to be built from concrete.

1 Different mixes of concrete are tested for strength.
The best mixes are tested with different types of reinforcing bars inside.
2 Reinforced concrete beams are tested in different conditions of damp and change of temperature. This is to see if there is any danger of the concrete cracking and the reinforcing bars going rusty.
3 Calculations are done of the stresses in the car park building with the different types of concrete. The most suitable type is chosen.

Computers are used:

1 To acquire data on materials being tested. Sensors can be fitted to a material. These sensors can then be directly connected to a computer. Often the sensors are analogue and are connected to the computer via analogue-to-digital converters. The sensors may provide data on:
(a) Loads or stresses or movement of a material.
(b) Temperature, pressure and humidity – this may affect a material being tested for endurance.
The computer records data from the sensors over a period of time. This is an example of data logging (see Unit 19.2).
2 To analyse the data from tests. A computer can help by:
(a) Rapidly carrying out calculations.
(b) Showing the results in the form of tables and graphs.

Example

Testing wooden beams for strength.

The diagram in Fig. 19.1 shows a rig for testing wooden beams. Each beam is moved into position and then a ram bends it slightly by a set distance. The force needed to do this is measured. This is done at a number of points along the beam. The beam is marked with paint to indicate how strong it is. The rig is controlled by a microcomputer which:

1 Receives signals from a light sensor indicating when the beam is in position to start testing.
2 Controls the rollers which move the beam.
3 Operates the hydraulic ram which bends the beam.
4 Monitors the force applied by the hydraulic ram.
5 Operates the paint sprayer which makes paint marks on the beam.

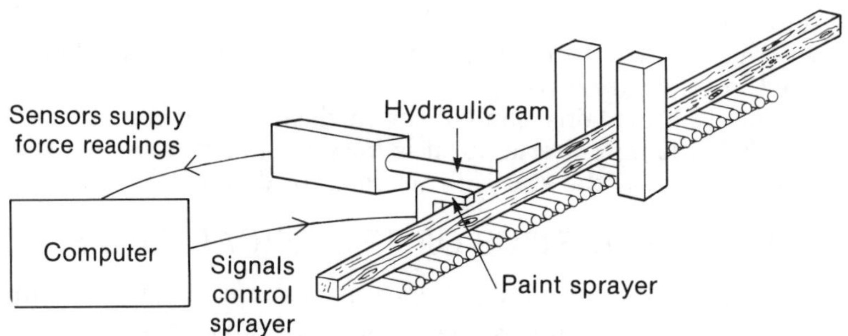

Fig. 19.1 A rig to test wooden beams for strength

STRUCTURAL DESIGN

Structural design is the design of mainly large structures such as dams and bridges.

The main role of computers in this field at present is in analysing designs. A structural engineer produces a design. The computer then does calculations to check that the design is safe. The engineers can then use the results to modify their designs if they so wish. For example, there are programs which help with bridge design by calculating the stress that would be found in various parts of the bridge.

GEOTECHNICAL DESIGN

Civil engineering does not just involve the materials used in construction. The soil and rocks on which a structure is built are also important. In the case of a road or a tunnel they may be very important. **Geotechnical design** refers to the design of the environment in which a structure is placed.

There are difficulties in applying computers in this area. Soil and rock are often more complex in structure than, say, concrete and steel. Applications include:

1 Working out whether a slope of a particular soil is stable or is likely to slip.
2 Finding the pressure produced by earth on a retaining wall – that is a wall built to stop the earth from slipping.
3 Analysing how water drains through different types of soil.
4 Using microprocessor-controlled instruments in the field.

Example of a geotechnical problem

When a new road is built large quantities of soil have to be moved. In some places the road cuts into hills and soil has to be removed. In other places the road is above ground level so that soil has to be added to build the road up. A computer can be used to work out the heights of the road so that soil does not have to be moved large distances.

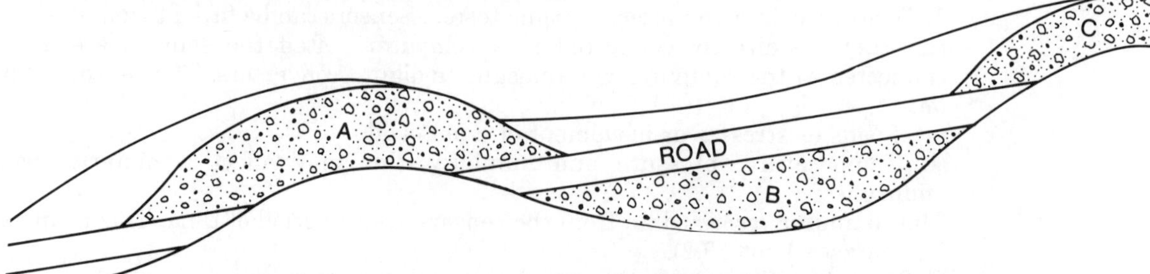

Fig. 19.2 A road showing soil movements. Soil from the cuttings at A and C is moved to make an embankment at B

The calculation is complicated by:
1 The need to make a road fit into the environment – it cannot be built up above the countryside just to get rid of some soil.
2 The fact that soil dug out may not be suitable for building up the road.
3 The need to keep the slope of the road to a fairly gentle gradient.

COMPUTERS IN THE WATER INDUSTRY

1 The introduction of the microcomputer has meant that it is now possible for individual depots to make local measurements of the quantity and quality of water.

Example

Burst mains are more easily detected so that less water is lost through leakage.

2 The revolution in communication technology has meant that data collected from remote locations can be monitored centrally. It has also meant that what happens at such locations can be directly controlled from a central point.

Example

Many of the large old pumping stations have been replaced by small automatic stations.

OTHER USES

Other uses of computers in civil engineering include:
1 Computer-aided design (see Unit 19.3).
2 Information retrieval from databases (see Unit 13.7).

Information available to civil engineers includes data provided by the British Standards Institute.

19.2 Data Logging

Data logging is the automatic recording of data as it is produced. A process is monitored continuously by instruments and the readings are recorded. When a computer is used the sensors are usually connected to an interface board which in turn is connected to the computer. As data is produced by the instruments it is stored by the computer on magnetic tape or disc. The data can then be analysed later.

Gathering data for a data logging system is called **data acquisition**.

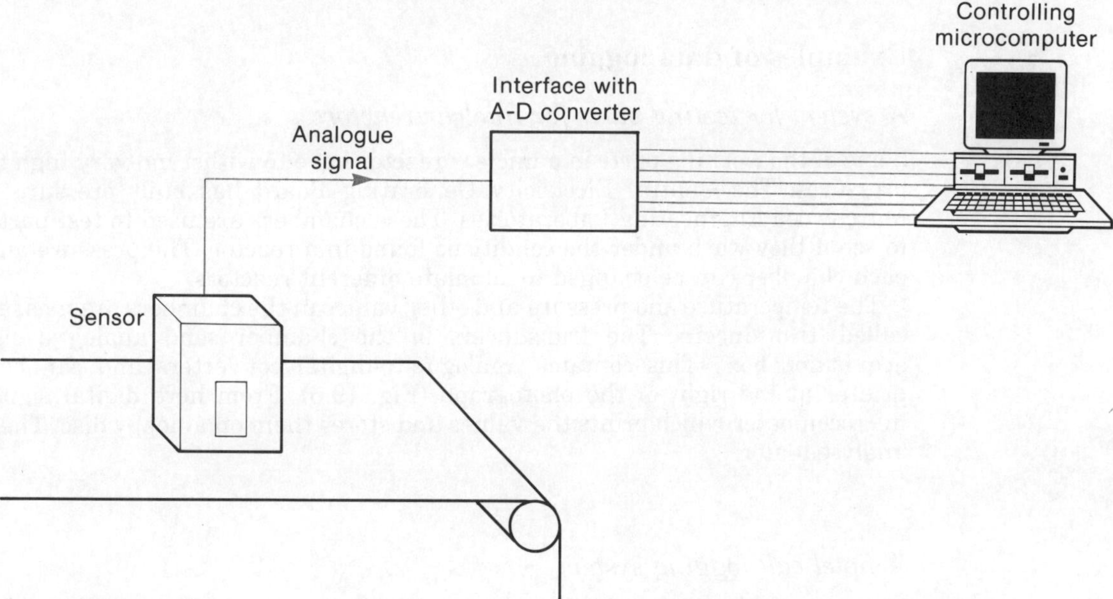

Fig. 19.3 A simple data logging system

In some data logging applications the data is displayed as it is being recorded:
1 As a set of numbers on a printer (as in Fig. 19.6).
2 As a graph produced on a drum plotter or a chart recorder.
3 As a constantly changing screen display.

Figure 19.4 shows the screen display for a data logging system to monitor conditions inside a petrochemical plant. Sensors monitor the temperature in a boiler, the flow at two critical points and the output produced. Each of the vertical columns on the graphs represents one minute. After each minute the four values are recorded for future analysis by the computer. At the same time the four graphs on the screen are each adjusted to take account of the new reading.

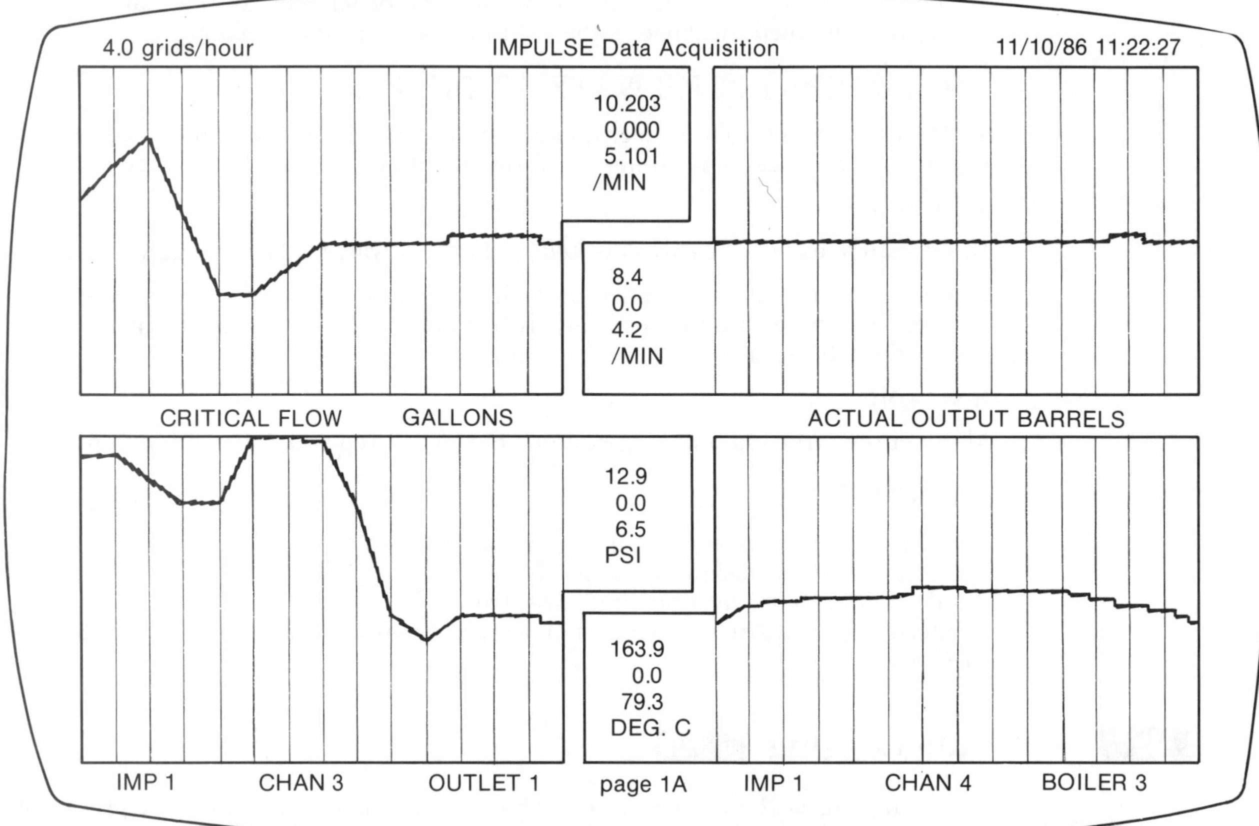

Fig. 19.4 Screen display using graphs to show the data for a data logging system as it is being recorded. The system shown is installed at a petrochemical plant (*By kind permission of Solartron Instruments*)

Examples of data logging

A system for testing parts for nuclear reactors

Some of the working parts in a nuclear reactor have to withstand very high temperatures and pressures. The Central Electricity Generating Board has built pressure chambers at the Marchwood Engineering Laboratories. These chambers are used to test parts for the reactors to see if they work under the conditions found in a reactor. The pressure and temperature in each chamber can be changed to simulate different reactors.

The temperature and pressure and other values in the chambers are measured using devices called 'transducers'. The transducers in the chamber send analogue signals to a 'data acquisition box'. This contains analogue-to-digital converters and can be seen under the printer at the right of the photograph (Fig. 19.6). From here digital signals are sent to a microcomputer which prints the values and stores them on a floppy disc. The data can then be analysed later.

A hotel call logging system

This is a very different type of data logging. Callstar (produced by Feeline Management Ltd) is a system which uses a microcomputer to log telephone calls made by hotel guests. The system is connected to the hotel's exchange. For any call made from a hotel room it can automatically record:

1 The room from which the call is made.
2 The number which has been dialled.
3 The length of time the call takes.

From this information the system can calculate the costs of calls and decide who is to be charged. The computer produces various reports for the hotel management. It also produces an up-to-date telephone bill as the guest checks out (see Figure 19.7).

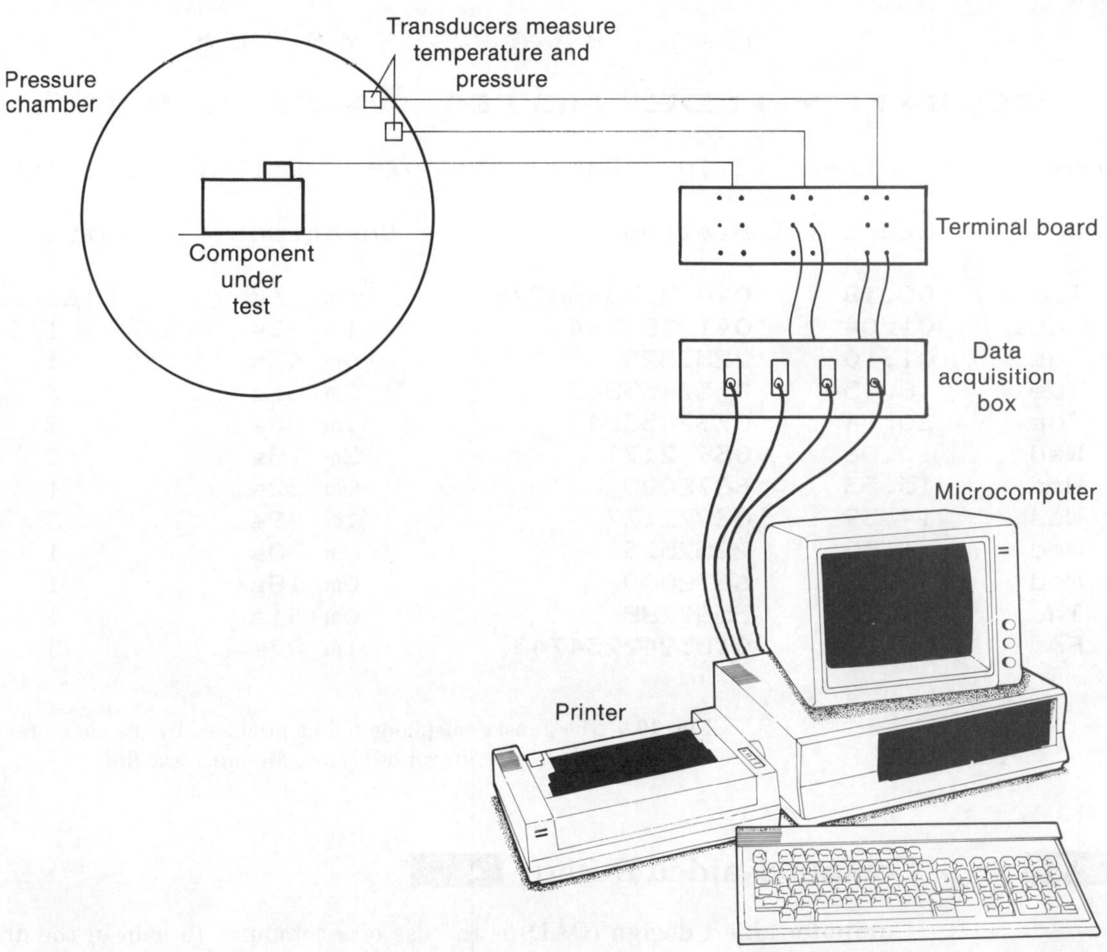

Fig. 19.5 A system for testing parts for nuclear reactors

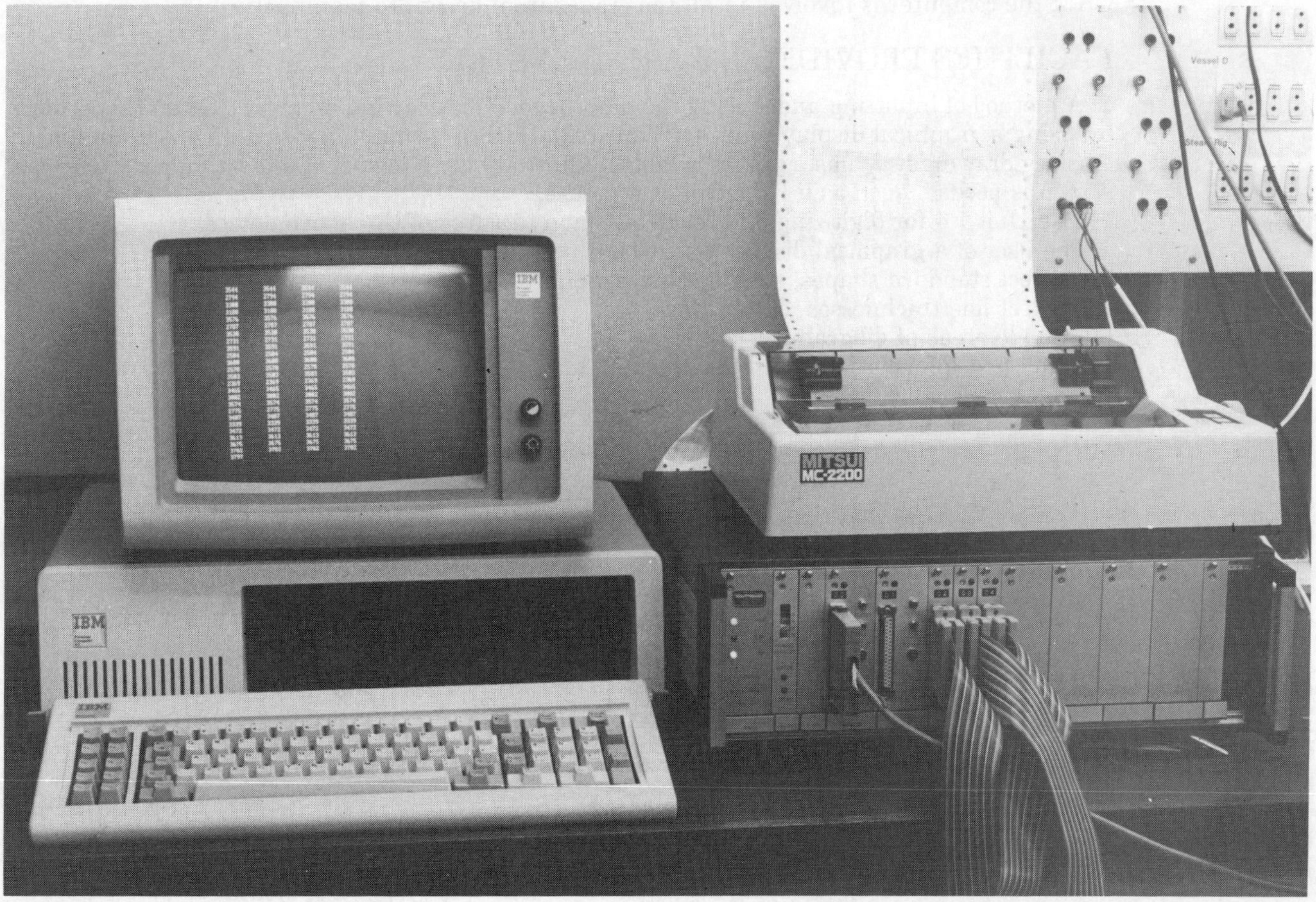

Fig. 19.6 The computer and the data acquisition box in a system to test parts for nuclear reactors (*By kind permission of Marchwood Engineering Laboratories*)

CALLSTAR SYSTEM 1301

COUNTRYWIDE HOTEL AND GOLF CLUB

Room: 136 Time: 12.10 Date: 01/02/86 Calls: 12 Total: £25.72

Day	Start	Dialled	Duration	Units	Cost
Tue	00.18	01012133450848	16m 6s	161	20.82
Tue	01.04	0412485744	1m 2s	1	0.14
Tue	01.10	2252525	0m 43s	1	0.14
Tue	18.15	0732453843	2m 01s	3	0.42
Tue	20.04	0732453843	1m 08s	2	0.28
Wed	10.06	03972177	2m 18s	12	1.68
Wed	13.53	6678000	0m 32s	1	0.14
Wed	14.39	03972177	1m 49s	3	0.42
Wed	16.58	2252525	0m 30s	1	0.14
Wed	19.21	6678000	0m 18s	1	0.14
Thu	14.38	5567788	0m 41s	1	0.14
Fri	08.20	0103942254743	1m 07s	9	1.26

Fig. 19.7 The guest's telephone bill as produced by the computer (*By kind permission of Feeline Management Ltd*)

19.3 Computer-aided Design

Computer-aided design (CAD) is the use of a computer to help in the drawing of designs from which objects are going to be constructed or manufactured.

CAD/CAM is short for computer-aided design and computer-aided manufacture. In CAD/CAM the computer is involved in all the stages from design to manufacture.

FACILITIES PROVIDED BY A CAD SYSTEM

1 A method of inputting and storing the data needed for drawing an object. Often this is done by using a graphical display unit (see Unit 6.2). Such a terminal needs a means of digitizing existing drawings such as a graphics tablet. Alternatively a means of indicating positions on a screen is needed, such as a light pen or a mouse.

(See Unit 7.4 for digitizing and for details and pictures of the above devices.)

The user of a graphical display unit would normally be able to:

(a) Select standard shapes, such as circles, squares, etc.
(b) Select line thicknesses, dotted lines, etc.
(c) Shade areas of diagrams.
(d) Add text information.

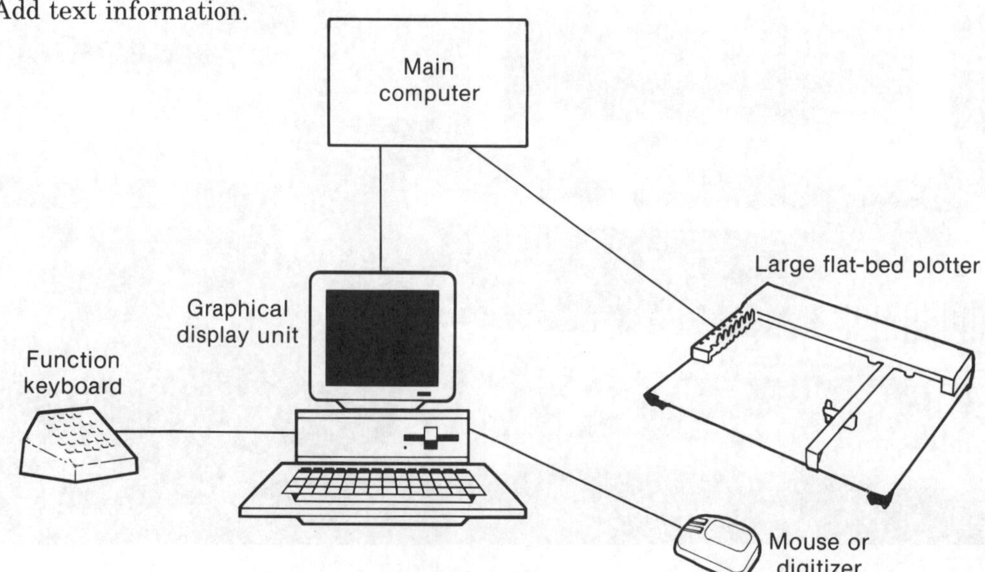

Fig. 19.8 The hardware used in a typical computer-aided design system

2 A means of editing designs once they have been produced. It would usually be possible to improve freehand lines, delete areas, change scales, etc.
3 The ability to display objects clearly. This can be done:
(a) By showing a 'three-dimensional' view, possibly with the object able to rotate on the screen.
(b) By showing different 'elevations' of the object – i.e. a set of views of it from certain different directions.
4 A means of drawing designs accurately on paper. Usually the hardware would include a large flat-bed plotter for this purpose.

Often the software would include further facilities associated with the object being designed, e.g.:
1 Costing of materials used.
2 Simulated tests of the object being designed (see Unit 19.4).

Examples of the use of CAD

In civil engineering

In highway construction, programs have been developed to aid design. One of these, MOSS, is based on superimposing the planned road on a computer 'map' of the area. The program helps spot potential difficulties and can calculate various costs. It has been found that use of CAD has meant that designs for new roads have been produced three times more quickly.

It is hoped that in the future CAD programs will, in conjunction with others, be able to produce specifications and estimates of quantities of materials required.

In kitchen design

Kitchen designers can use a program to help a customer to decide on their kitchen layout. The dimensions of the kitchen are entered into the computer. The computer has on file the shapes of various standard units, such as cupboards, cooker, sink, etc. These can be manipulated on the screen until the customer is satisfied with the result. The computer can then be used to work out the cost of the units chosen.

Design of machine parts

Packages are available which allow parts which have been designed separately to be connected together on the screen.

Advantages of CAD over manual design

1 Some types of drawing can be produced more quickly.
2 Top quality drawings can be produced with clear lettering by someone who is not a skilled draughtsman.
3 If a series of similar drawings has to be made this can be done very quickly.
4 The computer can check for obvious errors in drawings.
5 Once a design is stored in the computer, calculations can be done on the data – such as costing, etc.

19.4 Simulations

To **simulate** a system is to produce a model of it which has the same characteristics. By studying the behaviour of the model it is possible to find out how the actual system would behave in similar circumstances. Very often a simulation consists of a computer program which mimics a real-life situation. Usually the program is based on a number of formulae which form a mathematical model of the actual system.

Example of a simulation – traffic lights

A council is considering situating traffic lights at a busy road junction. It is not clear whether this would improve the situation at the junction or not. A survey is done to find out:
1 The number of cars per hour reaching the junction from each road at different times of the day.
2 The length of queues of cars waiting at the junction.

A computer program is written giving a simulation of the cars arriving at the junction and leaving it. The simulation can include the effect of traffic lights and shows:
1 Cars arriving each minute along the roads leading to the junction. For this the computer chooses a number of cars which is random but is within the range of numbers found in the survey.
2 The traffic lights changing. The model allows the timing of the lights to be changed.
3 Queues of cars waiting at the lights. The computer shows each queue getting bigger when

the lights are red. It then shows them getting smaller or disappearing when the lights are green.

First the simulation is run without any traffic lights. The queues of cars formed should be about the same as the real queues found in the survey. This shows that the model used in the simulation does work.

Then the program is run with some traffic lights included in the model. Different timings are tried in the simulation. If the council officials find that they can reduce the traffic delays, then they know it is a good idea to install the lights.

STAGES IN PRODUCING AND USING A COMPUTER SIMULATION

1 The problem to be solved must be fully understood.
2 Data from the real-life situation is collected if possible.
3 The model is formulated. This may involve a set of mathematical equations.
4 The computer programs are written and tested.
5 The program is run with data chosen such that the computer predictions can be compared with real-life events. This stage is called the **validation** of the model.
6 The computer is now ready to answer 'What if . . . ?' questions. The model is used with different data to make predictions about what would happen to the real system in a new situation.

In this case there are no real-life results for comparison. It is necessary to rely on the computer and on the model which has been made.

It will not always be possible to carry out all the above steps. It may not always be possible to collect data from the real-life situation beforehand. In this case validation of the model may not take place until after the first predictions have been made.

SITUATIONS WHERE SIMULATIONS ARE USED

1 Where conditions are too dangerous for real experiments to be carried out (e.g. studying the behaviour of a nuclear reactor if changes are made to the fuel rods).
2 Where a decision has to be reached and there are several possible courses of action (e.g. a model of the national economy). Ministers and Treasury officials can try various budget changes to see what their effect would be.
3 In designing. For example extensive simulation work was carried out in the planning of the proposed new airport for London. Features incorporated into the model included:
(a) Flow of people through the airport buildings.
(b) Flow of traffic on the proposed site and in the surrounding area.
(c) The effects of the noise of the aircraft engines.
4 Where a study being carried out is entirely theoretical and the performing of real experiments is an impossibility. A good example of this is the study into the origins of the universe. Theories such as the 'Big Bang' can be modelled and the consequences of the theory investigated.
5 In education and training. By interacting with a model of a situation a student or trainee can become familiar with the situation.

Further examples of simulations

1 Military operational research models. These are used for assessing weapons and tactics under various conditions (e.g. difficult terrain, adverse weather).
2 Economic models. These are used to analyse and predict the behaviour of firms, industries or even national economies.
3 International relations models. These simulate the state of relations between different countries of the world. They could be used, for example, to attempt to predict the outcome of certain military action by an individual country.
4 Educational simulations. These are widely available for microcomputers. One such simulation involves the user taking on the role of the owner of a small delivery service. The simulation then takes the user through the various stages in organizing deliveries efficiently. The user has to take decisions based on the information provided. The aim of the simulation is to teach the user something about vehicles and the road system as well as encouraging logical thought and good decision making.
5 Circuit testing. Computer simulation is being used to help in the design of new computers. It is no longer necessary to make an actual test circuit for any new chip which is designed. The new designs are instead tested by simulation. If the results of the simulation are satisfactory then production can be started.

FLIGHT SIMULATION

As early as the 1940s pilots where given some training in mock ups of real aircraft cockpits. Later, when the first multi-engined jet airliners were introduced computer-controlled flight simulators were employed. The 'cockpit' was mounted on hydraulic rams. The rams were under the control of a computer whose program simulated various flying conditions. The crew under training had to respond by referring to their instruments and operating their controls.

In these early simulations the 'view outside' was not very realistic. Advances in computer graphics have meant that visual images are now available to improve the authenticity of the simulations.

Techniques have improved so much that it is now possible for the training of military pilots to include the experience of enemy attacks. The attacks have a random factor in them so that the pilot is forced to respond not only quickly, but in a flexible way.

Civil pilots are able to practise landing and taking off. Accurate images of real airports appear in the simulation. Again random elements are introduced into the simulation so that the pilot has to respond to, say, a burst tyre on landing.

Flight simulation programs of a less complex nature are available for microcomputers. Some merely provide amusement, but others provide a serious exercise for would-be pilots.

19.5 Medical Uses of Computers

Computers are used in the medical field for a variety of purposes.

MEDICAL ADMINISTRATION

There are a large number of examples in this country of the computerization of medical records of patients. It would be possible for the computers involved to be linked. Then all health records for each person could be compared. This has not become common practice so far and the examples given mainly use unconnected systems.

Examples of the use of computers to store patient records

In hospitals

Computers are used to keep records of:
1 Casualty patients.
2 Outpatients receiving courses of treatment.
3 Patients resident in the hospital.

In doctors' surgeries

Records are still kept manually in many cases.

Where computers are used in surgeries they usually deal with:
1 The medical history of each patient – the system stores details of all patients on the doctors' lists. The data is more organized than when it is kept on paper files. Details of prescriptions, results of tests and any previous illnesses are readily available to the doctor.
2 Appointments – the computer stores a diary for each doctor. When a patient rings up to make an appointment, the receptionist uses a work station to check for a free time and to make the appointment.
3 Reminders to patients – some patients are subject to regular checks or they may be due for immunization or vaccination or some form of treatment. The computer can produce a reminder to be sent to them and make an appointment.
4 Prescriptions – the details of drugs prescribed for patients can be used to print prescriptions which the doctor then signs.

To store data on organ transplants

Some people have a defective organ such as their liver, kidneys, heart or lungs. This may be caused by disease or by an accident. In some cases it is possible for surgeons to transplant a healthy organ from a patient who has died. For some organs such as kidneys these transplants are very successful.

In this country data on all patients requiring new organs is stored on a computer by the United Kingdom Transplant Service in Bristol.

The information stored on each patient includes:
1 Their tissue type – an organ can only be transplanted from one person to another if their tissues match.
2 Their blood group.
3 Their clinical status – how ill they are.

If an organ becomes available then the computer is contacted to find a patient who needs one and whose tissues match.

If an organ is of a rare tissue type records can be checked throughout Europe. The Bristol computer has direct links with the EuroTransplant computer in Leiden, Holland and with ScandaTransplant in Scandinavia.

INFORMATION RETRIEVAL

As in many scientific subjects, doctors and consultants have great difficulty in keeping up with research. Research is being carried out throughout the world. The results of this are produced in papers, in reports and as articles in medical journals. It is very difficult to locate results of research on any chosen subject. For this reason large databases are set up containing all the articles produced, or in some cases abstracts from them. An abstract is a summary which contains all the important terms and references from an article.

In order to find a reference it is necessary to connect by terminal to the computer containing the data bank. The computer can then be asked to search for all articles containing certain keywords. For instance information about tissue typing and kidney transplants could be obtained by asking the computer to search for 'tissue' and 'kidney'.

CONTROL OF EQUIPMENT

Equipment in hospitals may be connected to a computer:

1 As a form of data logging (see Unit 19.2) so that data can be analysed later.
2 To adjust temperature, etc in an environment – e.g. for patients in intensive care.
3 To improve the accuracy with which equipment can operate. Figure 19.9 shows a computer being used to control and record brain scans.

(a)

(b)

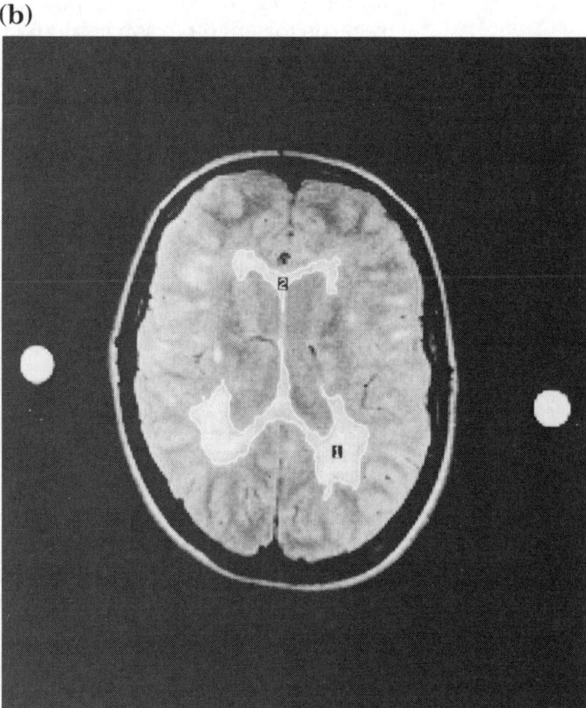

Fig. 19.9(a) A body scanner. For each scan the operator has to enter the patient's name, the operator's name, the patient's position for the scan, etc. **(b)** A brain scan (*By kind permission of IBM*)

20 USE OF COMPUTERS IN INDUSTRIAL PROCESSES

DEFINITIONS

A **sensor** is a monitoring device which measures some physical quantity and sends signals back to the processor. The sensors used are often analogue devices called transducers (see the first example in Unit 19.2).

Examples of sensors

1 A thermocouple—a device which produces a voltage proportional to its temperature. This is an analogue sensor because it produces a continuous range of voltages.
2 A pressure pad at a traffic light. This produces a signal if a car goes over it. It is a digital sensor because it is either on or off.
3 An infra-red sensor on a house alarm system. An infra-red beam is directed at the sensor. If the beam is broken by a burglar the sensor no longer detects light and the alarm goes off.

An **actuator** is a device which can produce a movement when given an electrical signal. Actuators are used by a computer to control equipment.

Feedback generally means using output from a system to influence the input.

In industrial processes feedback involves data from a sensor being used by a processor to control an operation.

Examples of feedback in everyday life

1 Sound from a microphone is amplified and fed through loudspeakers. Sound output from one of the speakers is accidentally directed at the microphone. This sound is input back through the microphone and is amplified and output again. The sound very quickly becomes too loud for the speakers to cope with and a loud whistle results.

This is an example where the feedback makes the system unstable. It is called **positive feedback**.

2 A cyclist starts to overbalance to the right. This is sensed by his ears and a message goes to the brain. The cyclist unconsciously shifts his weight towards the left and steers slightly to the right. This corrects the overbalancing.

In this example the feedback is used to make the system stable. This is **negative feedback**.

DIFFERENT WAYS IN WHICH COMPUTERS ARE USED IN INDUSTRIAL PROCESSES

Data logging

At this level the computer merely collects the data from sensors and records or displays it (see Unit 19.2 for details).

Quality control

In this case the computer not only monitors the process, but can take some action. Signals received from the sensors are compared with values stored in memory. If the results show the process is not working properly a message is sent to the operator. Examples are:

1 Checking raw materials for size and quality in the chemical industry.
2 Testing printed circuit boards. Such a technique replaces a large number of meter readings.

Process control

In process control the computer uses feedback to change the process itself if necessary. This is dealt with in detail in Unit 20.1.

Distributed systems and remote systems

Modern communication techniques can be used to link together separate processes. Often microprocessors have local control over individual operations. A large computer may have control over the whole network. When data from all parts of the system have been analysed new instructions will, if necessary, be sent to the local microprocessors. Such as system is an example of distributed processing.

Examples include:

The grid of pipelines and pumping stations operated by a gas board

As consumers use gas the pressure has to be maintained at a fixed level throughout the grid. This is done by pumping gas to those areas where the pressure is dropping. The whole grid is controlled by a computer at the board's headquarters. Each pumping station has a microprocessor and pressure sensors. Communication is by microwaves. The main computer sends a signal to a pumping station asking for pressure readings. The microprocessor sends results back. These are analysed and the main computer sends signals to the microprocessor to adjust the pumps.

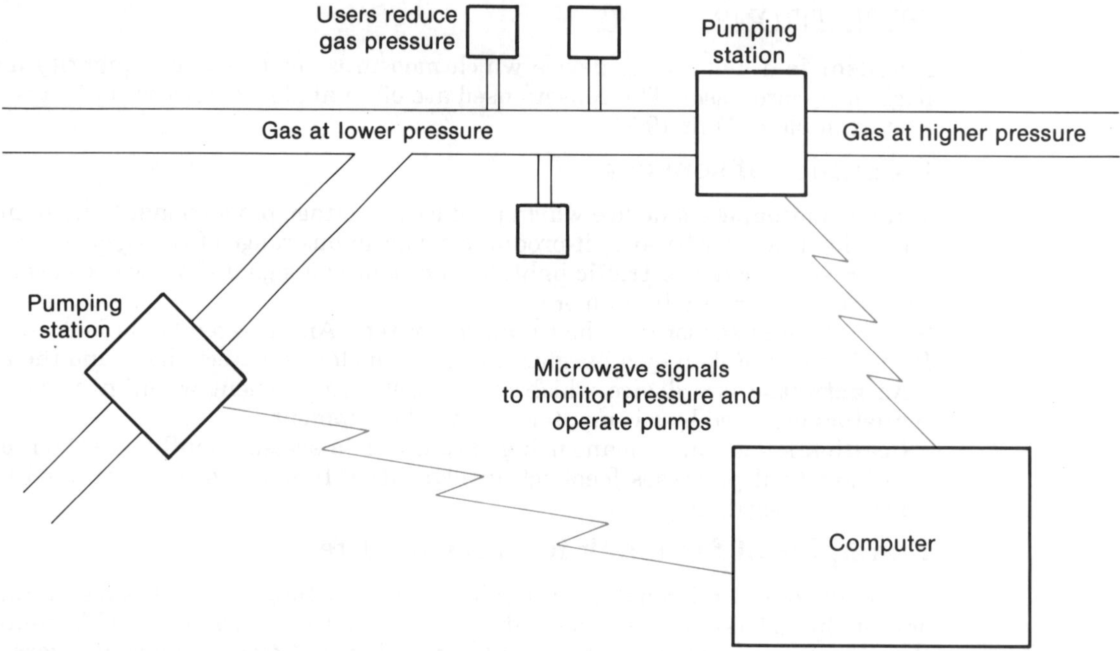

Fig. 20.1 Control of the pumping stations on a gas grid

An engineering plant

A central computer controls operations and monitors production. It also ensures that each machine is provided with tools, materials and instructions. Each individual machine is itself under microprocessor control.

20.1 Process Control

Process control means automatic control of an industrial process.

Usually the controller consists of a dedicated computer- or a microprocessor-based circuit. The computer may control the supply of materials and the timing of each part of the process. Usually the control process uses the feedback principle (see introduction to this Unit).

Some more sophisticated systems allow for 'learning' to take place. The microprocessor 'remembers' how the best results were obtained and attempts to reproduce those results.

Process control systems use negative feedback to keep the process stable. Control is carried out as follows:

1 Output from the process is monitored, signals being sent back to the computer.
2 The computer uses this data to adjust the process so that the output remains constant.

In a computerized process control application the following items are generally required:

1 A processor.
2 Display devices (e.g. VDU screens, LED or LCD displays) so that a human operator can check the system.
3 A printer to provide hard copy when required.
4 Sensors to provide information on the process under control (usually analogue in form).
5 Actuators to carry out control action in response to signals from the processor.
6 Digital-to-analogue and analogue-to-digital converters.

Examples of process control

Cement mixing

The computer controls the monitoring and weighing of materials and the speed of mixing.

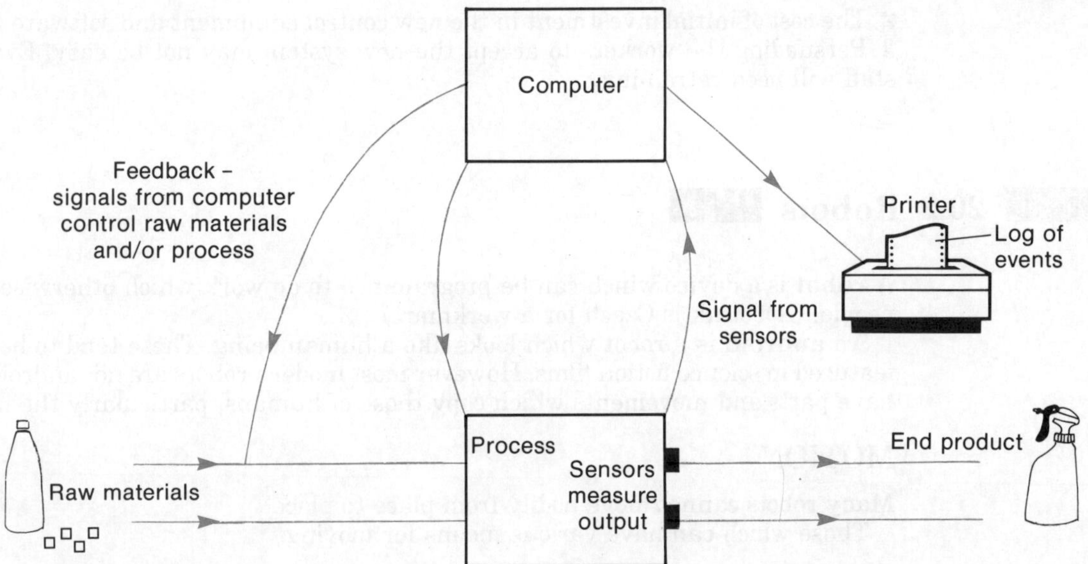

Fig. 20.2 A process control system

Various mixing recipes are held in memory and these can be changed, or new ones added, when required.

Chemical plant

It is the speed of the microprocessor which is important in this example. Inputs from sensors are received very frequently. This means that control actions can take place swiftly in response to changes. It is usual for every operation in the plant to be monitored at least once per second.

Computer numerically controlled machinery (CNC)

New machines are often built incorporating CNC. An alternative is to fit control equipment to existing machinery, this is called retrofitting. The second option has proved cheaper (about 30 per cent of the cost) and consequently more popular.

CNC machinery is used, for example, in woodworking. The patterns or the original to be copied are traced out and the tracing stored in memory. The tracing in memory is then used to control the cutting of the pattern into the final material.

Advantages of introducing computers to control processes

1 Labour costs are lower. Fewer operators and maintenance staff are required. Often maintenance work is put out to contract.
(**Note:** All this may not be seen as an advantage by the workers.)
2 A computer-controlled system is more flexible. This means the manufacturer can easily change the product to suit the customer.
3 The system is more reliable. Microprocessors rarely fail and when they do replacement is a relatively simple process.
4 Quality is improved. The quality of raw materials can more easily be monitored. More tests can be carried out during the process and those tests can be carried out more often. This improves the quality of the end product.
5 Safety is improved. The general level of control is improved. In particular 'fail safes' can be incorporated into the programs to deal with dangerous conditions. It is also possible to put control equipment into places where it would be unpleasant or even dangerous for a human being to go.
6 Energy is saved. Microprocessors can help ensure that energy is not wasted by monitoring and controlling its use. Where there are no people present there is less need for heating and lighting.
7 Raw materials are saved. When materials costs are significant the microprocessor can be programmed to minimize wastage. For example accurate weighing in the food industry can contribute to considerable savings.
8 For the workers who are left, jobs and conditions are improved. Because an operator is responsible for more than one machine that responsibility is higher. This could mean the pay is higher. Workers usually have cleaner, less hostile conditions.

Disadvantages of introducing computers to control processes

1 Although less staff are required, those that are needed are highly skilled and difficult to find.

2 The cost of initial investment in the new control equipment and software for it may be high.
3 Persuading the workers to accept the new system may not be easy. Even if it is accepted staff will need retraining.

20.2 Robots

A **robot** is a device which can be programmed to do work which otherwise has to be done by people. (Robotnik is Czech for a workman.)

An **android** is a robot which looks like a human being. These tend to be the type of robots featured in science fiction films. However most modern robots are not androids, although many have parts and movements which copy those of humans, particularly the human arm.

MOTION

Many robots cannot move bodily from place to place.

Those which can have various means for moving:

Wheels

Small wheels are suitable for fast movement on flat surfaces.
Large wheels can be used for slow movement on rough surfaces.
A large number of wheels makes a robot stable.
A small number of wheels gives better control of movement.

Examples of robots with wheels

1 PENMAN – a device which is connected to a computer by a cable and used to draw graphics on paper. It only has two wheels so that it is very manoeuvrable.
2 A robot for moving parts around a factory.

Caterpillar tracks

This is a continuous belt, as on a tank.

Fitted to robots which have to move slowly, possibly over difficult terrain. Movements can be controlled accurately.

Examples of robots with caterpillar tracks

1 The BBC Buggy – this is an educational robot which can be controlled by a BBC computer (see Fig. 20.3).
2 The robot used by the British Army in Northern Ireland to detonate bombs.

Legs

It is relatively difficult to make a robot walk on two legs because every time it raises one leg it has to balance on the other one. Robots with several legs are used for slow movement over very rough ground.

Gantry

In some factories and warehouses a robot which has to move within a small area can be suspended on a framework moved by cables.

STATIONARY ROBOTS

Many industrial robots are fixed in position.

Usually the parts and movements are similar to those of a human arm (see Fig. 20.4) – they have a waist, a shoulder, an elbow, a wrist and a hand. The ability of a robot to move is measured by its degrees of freedom.

A **degree of freedom** is the ability to swing or to rotate in a particular direction at a particular joint.

Each main joint of a robot may allow any of the following three movements (see Fig. 20.5):
1 **Pitch** – movement vertically up and down,
2 **Yaw** – movement left or right across the joint,
3 **Roll** – rotation clockwise or anticlockwise.

Examples of degrees of freedom

1 A wrist normally has three degrees of freedom. The hand can pitch and yaw and roll.
2 A simple industrial robot usually has seven degrees of freedom. It has one at the waist (rotation), one at the shoulder (pitch), one at the elbow (pitch), three at the wrist and one at the hand (opening and closing) (see Fig. 20.5).

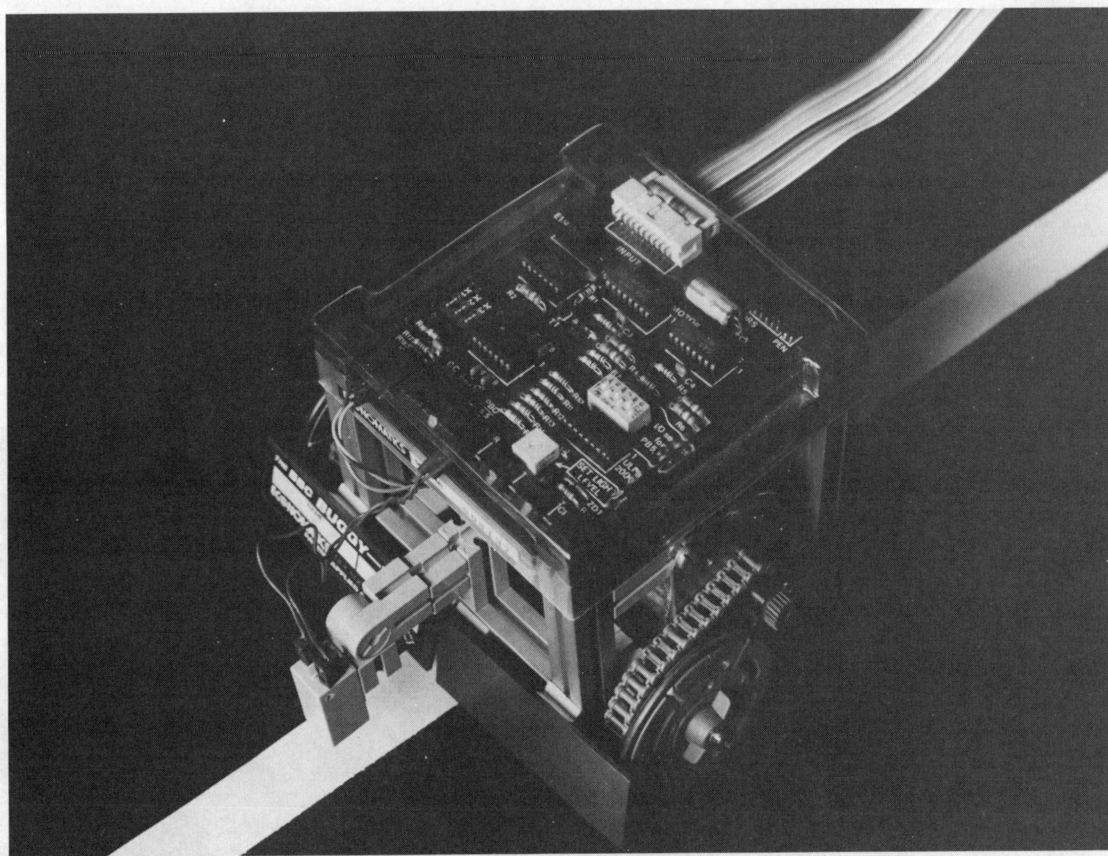

Fig. 20.3 The BBC Buggy is using a light sensor to measure the intensity of light. The computer uses these results to make the Buggy follow the white line.

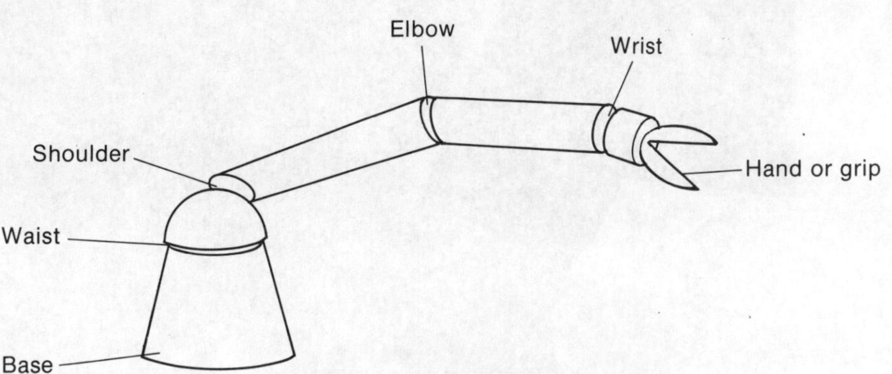

Fig. 20.4 A robot arm showing the main parts

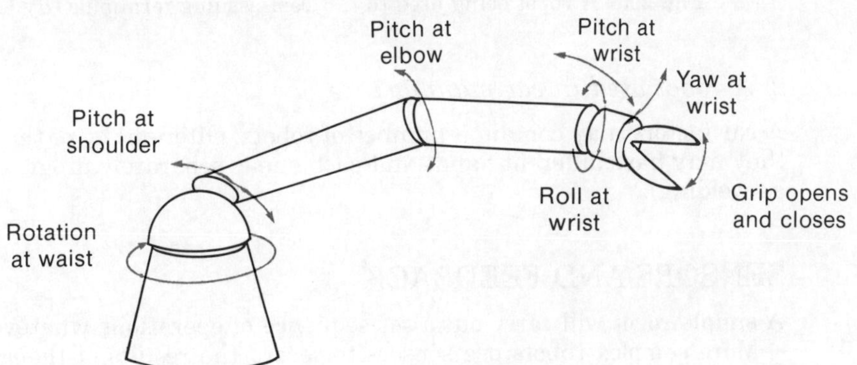

Fig. 20.5 A robot arm showing the main directions of movement

Examples of stationary robots

1 A robot to test cash issuing terminals before they are installed at banks (see Unit 6.2)

Each terminal has to be tested for several hours before being installed in a bank. The robot inserts cards and presses the appropriate buttons on the terminal, taking the money and stacking it (see Fig. 20.6). It selects a card from 10 different cards and carries out different types of transactions so that the test simulates real use by customers.

The terminal does not have to be positioned very carefully as the robot can find the terminal and memorize where it is.

This robot will only work when no one is near it. To avoid hurting anyone the robot moves to a safe point and stops when anyone approaches.

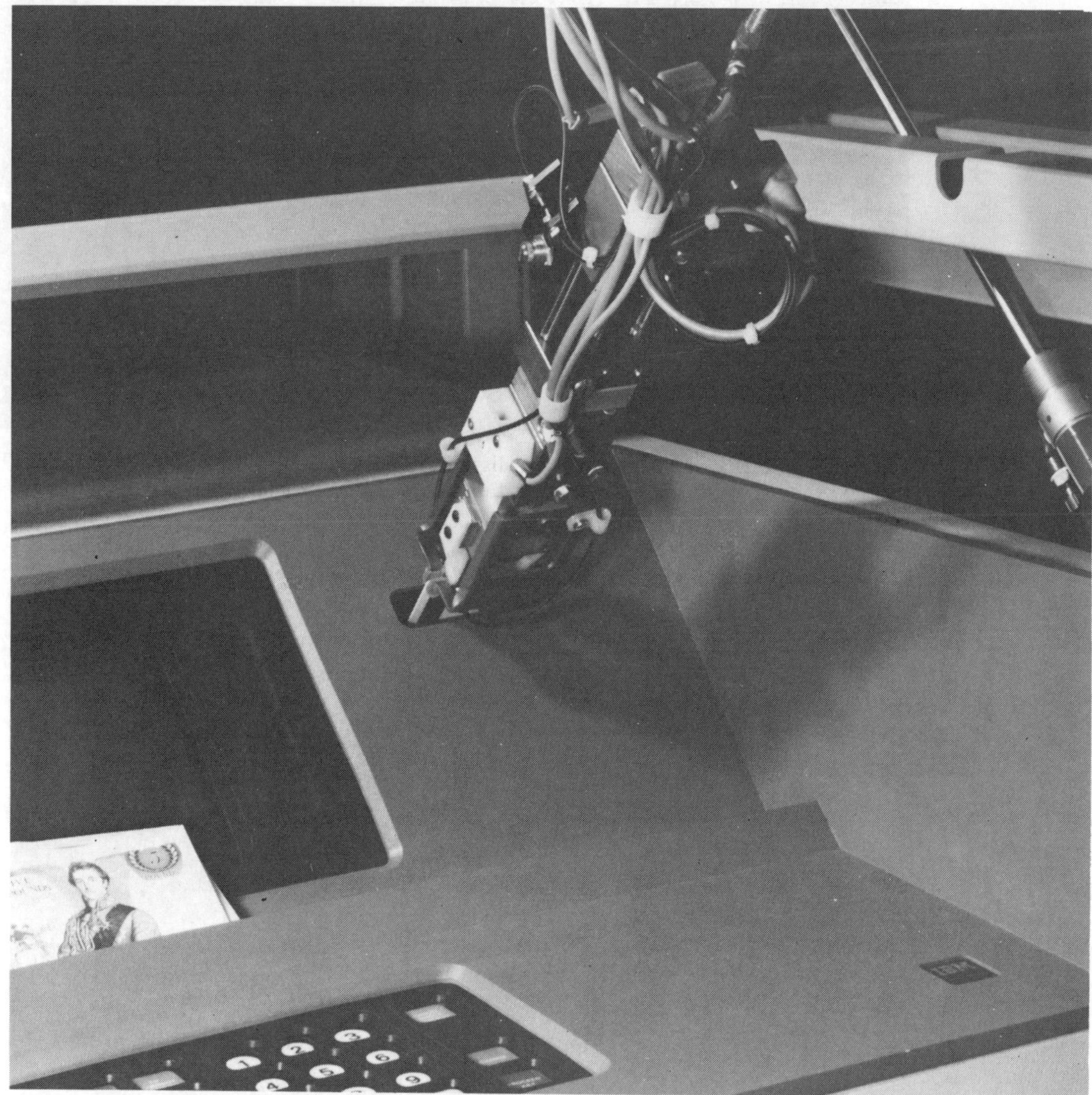

Fig. 20.6 A robot being used to test cash issuing terminals (*By kind permission of IBM*)

2 A robot used in car manufacture

A car factory may contain a number of robots. Often many of them are of the same type, but they may have different hands and each one is separately programmed for its own task (such as welding).

SENSORS AND FEEDBACK

A simple robot will carry out a set sequence of operations whatever happens.

More complex robots use sensors to record the results of their actions. They then use the feedback principle to change their actions to suit the situation (for feedback see the introduction to this Unit).

Examples of the use of sensors and feedback

1 (a) A simple robot designed to paint metal panels will only paint the shape it is programmed to paint and if the conveyor supplying it with panels is stopped it may paint thin air.
(b) A more complex robot also paints metal panels. This one is fitted with a video camera to record the shape of a panel. It can paint panels of different shapes and its sprayer is automatically switched off if no panel is present.
2 A mobile robot carrying parts in a car factory has a light sensor and uses it to follow a white line on the factory floor. If the sensor shows a low light reading the robot is not properly following the line. The processor adjusts the direction until the light level rises again, showing that the line is being followed.

PROGRAMMING

The computer processor controlling a robot may be contained in the robot or it may be separate. If separate it may be connected by a cable or it may send signals to the robot, for instance by radio waves or microwaves.

The computer is programmed to control the robot. Even if the program does not include any feedback the program will contain a large number of instructions.

Methods of entering a program include:

1 Writing a program of movements and typing them at a keyboard.
2 Switching the robot into 'learn' mode. Its arm can then be moved through the necessary sequence of movements and the computer memorizes them. The arm can be moved by hand or remotely using a joystick.

Advantages of robots

1 They can carry out a task repeatedly for hours without stopping.
2 They can operate in situations where humans cannot easily go (e.g. on other planets, deep in the ocean, probing explosives).
3 They do not make errors due to tiredness or lack of concentration.

Disadvantages of robots

1 They are expensive initially.
2 They can only cope with the particular situations they are built and programmed for.

21 SOCIAL IMPACT OF COMPUTERS

Assessment Objective E of the GCSE National Criteria in Computer Studies states that a candidate should be able to:

'demonstrate some understanding of the social and economic effects of the use of computerized systems on individuals, organization and society'.

This is difficult to do because the situation is complicated. Even experts cannot agree on the social effects of computers. For instance we have a very high level of unemployment. Often firms which introduce computers lay workers off because they need fewer people to do the same work. On the other hand some firms which have not introduced computers cannot compete and they have to make people redundant as well. It is very difficult to say clearly what effect computers have on the unemployment situation (see Unit 21.3).

To show an understanding of the effects of computers you need to:

1 Know the facts about each situation – you should be clear what the effects are and what features of computers give rise to them.

2 Be able to put forward arguments for both sides where there is a doubt about the benefits.

For this reason each section of this Unit contains facts, examples and arguments.

21.1 Changes in Business and Society

FACTS

Computer developments during the past five decades can be summarized as follows:

1940s The first few working electronic computers.

1950s The first few computers for sale.
High-level computing languages developed.

1960s Fairly large numbers of mainframe computers sold.
Stock control, payroll and accounts are the most common applications. Most computing is done by batch processing. The first multi-access systems using typewriter terminals.

1970s The introduction of minicomputers and then microcomputers. Much more varied applications.
Dramatic increase in numbers of VDU terminals and of interactive computing.

1980s The spread of the use of computers into every part of life – shops, offices, schools, factories, our homes.

In the 1980s there has still been a large scale use of mainframe computers. However the huge growth in information technology has been due to the use of:

1 Microprocessors for control purposes.
2 Computers for word processing and other office applications.
3 Modern communications.
4 General-purpose microcomputers in homes, schools, business, etc.

Examples of uses of information technology

1 To monitor and control the operation of equipment, e.g.
(a) A 'robot' programmed to weld the joints on a car during manufacture.
(b) A fully automated greenhouse, in which the temperature and humidity are kept constant; a microprocessor controls the ventilators, the watering and the heating.
(c) Controlling the fuel flow in a car to lessen petrol consumption and lessen the pollutants in the exhaust fumes.

2 In offices an array of equipment is available which together is being referred to as the 'electronic office', (see Unit 18.4) e.g.
(a) Word processors.
(b) Work stations which can communicate with other work stations and can store information, eliminating a lot of the previous requirement for paperwork.

3 In the home, e.g.
(a) Many new models of automatic washing machine are microprocessor-controlled.
(b) In video game devices.
(c) In home computers.
(d) In devices for communicating outside the home (e.g. with information systems such as Prestel).

4 In small business computers, e.g.
(a) In newsagents and other shops.
(b) In estate agents.
5 In schools. In the early 1970s computers were far too expensive for ordinary schools to buy them. The microcomputer has changed that completely. Now most primary schools have computers and many secondary schools have networks.

TRENDS WHICH RESULT FROM THE USE OF INFORMATION TECHNOLOGY

The increased reliance on communications

It has been possible to conduct business at a distance for some time. This has been due to improved transport, post, telephones and telex. Now however information can be transmitted far more quickly and cheaply in the form of computer data. Business can be run in a different way. Examples:
1 People are increasingly working from their homes; this improves the chances for employment of housewives, the disabled, etc.
2 Companies can set up offices which are distant from one another.
3 Industries can control operations automatically at a distance – e.g. water pumping stations, electricity grids.
4 Shopping chains can control their stock and accounts from a central computer (Unit 17.1).
5 Clients of banks and building societies can handle their money from cash dispensing terminals.

The decreased use of cash

People can be paid their wages and spend them without handling any actual money. It is becoming possible to use **electronic funds transfer (EFT)**.

Electronic funds transfer is the moving of money from one bank account to another using data communications and without any paper transactions.

For example, in some shops the customers can submit their bank card to be inserted into a reader attached to the point-of-sale terminal. The card is checked by the customers' bank computer. The amount registered on the till is then automatically transferred from the customers' bank account to the shop's bank account. This is known as **electronic funds transfer at point of sale (EFTPOS)**.

It must be said that progress towards a 'cashless society' is slow. Many people prefer to handle cash. In fact many people do not have bank accounts.

ARGUMENTS

The main arguments here are about:
1 How much effect the 'information revolution' will have on the lives of most people.
2 Whether the changes are of benefit to us.

The following are three completely different points of view which people hold:
1 That the integrated circuit manufacturers are having difficulty finding things for us to do with their products, and that their major impact on the average home is in computer games. The new technology will make life easier but it will not really change it significantly. **Or:**
2 That this new revolution is more important than the Industrial Revolution. It will:
(a) Give us more leisure time.
(b) Improve the quality of our lives.
(c) Completely change our job structure, creating interesting jobs in the 'information industry' as boring ones are lost from traditional manufacturing.
We must enter the new age with enthusiasm or the rest of the world will leave us behind. **Or:**
3 The changes taking place are harmful to society:
(a) The centralization of information by large companies and Government departments may help them, but it makes them inaccessible to us and takes away our privacy.
(b) The technology is being used to divide society – to improve the quality of life of the rich but not of the poor.

Which of these three is nearest the truth remains to be seen, and may still be argued about when the 'revolution' is over.

21.2 Personal Privacy

Information is stored about each of us on a large number of computers. Such information has been stored in the past on paper but now it is stored electronically. It is therefore technically possible:

1 To use modern communications to send data about us from one computer to another.
2 To use the power of computers to process the data. For instance:
(a) All the facts stored about a given person could be brought together to provide a complete dossier.
(b) Records relating to financial problems or court appearances could be used by prospective employers, etc.
(c) Lists could be produced of all people in certain categories. These could be used for political or other purposes.

Many people feel that we should have the right:
1 To withhold information about ourselves.
2 To stop data being passed from one database to another without our knowledge or consent.
3 To find out what data is stored about us.
4 To have inaccurate data corrected.

FACTS

1 Examples of centrally held data files

(a) Any British family could expect details about them to be held on numerous data files. Examples are:
(i) their health records on files at the doctor's surgery, the local hospital and the local health authority,
(ii) their income on computers owned by their employer and by the income tax office,
(iii) the state of their accounts on bank and building society computers,
(iv) the amounts they spend on electricity, gas, water, etc. are stored on files of the appropriate companies.

In fact often when people buy furniture or pay for a holiday or subscribe to a magazine, etc. their name and address go on computer file. Lists of these names and addresses can then be sold to advertising and similar companies.
(b) Police records – the police hold records on large numbers of people. These records include:
(i) The Police National Computer, which has information on about 23 million people and includes data on:
people with criminal records,
fingerprints,
stolen or suspect vehicles,
vehicle owners.
(ii) The Special Branch Computer, which stores data on over 2 million people, many of whom are not criminals or even suspected of crime.
(c) The Driver and Vehicle Licensing Centre at Swansea. Information about all drivers and their cars is now held at this centre. Uses of this data have included:
(i) tracing owners of a particular make of car for the manufacturer so that they can be recalled for checking,
(ii) finding the most recent addresses of people who are dodging Income Tax.

2 Data laws in other countries

(a) *Sweden* – the Data Act of 1973 gives a citizen the right to be present while an official checks centrally held information. If the citizen objects to anything, an independent arbitrator decides what should be changed.
(b) *USA* – a 1974 amendment to the Freedom of Information Act gives citizens the right to be shown all information held about them by Government agencies.
(c) *France* – a law passed in 1978 bans references in computer files to citizens' religion, politics, race or health. Anyone has the right of access to data about themselves if they think the information held infringes the privacy law. It is thought each person in France is referred to in about 500 files.

3 The Data Protection Act in Britain

The Data Protection Act was passed in 1984.

(a) This Act refers to:
(i) the **data user** – anyone who stores and processes computer data about people,
(ii) the **data subject** – anyone who has information about them stored by data users.
(b) The Act created:
(i) a Data Registrar, who is the person who sees that the Act is enforced.
(ii) a Data Protection Tribunal, to which people can appeal against the Registrar's decisions.
(c) Any data user and any computer bureau has to apply to the Data Registrar before they can store and use data about people. There are some exceptions such as payroll data or data held for 'national security' purposes. Those applying have to state what data they are storing, and

what they intend to use it for. If their application is accepted then their name and details of the data held goes into a register. This register will be in large public libraries and anyone can go and have a look at it.

(d) The Act has some guiding principles of which the main ones are:

(i) data must be obtained fairly and lawfully,

(ii) data must only be held or used or disclosed in the way that has been registered,

(iii) data must be accurate,

(iv) people must be allowed to have information about them disclosed if they request it; if they can prove it is wrong it must be changed or deleted,

(v) data users and computer bureaux must protect the data they hold.

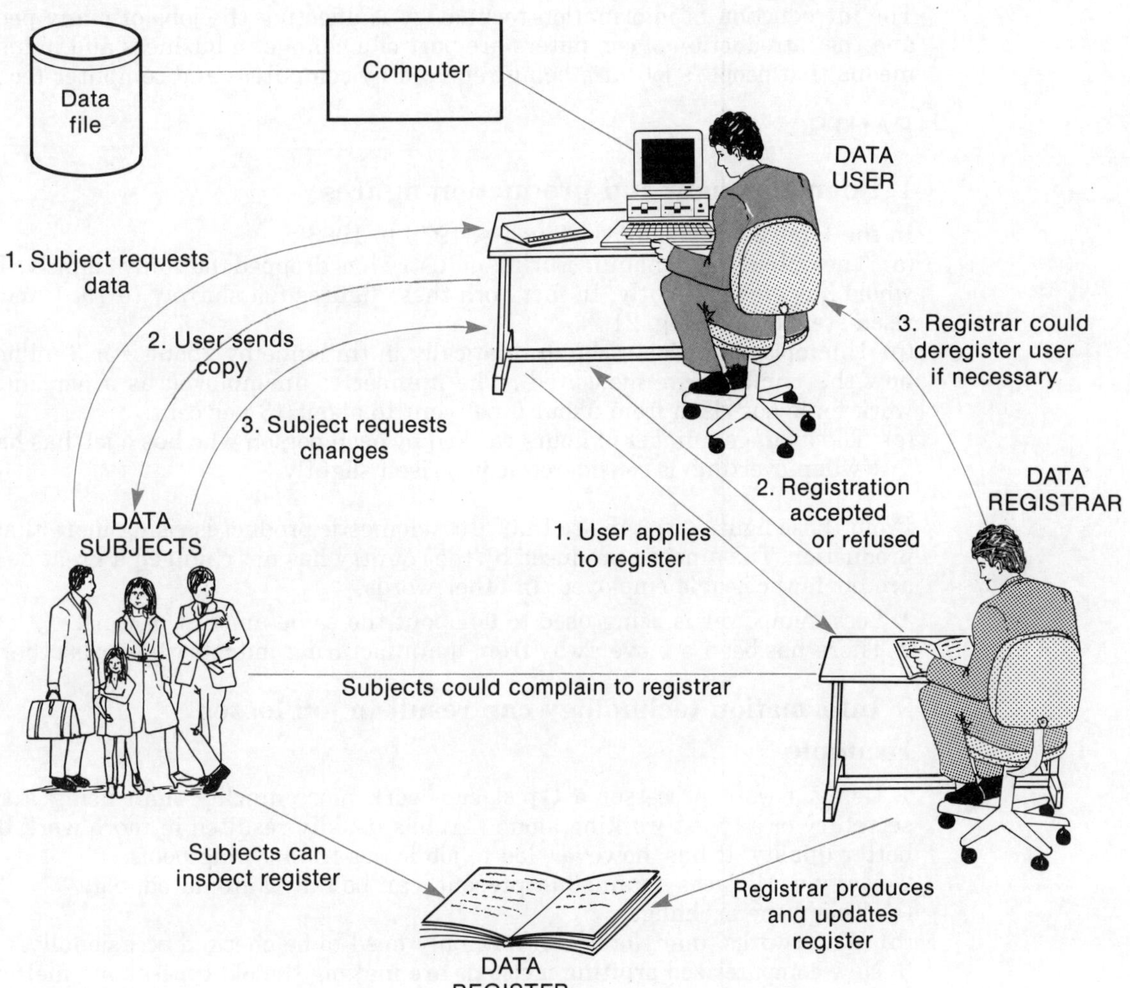

Fig. 21.1 How the Data Protection Act works

ARGUMENTS

In favour of more rights for individuals

1 The Data Protection Act is not strong enough.

(a) The Act only deals with computer data and not with paper files.

(b) There are large numbers of organizations who hold data but who have not registered.

(c) Data subjects cannot complain about uses or disclosures of data if the data user is registered for that use.

(d) Data subjects can only complain about the inaccuracy of data if they have 'suffered damage' from it.

(e) Data can be held for 'National Security' purposes which people cannot gain access to.

2 If we had a 'Police State' the data could be used to people's disadvantage. This is not so impossible even in this country. Other countries, such as Chile, with a long history of democracy, have been taken over by dictatorships.

In favour of the free use of information

1 The Data Protection Act is largely unnecessary.

(a) The registration process costs a lot of money and is a lot of trouble to data users.

(b) A lot of people are likely to break the law unintentionally because they haven't registered properly.

(c) People should have the right to store some data about employees, pupils, etc. without them knowing about it.
(d) Stories about misuse of data or inaccurate data are exaggerated. There have been very few complaints to the Data Registrar so far about data users.
2 We would never have a police state in this country. The authorities only use their files against those who break the law. In other words they are used to protect the rest of us.

21.3 The Effect on Unemployment

The introduction of information technology is affecting the jobs of many people. Automation and the introduction of computers are part of a change in business and industry. This change means that people's jobs are being replaced by computers and computer technology.

FACTS

1 Unemployment and production figures

In the United Kingdom over 8 years (1979 to 1986):
(a) The output from manufacturing industry has dropped, but only slightly. The economy as a whole has grown slightly. In fact both these figures fell sharply to 1981 and since then have risen steadily (see Fig. 21.2).
(b) Unemployment has risen dramatically in this time by about 2 or 3 million (depending on how the numbers are measured). The number of unemployed as a percentage of the whole work force has risen from about 5 per cent to about 13 per cent.
(c) The average number of hours worked by each person who has a job has hardly changed. In fact when overtime is considered it has risen slightly.

From these figures we can see that gross domestic product is rising more than manufacturing production. The amount produced by the country has not changed a great deal although there are far fewer people employed. In other words,
1 Less manpower is being used to do about the same amount of work.
2 There has been a move away from manufacturing industry towards other work.

2 Information technology can result in job losses

Example

1 Using a word processor a typist can work more quickly than using a typewriter. For a secretary or a typist working alone this has usually resulted in more work being done and of better quality. It has, however, led to job losses from typing pools.
2 Many workplaces, manned at present, can be fully automated. e.g.
(a) Telephone exchanges.
(b) Waterworks, many of which now only need to be checked occasionally.
3 New computerized printing methods are making the old typesetting methods obsolete. This has caused great problems in the newspaper industry. New cheap 'desk-top publishing' systems threaten to produce more changes.

3 New jobs are created within the information industry

Examples

1 All the new equipment has to be designed and manufactured. These new industries need designers, production workers, managers, sales and maintenance staff, etc.
2 Someone has to produce all the computer programs. There has been a growth in the software industry.
3 Firms need advice on new systems. This has meant an increase in systems consultants.
4 The new equipment needs staff to run it.

ARGUMENTS

In favour of the technology

1 Other countries are introducing new technology. If we do not compete with them we will have even greater unemployment. Computers can be used to increase productivity, so that the same number of people are needed, but more work is done.
2 As more and more work is done by machines there will be more leisure time for all of us. Society's attitude to being unemployed will change. People without work will no longer be ashamed of it – or short of money.

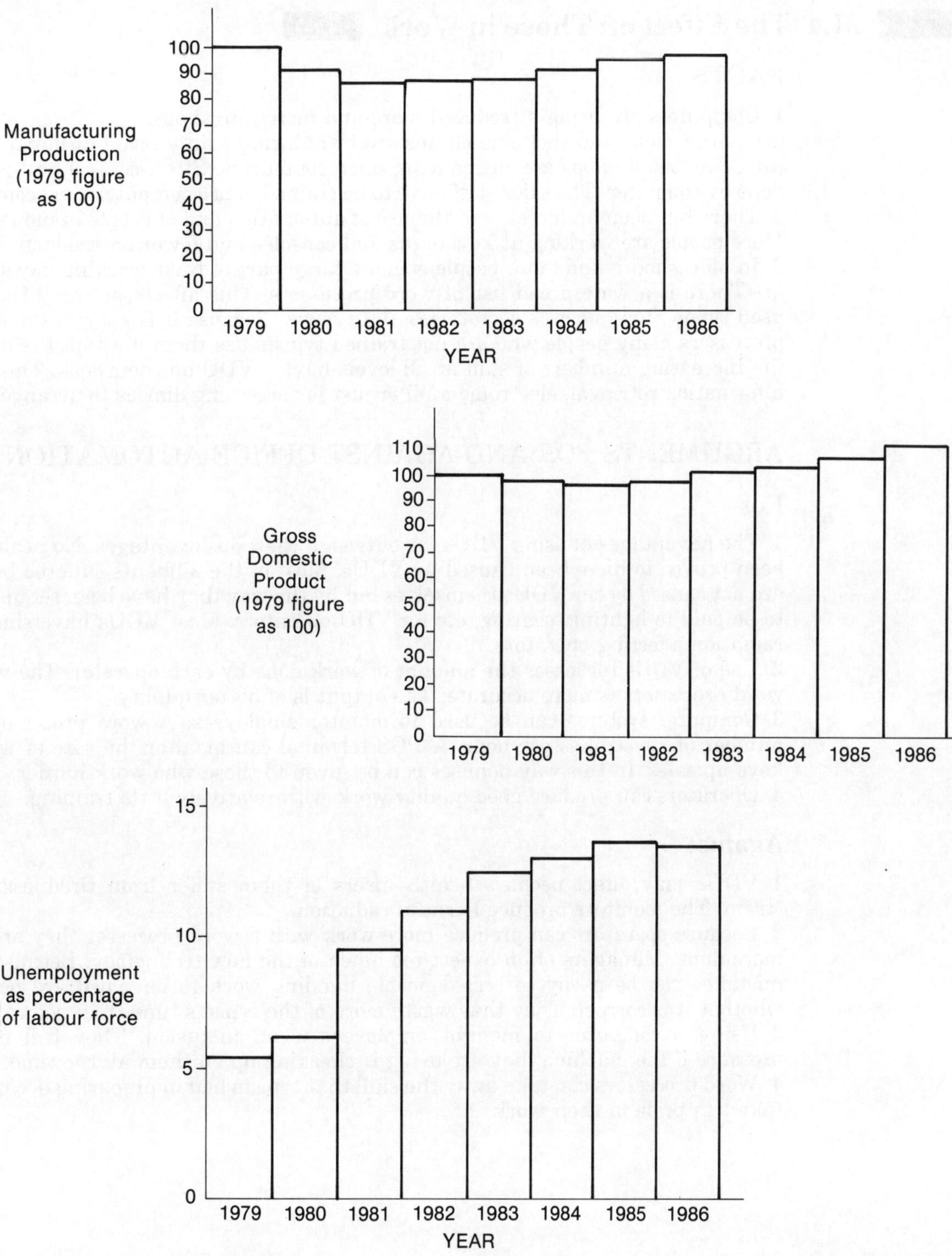

Fig. 21.2 The changes in the economy, manufacturing output and unemployment 1979–86

3 The introduction of computers gets rid of all the boring jobs and produces new and more interesting ones. People are released from repetitive tasks and so their work can become more creative. Someone has to design and make all the new devices and program the computers.

Against the technology

1 The economies of Britain and other countries are only growing very slowly. In this situation if one firm uses new technology to produce more, then someone somewhere else is put out of work.

2 There has not been any sign of the 'Age of Leisure' yet. Those with jobs work just as long, and the unemployed have so little money and are so worried by their situation that they cannot enjoy the extra time they have.

3 (a) The interesting jobs are all being created for skilled and highly qualified people. Those who previously did the boring jobs either have lost their job or it is less rewarding than before.

(b) Even if the introduction of new equipment does create new and interesting jobs, these cannot be done by the people whose jobs are replaced.

21.4 The Effect on Those in Work

FACTS

1 Computers are being introduced more and more into shops.
(a) Large shops and shopping chains are introducing point-of-sale terminals (see Unit 17.1).
(b) Some small shops are introducing microcomputers. Stock control and accounts are then done by computer. The sales staff have to be trained to use computers and computer terminals.
2 There has been an increase in the use of automation and of robots in industry (see Unit 20). More people are working at keyboards and consoles and fewer on production lines.
3 In offices more and more people spend a large part of their working day sitting at a VDU.
(a) There is a widespread use of word processors. This affects not only those who formerly used typewriters such as secretaries and typists. Because it is easy to correct work on word processors many people who are not trained typists use them if a typist is not available.
(b) Increasing numbers of staff at all levels have a VDU on their desk. This may be used for information retrieval, electronic mail or just for accessing diaries to arrange meetings.

ARGUMENTS FOR AND AGAINST OFFICE AUTOMATION

For

1 The advantages of using VDUs far outweigh their disadvantages. No health problems have been proved to have been caused by VDUs. Most of the ailments suffered by VDU operators are not caused by the VDUs themselves but by the way they have been set up. Attention needs to be paid to lighting, seating, etc for VDU operators. Most VDUs have shielding to prevent radiation affecting operators.
2 Use of VDUs increases the amount of work done by each operator. The work produced by word processors is more accurate. The output is of better quality.
3 Computer systems can be used to monitor employees. A word processor can record the number of keystrokes per hour. A POS terminal can monitor the rate at which an operator keys up sales. In this way bonuses can be given to those who work harder.
4 Operators can produce good quality work with relatively little training.

Against

1 VDUs may affect people's health – users of them suffer from tiredness, discomfort, eye strain. The monitors produce harmful radiation.
2 Because operators can produce more work with a word processor they are expected to get more done. Managers often expect too much of the new technology. Because they know that mistakes can be easily corrected people handing work to be typed are not so fussy about whether it is correct. They thus waste more of the typist's time than before.
3 Using a computer to monitor employees is an intrusion. They feel under continuous pressure if the machine they are using is checking up on them all the time.
4 Word processors can take away the skill that typists had in preparing documents. Operators take less pride in their work.

EXAMINATION QUESTIONS

This section contains a selection of examination questions. The source of each question is given in italics next to the question number. Answers are found in the next chapter. The questions are in the order of the core units. Where a question involves work in more than one unit, it has been put with the unit which is most important in answering it.

Acknowledgements

The author is grateful to the following Examining Boards and Groups for their kind permission to publish questions:

London East Anglian Group	(LEAG)
Midland Examining Group	(MEG)
Northern Examining Association	(NEA)
Northern Ireland Schools Examinations and Assessment Council	(NISEAC)
Scottish Examination Board	(SEB)
Southern Examining Group	(SEG)
Welsh Joint Education Committee	(WJEC)

Grades

Grades have been written against some of the questions to give you some idea of their difficulty. The grades used are based on the way the various examining groups have designed their papers:

1 SEG and NEA candidates are expected to do all the papers set. No grades have been given against these questions.

2 All WJEC candidates sit Paper 2, so no grades have been given against these questions. Candidates then have to decide whether to sit Paper 1 (grades C to G only) or Paper 3 (Grades A to E).

3 In the MEG papers each question is in a section aimed at a particular grade. This is the grade which has been used here.

4 Candidates for the LEAG, NISEAC and SEB Standard examinations are allowed to take various combinations of papers. Each different combination can lead only to certain grades. The grades shown are the complete range of grades which could be given for the paper the question is in.

Further details of the examinations set by the different groups can be found in the Table of Analysis of Syllabuses at the start of this book.

Case Study Questions

General notes on how to tackle Case Study examinations are given in the section on Projects, Coursework and Case Studies which follow the answers to these questions at the back of the book.

Any of the questions selected here which involve a Case Study have been marked **CASE STUDY**.

The applications chosen and Case Study subjects vary from syllabus to syllabus and from year to year. The applications involved in the questions chosen here are:

LEAG A video club called 'Moviehome' from which members can hire videos. Information is kept about the members in the *member file* and about the videos in the *video file*. Megan owns the club and Anil works there.

NEA The library system of City Cultural Services.

SEG The use of computers in the retail banking service offered by major high street banks and many building societies.

1 Information Processing

1 *MEG 1991, Paper 1 No 6* *Grade G*

A pelican crossing has input, processing and output. Ring *one* of the words which describes each of the following.

Bleeper	input	process	output
Button	input	process	output
Red light	input	process	output

2 *SEG 1991, Paper 1 No 2*

Dates are read into a computer in the following format:

Two digits for the day
Three letters for the month
Two digits for the year

For each of the dates below, state whether it is in a correct format, and if not, why it is wrong.

91APR23
03FEB91
26JUNE90

3 *WJEC 1988, Paper 1 No 15* *Grades C–G*

A school uses a computer to store information on its pupils. One of the files holds information in coded form regarding the examination results of the pupils. Some of the fields used are as follows:

Subject Level Mark obtained Date of examination

The codes used for each field are:

Subject *001 = English*
102 = Maths
304 = Physics

Level *02 = GCSE*
03 = A Level
04 = Oral

The '**mark**' is a 3 digit number in the range 000 to 100.

'**Date of examination**' is written in the following way:

1087 = October 1987
0686 = June 1986

(a) Interpret the following codes

(i) **102020560585**

(ii) **001040831187**

(b) Encode the following: a mark of 65 in an 'A' level Physics examination taken in June 1984.

(c) Errors can be made on entering information. Give *one* example of an incorrect entry to:
(i) The date field
(ii) The mark field

(d) Suggest *one* extra field that might be useful and give a reason for your choice.

4 *MEG 1988, Paper 1 No 6* *Grade G*

Ring *two* of these items which are methods of data collection for input to a computer system.

Survey forms Bar codes Printers Televisions ROM

5 *NEA 1988, Paper 1 No 10*

Description: The action involved in collecting data for a particular computer process, such as the continuous collection of temperatures in a chemical process.

Term:..

6 *WJEC 1991, Paper 2 No 19*

Sian Edwards has left school but wishes to take two GCSE examinations in computer studies and music. She has applied to the Cambrian Examining Board, who have sent her a form. She has filled in most of it as you can see below.

CAMBRIAN EXAMINING BOARD
CANDIDATE ENTRY FORM FOR 1992 EXAMINATIONS

Surname: E D W A R D S

Forenames: S I A N
J U L I E

Address: 8 4 B R O A D S T
A N Y T O W N
P O W Y S

Post code: A N 4 3 L T

Date of birth: 1 5 0 5 7 4 Sex (M/F): F

Enter number of subjects to be attempted: 0 2

Enter subject codes (see key below)

Art	AR	Computer studies	CO	Human Biology	HB
Biology	BI	Economics	EC	Mathematics	MA
CDT	CD	English	EN	Music	MU
Chemistry	CH	French	FR	Physics	PH
Classical studies	CL	Geography	GG	Religious knowledge	RK
Combined science	CS	German	GE	Sociology	SO

(a) Complete any other boxes needed.
(b) Why are boxes used?
(c) Why are codes used instead of subject names?
(d) Why are candidates asked to write down the number of subjects as well as the code?

7 *WJEC 1988, Paper 3 No 4* *Grades A–E*

An electricity board uses a computer-based system to charge customers for the electricity they use. Each customer has a meter which records the amount of electricity used (see diagram below). Every three months a meter reader visits the customer's house to read their meter. The new meter reading is written on a data collection form next to the customer's account number. Using the new meter reading and the previous meter reading the actual electricity used can be calculated. The customer is then sent the bill for the electricity used.

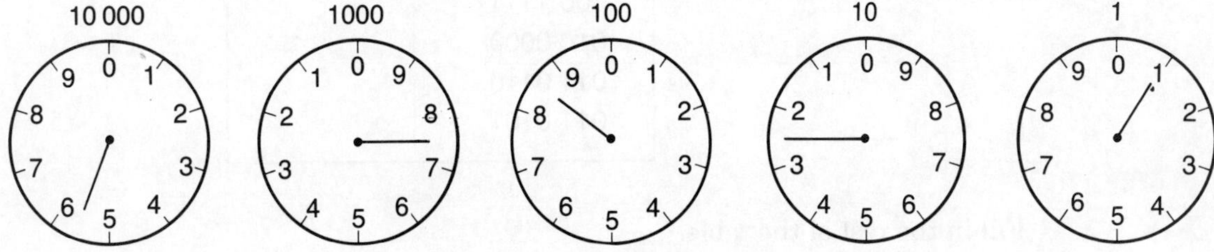

A typical electricity meter

This would be recorded on a data collection form as

5	7	8	2	1

(a) Design a suitable data collection form to allow the meter reader to visit each customer and record the new meter reading. Show clearly which information is printed by the computer and which is written by the meter reader.

(b) The electricity board keeps a record of each customer's details. Describe the different fields you would expect to find in each customer's record that enable the system described above to function.

(c) A customer receives an incorrect bill for about £1,000,000.
(i) Explain how this could happen.
(ii) What steps could be taken to prevent this?

(d) Customers often telephone the electricity board to enquire about bills, etc. The telephone operator must be able to access each customer's details immediately in order to answer their enquiries. Describe a suitable computer-based system to achieve this. Make specific reference to the required hardware, operating system features and method of access to the data files.

2 Representation of data

8 *LEAG 1991, Paper 3 No 9a* *Grades C–F*

This table shows the binary codes used for storing characters in the memory of the computer.

Binary Code	*Character*	*Binary Code*	*Character*
010 0000	Space	100 0111	G
011 0000	0	100 1000	H
011 0001	1	100 1001	I
011 0010	2	100 1010	J
011 0011	3	100 1011	K
011 0100	4	100 1100	L
011 0101	5	100 1101	M
011 0110	6	100 1110	N
011 0111	7	100 1111	O
011 1000	8	101 0000	P
011 1001	9	101 0001	Q
010 1011	+	101 0010	R
010 1101	-	101 0011	S
011 1101	=	101 0100	T
100 0001	A	101 0101	U
100 0010	B	101 0110	V
100 0011	C	101 0111	W
100 0100	D	101 1000	X
100 0101	E	101 1001	Y
100 0110	F	101 1010	Z

Rita is a computer programmer. She is changing some binary codes into characters. She makes and table and starts to fill it in.

Binary Code	*Character*
100 0111	G
100 1111	O
101 0100	
100 1111	
010 0000	
011 0110	
011 0101	

Fill in the rest of the table.

9 *MEG 1988, Paper 1 No 11* *Grade G*

Write the number 6 in binary.

10 *WJEC 1991, Paper 2 No 18*

In a certain computer, positive and negative whole numbers are represented by a 12-bit word. The first bit is a sign bit, with 0 for a positive number, and 1 for a negative number. The rest of the word represents the magnitude of the number in binary.

For instance the number –6 is represented by:

1	0	0	0	0	0	0	0	0	1	1	0

(a) What do the following numbers represent in denary (decimal)?

(i)

0	0	0	0	0	0	0	0	0	1	0	1

(ii)

1	0	0	0	0	0	0	1	0	0	1	0

(b) Show, in the grid below, how the number –15 would be represented.

(c) Write down the largest positive number that can be represented:

(i) In binary, in the grid below

(ii) In denary (decimal).

11 *SEG 1991, Paper 1 No 14*

A storage location within a microcomputer has the following binary pattern in it.

0	1	0	0	1	0	1	1

(a) (i) What two's complement number does this represent?

(ii) Write down the binary pattern for the negative of this number in two's complement form.

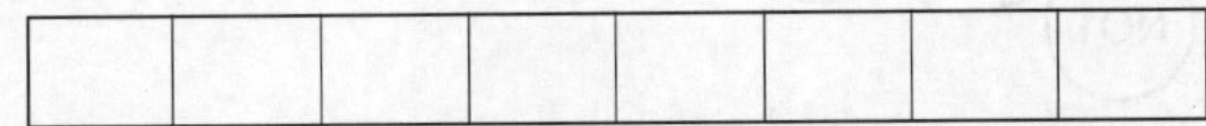

(b) Write down the hexadecimal equivalent of this number.

(c) Instead of representing a number, this location could be interpreted in other ways. Give *two* other possible interpretations, with an example for each.

12 *SEG 1988, Paper 1 No 33*

What is the decimal equivalent of the hexadecimal number represented by E?

A 5
B 8
C 14
D 15

13 *NEA 1991, Paper 2 No 4(a)*

Digital computer systems use patterns of binary digits to represent characters and integers.

What name is given to:

(i) A single binary digit?

(ii) The collection of binary digits used to represent a character?

(iii) A method used to represent both positive and negative integers?

(iv) A special memory location used to hold the result of a calculation?

14 *NISEAC* *Grades E–G*

Below is a diagram of an output port on a washing machine e.g. when the number 24 (0001 1000) is output the machine is 'told' to spin and to pump.

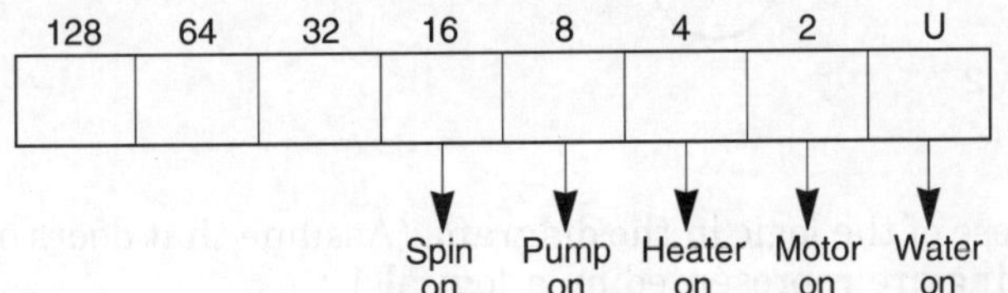

(a) Describe what happens when:
 (i) 7 is output.
 (ii) 1 is output.
 (iii) 0 is output.

3 Digital Logic

15 *NISEAC* *Grades E – G*

A drinks machine measures the size and the weight of each coin as it is entered. It only accepts any coin which has the correct size *and* weight. Complete the table below using 1 for accept or 0 for reject.

	Size not correct	Size correct
Weight not correct		
Weight correct		

16 *MEG 1988, Paper 2 No 13* *Grade C*

Complete the truth table using the logic network given below.

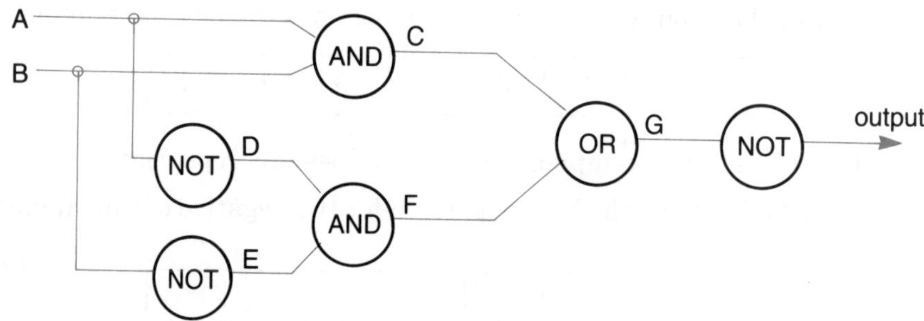

A	B	C	D	E	F	G	output
0	0	0	0				
0	1	0	1				
1	0	0	0				
1	1	1	0				

17 *MEG 1988, Paper 3 No 1* *Grade B*

A room has two doors and two windows. There is a burglar alarm system wired up using the following logic diagram.

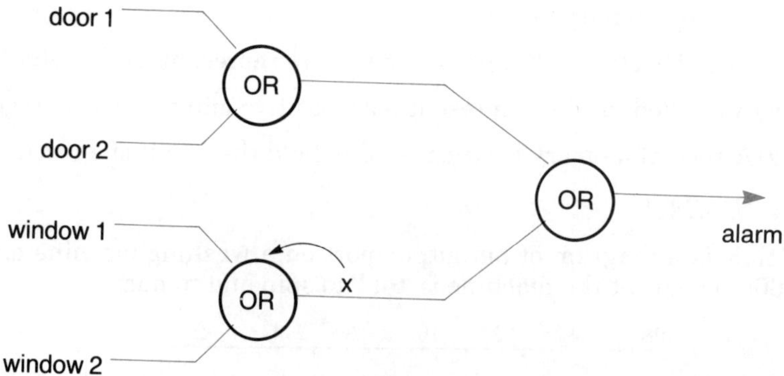

(a) Explain the purpose of the logic in the diagram. (Assume that doors or windows being open and the alarm sounding are represented by a logical 1.)
(b) The logic gate labelled X is changed to an AND gate. Write down what bad effect this has.

4 Computer Hardware – Introduction

18 *NEA 1991, Paper 2 No 1* *Grades A, B*

(a) Name the three main components of a central processing unit (CPU).
(b) Describe the function(s) of each component of a CPU given in part (a).

19 *MEG 1988, Paper 1 No 14* *Grade F*
For *each* of the following devices ring whether it gives an analogue or digital output.

Device	*Type of output*	
joystick fire button	analogue	digital
sundial	analogue	digital
radio loudspeaker	analogue	digital

20 *WJEC 1988, Paper 1 No 6*

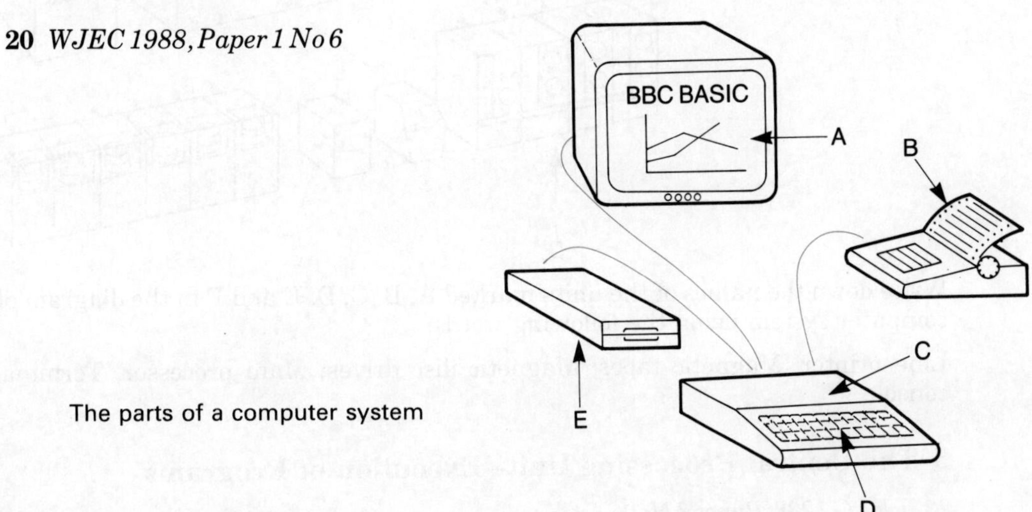

The parts of a computer system

The diagram shows a typical micro computer system. Using the words secondary storage, input, cpu, output complete the following table. *One* of the words is used twice.

Label	*Description*
A	Output
B	
C	
D	
E	

21 *NEA 1988, Paper 1 No 16*
Many electrical devices at home and at work now contain microprocessors.
(a) Name *four* devices that are now likely to contain microprocessors.
(b) Using microprocessors in electrical devices will change the way these devices are designed, manufactured and repaired. Describe these changes.
 (i) Design.
 (ii) Manufacture.
 (iii) Repair.
(c) The terms microprocessor and microcomputer are often confused. What are the differences?

22 *WJEC 1988, Paper 1 No 1* *Grades C – G*

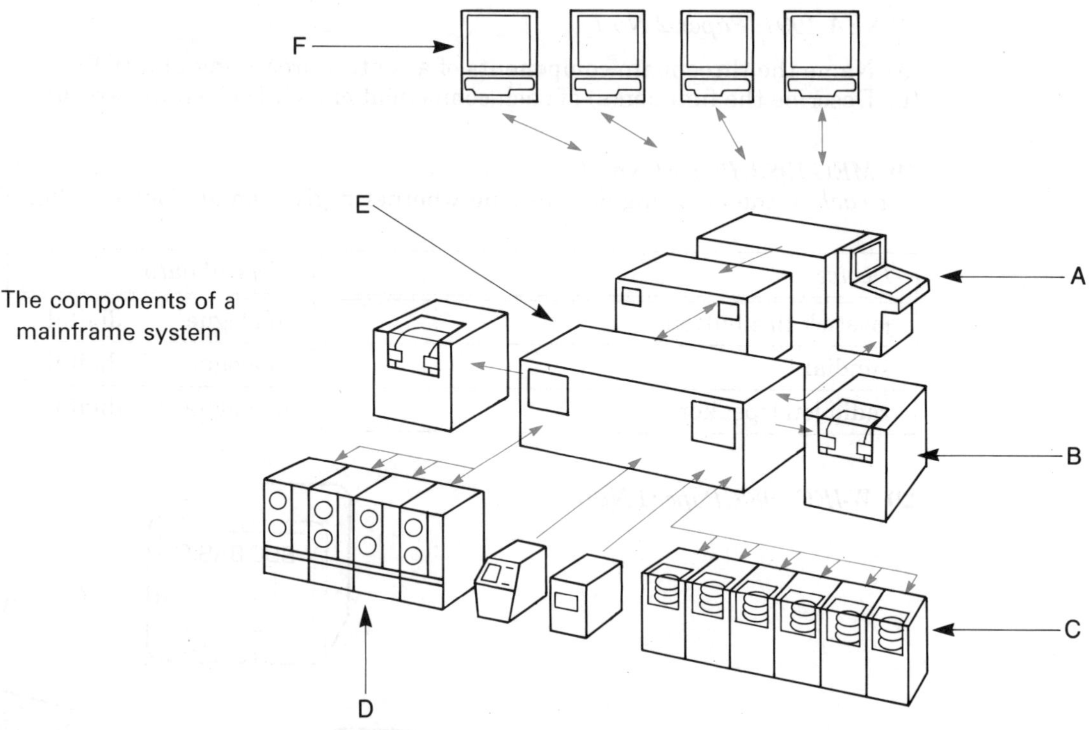

Write down the names of the units marked A, B, C, D, E and F in the diagram of a mainframe computer system using the following words:

Line printer; Magnetic tapes; Magnetic disc drives; Main processor; Terminals; Operator's console.

5 The Central Processing Unit – Execution of Programs

23 *LEAG 1988, Paper 3 No 1* *Grades C to F*

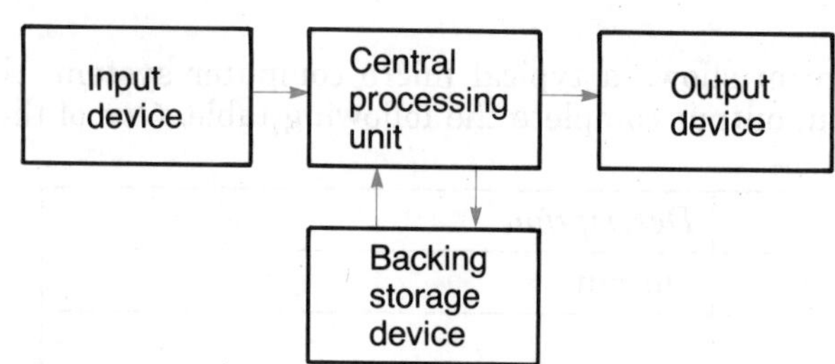

(a) The diagram shows the flow of data in a computer system. In which part would you expect to find the Immediate Access Store?
(b) Give *one* use for the Immediate Access Store.
(c) (i) An instruction word has been copied from the Immediate Access Store under the direction of the control unit. Where would it have been copied to?
(ii) What part does the program counter play in the above event?
(d) Some instructions make use of the accumulator. Describe briefly one use of the accumulator.

24 *NISEC Specimen Paper 4 No 10B* *Grades A – D*

Indicate the function of the Sequence Control Register and the Instruction Register in the CPU.

Describe a typical fetch-execute cycle in the execution of a program instruction, with particular reference to these two registers.

25 *MEG 1988, Paper 1 No 24* *Grade E*

Complete the following table by filling in the correct instruction type chosen from the list.

arithmetic logic control data transfer

Instruction	*Type*
Save	
Or	
Jump	
Subtract	

26 *LEAG 1991, Paper 5 No 5* *Grades A, B*

The Central processing unit (CPU) of a simple computer includes:

A program counter
An accumulator
A memory with addresses starting at ONE.

The program instructions of the processor include:

LOAD address – Loads the contents of the specified address into the accumulator.
STORE address – Stores the contents of the accumulator into the specified address.
ADD address – Adds the contents of the specified address to the accumulator; leaving the result in the accumulator.
HALT – Stops the execution of the program.

The diagram below shows the state of the CPU just before it is about to fetch the instruction in memory address 3.

Program counter
3

Accumulator
0

Memory address	*Contents*
1	+15
2	0
3	LOAD 1
4	ADD 1
5	ADD 1
6	STORE 2
7	HALT

The next diagram shows the state of the CPU just after it has executed the instruction in memory address 3.

Program counter
4

Accumulator
+15

Memory address	*Contents*
1	+15
2	0
3	LOAD 1
4	ADD 1
5	ADD 1
6	STORE 2
7	HALT

(a) (i) Describe the purpose of the program counter.
(ii) Draw a diagram to show the state of the CPU just after it has executed the instruction in memory address 4.
(iii) Describe the purpose of the accumulator.
(iv) State the contents of memory address 2 once the HALT instruction has been executed.

(b) Mr Duncan is a teacher of computer studies.
Some of Mr. Duncan's pupils find it difficult to understand what the central processing unit does. Mr Duncan decides to write a program which will produce a diagram on the screen to illustrate a CPU in action.

Mr Duncan wants his pupils to be able to control the program.

(i) Explain why it would be a good idea for the pupils to be able to control the program.
(ii) State one way in which a pupil could interact with the screen display in order to control the program.
(iii) Draw a detailed layout for the screen display that Mr. Duncan wants.

Note that the layout must:

show the program counter, the accumulator and the memory addresses
indicate which parts could change
show how the pupils could control the program.

6 Communications Hardware – Terminals and Interfaces

27 *NEA 1991, Paper 2 No 3* *CASE STUDY*

Many computers, such as those in the Case Study Library System, communicate with each other using special interfaces such as modems and multiplexors.

(a) (i) Give two reasons why an interface is used when computers communicate with each other.
(ii) What task(s) does a multiplexor carry out?

(b) The diagrams below show different applications which use communications interfaces. Complete each diagram.

(i) Two stand-alone microcomputers communicate by sending signals along telephone wires.

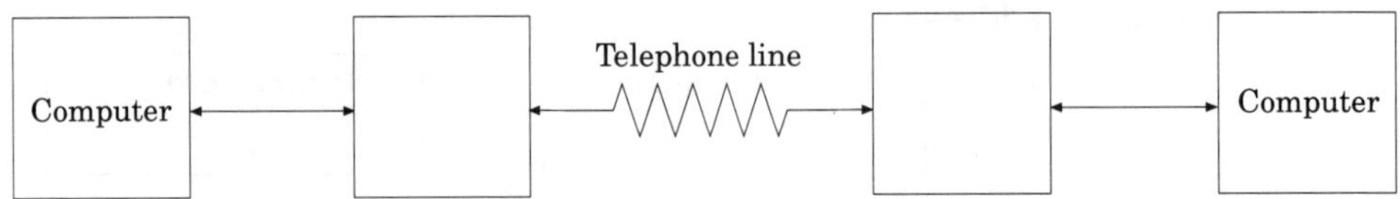

(ii) A mainframe computer used for mail order shopping is connected to many terminals in the same building.

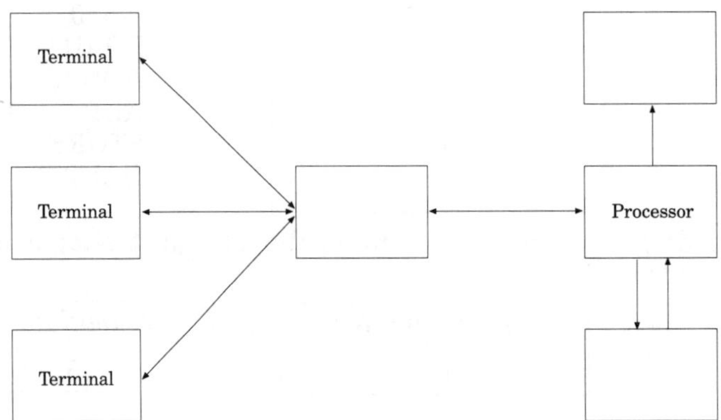

28 *MEG 1988, Paper 1 No 15* *Grade F*

A supermarket uses point-of-sale terminals.

(a) Number the following steps in the order they will be carried out at the terminal when an item is being purchased.

Step	*Step number*
Look up price	
Input item code	
Work out change	
Input money given	

(b) Write down *two* methods by which the item code could be input at the terminal.

(c) The record for each item on the computer file contains its price and the number left in stock. What change is made to this record when an item is sold?

29 *SEG 1988, Paper 2 No 6*

All computers need devices for input, output and storage.

(a) Name *one* device used only for input.
(b) Name *one* device used only for output.
(c) Name *one* storage device.
(d) Explain why an *interface* is necessary when using a peripheral device.

7 Data Preparation and Input

30 *LEAG 1988, Paper 1 No 11* *Grades D–G*

A keyboard operator is entering information into a computer system. Information is read from the data capture forms and typed in. Describe a method of verification which would help to reduce errors.

31 *WJEC 1988, Paper 1 No 5* *Grades C–G*

The following table contains a list of devices and media. Show whether each is used for input or output, by means of a tick (√) in the correct column.

Device/media	*Tick (√) input*	*Tick (√) output*
Mouse		
Graph plotter		
Line printer		
Magnetic ink character reader		

32 *NEA 1988, Paper 1 No 2*

Which *one* of the following devices is most likely to be used off-line to a main computer?

A Magnetic tape unit
B Disc drive
C Key-to-disc unit
D Operator's console
E Graphical display unit

33 *NEA 1988, Paper 1 No 11*

Many computer applications make use of optical methods such as mark sensing and OCR (optical character recognition) to input data.

(a) Name an application that uses mark sensing. State what data is input using mark sensing.
(b) Name an application that uses OCR. State what data is input using optical character recognition.
(c) Both of these methods of input have advantages. Give one advantage of each method of input.
  (i) Mark sensing.
  (ii) OCR.

34 *SEG 1991, Paper 2 No 1a, b, c* **CASE STUDY**

Here is a picture of a bank cheque

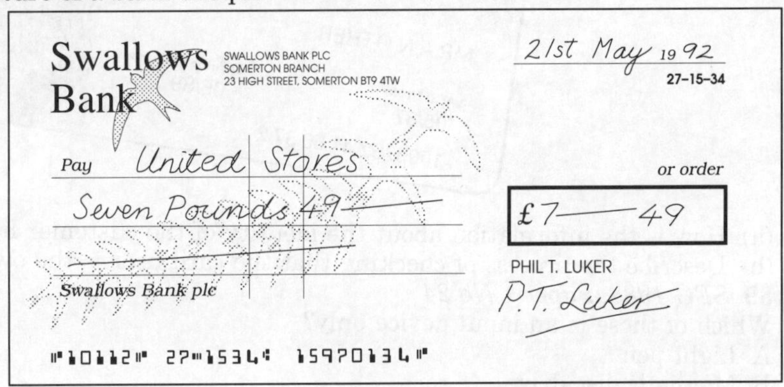

(a) What is the full name of the special characters printed at the bottom of the cheque?
(b) Name the *three* items of data contained in those special characters shown on the cheque above.
(c) After a cheque is paid into a bank, it has to be processed by a computer.
Before it is processed an extra item of data has to be typed onto the cheque into the blank space at the lower right hand side of the cheque.
What is that extra item of information?

35 *WJEC 1991, Paper 2 No 15*

(a) Input to computer at present is often by keyboard. Give *two* disadvantages of using keyboards.
(b) Input can be by voice recognition, (speaking to the computer). Describe *one* difficulty with designing such a system.

36 *NEA 1988, Paper 1 No 15*

The diagram above shows coded data that could be input into a computer

(a) Which one of the following is the name given to this method of input?
A Magnetic ink character recognition
B Optical character recognition
C Bar code reading
D Cash-card reading
E Mark sensing
(b) State *two* applications that would use this method of data input.
(c) For *one* of the applications you have given, state *two* items of information that might be represented by the coded data.
(d) State what hardware is needed to enter the coded data into a computer and describe how this hardware is used.

37 *WJEC 1991, Paper 2 No 24a, b, c*

Recently, a supermarket has started using point of sale (POS) terminals at its check outs, to help with stock control.

Every time an item is sold at the POS terminal, a pattern of lines is read by a laser scanner.

(a) Write down the name of this type of pattern.
(b) What information will the computer output to the POS terminal each time an item is passed over the scanner?
(c) What information will be input to the computer at this time?

38 *SEG 1988, Paper 2 No 3*
Many banks now issue plastic cards that can be used to get cash from cash machines.

(a) How is the information about the identity of the customer held on the card?
(b) Describe the process of checking that the card user is the owner of the card.

39 *SEG 1988, Paper 1 No 24*
Which of these is an input device only?
A Light pen
B Magnetic disc drive
C Printer
D Visual display unit

40 *WJEC 1988, Paper 2 No 7*
Name *two* devices which can be used for input only, describing a suitable use for each device.

8 Output

41 *WJEC 1991, Paper 2 No 8*

Imagine that an elderly relative or friend of yours, who writes a lot of letters on an old typewriter, is thinking of buying a microcomputer designed for word processing, but is not very confident about 'new technology'.

He/she has read a leaflet about this microcomputer, and has found *four* terms which he/she does not understand. Explain them in everyday language.

(i) Menu.
(ii) Cursor.
(iii) Search and replace.
(iv) Default.

42 *LEAG 1988, Paper 1 No 13* *Grades D–G*
All computer systems require at least one input device and at least one output device if they are to do a useful job. Below are three situations. Give an input device and an output device for each.

Situation
(a) A microprocessor system in a washing machine.
(b) An enquiry/booking system of a large airline.
(c) An arcade video game.

43 *MEG 1988, Paper 1 No 26* *Grade E*
A computer program is written such that the user makes selections from a menu.
Give *two* reasons, other than speed, why using a menu to select the commands might be better than typing in the commands themselves.

44 *WJEC 1991, Paper 2 No 8*
A word processor uses both a screen and a printer.
(a) Give *one* advantage of using a screen.
(b) Five *one* advantage of using a printer.

45 *SEG 1988, Paper 1 No 38*
A large city central library uses a computer to produce a catalogue of details for every one of the 500 000 books it contains. Copies of this catalogue are output and distributed once a month to all the smaller branch libraries around the city. The branch libraries do not have computer facilities of their own. Which form of output would be most suited to this task?
A Cassette tape
B Fanfolded printer paper
C Floppy disc
D Microfiche

9 Storage Devices and Media

46 *MEG 1988, Paper 1 No 2* *Grade G*
Would the program for an automatic washing machine be held in RAM or ROM?

47 *SEG 1991, Paper 1 No 8*
ROM and RAM are two different types of memory found in the IAS of a computer's CPU.
(a) What do these abbreviations mean?
(i) ROM.
(ii) RAM.
(iii) IAS.
(iv) CPU.
(b) Describe the differences between ROM and RAM, and give an example of the use of each.

48 *NEA 1991, Paper 2 No 5*
(a) Select, from the list below, the most suitable type of backing store for each situation described in the table. (You may use each type of backing store once only.)

CD-ROM | Exchangeable hard disc | Floppy disc
Fixed hard disc | Magnetic reel-to-reel tape | Magnetic cassette tape

Situation	*Most suitable backing store*
The main backing store for a network of microcomputers in a school	
A small lap top computer used for simple word processing	
A stock control application for a chain of supermarkets	
A stand-alone microcomputer used for a local history database in a library where users can retrieve documents, pictures and statistical information.	

(b) There are two types of backing store in the list above, which you have not used in answering part (a). Write these down. For each type of backing store give a different situation for which it is suitable and explain why it is suitable. (Do not repeat the situations given in part (a).)

49 *NISEAC* *Grades E–G*

Files held on disc have been compared to songs held on a long playing record and files held on magnetic tape have been compared to songs held on tape.

Give *one* advantage of holding files on tape. Give *one* advantage of holding files on disc.

50 *MEG 1991, Paper 2 No 5* *Grade D*

Explain two uses of backing storage in a computer system.

51 *MEG 1988, Paper 1 No 22* *Grade E*

Explain the meaning of serial access and direct access. Give an example of a backing storage device which uses each of these methods of access.

52 *WJEC 1991, Paper 2 No 23*

(a) The diagram above shows a 5¼" floppy disc in its protective cover. What is the purpose of

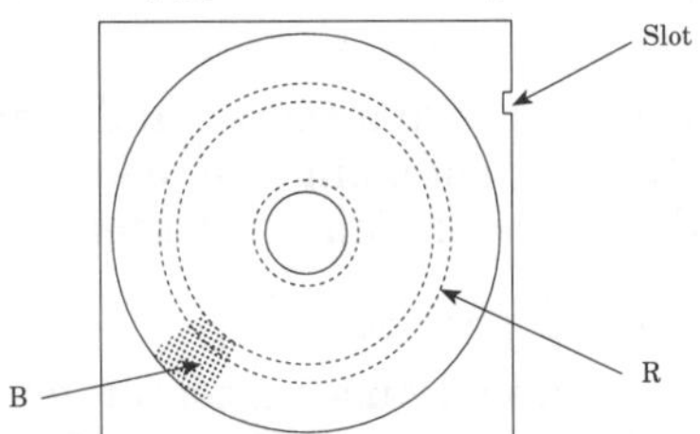

the small slot cut out of the side, which is sometimes covered with a small piece of tape?

(b) The diagram also shows the layout of data on the disc.

(i) What are the rings R called?

(ii) What are the blocks B called?

(c) When a disc is new, it has to be prepared for use by adding addressing information to it. Write down the name of this process.

(d) (i) Give *one* advantage that hard discs have over floppy discs.

(ii) Give *one* advantage that floppy discs have over hard discs.

10 Using Computers to Solve Problems

53 *LEAG 1988, Paper 5 No 1* *Grades A, B*

A software house is planning to release a new accounts package for small businesses. The package is designed to do the following tasks:

(i) Print out a bill for each order sent out by the business.

(ii) Print out a payment slip to go with all bills paid by the business.

(iii)Record the details of all the goods bought and sold by the business.

(iv)Keep a record of all stock held, and update this record when goods are sold or received.

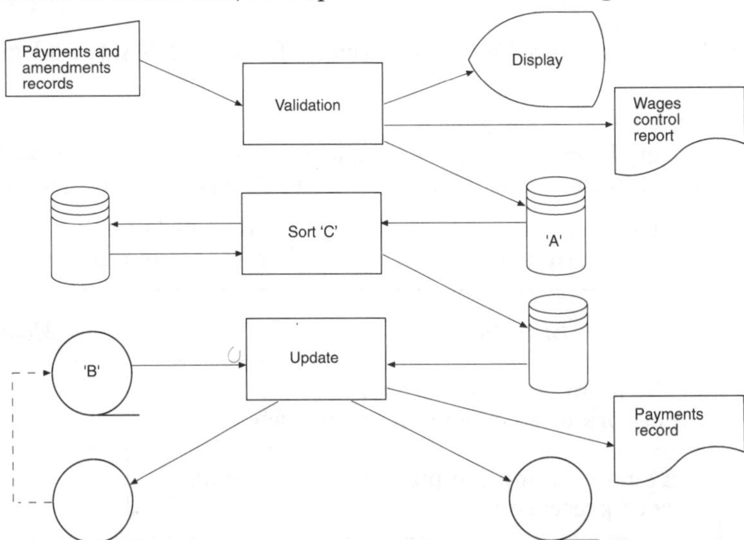

(v) Keep and update the financial records of the business, e.g. how much money is in the bank, how much is owed to the business, how much is owed by the business, profits, losses etc.

(a) Give *four* essential items of hardware that would be needed to run this sort of package.

(b) There are both advantages and disadvantages for small businesses in buying packages like this accounts package. State *two*advantages and *two* disadvantages, to a small business, of buying a ready made package from a software house, rather than commissioning one for its particular needs.

(c) The programmers employed by the software house have written a user manual to be supplied with the package. Describe *three* sections that should be included in this user manual and say what benefit the user might get from each of these.

(d) The programmers have also written the detailed program documentation which is kept by the software house. Describe *three* sections of this documentation and explain why they are included.

54 *LEAG 1991, Paper 2 No 1c* **CASE STUDY** *Grades D - G*

Megan decides to ask a systems analyst to advise her on a computer system for 'Moviehome'. This is a list of the tasks the systems analyst does:

Analyses Designs Implements Investigates Monitors

Choose words from this list to complete the sentences below.

First the analyst .... what the manual system does.

Second the analyst .... in detail the needs of 'Moviehome'.

Third the analyst .... a computer system for 'Moviehome' and recommends a software package.

Fourth the analyst .... the new computer system by installing it at 'Moviehome' and testing it.

Finally the analyst .... the new computer system to check that it is working well.

55 *LEAG 1988, Paper 3 No 8* *Grades C–F*

The figure on page 191 is a systems flowchart outlining a computerised payroll system.

(a) What are the media used to store files 'A' and 'B'?

(b) On the diagram find and label

(i) A scratch (work) file.

(ii) A master file.

(iii) A transaction file.

(c) Give one reason why the data is sorted in the process labelled 'C' on the diagram.

56 *NISEAC* *Grades A–F*

Programmers often spend more time maintaining programs than writing new ones. Give *three* reasons why program maintenance is necessary.

57 *MEG 1991, Paper 1 No 14* *Grade F*

Complete this diagram for the process of telephoning a friend by inserting the steps in the correct boxes.

Speak to friend Dial number Replace receiver Pick up receiver

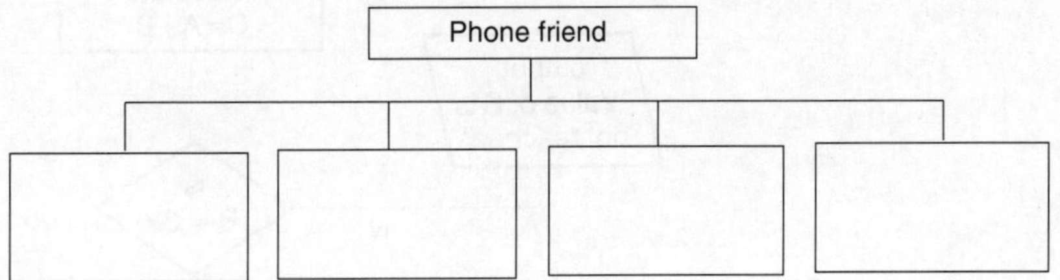

58 *WJEC 1991, Paper 1 No 13* *Grades C –G*

A computer program is to be written from the flowchart shown below.

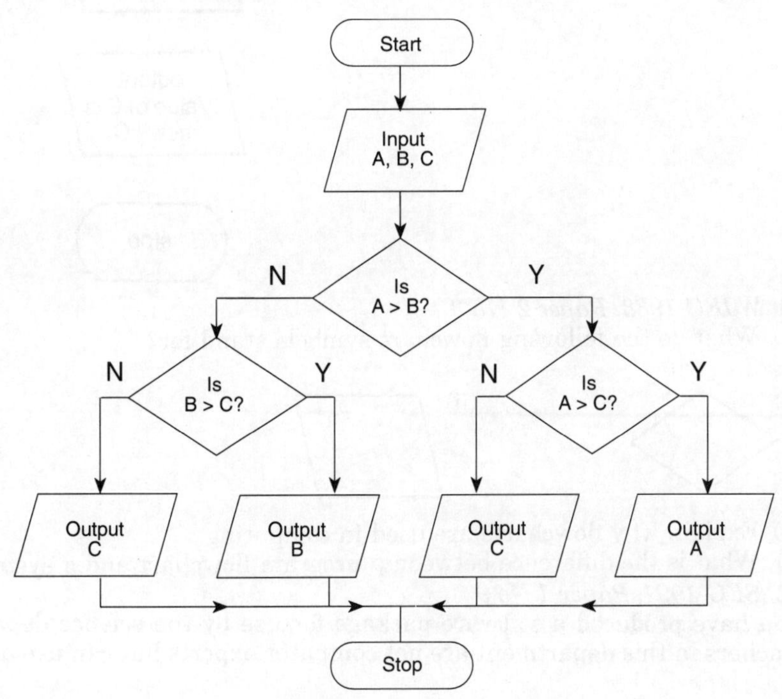

(a) Dry run the flowchart for the following three sets of data and write down the output produced in the appropriate column.

Input	*Output*
A = 11, B = 6, C = 4	
A = 11, B = 16, C = 2	
A = 4, B = 4, C = 7	

(b) Briefly describe the purpose of the program.

59 *WJEC 1991, Paper 2 No 20*

Systems analysis consist of various steps. Describe the *two* steps named below.

(a) Feasibility study
(b) Implementation

60 *WJEC 1988, Paper 1 No 8* *Grades C–G*

A computer program is to be written using the following flowchart. Dry run the flowchart and write down all the output produced.

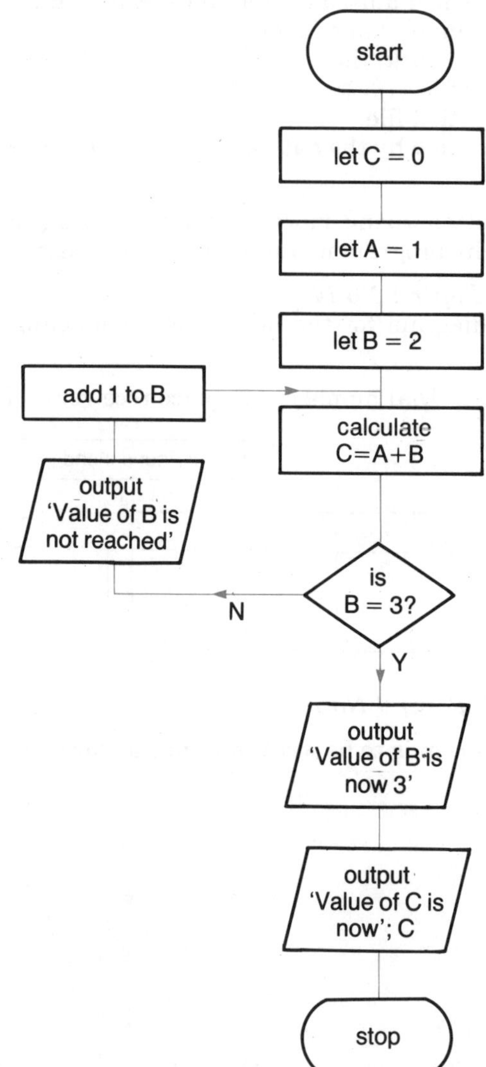

61 *WJEC 1988, Paper 2 No 3*

(a) What do the following flowchart symbols stand for?

(i) 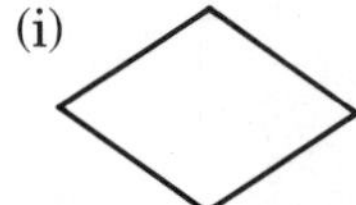

(ii) 

(b) Explain why flowcharts are used in computing.
(c) What is the difference between a program flowchart and a system flowchart?

62 *SEG 1991, Paper 1 No 9*

You have produced a software package for use by the science department in our school. The teachers in this department are not computer experts but can use a computer.

(a) Give *four* items of documentation that should be in the user guide for this package.
(b) You have also written some technical documentation for a computer specialist who will update the package when necessary.
Give *four* items of documentation that should be included in this technical documentation.

63 *MEG 1991, Paper 1 No 3* *Grade G*
Ring *two* items which are found in the user documentation of a computer program.

Loading instruction	Wiring diagram	Integrated circuit
Floppy disc	Example output	Operating system

64 *MEG 1991, Paper 1 No 13* *Grade F*
A software company is producing a new applications program.
(a) Ring *three* items which will be designed when producing the program.

Logic circuit	File structure	Laser	Wiring diagram
Screen layout	Processes	Keyboard	Chips

(b) Write down *three* items which should be included in the technical documentation of this program.
(c) Test data is used when producing a program. What is meant by test data?

11 Programming – Languages and Styles

65 *MEG 1991, Paper 3 No 3* *Grade B*
Programs are translated by compilers into machine code. Give two advantages of using compilers rather than programming directly in machine code.

66 *LEAG 1988, Paper 1 No 5*
(a) A high level language is slow to execute.
(b) A high level language is easy for people to read and write.
(c) This is because it is close to human language.
Write *three* statements like these about a low level language.

67 *LEAG 1991, Paper 1 No 9* *Grades D – G*
Rita has to write a program to do the payroll. She can choose to write the program in a low level language or a high level language.
(a) Give *two* reasons why Rita should choose the high level language.
(b) Rita writes the program in a high level language. The program has to be compiled. Explain why a program in a high level language is compiled.

68 *NEA 1988, Paper 1 No 5*
A program is written in a high level languages. Which one of the following statements is true?
A Each instruction in the program represents anumber of machine instructions.
B It is written in binary.
C It does not need to be translated before execution.
D It is translated by an assembler before execution.
E The language is called 'high level' because it is difficult to learn.

69 *WJEC 1991, Paper 2 No 9*
In the early days of computing, programs were normally written in assembly language. Today, programs are normally written in a high level language.
(a) Explain *one* advantage of a high level language to the programmer.
(b) An expert programmer has written a games program. Why might this programmer prefer to use assembly language?

70 *WJEC 1991, Paper 1 No 2* *Grades C – G*
FORTRAN, BASIC and COBOL are high level programming languages. Which of these languages is best suited for:
(i) Learning programming?
(ii) Scientific program writing?
(iii) Commercial program writing?

71 *MEG 1988, Paper 1 No7* *Grade C*
For each of these items of data ring its type.

Data	*Type of data*	
a town name, e.g. Banbury	numeric	string
the number of words in a sentence, e.g. 11	numeric	string
a car registration number e.g. J353 AXB	numeric	string

72 *MEG 1991, Paper 2 No 4* *Grade E*

(a) A routine in a program is described by this structure diagram.

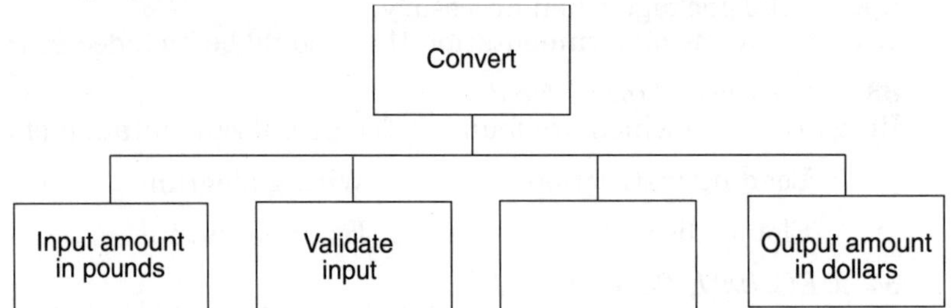

Write down what the empty box should contain.

(b) Another part of the program includes the following steps. For each step ring the correct type of construct.

Step	*Construct*		
If input is 9999 stop otherwise continue	sequence	selection	repetition
Continue accepting inputs until the escape key is pressed	sequence	selection	repetition

(c) Ring one phrase to complete the sentence.
The program is written in a high level language because:

It needs to use graphics / It needs accurate calculations /
It is easier to transfer to different machines / It will run faster/

73 *LEAG 1988, Paper 1 No 7* *Grades D–G*

Large programs are often written in modules. Give *one* reason why.

12 Errors

74 *SEG 1991, Paper 1 No 13*

When developing a computer program, a number of errors may occur. For each type of error below:

(a) Give an example of the error (with both correct and incorrect versions where appropriate).
(b) Describe how and when it should be detected.

(i) Syntax error.
(ii) Logical error.
(iii) Execution error.

75 *NISEAC* *Grades A–F*

A program is executed and produces results which are found to be incorrect. List *three* different methods the programmer can use to locate a mistake in the program.

76 *LEAG 1988, Paper 3 No 18* *Grades C–F*

A company records the workers clocking in and out times on time sheets. There is no night shift. The format for each sheet is: A five digit works number, followed by 5 or 6 pairs of times in 24 hour clock notation, (time of arrival followed by time of leaving), each field separated by a slash /. An example is shown below. It has three errors in it.

20023/0900/1703/1706/0859/0858/1659/0901/1702/0859/17084/0900/1330

(a) Find the three errors and underline each one.
(b) For each error give a validation rule that might be used in the data entry program to detect it.

77 *LEAG 1991, Paper 4 No 3a* **CASE STUDY**

The record of each video in the video pile includes the following fields:

Field name	Field description
Video reference number	A four digit number followed by A, B or C
Title	The title of the video
Playing time	Numeric field given in minutes. It must be between 30 and 200
Certificate	Must be one of: U - suitable for all PG - parental guidance 15 - only for over 15 year olds 18 - only for adults
Cost per day	Numeric field given in pounds

Below are the details of some videos that Anil has typed into the computer. The computer program validates the data to check for errors.

For each video given, state if the data is correct and if it is not correct, name the validation check that would detect the error.

Video reference number	*Title*	*Playing time*	*Certi-ficate*	*Cost per day*	*Correct Y/N*	*Name of validation check used*
1836A	Winnie the Pooh	15	U	1.00		
2172A	Ghostbusters II	90	PG	£2.5		
2180C	Turtles – The Killer Pizzas	45	U	1.50		
312B	Working Girl	75	15	1.50		
3472B	Phantom of the Opera	87	18	2000		

78 *MEG 1988, Paper 3 No 13* *Grade A*

A date is to be entered into a computer program in the form ddmmyy where dd is the day of the month, mm is the month and yy is the year. For exmaple 230481 would be the 23rd April 1981. Describe clearly the *three* following validation techniques that oculd be used to test the data:
(a) Length check. (b) Format check. (c) Range check.

79 *NEA 1991, Paper 1 No 8*

The terms in the grid are all data items.

1 An ISBN number on a book	2 A person's name on a cheque
3 An account number on a cheque	4 A price on a can of soup
5 A membership number on a library borrower's card	6 The number of cans of soup in stock in a supermarket

Which of these would
(i) Be printed as a bar code?
(ii) Be printed in magnetic ink?
(iii) Contain a check digit?
(iv) Never be validated by a range check?

80 *LEAG 1991, Paper 3 No 5e* *Grades C – F*

A modem does an automatic parity check on all the data. The modem checks these binary codes:

00000011
10100000
00111010
01000110
01101100

The binary codes should all have the same parity. One of them is wrong.
(a) Check the parity of these binary codes and underline the binary code which is wrong.
(b) Explain why the binary code you underlined failed the parity check.

13 Files

81 *WJEC 1991, Paper 2 No 22*

(a) Explain the meaning of sequential access and direct access to a file. Give *one* example of a storage device suitable for each type of access.
(b) Give *one* example of data which must be held in a direct access file.
(c) Explain why this particular data must be held in a direct access file.

82 *SEG 1988, Paper 1 No 5*

Which of the following is suitable for storing in a fixed length field of 6 characters?
A Address
B Birthplace
C Date of birth
D Name

83 *SEG 1988, Paper 3 No 5*

A stock file is held on magnetic disc so that records can be read and updated in any order.
(a) What is the name of this type of access?

84 *WJEC 1991, Paper 2 No 4*

Three versions of a file are often kept. These are sometimes known as Grandfather, Father and Son versions. Give *one* reason why this is done.

85 *SEB Standard* *Grades 5, 6*

(a) Peter has written a COMAL program for a project. He wants to make a back-up copy on another disc. His teacher gives him a disc. Explain why a new disc must first be formatted before it can be used to store programs.

(b) Peter has a computer system with one disc drive. He wants to make the back-up copy using the LOAD and SAVE commands. Write out a list of instructions for him to do this.

86 *MEG 1988, Paper 3 No 16* *Grade A*

A master file and a sorted transaction file are stored on magnetic tapes. The transaction file has been checked and is known to contain only new records to be inserted into the master file. Describe how a new master file can be generated using the existing master file and the transaction file.

87 *WJEC 1991, Paper 1 No 12* *Grades C – G*

An estate agent keeps a file of property tor sale on computer. Some of the information stored on each property is as follows.

Code	*Type*	*Class*	*Price (£)*	*Number of bedrooms*
AXY123	House	D	91420	4
AXY917	Bungalow	S	80000	3
AXX134	House	S	47500	3
AXZ912	Bungalow	D	120000	4

(a) The *class* field uses a single letter. D is a detached property and S is a semi-detached property. Suggest a helpful code for a terraced property.

(b) Name the key field.

(c) Every week the estate agent needs to update the file.
  (i) What does update mean?
  (ii) Which field is most likely to be affected when he updates his file?

(d) The estate agent decides to sort the records in his file on *price* in ascending order. Complete the following table.

Order before sorting	*Order after sorting*
AXY123	
AXY917	
AXX134	
AXZ912	

88 *MEG 1988, Paper 2 No8* *Grade C*

The contents of four files are shown below.

file A	*file B*	*file C*	*file D*
27	93	34	27
36	60	39	34
38	34	45	36
97	39	60	38
	102	93	39
	45	102	45
			60
			93
			97
			102

(a) State how utility routines could have been used to produce files C and D from files A and B.

(b) Describe the function of *one* other utility routine.

89 *LEAG 1988, Paper 1 No 19* *Grades D–G*

'Hacking' is where someone tries to gain illegal access to a computer system. This is usually done using a remote terminal or microcomputer.

(a) Give *one* example of harm that a 'hacker' might do if successful in breaking into a computer system.

(b) One method of protecting computer systems from 'hackers' is to have a system of passwords or codes. These should be secret and known only to legal users. Some people use names of people close to them because they are easy to remember. Why is this not a good idea?

(c) Give a suitable password for a remote access computer system. Say why you have given it.

(d) Give *one* further simple method of protecting a computer system from 'hackers' trying to use remote terminals.

90 *WJEC 1991, Paper 1 No 9* *Grades C - G*
(a) What is a database?
(b) Name *three* different applications of databases.

91 *SEG 1988, Paper 1 No 3*
Which of these is used to guard against accidental loss of data?
A Keeping back-up copies of files
B Keeping files under lock and key
C Keeping terminals under lock and key
D Using passwords

92 *NISEAC* *Grades A–F*
In an application three generations of the masterfile are kept. What are these three generations normally called and why are they considered necessary: Why is tis also necessary to keep generations of the transaction file?

14 Software

93 *NEA 1988, Paper 1 No 7*
Description: Programs and procedures, with their documentation, which can be implemented on a computer system.

Term:..

94 *LEAG 1991, Paper 2 No 6* **CASE STUDY**
The software package that Megan bought is made up from a number of modules. Some of the modules are applications packages, the others are utility programs.

When Anil switches on the computer each morning the following menu appears on the screen:

1 Set date and time
2 Video club management
3 Format floppy discs
4 Backup
5 Video club accounts

(a) Give *two* items on the menu that refer to applications packages.
(b) Give *two* items on the menu that refer to utility programs.
(c) Item 4 on the menu is for Anil to make a backup copy of the files. Explain why Anil needs to make back up copies.

95 *MEG 1991, Paper 1 No 4* *Grade G*
Ring *two* items which are application packages.

Merge routine	Payroll system	Disc copier
Structure diagram	Stock control system	Chip

96 *WJEC 1991, Paper 1 No 15* *Grades C – G*
The following software packages are available to teachers, pupils and office staff at Oaktree Comprehensive School

(i) Spreadsheet package.
(ii) Desktop publishing package.
(iii) Information retrieval package.

Describe briefly *one* application for each package within the school, indicating what it might be used for and an advantage of its use.

97 *NEA 1991, Paper 1 No 16a*
(a) Which of the following tasks would normally be carried out by an operating system?

A To transfer a file from one disc to another
B To calculate a person's pay
C To make an estimate of a company's profits
D To list a disc directory on a printer

(b) List *three* other tasks that you would expect an operating system for a mainframe computer system to perform.

15 Processing Systems

98 *SEG 1988, Paper 1, No 28*
Which of these applications is an example of a real-time computer system?

A Controlling a nuclear reactor
B Printing wage slips
C Producing gas bills
D Searching a database

99 *NISEAC* *Grades A – F*
A computer system with a single disc drive and printer allows up to 50 users simultaneous access.

If two or ore users attempt to print out reports at the same time, how would the system handle this?

100 *WJEC 1988, Paper 2 No 1*

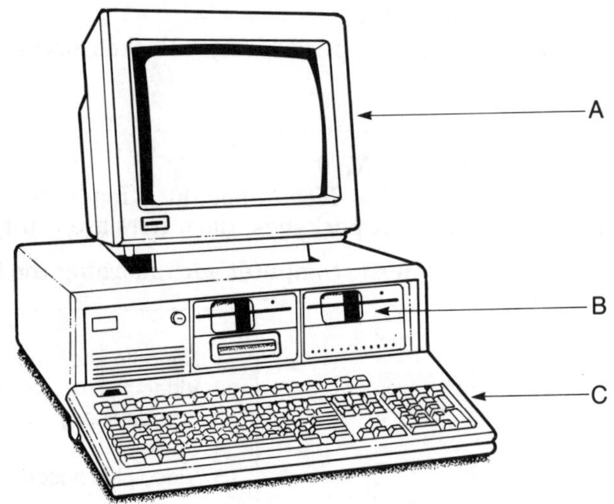

Write down the names of the units market **A**, **B** and **C** on the above diagram of a microcomputer.

101 *SEG 1991, Paper 2 No 6* **CASE STUDY**
Both batch and interactive processing take place in a banking computer system. Explain what each term means, and give an example of where it would be used in banking.

102 *MEG 1991, Paper 1 No 5* *Grade G*
Tick which of these applications may use batch processing and which must use on-line processing.

Application	*May use batch processing*	*Must use on-line processing*
Monitoring heart beats		
Producing electricity bills		
Robots making a car		
Printing class lists		

103 *WJEC 1988, Paper 1 No 11* *Grades C – G*
Some schools and colleges have networks of computers.
(a) Give *two* advantages of a network of computers.
(b) Give *one* disadvantage of using a computer network.

104 *WJEC 1991, Paper 1 No 8* *Grades C – G*
The following diagram shows a computer network consisting of workstations A, B, C and D together with a printer.
(a) Explain the term computer network.
(b) Workstations A, B and C have twin floppy disc drives and workstation D has a single floppy with a hard disc. Why does D have a hard disc?
(c) Give *one* advantage of a computer network over a stand-alone computer system.

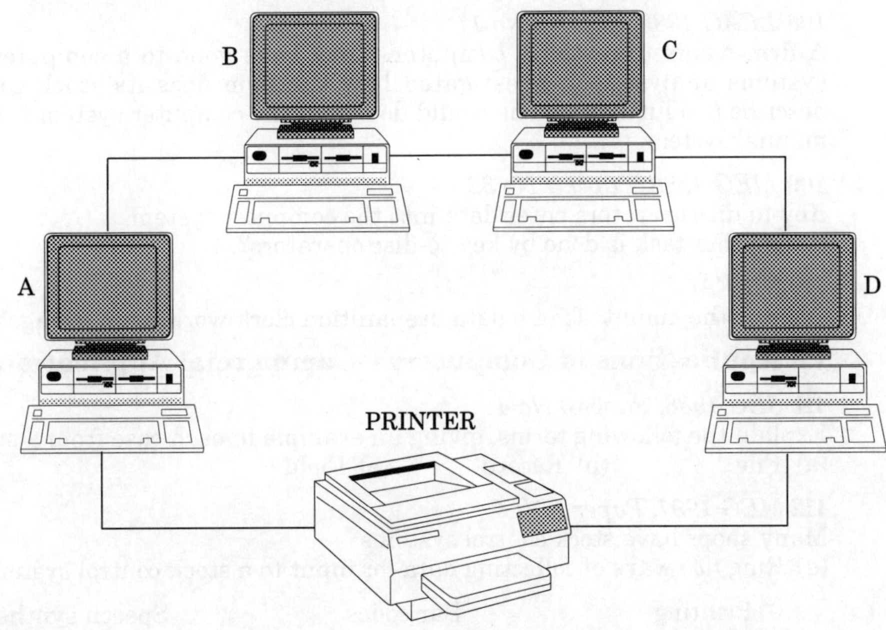

16 Jobs in Computing

105 *WJEC 1991, Paper 2 No 5*

NINIAN COMPUTER RECRUITMENT

DATA PROCESSING MANAGER — Gwynedd
At least 5 years' senior experience — To £20 000

COMPUTER OPERATORS
At least 12 months' experience with VAX/VMS — Mid Glam. £10 000+

Read the advertisement above, which appeared in a computer magazine.
(a) What does a data processing manager do?
(b) What does a computer operator do?

106 *SEG 1988, Paper 2 No 2*
Here is a list of job titles to do with computers:

Computer engineer	Computer operator
Data control clerk	Data processing manager
File librarian	Keyboard operator
Programmer	Salesman
Shift leader	Systems analyst

For each of the tasks below, write down the most likely job title of the person doing it. You can use a job title once, more than once, or not at all.

(a) Loading a line printer with paper.
(b) Coding a computer program.
(c) Appointing new staff in a data processing department.
(d) Correcting errors in a program.
(e) Finding the correct data tape.
(f) Testing a new computer system.
(g) Demonstrating a computer to a new customer.
(h) Keying in data.
(i) Repairing a faulty disc drive.

107 *SEG 1991, Paper 1 No 4*
Give a brief description of the work of each of the following people who work in a large computer installation.

(i) Computer operator
(ii) Keyboard operator

108 *LEAG 1988, Paper 3 No 11* *Grades C – F*

A firm wants to install a computer. They have gone to a computer company for help. The systems analyst has investigated how the firm does its stock control manually. List or describe *two* further jobs he would do before the computer system is fully ready to replace the manual system.

109 *MEG 1988, Paper 4 No 32* *Grade B*

Key-to-disc operators enter data into the computer system.
What other task is done by key-to-disc operators?

110 *NISEAC* *Grades E – G*

What is the main task of a data preparation clerk working in a wages office?

17 Applications of Computers – Commercial Applications

111 *SEG 1988, Paper 3 No 4*

Explain the following terms, giving an example in each case from a stock control system.

(a) File (b) Record (c) Field

112 *MEG 1991, Paper 1 No 7* *Grade G*

Many shops have stock control systems.

(a) Ring *two* ways of collecting data for input to a stock control system.

Printing	Bar codes	Speech synthesis
Magnetic strips	Passwords	Mouse

(b) Give *two* outputs from a stock control system.

(c) Ring *two* items to complete the sentence.

Details of each item in the shop are stored in a computer in .... and ....

Files	Packets	Screens
Records	Shelves	Keyboards

113 *MEG 1991, Paper 3 No 4* *Grade B*

A factory manager uses a payroll package to produce payslips for each employee. Here is the systems flowchart for the payroll system.

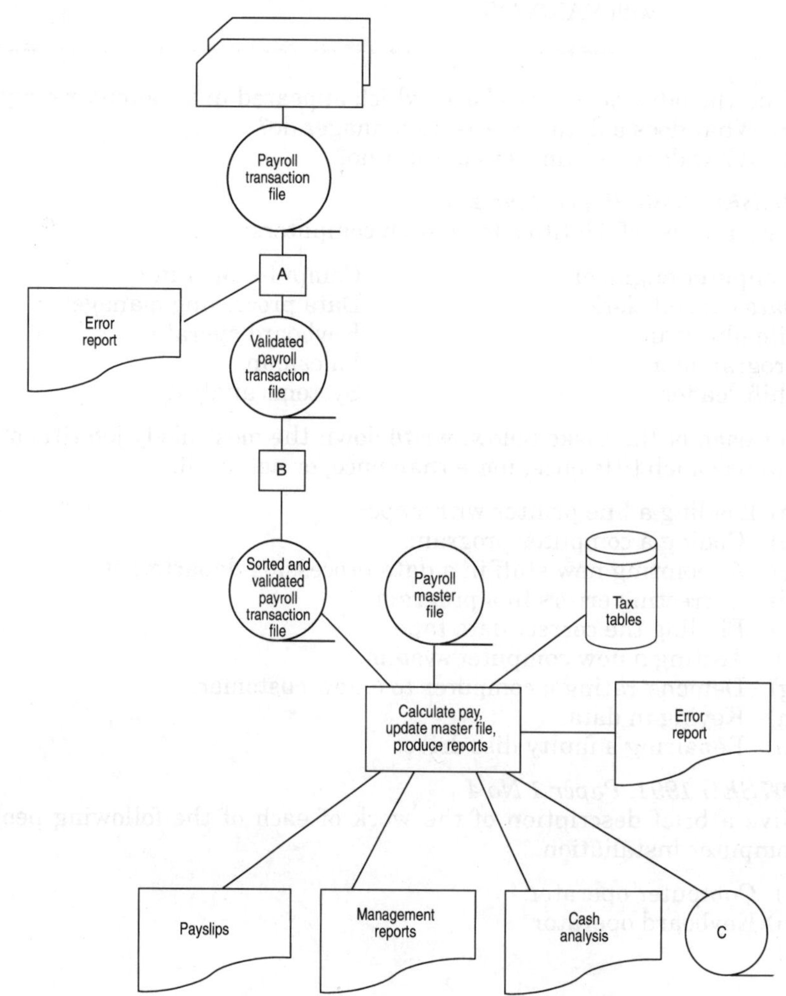

(a) Write an appropriate entry for boxes labelled A, B and C.
(b) Each employee has a record on both the payroll transaction file and the payroll master file. A B Smith works at the factory and some of the information stored about her is shown below.

1	Name	A B Smith
2	Department	Sales
3	Rate of pay	£6.50
4	Tax code	414H
5	Hours worked last week	37
6	Employee number	1903678
7	Pay earned so far this year	£1963

Using this information, list the numbers of the fields which would be stored in the master file record and those which would be stored in the transaction file record.
(c) Describe *two* ways in which the personal data held about employees at the factory could be misused.
(d) Payroll was one of the earliest commercial applications to be carried out using a computer. Give *two* reasons for this.
(e) Payslips are printed using preprinted stationery.
(i) Explain why preprinted stationery is used.
(ii) Explain why an example of the preprinted stationery is important to a person who develops or modifies payroll software.
(f) (i) Name a suitable output device for producing the payslips and give *one* reason why it would be better than using a daisywheel printer.
(ii) Most peripherals have standard interfaces. Explain what is meant by an interface.

114 *NEA 1991, Paper 1 No 17*
For an airline booking system, records of available seats are kept on a central computer.
(a) Give *three* examples of outputs that the system would be expected to produce.
(b) Give *two* examples of different master files that the system would be likely to use.
(c) Give *two* advantages of a computerised airline booking system over a manual one.

18 Communication Systems and Word Processing

115 *WJEC 1991, Paper 2 No 11*
Explain why an airline booking system needs to use a real-time computing system.

116 *SEG 1991, Paper 1 No 6*
(a) Name a teletext service available through an ordinary television signal.
(b) Name a widely used public viewdata service that uses the telephone network.
(c) Describe *two* main differences between these two forms of videotext, apart from costs and equipment used.

117 *SEG 1991, Paper 1 No 7*
A large company is installing an electronic mail system into its offices, which are spread throughout the world.
(a) Give *one* advantage of using electronic mail rather than using the postal service.
(b) State, with reasons, *two* advantages of using electronic mail rather than the telephone.
(c) Give *one* disadvantage of using an electronic mail system.
(d) Pictures cannot be sent by many electronic mail systems. Name a method by which pictures can be sent quickly to another place.

118 *NEA 1991, Paper 1 No 12*
Prestel is an interactive viewdata system that uses a modem. One feature of the system is electronic mail.
(a) (i) Give two different types of information that could be obtained from Prestel.
(ii) Give two different transactions that could be carried out using Prestel.
(b) Explain what is meant by:
(i) Interactive.
(ii) Modem.
(iii) Electronic mail.
(c) Ceefax is a teletext system. Describe *four* ways in which teletext systems differ from interactive viewdata systems.

119 *WJEC 1991, Paper 1 No 4* *Grades C – G*
Many offices are replacing typewriters with word processors.
(a) Give *two* advantages of word processors compared with typewriters.
(b) (i) Describe *one* problem that might arise when word processors are introduced in an office.
(ii) Explain how this problem could be overcome.

120 *SEB Standard* *Grades 3, 4*

(a) The secretary at Freeman and Cumming uses a typewriter to type letters, legal documents and notes of meetings.

Some of the letters and legal documents are of the same basic form with individual client's details added. The final copy of legal documents must always be free from typing corrections. Some of these documents are very long.

Describe *four* facilities of a word processor that would be of particular help to the secretary to get through her work more quickly.

(b) Mr Freeman and Mrs Cumming are wondering whether to buy a word processor or employ an assistant secretary instead.

This is what Mr. Freeman thinks:

> I am against the idea of buying a word processor for these reasons.
> 1 We would need to spend a lot of money immediately on a word processor.
> 2 Our present secretary would have to go on a long and expensive training course.
> 3 An assistant secretary would, in the end, cost use more money but could do other office jobs like filing. A word processor could only be used to produce letters and documents.
> I would therefore prefer to appoint an assistant secretary.

Mrs Cumming would prefer to buy a word processor. She intends to reply to Mr. Freeman explain why she agrees with some of these points but disagrees with other. What should she say in reply?

(c) Mrs Cumming and Mr Freeman decided in the end to buy a word processor and they sent their secretary on a training course. She found the word processor very easy to use. Describe two features that could make word processing packages user-friendly.

121 *SEG 1991, Paper 1 No 1*

You have just entered the word processor and see the menu shown on the diagram below. A letter is stored on disc. You need to produce a copy of this letter with some changes.

Write down the order in which the options should be used.

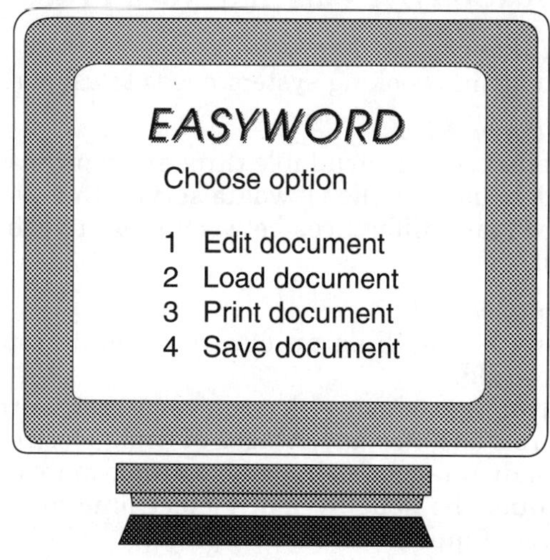

19 Technical, Scientific and Other Uses

122 *LEAG 1988, Paper 1 No 18* *Grades D–G*

A runner is training for a 1500 m race. The coach is worried about the effects of running on the athlete's heart and lungs. To monitor the runner there is a microcomputer system worn on a belt around her waist. There are sensors that will measure the following:

1 Breathing rate.
2 Heart rate.
3 Stepping rate.

These sensors are connected to the microprocessor. The microprocessor is connected to a radio transmitter. The transmitter sends the information collected to a track side computer system. This is shown in the diagram on the next page.

(a) What inputs are required for this data logging system?

(b) There is an output devices connected to the belt microprocessor. This output device is not shown on the diagram. It gives urgent information to the runner.

(i) Describe or name a suitable device

(ii) Give *one* use for this device.

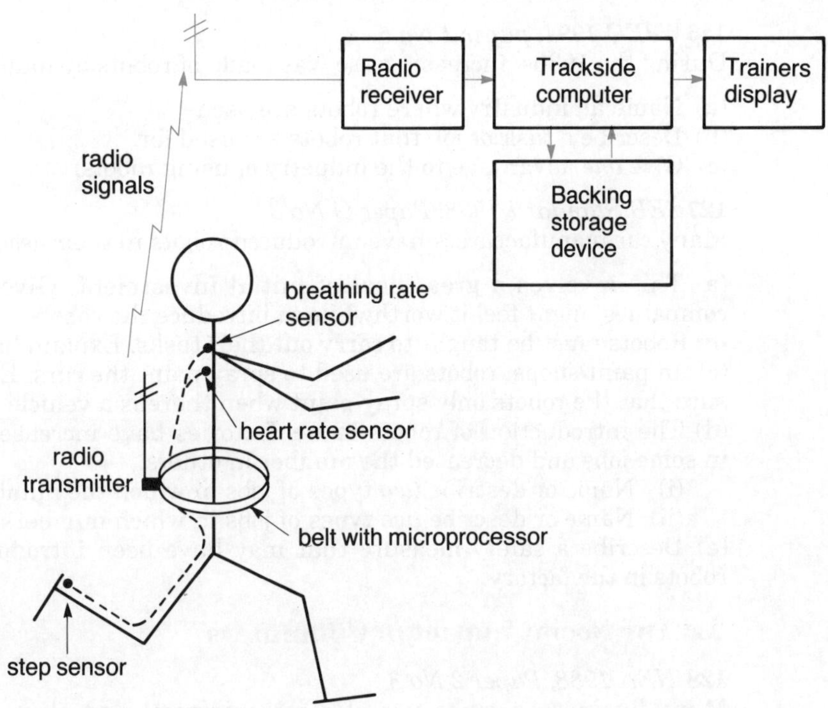

(c) The track side computer system also has an output device.
 (i) Describe or name a suitable device.
 (ii) Give *one* use for this device.
(d) Give *one* reason why there is a backing storage device provided on the track side computer.

123 *SEB Standard* *Grades 3, 4*
(a) Mr and Mrs Glen wish to move to a new house. They are planning their dream home. Dream Homebuilders Ltd build houses to customers' own specifications. They draw up plans and build models to give customers an idea of what their houses will actually look like. If customers are not happy then plans are redrawn and new models built.

Mr and Mrs Glen contact Dream Homebuilders Ltd. Mrs Glen, who is a computer consultant, is surprised to find that the firm does not use computers in designing houses. She tells them about Computer Aided Design systems.

Describe *two* input and *two* output devices that the firm might need if they were to install such a system.
(b) Describe how a Computer Aided Design system could be used to make changes to existing plans and produce new copies of them.
(c) Describe the advantages of the computerized system by comparing it with the manual system.
(d) Despite the cost of equipment and training, Dream Homebuilders Ltd decide to install a Computer Aided Design system. They also plan to keep on all of their existing employees. How can this be financially worthwhile?

20 Use of Computers in Industrial Processes

124 *MEG 1991, Paper 2 No 8* *Grade D*
(a) A greenhouse contains a temperature sensor and an electric heater. Describe how these can be used with computer control to keep the temperature inside the greenhouse above freezing.

(b) Give *two* ways in which the work of the gardener could change through the use of computer control in the greenhouse.

125 *MEG 1991, paper 1 No 5* *Grade A*
A computer is being used in a hospital to monitor and regulate the rate of a patient's heartbeat. A drug which will increase the heartbeat is being pumped into the patient at a variable rate controlled by the computer.

(a) Explain how feedback is used in this system to maintain a satisfactory heartbeat rate.
(b) The system involves the conversion between analogue and digital data. Explain why it is necessary to convert:

(i) From analogue to digital data.
(ii) From digital to analogue data.

126 *WJEC 1991, paper 1 No 5* *Grades C – G*
During the 1980s, increasing use was made of robots by industry.

(a) Name an industry where robots are used.
(b) Describe a task or job that robots are used for.
(c) Give *one* advantage to the industry of using robots.

127 *SEB Standard 1988, Paper G No 3* *Grades 3,4*
Many car manufacturers have introduced robots to their assembly lines.

(a) This involves a great deal of initial investment. Give *two* financial reasons why the companies might feel it worthwhile to introduce the robots.
(b) Robots must be taught to carry out their tasks. Explain how this is done.
(c) In paint shops, robots are used to spray paint the cars. Explain what can be done to make sure that the robots only spray paint when there is a vehicle there.
(d) The introduction of robots in car factories have increased the number of people required in some jobs and decreased the number in others.
(i) Name or describe *two* types of jobs in which the numbers have increased.
(ii) Name or describe *two* types of jobs in which numbers have decreased.
(e) Describe a safety measure that may have been introduced as a direct result of having robots in the factory.

21 The Social Impact of Computers

128 *NEA 1988, Paper 2 No 3*
Many businesses make use of electronic mail and electronic funds transfer to improve efficiency, reduce costs and speed up communication.

(a) State *one* advantage of using electronic mail instead of having a telephone conversation.
(b) State *one* difference between electronic mail and electronic funds transfer.
(c) Name *two* applications that might use electronic funds transfer.
(d) Describe how electronic mail and electronic funds transfer might change the work patterns and lifestyles of people using them.

129 *NGA 1991, Paper 2 No 9*
Many organisations have computer databases that store personal information about individuals. Some of these organisations are listed below.

Banks	Employers
The Department of Social Services	The Inland Revenue

(a) List *four* other organisations that store personal information about individuals.
(b) When organisations collect and store personal information on computer they must take precautions to protect the rights of individuals. One precaution is to make sure that data has been obtained fairly and for lawful purposes.

Describe *four* other precautions that organisations must take.

(c) These computer databases can be easily linked together to exchange data. List three developments in hardware or software that have made this possible and explain how each development made the exchange of data easier.

130 *WJEC 1991, Paper 2 No 14*
In a shop, records of the customers are kept on magnetic disc.

(a) A customer wishes to see his record. The shopkeeper must show it to him. Explain why.
(b) What would his rights be if he discovered some of the information as wrong?
(c) If this information were held on paper files instead, explain what difference this would make.

131 *NISEAC* *Grades A–D*
The argument that computers help increase unemployment is sometimes countered by saying that the new microchip based technologies create job opportunities that were unheard of 20 years ago.
(i) Describe how computers are replacing people in two distinct areas of employment.
(ii) Describe two broad areas of employment that did not exist before computers became available (excluding data processing).
(iii) Comment on the changes in employment patterns that have resulted from the development of computer technology.

132 *WJEC 1991, Paper 2 No 12*
A factory makes components for car engines. When one part of the factory is automated, fewer workers are needed than before.

(a) Name one new job which will be needed with the new machines in the factory.
(b) A person who has been working in the factory is hoping to get one of these new jobs. Why might this be difficult for him or her?
(c) If the factory had decided to keep the old manual system instead, all the workers might have kept their jobs in the short term. What might be the longer term result of this?

133 *NEA 1991, Paper 1 No 15*
When computers are introduced into organisations they usually affect the work and jobs of staff. Describe the possible effects of computerisation on the jobs and the work of staff in the work places below.

(i) A motor car factory.
(ii) A supermarket.

ANSWERS

This section contains hints and/or answers to the questions in the previous section.

For many of the questions the answer can be found easily by looking up the topic in the main text of Units 1 to 21. In these cases the only hint given here is a reference to the appropriate section in the text.

The items in **bold type and brackets** are hints and are not part of the answer.

All hints and answers are solely the responsibility of the author. They were not supplied by the Examining Boards and they may not give the only way of doing the question.

1 Bleeper: output; Button: input; Red light: output.

2 91APR23 Incorrect. Year has been put first
03FEB91 Correct
26JUNE90 Incorrect. Not three letters for the month.

3 (a) (i) Maths/GCSE/56/May 1985. (ii) English/Oral/83/November 1987.
(b) 304030650684.
(c) (i) 13 **(or any number not in the range 01 to 12)**. (ii) 360. (d) Candidate number. To identify the pupil.

4 Survey forms, bar codes.

5 Data capture. **('Data acquisition' is an acceptable answer)**

6 (a) CO in first pair of empty boxes, MU in next pair.
(b) To make it easy to key data accurately.
(c) To standardise what is typed. To save writing, keying and storage.
(d) As a check that the form is filled in correctly.

7 (a) **(Draw a simplified version of the meter reading form in Unit 1.3-Fig. 1.3. Show the meter number, the customer's name and address and a space for the meter reading. Indicate the reading as written by the meter reader, the rest as written by the computer)**
(b) Customer's name, address, telephone number, meter number, last meter reading, meter reading dates, account number and the state of the account.
(c) (i) Completely incorrect meter reading e.g. a reading smaller than the last one taken.
(ii) The computer should make estimates of possible highest and lowest reading. Any reading not in this range should be rejected so that it can be checked manually. (d) **(The system described should be a mainframe computer with an operating system which allows batch running to process the meter slips. It will also allow multi-access so that the telephone operators can use terminals. The customer files will have to be on disc so that direct access is possible).**

8 Completed table will read: GOTO 65.

9 110.

10 (a) (i) +5 (ii) −18. (b) 10000001111
(c) (i) 011111111111. (ii) 2047.

11 (a) (i) +75. (ii) 10110101 (b) B5.
(c) An ASCII character: e.g. 01000001 would be letter A.
An address of a location: e.g. 00000111 could refer to location 7.

12 C.

13 (i) Bit. (ii) Byte. (iii) Two's complement. (iv) Accumulator.

14 (a) (i) 7 in eight-bit binary is 00000111.
The machine would have heater, motor and water all on.
(ii) 1 in eight-bit binary is 00000001. The machine would have only its water on.
(iii) If 0 is output all the bits are 0, so nothing is on.
(b) When the number is 00011010 the machine will spin and pump and its motor will be on.
(It has been assumed that the washing machine can do this – it could be an error condition if this means the machine is trying to wash, spin and pump all at the same time)

15 (This is a truth table, but not set out in the usual way. This is an AND gate-compare with the truth table for AND in Unit 3.2)

	Size not correct	*Size correct*
Weight not correct	0	0
Weight correct	0	1

16

A	B	C	D	E	F	G	output
0	0	0	1	1	1	1	0
0	1	0	1	0	0	0	1
1	0	0	0	1	0	0	1
1	1	1	0	0	0	1	0

17 (a) If any door or any window is opened the alarm will sound.
(b) If the doors are kept shut and just one window is opened the alarm will not sound.
18 (see Unit 4.1)
19 Digital (fire button), analogue (sundial), analogue (loudspeaker).
20 B: Output, C: CPU, D: Input, E: Secondary storage.
21 (a) Car, washing machine control system, central heating control system, camera (or etc). (b) Design: Smaller, neater, with fewer mechanical parts and capable of more complex tasks. Manufacture: Can be more easily automated because the device has fewer parts. Repair: Should be less frequent. Requires less skill as there are fewer parts to go wrong.
(c) A microprocessor is just a chip. A microcomputer is a complete computer which contains a microprocessor to do its processing. **(See Unit 4.2)**
22 A: Operator's console, B: Line printer, C: Magnetic disc drives, D: Magnetic tapes, E: Main processor, F: Terminals.
23 (a) In the Central processing unit. (b) To store a program while it is being run.
(c) (i) Current instruction register. (ii) **(See Unit 5.2)** (d) **(See Unit 5.2)**
24 (See Units 5.1, 5.2)
25 SAVE: data transfer, OR: logic, JUMP: control, SUBTRACT: arithmetic
26 (a) **(For parts (i) and (iii) see Unit 5.2)**
(ii)

Program counter
5

Accumulator
+30

Memory address	*Contents*	
1	+15	
2	0	
3	LOAD	1
4	ADD	1
5	ADD	1
6	STORE	2
7	HALT	

(iv) +45.
(b) (i) So that they can edit the program and execute it a step at a time.
(ii) Select menu options and indicate which registers and locations to change with a mouse.
(iii) Your diagram should be like that given, have menu boxes marked EDIT, RUN, STEP and QUIT and should show the contents of the program counter, the accumulator and the contents of the locations as highlighted or coloured.
27 (a) (i) **(See introduction to Unit 6.4)** (ii) **(See last item in Unit 6.3)**
(b) (i) Label each empty box 'modem'.
(ii) Label box in the middle 'multiplexor', box at the top 'printer' and box at the bottom 'disc unit'.
28 (a) Look up price: 2, Input item code: 1, Work out change: 4, Input money given: 3.
(b) Read from bar code using laser scanner; typed at keyboard.
(c) Number left in stock is decreased by one.
29 (a) Keyboard **(or mouse, light pen, etc)**.
(b) Plotter **(or any type of printer)**.
(c) Disc drive **(or magnetic tape unit)**.

(d) **(See introduction to Unit 6.4)**
30 (See introduction to Unit 7)
31 Mouse: input, Graph plotter: output, Line printer: output, MICR: input.
32 C.
33 (a) Application: Checking answers to multiple choice examination questions. Data input: Marks indicating choices made by the candidates.
(b) Application: Inputting meter readings for gas board. Data input: Number indicating the reading on the meter.
(c) Advantage of mark reading: few recognition failures. Advantage of OCR: handwritten characters can be recognized.
34 (a) Magnetic Ink Character Recognition **(Font E13B acceptable)**
(b) **(See 'Uses of MICR' in Unit 7.2)**
(c) The amount of money.
35 (a) They cannot easily input graphics. Data which is already printed on paper has to be retyped.
(b) People's voices differ from one another.
36 (a) C (Bar code reading).
(b), (c), (d) **(See Unit 7.3–'BAR CODES')**
37 (a) Bar code.
(b) Price and name of item.
(c) Number codes for the country of origin, manufacturer and an item number for the product.
38 (a) As binary codes stored on a magnetic strip.
(b) The user inserts the card in the cash machine when requested. Numbers which identify the user are read from the card by the machine. The user is asked to key in an identification number and does so. A computer checks the number keyed in against the user's correct identification number.
39 A.
40 (Possible answers would be a mouse and a joystick. See Unit 7.4 for suitable uses)
41 (i), (ii) **(See Unit 8.1)**
(iii) Find all the places a chosen word occurs and replace it with another word.
(iv) What the computer will choose for an option if you don't make a choice yourself.
42 (a) Input: Control panel. Output: Motors, valves and heaters.
(b) Input: Keyboard of a travel agent's terminal. Output: Display screen of the terminal.
(c) Input: Buttons, joysticks, etc. Output: Display screen.
43 Reason 1: Choice can be made simply – pressing one key or using a mouse.
Reason 2: There is no need to remember the possible commands.
44 (a) A user can move around the text on the screen and edit any part of it.
(b) It gives a hard copy to take away or to send to others.
45 D.
46 ROM.
47 (a) **(See Unit 4.1)**
(b) **(See Unit 9.1)**
48 (a) Fixed hard disc; Floppy disc; exchangeable hard disc; CD-ROM.
(b) Magnetic cassette tape: Backing up a network file server. It stores a great deal of data on a small cassette.
Magnetic reel-to-reel tape: To store the master file for a payroll application. Stores more than a cassette, suitable for storing sequential files.
49 (See Unit 9.3–'Comparison between magnetic tape and exchangeable hard discs')
50 (See Unit 9.2)
51 (See Unit 9.2 for explanations and devices)
52 (a) **(See Unit 9.2 - Fig 9.5)**
(b) **(See Unit 9.2 - Fig 9.4)**
(c) Formatting.
(d) **(See Unit 9.3)**
53 (a) Keyboard, visual display monitor, disc unit, printer.
(b) Advantages: Package would be cheaper; it would be available quickly.
Disadvantages: Package might not exactly fit the requirements of the business; it could not easily be changed to fit new requirements.
(c) **(See Unit 10.6–'DOCUMENTATION FOR THE USER')**

(d) **(See Unit 10.6–'DOCUMENTATION FOR A PROGRAMMER')**
54 Investigates; Analyses; Designs; Implements; Monitors.
55 (a) 'A': Magnetic tape; 'B': Magnetic disc.
(b)

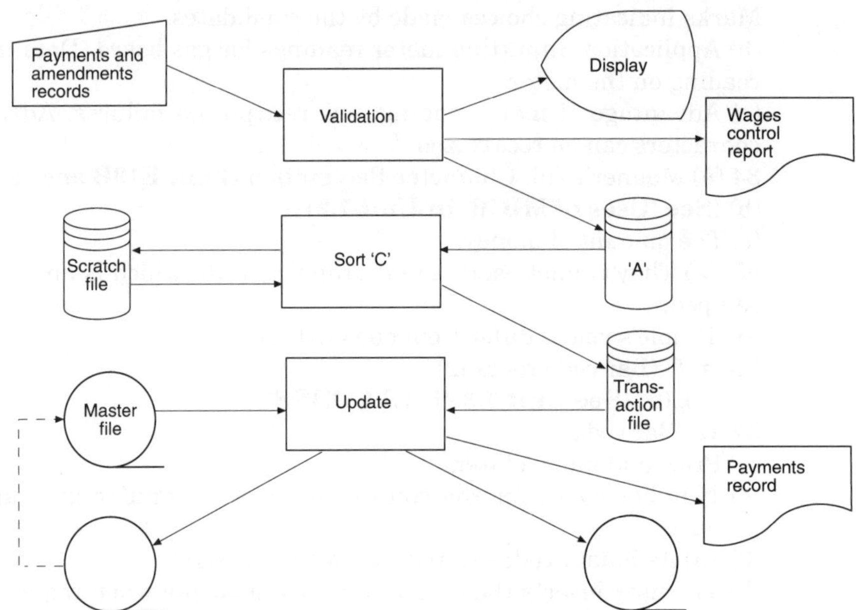

(c) The data in the transaction file is sorted so that it is in the same order as the records in the master file. The records in the master file can then be updated in their correct order.
56 Program maintenance is necessary:
(i) To correct errors which the software contains.
(ii) To improve the facilities offered by the programs.
(iii) To ensure the software still runs with new hardware.
57 Left to right: Pick up receiver; Dial number; Speak to friend; Replace receiver.
58 (a) 11; 16; 7.
(b) To find the largest of three numbers.
59 **(See Unit 10.2)**
60 Value of B is not reached.
Value of B is now 3.
Value of C is now 4.
61 (a) (i) Decision box (ii) Input or Output.
(b) System flow charts are used to represent the operations on data in an information processing system. Flow charts of algorithms may be used to help with the design of algorithms or programs. They are also included in program documentation to help explain how a program works.
(c) **(See Unit 10.3 – 'FLOWCHARTS')**
62 **(See Unit 10.6)**
63 Loading instruction; Example output.
64 (a) File structure; Screen layout; Processes.
(b) **(See Unit 10.6)**
(c) **(See Unit 10.4 – 'Testing and Debugging')**
65 Advantage 1: Programmers write in high level language which is easier to write.
Advantage 2: The programs will work on a variety of machines.
66 (a) A low level language program is fast to execute.
(b) A low level language is difficult for people to read and write.
(c) This is because it is close to machine language and not like human language.
67 (a) Reason 1: The program will be easier to write.
Reason 2: The program will be easier to understand and modify.
(b) The computer can only run machine code programs. The compiler is needed to translate Rita's program into machine code.
68 A
69 (a) High level languages are easier to use because they use words suitable for the problem being solved.
(b) The assembly language program will run faster than a high level program.

70 (a) BASIC. (b) FORTRAN. (c) COBOL.
71 Town name: string; Number of words: numeric; Car registration: string.
72 (a) Multiply input by conversion ratio.
(b) Selection; repetition.
(c) It is easier to transfer to different machines.
73 So that someone reading a program can easily understand its structure.
74 (a),(b) **(See Unit 12.1)**
(c) **(See Unit 12.2)**
75 **(See Unit 12.2)**
76 (a) 20023/0900/1703/1706/0859/0858/1659/0901/1702/0859/17084/0900/1330
(b) (i) Time of arrival should be less than 1200.
(ii) Time of leaving should be greater than time of arrival.
(iii) Each time should have exactly four digits.
77 1836A: N Range check (time).
2172A: N Type check (cost).
2180C: Y.
312B: N Length (Reference No).
3472B: Y.
78 (a) Check that the number of characters in the date is six.
(b) Check that each character in the date is a digit.
(c) Check that mm is between 01 and 12 inclusive. Check that dd is a possible day for the given month, e.g. if mm = 01 (January) that dd is between 01 and 31 inclusive.
79 (i) 1 (ii) 3 (iii) 5 (iv) 2
80 (i) 01000110 has wrong parity.
(ii) All the others have even parity. This one has odd parity.
81 (a) **(See Unit 13.1)**
(b) Data in a large on-line database.
(c) Searching the database would be too slow if access to it was sequential.
82 C
83 (a) Direct.
(b) No: data can only be read for different parts of a magnetic tape by continually winding and rewinding it – a very slow process.
84 So that if data is lost or incorrectly updated it can be recovered.
85 (a) The disc must be formatted because, before this is done, the disc has no addressing system to enable the computer to store or find files.
(b) Put the original disc in the drive; load the program; put the new disc in the drive; save the program.
86 OPEN both files and read a record from each.
REPEAT
IF master file record comes before transaction file record THEN write the master file record to new master file; read a new master file record or find the end of the master file,
ELSE write transaction file record to new master file; read a new transaction file record or find the end of the transaction file.
UNTIL end of master file OR end of transaction file.
IF end of transaction file is reached first THEN read the remaining records from the old master file; write them onto the new master file.
ELSE read the remaining records from the transaction file; write them on to the new master file.
CLOSE both files.
87 (a) T (b) CODE (c) (i) **(See Unit 13.4)** (ii) *Price.*
(d) AXX134; AXY917; AXY123; AXZ912.
88 (a) File C has been produced from file B using a short routine. File D has been produced from files A and C using a merge routine.
(b) **(See Unit 14.2–'Examples of utility programs')**
89 (a) Delete data files: accidentally or otherwise. (b) The hacker may know the person involved and know their friends. In any case names are easier to guess than random selections of characters. (c) SIVEN57: This is an apparently random sequence of letters and digits and yet it is something that could be remembered easily. (d) Keep all terminals in protected areas and scramble all data to and from them.
90 (a) **(See Unit 13.7)**
(b) Any three sensible applications, e.g.
(i) Storage of pupil records for a school, (ii) Storage of records of court cases so that lawyers

can check on past decisions, (iii) Storage by a firm of all data referring to stock.

91 A.

92 (i) **(See Unit 13.6–'Methods of protecting data')**

(ii) Generations of the transaction file are kept so that if the son master file was corrupted it could be recreated using old versions of the master and the transaction file.

93 Software.

94 (a) Video club management; video club accounts.

(b) Format floppy discs; backup.

(c) So that if any of the files get lost or corrupted there is another copy of the data.

95 Payroll system; stock control system.

96 (Any sensible examples e.g.)

(a) Keeping records taken of the weather by a Geography class. The spreadsheet could be used to work out average temperatures and total rainfall. Formulae can be easily written for these calculations.

(b) Editing and arranging a school magazine. The desktop publishing package makes it easy to bring together text and pictures and arrange them into pages.

(c) Storing titles and authors of books in the library. A pupil or teacher can search for books by chosen author or chosen subject. The information retrieval package allows a variety of searches to be made.

97 (i) A, D (ii) **(See Unit 14.3 - the section 'For larger computers and networks')**

98 A.

99 Work to be printed out would be stored as a queue on the disc. Files from the queue would then be printed out one at a time.

100 A: Display screen (or visual display monitor), B: Disc unit, C: Keyboard.

101 (a) **(For explanation see Unit 15.3)** Use in banking: Sorting cheques.

(b) **(For explanation see last paragraph of Unit 15.4)** Use in banking: Taking out money at a cash issuing terminal.

102 Batch processing: Producing electricity bills; Printing class lists.

On-line processing: Monitoring heart beats; Robots making a car.

103 **(See Unit 15.5–'Advantages and disadvantages of local area networks')**

104 (a) **(See introduction to Unit 15.5)**

(b) D acts as a file server for the network.

(c) All the workstations can share files and printers.

105 (a) **(See Unit 16.1)** (b) **(See Unit 16.5)**

106 (a) Computer operator.

(b) Programmer.

(c) Data processing manager.

(d) Programmer.

(e) File librarian.

(f) Computer engineer.

(g) Salesman.

(h) Keyboard operator.

(i) Computer engineer.

107 (a) **(See Unit 16.5)** (b) **(See Unit 16.6)**

108 **(See Unit 16.2)**

109 Verifying data which has been keyed in previously **(or keeping a record of the data dealt with).**

110 Batching together payroll data ready for keyboard operators to key.

(The person doing the keying would be called an 'operator' rather than a 'clerk'.

111 (a), (b), (c) **(Terms 'file', 'record' and 'field' explained in the introduction to Unit 13).**

Examples from a stock control system for one branch of a supermarket chain:

(a) Stock file containing data on the status of all items stocked in the branch.

(b) A record from the stock file containing details of one type of item stocked in the branch.

(c) One field from this record – such as reference number or quantity in stock.

112 (a) Bar codes; Magnetic strips.

(b) 1 Lists of goods to be ordered from each supplier; 2 Records of sales and forecasts for management.

(c) Records ... files.

113 (a) A Validate transaction data; B Sort transaction data; C Updated payroll master file

(b) Master File Record: 1,2,3,4,6,7. Transaction File Record: 5,6.
(c) It could be shown to banks or credit companies. Employees could find out how much others earn.
(d) Reason 1: All firms want to calculate a payroll. Reason 2: Payroll programs can be batch processed.
(e) (i) Most of the printing on a payslip is the same for everyone; it would be wasteful and time consuming for the computer to keep printing this each time.
(ii) A person modifying the program needs to know where all the fields are on the payslip.
(f) (i) Line printer: Much faster than a daisywheel printer.
(ii) **(See Unit 6.4)**
114 (a) Tickets; Invoices; Flight display at the airport.
(b) Timetable file; Booking agent file.
(c) System works in real time: it is kept continually up to date, with no danger of a clash of bookings. The computer can integrate flights, bookings and passenger details.
115 All details can be kept continually up to date so that two agents cannot book the same seats.
116 (a) CEEFAX **(or ORACLE)**
(b) PRESTEL **(or CAMPUS)**
(c) **(See Unit 18.3)**
117 (a), and (c) **(See Unit 18.3)** (b)(i) One message can be sent to a number of people.
(b)(ii) A message can be sent to a person who is out. (d) FAX.
118 (a) (i) 1 Details of sports fixtures. 2 Insurance rates.
(ii) 1 Book theatre tickets. 2 Book holidays.
(b) Interactive: the computer and the user communicate with one another in a conversation.
Modem: a device which converts between analogue and digital signals so that computer data can be sent via telephone lines.
Electronic mail: **(See definitions at start of Unit 18).**
(c) **(See Unit 18.3)**
119 (a) (i) The user does not have to worry about ends of lines.
(ii) Mistakes can be easily corrected.
(b) (i) Typists might not like them.
(ii) Sensible training and education beforehand.
120 (a) **(Any editing facilities could be mentioned for three of these – See Unit 18.4)**
Adding names from a stored list to personalize a document.
(b) 1: The word processor would soon save the money spent.
2: Word processors are very reliable.
3: True.
4: True, but a computer with a word processing facility could be purchased which would do a lot more than just produce letters and documents.
(c) The use of menus from which the user selects commands;
a 'help' facility so that the user can ask the computer for help with any command.
121 2, 1, 4, 3.
122 (a) Breathing signal, Heart beat signal, Step signal.
(b) (i) A device with two 'beepers' and LEDs which sound and flash if heart rate or breathing rate rise above a certain level.
(ii) If the runner's heart rate rises too high he will be warned by the LED and beeper and can lower his running rate accordingly.
(c) (i) A chart recorder or drum plotter.
(ii) To make continuous graphs against time of breathing rate,.heart rate and stepping rate.
(d) To store readings from the sensors so that they can be analysed by the computer after the run.
123 (a) Input – graphics function keyboard and mouse. **(See Units 6.2 and 7.4)**
Output – high-resolution monitor and flat-bed plotter. **(See Units 8.1 and 8.3)**
(b) **(See Unit 19.3 – 'Facilities provided by a CAD system')**
(c) (See Unit 19.3 – Advantages of CAD over manual design')
(d) Presumably Dream Housebuilders expect the new system to lead to increased business which would still be handled with the same staff using the new system.
124 (a) The computer inputs sensor readings. If the reading approaches zero the computer sends a signal to switch the heater on. When its rises well above freezing the computer outputs a signal to switch the heater off.
(b) 1 The gardener would not have to switch the heater on and off (or adjust ventilators etc.).
2 The gardener would not have to be available in the evening.

125 (a) **(For definition of feedback see introduction to Unit 20).**
When the patient's heart beats a sensor attached to the heart sends a signal to the computer. The computer calculates the heart beat rate and the amount of drug required to return it to normal. It sends signals to the pump controller at the correct time intervals. This is negative feedback because the computer outputs signals to correct the heart beat and so adjust the input from the sensor.
126 (a) Car industry.
(b) Move parts after one process and place them in position for the next process.
(c) They can carry out a task repeatedly for hours without stopping.
127 (a) 1: Once robots have been paid for it does not cost very much to run them.
2: Using robots the company needs fewer workers to produce the same number of cars, and saves wages. (b) **(See Unit 20.2–'PROGRAMMING')**
(c) **(The system with a video camera described in Unit 20.2 - 'SENSORS AND) FEEDBACK' could be given as an answer)**
(d) (i) 1: Robot maintenance 2: **(Any job could be given which does not use robots such as manufacturing the car parts)**
(ii) **(Any jobs could be given which have been replaced by robots such as painters and welders)**
(e) Emergency stop buttons on the power supply to the robots.
128 (a) A message can be sent by electronic mail if the person receiving it is not available to use the telephone.
(b) **(There are many differences but one obvious one is:)**
Electronic mail involves transfer of information, electronic funds transfer involves transfer of money.
(c) EFTPOS: using a card to pay direct via a supermarket POS terminal. Cash withdrawal at a bank dispenser.
(d) Use of electronic mail makes it easier for some people to work at home and for people to have a permanent record of correspondence without the use of paper. Electronic funds transfer allows people to handle their finances with little use of cash or cheques.
129 (a) The doctor's surgery; Credit companies; The police; The Driver and Vehicle Licensing Centre.
(b) To ensure that information is accurate; To register to use personal information; To use data only for the purpose registered; To protect data that they hold.
(c) Improved communications: large amounts of data can be sent at high speed on data links. Improved disc and tape manufacture: large amounts of data can be stored and sent on small discs and tape cartridges. Open systems: computers of different types are able to communicate with one another.
130 (a) The Data Protection Act says that data users must disclose information about him if he requests it.
(b) He could ask for it to be changed. If the shopkeeper refuses he could complain to the Data Registrar.
(c) He would not have any rights under the Data Protection Act.
131 (Part (i) you could take many possible jobs where the same production is achieved with fewer workers because computers are used–the printing industry introducing computerized typesetting and offices with word processors are obvious examples. In Part (ii) there are also plenty of examples e.g. micro-computer shop employees, salesman for computer games machines, etc. For Part (iii) see Unit 21.3 and 21.4)
132 (a) Engineer maintaining the new equipment.
(b) Lack of the necessary skills and qualifications.
(c) The factory may lose orders to its competitors and be forced to close.
133 (Any realistic suggestions would do e.g.) Motor car factory: Each worker would produce more; The factory would produce more cars and employ fewer workers; Robots would probably do more of the labour-intensive jobs. The remaining jobs would involve understanding and monitoring new equipment. Supermarket: Till staff would do less writing and less calculation; Floor staff would have to do less counting of goods on shelves; Jobs would be generally more skilled.

PROJECTS COURSEWORK AND CASE STUDIES

All syllabuses require candidates to submit coursework or a project. This counts towards your total mark in the subject (the actual percentages are given in the Table of Analysis). The work is assessed by your teacher and it is then 'moderated'. This means that some or all of the coursework from your school is compared with the work from other schools and the marks adjusted if necessary.

In most cases the project work required involves using a computer to solve a problem. The problem chosen can be solved in one or both of two ways:

1 By designing and writing a program yourself in a high-level programming language.

2 By using an application package, that is, a program written by someone else.

Programming Projects

1 The requirements for these vary from one syllabus to another. Often your teacher is allowed to give you a copy of the mark scheme for the project. If so, this is very helpful as it enables you to see how much work to do on each aspect of the project, and you should be careful to produce all of the items listed there.

2 Usually the programming itself is not so important as the design, testing and documentation stages. If this is so, it is vital to spend the proper amount of time on them. Everyone designing a program wants to get it right but you must discipline yourself to leave enough time for:

(a) Documentation (see Unit 10.6).

(b) Testing the program. This means working out beforehand a set of data which will test the program thoroughly (see Unit 10.4).

(c) Making sure the program is easy to read by rearranging it and adding remarks to it (see Unit 11.8 on program design and layout).

3 When tackling a programming project, regard yourself as a systems analyst/programmer who has been commissioned to design a new system and to write, test and document a program to fit a user's requirements (see Unit 10.2 on designing and programming and Units 16.2 and 16.3 on the duties of a systems analyst and a programmer).

4 When writing a piece of documentation get it clear in your own mind who it is for. Is it for a user of the program or a programmer or an examiner? Thus instructions on how to use the program should not be mixed up with details of lines in the program or comments about the difficulties you encountered in getting it to work.

Use of packages

The majority of people using computers do so by using packages, rather than by writing programs themselves.

1 If you choose this option you should, if possible, study the mark scheme or other guidance provided by the board and make sure that you do what is required.

2 Choose a problem which you can hope to solve in the time available and with the equipment at your disposal. If the task obviously needs a graph plotter and you are not sure that you will be able to use one, then choose a more suitable problem. You will be heavily penalized if your choice is not a sensible one.

3 It is usually best to use the package to carry out a definite task which somebody wants done. You must make it clear:

(a) **Who the user is.** You will learn more and write a better report if the user is, or is imagined to be, a person who does not know much about computers.

(b) **What the task is.** An account of how the package was used for a specific purpose is more likely to gain good marks than if you write a general review of the package.

4 Assume that the report is for an examiner who is familiar with computers generally but that you have to convey to him what computer system you are using and what the package can do. The examiner does not want to have to read the manual before reading your report, so make a brief but clear summary of those features of the package which are needed for your problem.

5 Explain clearly how data was collected. The examiner will be checking whether you:
(a) Take steps to reduce errors in the data.
(b) Take into account possible inaccuracy of the input data in interpreting the results.

6 For most boards you will have to produce evidence that the package has been run on a computer system. If you are controlling motors or other devices, or if you are displaying something on the screen, you may need to take photographs as proof. If you do then make sure plenty of time is allowed for this.

7 Most non-technical users find it difficult to follow documentation, particularly that explaining how to use the computer system. They will usually have less difficulty with the program documentation. Your account should explain any weaknesses you found in the documentation and the problems this caused.

8 The final section of the report should be an overall account of how well the package met the user's needs.

9 When looking for suitable packages you will find that some programs can be applied to a wide range of problems. Two examples of this are:
(a) A file enquiry program.
(b) A spreadsheet program.

An example of the use of each of these for a project is given in Unit 14.1, together with more general notes on the evaluation of software.

Case Study Examinations

Some boards set a written paper on a particular application. This is called a Case Study Examination. (Candidates for the Scottish Standard Grade should note that this is not the same as the Case Study they do as part of their classwork.) In most cases, but not all, candidates are told before the examination some of the details of it. (See the Table of Analysis.)

A case study examination tests your ability to:

1 Work out what information is needed by the system which has been described.

2 Decide how to translate this information into data so that the computer can process it, and then how to interpret the results.

3 Choose appropriate hardware to support the system.

4 Design suitable input and output formats.

5 Design simple non-computer procedures.

Before the examination you should spend some time working out as much as you can about the system.

1 List the information which the system outputs and the information required as input. Include any files in your list.

2 For any files described, decide as much as you can about the length and type of fields and records. For example, if a name has to be stored, decide whether it should be in a fixed or variable length field and, if it is fixed, what length it will be.
Decide on any coding which you think is necessary. For example, with a program for allocating pupils to subjects, it would obviously waste storage and typing time if *Geography* was stored in full. A code would be used such as 'G' or 'GEO' and there would have to be a method of translating to and from the code, such as by using a look-up table.

3 Work out what hardware could be used by the system. You will need a rough idea of the relative capabilities of different devices as you might have to compare them. (If you are asked to decide between devices, marks will be awarded not so much for the choice you make but more for how you justify your choice, and you should list both the good and the bad points of the devices you are asked to consider.)

4 Design carefully the format for any input and output, such as input documents or screen layouts. You should also work out any validation checks that could be used for the input data.

5 Work out any manual procedures which may be necessary and try to make sure that they can reasonably be done by the type of person likely to have to carry them out.

When you do the paper you may well be required to produce an algorithm for solving one of the problems posed by the system which has been described. It will be assumed by the examiner that it takes you some time to work out the solution before you start writing it down, so that your answer should not be too long. It is important not to produce a detailed answer in the form of a flowchart unless you are specifically asked to. Ordinary sentences in English would be better and you should avoid the use of simplified variable names and BASIC-type statements.

INDEX